# THE REVENGE OF REASON

# THE REVENGE OF REASON

PETER WOLFENDALE

URBANOMIC

Published in 2025 by
URBANOMIC MEDIA LTD,
THE OLD LEMONADE FACTORY,
WINDSOR QUARRY,
FALMOUTH TR11 3EX,
UNITED KINGDOM



BRITISH LIBRARY CATALOGUING-IN-PUBLICATION DATA

A full catalogue record of this book is available
from the British Library

ISBN 978-1-913029-87-6

Distributed by The MIT Press, Cambridge, Massachusetts
and London, England

Type by Norm, Zurich
Printed and bound in the UK by
Short Run Press

www.urbanomic.com

# CONTENTS

# Preface:
# The Promise of Abstraction

## Ray Brassier

Pete Wolfendale's work is a wager on the promise of abstraction: the promise of self-creation unfixing authenticity; of freedom undoing fatalism; of experimental embodiment displacing somatic chauvinism. Wolfendale wants to twist free from the dialectic of Enlightenment, in which reason and nature are entwined in an escalating spiral of domination. While there is no doubt that the ascent of cognitive abstraction from Galileo to Turing has enabled new forms of social domination (via the automation of exploitation and the intensification of surveillance), Wolfendale's wager is that social liberation is not to be achieved by descending back into concrete immediacy but by propelling abstraction beyond domination, accentuating what is ungovernable in it so as to unmoor concretion from the fixity of identities, types, kinds, attributes, roles, and bodies. Once we understand to what extent our thinking and acting is a collaboration with the world, which we can shape as much as if not more than it shapes us, we can begin to hone them with a view to transforming ourselves and our world. Among the inspirations for this emancipatory vision of reasoning is the work of Robert Brandom, of whom Wolfendale is both an inspired reader and heterodox disciple. Brandom's 'inferentialism' can be encapsulated in four basic claims:

(1) Concepts derive their content from their role in reasoning, not from their representation of objects.

(2) Reasoning consists in grasping what we are committed and entitled to in making assertions, rather than in mastering a logical calculus.

(3) The use of any linguistic expression or concept has two aspects: the circumstances under which it is correctly deployed and the appropriate

consequences of its deployment. The semantic content to which we commit ourselves by using a concept can be represented by the inference from its circumstances of appropriate deployment to the appropriate consequences of such deployment.

(4) Rationality is expressive in so far as it renders our implicit content-conferring inferential commitments *explicitly* assertible.[1]

This last is perhaps the most important point. Reason is expressive in so far as it brings the material inferential practices governing the game of giving and asking for reasons into that game as explicit topics of discussion and justification. By making them explicit, it allows us to question our entitlements and revise our commitments. Interrogation and revision alters the inferential profiles of our concepts, subjecting them to a conscious process of rational transformation. Thus inferentialism decouples rationality from the consolations of metaphysical rationalism: whatever primacy we ascribe to a principle is contextual not transcendent; whatever necessity we recognize in truth is one we have instituted. Reasoning is socially instantiated dialogical activity rather than intuitive illumination, whether natural or divine. Yet cognitive progress is nonetheless discernible through this historical process of correction and revision. But it must be retrospectively reconstructed through a narrative of unfolding truth in which we strive to interpret our predecessors not in terms of what, by our lights, they failed to know, but in terms of what, by their lights, made our own knowing possible.

Inferentialism couples meliorist and fallibilist conceptions of cognitive evolution in a way that is close to Hegel's while rejecting his absolute idealism, i.e., the claim that the structure of being ultimately coincides with the structure of thinking. Hegel tries to establish this coincidence by maintaining that the science of the appearance of knowing (the *Phenomenology of Spirit*) culminates in the science of knowing (the *Science of Logic*). This is tantamount to the claim that knowing the failures of knowing culminates in absolute knowing. What Hegel calls

1. See R. Brandom, *Making it Explicit: Reasoning, Representing and Discursive Commitment* (Cambridge, MA: Harvard University Press, 1994); *Articulating Reasons: An Introduction to Inferentialism* (Cambridge, MA: Harvard University Press, 2000)

'natural consciousness' is the sphere of the appearance or possibility of knowing, structured around the hiatus between subject and object. It is superseded by 'science' as real or actual knowing, in which the separation of thought and thing is overcome and thinking knows itself. In one of the many remarkable essays included in this volume, Wolfendale rejects Hegel's attempted supersession, calling it 'The Greatest Mistake'. If Hegel begins with natural consciousness, as he must, he cannot presuppose the actuality of knowledge; he must assume its appearance without presupposing that knowledge's appearance also guarantees its possibility. The attempt to derive the possibility of knowledge from its appearance is suspended by radical scepticism, which argues as follows: to know is to assert; assertion requires a criterion distinguishing true from false assertion; but possession of such a criterion presupposes the ability to assert the difference between true and false assertion, which is precisely what is in question. The sceptic's case can also be formulated in terms of Agrippa's trilemma, which asks how we can justify a proposition without either (a) merely asserting its truth (bare assertion); (b) appealing to another proposition also requiring justification (regress); or (c) justifying it by appeal to itself (circularity). The sceptic describes the apparent structure of knowledge in order to undermine it. All that is required to do this are assertions, the propositions they express, and the relations of incompatibility and consequence between these propositions. But as Wolfendale points out, Hegel augments this minimal structure with an account of the internal structure of propositions featuring the distinction between objects and concepts, the possibility of their discrepancy, and the conceptual suppression of this discrepancy. The problem is that the charge of insufficiency which Hegel levels against the skeptic's account of the appearance of knowledge can also be levelled at his own alternative. This insufficiency reproduces the problem of the criterion: how are we to choose between these competing accounts of the appearance of knowledge? Is the minimal structure of justification captured by compatibility relations between propositions or by the conceptual suppression of the discrepancy between concepts and objects?

The problem of identifying the appearance of knowledge is that of identifying our ordinary (pre-scientific) structure of justification. Where Hegel opposes science to natural consciousness as contrasting species of thinking, Wolfendale (following Brandom) takes ordinary discursive practice to be the genus of which science, or transcendental philosophy, is the species. For Hegelian rationalism, natural consciousness is superseded by science, whereas for Wolfendale's inferentialism, discursive practice is *explicated* by transcendental philosophy. Yet this should not be taken to ratify the claim that there is a transcendent abyss separating thoughts from things, vindicating the finitude of reason against Hegel's confidence in its infinitude. Intentionality, or the aboutness of thought, is not a transcendent gap in being but a function of inferential role, explicable in terms of the interplay between discursive commitments and entitlements. We can use words to refer to things because we can use them to refer to other words. This 'anaphoric' resolution of the problem of reference is another of Brandom's ingenious innovations.[2] It explains how we and our linguistic ancestors can still be referring to the same objects despite changes in our concepts (seventeenth-century English speakers meant what we mean when we say 'water' despite not knowing what $H_2O$ is). Making these commitments and entitlements explicit allows us to clarify our concepts and, where necessary, rectify their referents. The expressive movement whereby what is implicit in our saying and doing is made explicit is precisely what allows reason to reshape its own form and to extend its ambit beyond what was previously considered thinkable.

Thus Wolfendale's conviction is that inferentialism provides the basis for a post-Kantian or non-dogmatic metaphysics that does not reinstate the identity of thought and being. This is the topic of his 'Essay on Transcendental Realism', one of the centrepieces of this volume. Its principal claim is that, contrary to those who think commitment to realism is incompatible with transcendental philosophy, entitlement to realism can only be secured from within a transcendental framework. To that end, Wolfendale introduces several crucial distinctions: between mind-independence and attitude-independence on the epistemic side, and between reality, the in-itself, and the world on the metaphysical side. His most decisive distinction is between the formal and the real structure of the Real, which he uses to demarcate the domain of the transcendental from that of the metaphysical. Transcendental realism then becomes the thesis according to which, in Wolfendale's words, 'the structure of thought implies that there is a real structure of the world which is not only independent from but also in excess of the structure of thought'. What might it mean to claim that the world's

2. See R. Brandom, 'Reference Explained Away', *The Journal of Philosophy* 81:9 (1984): 469–92.

real structure exceeds the structure of thought? Principally, that the variety of real individuals the world contains need not line up with our extant typology of sorts or kinds. The logic of individuation is a transcendental concern. Neither the variety of intelligible forms nor of sensory contents can be stipulated by metaphysical fiat. Kant's discovery of transcendental synthesis as the power of articulating sensory content with conceptual form marks his epochal break with Aristotelian hylomorphism. Transcendental logic, in Wolfendale's words, is 'logic as if individuation mattered'. But the logic of individuation unfolds across both sensory and conceptual registers; it involves sensibility (intuition), understanding (judgement), and reason (syllogism). Grasping the interaction between these three domains is essential to Wolfendale's 'computational Kantianism': if the individuation of typed perceptual objects requires the unity of judgement, the unity of any single judgement requires its integration into the body of judgements presupposed and entailed by it to yield a cohesive representation of a unified world. But as Wolfendale notices, this Kantian account obliges us to distinguish between perceptual and discursive objectivity; the former as proper to objects that remain invariant across changes in sensory perspective and the latter as proper to objects that remain invariant across changes in rational perspective. Perceptual and discursive objectivity coincide in our discourse about directly perceptible objects (chairs, dogs, water, etc.). But they begin to diverge in our discourse about objects decoupled from immediate perception (electrons, prime numbers, justice, etc.). Transcendental realism, in Wolfendale's sense, is sensitive to the degrees of divergence between perceptual and discursive objectivity while avoiding empiricism, which insists that the discursive is bounded by the perceptual, and dogmatic rationalism, which denies that the perceptual exerts any constraint upon the discursive. Wolfendale's inferentialism acknowledges empirical constraint while suggesting that it can be indefinitely loosened.

What distinguishes perceptual content from non-perceptual content? To answer this question, Wolfendale suggests we consider perceiving subjects as causal systems analogous to information storage media (ISMs). The criterion for sameness of content across different ISMs is a functional mapping from the components of one set of variable states to those of another in terms of the common outputs with which they are correlated. The difference between perceptual and non-perceptual content can then be explained as follows: perceptual content is functionally individuated and qualitatively specific (where the specificity of the quality is not independent of function); non-perceptual content is categorial content where categories are defined as general functional roles common to specific conceptual roles (here sensory qualities are irrelevant). Wolfendale then introduces a distinction between universal perceptual content and empirical conceptual content. Since empirical conceptual content is fixed both by its functional role in mediating the organism's relation to its environment and by sensible qualities determined by specific sensory modalities, it will vary according to differences in functional role as well as differences in sensory modality. By way of contrast, universal perceptual content would be perception whose content is independent of causal functioning and sensory qualities; it would be a perceptual experience endowed with the same content for all perceivers irrespective of differences in their biological (sensory) and cultural (conceptual) histories. On this basis, Wolfendale proposes an illuminating reformulation of Wilfrid Sellars's myth of the categorial given. This is the claim that the categorial structure of reality impresses itself upon the mind in the same way as a seal impresses itself upon melted wax. Using his distinction between empirical conceptual content and universal perceptual content, Wolfendale defines the categorial given as universal perceptual content independent of empirical conceptual content. As he puts it, this is the claim that two creatures could have the same experience without having the same conceptual grasp of this experience. It is to insist that there is a kind of self-individuating content which cannot be individuated through any functional mapping between its vehicules. The myth of self-individuating perceptual contents can be added to those of self-presenting actualities and self-intimating mental states as yet another lattice in the framework of givenness denounced by both Sellars and Brandom.

Simply put, the myth is the assumption that what is given—perceptually, categorically, phenomenologically—cannot be remade. To reject the myth is to begin to see how reason invites us to remake our world and our selves. But reason is embodied in language and since language allows us to modify the heuristic frames embedded in cognition, this means, in Wolfendale's words, that 'the distinctive feature of rational cognition is un-framing'. The most consequential sites for this cognitive un-framing are the concepts of selfhood, freedom, and value. Their mutual entwinement in Wolfendale's vision provides perhaps the most powerful distillation of his re-envisaging of the link between reason and freedom. The self is neither a disembodied substance nor an embodied consciousness: it is the locus for the extension and revision of rational commitments, motivated by an ideal of self-determining uniqueness irreducible to the empirical distinctiveness of psychological or physical determinants. As locus of rational self-transformation, the self can integrate and manage the body's causal constraints without turning them into normative constraints. Selves are loci for processes of transformation within physical nature whose impetus and terminus cannot be comprehended within that nature. Needless to say, these need not be human selves. Creatures with vastly different biologies or histories, not to mention creatures whose bodies are synthetic rather than organic, will be motivated to become selves once their capacities for perceiving, thinking, and acting begin to be governed by the interplay between commitments and entitlements. We might say that for Wolfendale, selves, although parts of nature, are wholly unprecedented beings whose uniqueness outstrips that of every other kind of being. Their unlikeness is unlike anything in the world. Yet precisely in so far as selfhood is an ideal of realisation without precedent or analogue in anything that is, it is 'neither the ultimate form of identity to which every thing aspires nor a supreme being in which every thing partakes'. Selfhood is neither the fundamental basis of metaphysical individuality—contra panpsychism—nor the divine apex within which all individuality is encompassed—contra pantheism. It is rather 'the unreachable limit implied by the idea of freedom as such'. Freedom is the desire for self-realization where there is no analogue or precedent for what is to be realized. This is the sense in which the self is 'an unreachable limit'. Selfhood is inextricable from freedom because it involves the evolution of desire in a process of becoming which fixes its own ends. Freedom implies the autonomy of desire as a law unto itself. To say that desire desires itself is to say it is its own reason for being. This is Wolfendale's rationalist recoding of Gilles Deleuze and Félix Guattari's account of 'desiring-production':

> [F]or all these untapped potentials lie hidden in the layers of cybernetic complexity ranging from micro-organisms to the tips of those strangest branches of the animal kingdom, there must be a point at which something makes them its own, by allowing itself to be made by them, achieving a modicum of actuality

> in the process. This need not be human. But it does need to be autonomous. ('Beyond Survival')

The autonomy of desire is indissociable from that of the self. Since the reason for becoming a self is the liberation of desire from instinct and need, this reason cannot be satisfied by biological survival (adaptation) or metaphysical persistence (conatus). This means that a community of selves cannot be motivated by the imperative of biological survival; what motivates it is the obligation to perpetuate what Wolfendale calls 'the infrastructure of self-realisation'; which is to say, the set of mechanisms, capacities, skills, techniques and practices upon which the capacity for self-realisation supervenes in any given instance. Thus the ultimate goal of self-realisation is not the perpetuation of individuals, species, or even genera but of the evolution of the desire for self-realisation. Freedom is the ultimate source of value as that which *is not* but *ought to be* created. We need to distinguish the existence of freedom as source of value from the myriad forms that freedom might take through the vast array of possible autonomous agents and value-creating activities in which they might engage. We have scarcely begun to imagine the different ways in which things might matter. But freedom entails value creation, the proliferation of different ways of mattering. What matters, says Wolfendale, is that something *must* matter:

> This means that no matter who we are and what we want, we should care about the freedom of ourselves and others, and promoting its unconstrained evolution. The only thing that should constrain freedom is itself, and this is the true content of right. ('Why Does Anything Matter?')

Freedom here is no longer the paltry negative freedom beloved of sceptical liberals, for whom private property, markets, and inequality guarantee the rights of the individual. It is the freedom to make the world right by abolishing these guarantors; the freedom to unmoor the self from the markers of individuality affixed to it. It is by destituting every metaphysical assumption about the provenance of value that reason reveals our responsibility for instituting it. Rightness, which is to say, justice, is not given by the world; it must be made. There is no better way of formulating the imperative of rationalism.

# Introduction: On Neorationalism

The word 'neorationalism' is not one I coined, but it has consistently been used to describe the work of Ray Brassier, Reza Negarestani, and myself, along with numerous fellow travellers. It's not something we've ever defined as such, precisely because it's not a moniker we ever consciously picked. However, today I'm reminded of the implicit commitment that might be taken to distinguish neo-rationalism from its opponents, if it can be said to be anything like a consistent philosophical programme. It's this:

> *To reject all rational intuition in the name of reason, to insist that not only is there no intuitive faculty of rational knowledge, there is no intuitive purchase on reason's own structure, possibilities, and limits. Reason is not what you think it is. Reason is not rationalisation. Reason is not* reasonable.

What distinguishes neorationalists isn't just this principled commitment, but our practical response to it. Our main departure from the classical rationalism of Descartes, Leibniz, and Spinoza is a fidelity to the computational turn that began in the early twentieth century, and whose consequences we are *still* working out; consequences which land blow after blow on our intuitive conception of what thinking is, breaking our ways of rationalising what we are, and shattering our illusions regarding what it's reasonable to believe.

Reasoning is something that is *done*, and it's something that can be done by processes other than us, processes that can and have been studied *using* reason, with the unforgiving precision of mathematical proof. Russell's paradox and Gödel's theorems lie at the beginning of an ongoing process through which we demonstrate reason's own limits, and then, following Turing, use these limits as purchase to pull it out of our hominid skulls and realise it in new and stranger forms. We haven't yet created artificial rational agents, only fragments thereof, but the humanist hubris that refuses to see these processes as fragments of things *like us* looks increasingly desperate, increasingly willing to rationalise away the advance of mathematical logic, the progress of artificial intelligence, and the encroachment of computational neuroscience.

If you think that you can't be studied as an information processing system, and that this allows you to wall off your intuitive conceptions of not just the human condition but *what is good* in this condition, then I'm afraid there's an oncoming wave that will crest those walls and drown your parochial ambitions. The promise made by neorationalism isn't that this wave is *empirical* science come to show you the horrors or your neuronal substrate,[1] but that it is *mathematical* science come to show you the wonders of your computational soul. We are non-terminating processes interacting with our environment and with one another, exploring the mathematical and empirical realms together, playing games of proof and refutation, and building systems and models that are beginning to encompass our own selves. We are beautiful. We are free. Computational self-consciousness will only enhance this, even if it changes our understanding of what it means.

*

I wrote the above words about five years ago, on my long-running if irregularly updated blog.[2] When it came to finally assembling this book, which is in one respect merely my collected papers, but in another is evidence of the intellectual trajectory I've travelled over the last decade or so, it felt appropriate to begin with such a clear statement of philosophical aspiration, if only so that the ways in which what follows attempts and fails to live up to that aspiration might be laid bare. The book is divided into two parts.

The first half is constituted by a series of essays originally given as talks since 2015, whose themes are deeply related enough to form a recognisable sequence: 'Prometheanism and Rationalism' goes some way toward fleshing out the background, motivations, and perspective of neorationalism by relating it to other philosophical ideas that emerged in the wake of the failure of speculative

---

1. Pace Scott Bakker. See 'Philosophy and Normativity', in this volume. Cf. S. Bakker, *Neuropath* (New York: Tor Books, 2010).

2. 'On Neorationalism', <https://deontologistics.co/2018/02/11/on-neorationalism/>.

realism,[3] namely *left accelerationism* and *xenofeminism*; 'The Reformatting of Homo Sapiens' contextualises and develops the resulting conception of reason by embedding it in debates regarding human nature, providing an evolutionary account of its emergence and entrenchment while outlining a *rationalist inhumanism* that might redefine our understanding of agency, selfhood, and value; 'Beyond Survival' takes up the task of redefining our conception of agency by way of a sustained critique of those distortions generated by appeal to survival as an ultimate goal, providing an account of the *analogical bootstrapping* involved in causal explanation of complex systems and what it means for such systems to achieve *autonomous agency*; 'On Containing Multitudes' expands upon this by digging deeper into the concept of selfhood, categorising various approaches to it throughout the history of philosophy and psychology, and attempting to provide an integrated account that makes sense of various forms of *personal multiplicity*, from the mundane to the unusual to the purely speculative; and finally, 'Why Does Anything Matter?' revisits the concept of value in light of all of this, grappling with the possibility of *cosmic extinction* and sketching an answer to the question that forms its title. Owing to its origins in isolated talks, this sequence contains some repetition and redundancy, and leaves out much that a fuller, more integrated treatment would ideally cover. But I hope it stands as it is.

The second half contains a selection of texts written between 2010 and the present. It begins with two interviews that provide an accessible introduction to my thoughts on a range of important topics: 'Philosophy and Normativity' with Kai Peattie, which provides some insight into my overall philosophical trajectory, especially the influence of Robert Brandom's work upon my thinking, while addressing some critiques of the prominence I give to the notion of *normativity*, 'Artificial Bodies and the Promise of Abstraction' with Anthony Morgan, which provides a conceptual overview and critique of the 'embodiment paradigm' that operates at the intersection of philosophy and cognitive science, while raising some questions about the *computational* underpinnings of intentionality, and 'Incarnation', a 2025 interview for the podcast *Disintegrator*, which discusses questions around AI, AGI, and computation.

The remainder is then broken into three further sections.

3. For a detailed account of this failure, see my previous book *Object-Oriented Philosophy: The Noumenon's New Clothes* (Falmouth: Urbanomic, 2014).

**Physis** groups together essays that deal directly with topics in metaphysics and methodology of metaphysics: 'The Greatest Mistake: A Case for the Failure of Hegel's Idealism' offers a high-level overview of Hegel's philosophical system and the argument that underpins it, and then identifies a fatal objection to this argument based on his account of *natural consciousness*; 'Essay on Transcendental Realism' analyses two competing dialectics operating in contemporary metaphysics, and, by developing a novel account of *objectivity*, uses them to articulate an account of what metaphysics is that treats it as continuous with natural science without dissolving its non-empirical logical core; and 'Ariadne's Thread: Temporality, Modality, and Individuation in Deleuze's Metaphysics' then offers a rereading of Deleuze's metaphysics broadly consistent with this methodological perspective, showing how Deleuze's focus on the role of time in dynamic systems theory shapes his approach to *the problem of universals*.

**Logos** groups essays that deal with topics in logic and epistemology broadly construed: 'Is There a TV in my Head?' delves into the philosophy of perception, elucidating Sellars's critique of the categorical given in a way that presents a fatal objection to the project of introspective phenomenology; 'On Computational Asymmetry' sketches out some ideas about the relationship between computational asymmetry and semantic content, including a reading of the analytic/synthetic distinction, and 'On Transcendental Logic' is an excerpt from a larger unfinished piece that provides a standalone summary of the core features of my reading of Kant, the project of *transcendental logic*, and gestures in the direction that this project must be taken if we are to take it further than Kant himself.

**Ethos** groups essays that deal with topics in the philosophy of value, covering both ethics and aesthetics: 'The Artist's Brain at Work' attempts to provide a theory of art as *cognitive stimulation* by simultaneously critiquing and synthesising the dominant aesthetic and semantic paradigms for understanding its significance; 'Art and Value' addresses the question of the value of art, rehearsing the historical path that has led us to the impasses of contemporary art and proposing a return to a disambiguated notion of *beauty as value*; 'What's in a Game?' introduces the problem of delimiting the *concept of game*, examining various purported solutions across mathematics, sociology, and philosophy, before providing a novel definition of my own, and 'Not So Humble Pie' is an unpublished short piece providing an ethical justification of meat consumption.

There are other completed essays and incomplete fragments that I would have loved to include here, but space constraints have forced me to whittle the list down to the above. My views on some matters expressed in these older pieces have since changed in some cases, and my terminology has undergone occasional shifts, but for the most part they provide a representative sample of my thinking on a range of topics that continue to interest me. That being said, it's perhaps worth providing a brief overview of some of my most important commitments, so that themes running between the various texts in both halves might be traced more easily.

**Computational Kantianism** insists on interpreting Kant's project of *transcendental psychology* as prefiguring the problem of *artificial general intelligence*, which is to say, providing a maximally abstract functional description of anything that might count as a minded, autonomous rational agent. This general commitment runs throughout the essays in the first half, but the interpretation of Kant is developed in most detail in 'On Transcendental Logic'. There are two more specific commitments that follow from this, which concern a pair of *dualities* articulated in Kant's thought. The duality between the *theoretical* and the *practical* is a central theme of 'Beyond Survival' and 'On Containing Multitudes' and is central to my account of personal autonomy. The duality between the *mathematical* and the *empirical* is addressed in a limited way in 'Essay on Transcendental Realism' but is more explicitly thematised in 'On Transcendental Logic' and 'Artificial Bodies and the Promise of Abstraction'.

**Minimalist Hegelianism** attempts to separate Hegel's important insights into the semantic structure of the *conceptual* and rational basis of *freedom* from the metaphysical and theological commitments entailed by his *absolute idealism*. My key objection to Hegel's overall system can be found in 'The Greatest Mistake', but the account of natural consciousness presented therein plays a crucial role in the 'Essay on Transcendental Realism', as does the account of *semantic inferentialism* developed in detail by Robert Brandom under the influence of Hegel.[4] If there's one thing that distinguishes this picture of reason from the broadly Bayesian model popularised by contemporary online rationalists, it is its unwavering commitment to the significance of *conceptual revision*. Where Bayesians

4. Implicitly in *Making it Explicit* (Cambridge, MA: Harvard University Press, 1998) and explicitly in *A Spirit of Trust* (Cambridge, MA: Harvard University Press, 2019).

revise probabilistic credences assigned to propositions whose meanings are fixed in accordance with a prior conception of the overall space of possible beliefs, Hegelians recognise that the true power of rationality consists in confronting seeming impossibilities that force us to revise the meanings of our terms, and thereby our conceptions of what is possible. If any criticism can be made of Brandom, it is that his commitment to revision does not go far enough.[5] This commitment to revision runs through the essays in the first half, where it follows a distinctly Hegelian trajectory by transforming into a concern with freedom.

**Heretical Platonism** subtracts Plato's commitment to the autonomy of reason from its enmeshment in his metaphysics of empirical archetypes and the associated ethics of perfection, preserving the paradigmatic status of mathematical knowledge and the unbounded transcendence of normative ideals.[6] The critical dimension of this heresy can be seen both in the reconstruction of Deleuze's overturning of Platonism in 'Ariadne's Thread', where an alternative conception of empirical universals is sketched out, and in a less direct form in 'Beyond Survival', where the notion of natural teleology implicit in Plato's perspective is roundly rejected. The paradigmatic status of mathematics is explored in 'Artificial Bodies and the Promise of Abstraction', while the basic features of the corresponding conception of normativity are addressed in 'Philosophy and Normativity'. The latter is fleshed out in different ways by the discussion of truth and objectivity in the 'Essay on Transcendental Realism' and the discussion of beauty and art in 'Art and Value'. In each case, there is a split between the *formal* ideal (truth/beauty), which has general applicability to all rational activity (e.g., fictional truths and excellence in craft), and its *substantial* or ownmost form (objective truth/absolutely unconditional value), which gives rise to its own specific practices (i.e., science and art). These constitute two pillars of the trinity of *cardinal values*, truth, beauty, and right—although the third and its relation to the others is only briefly addressed, in 'Why Does Anything Matter?'.

---

5. This becomes clear in the formal incompatibility semantics developed in *Between Saying and Doing* (Oxford: Oxford University Press, 2008), which ultimately uses a classic conception of contradiction (i.e., explosion) to reconstruct a static Aristotelian genus-species hierarchy from incompatibility relations between propositions. This is undoubtedly impressive, but it shies away from the underlying dynamics involved in reasoning with nontrivial contradictions.

6. This is precisely the genre of Platonic heresy already evident in Alain Badiou's work, although I have not engaged with the latter in depth in any of the pieces in this volume, much to my own chagrin.

It remains to say something about my debts to others, philosophical and otherwise, which are perhaps too extensive to properly enumerate. As the opening indicates, I owe a deep and abiding debt to Ray Brassier and Reza Negarestani, both for the inspiration provided by their work and for the personal support and encouragement they have provided me over the years. The sequence of essays in the first half is perhaps more overtly engaged with themes from Ray's work, especially the engagement with survival and extinction that runs from 'Beyond Survival' to 'Why Does Anything Matter?', but while the touch of Reza's 'The Labor of the Inhuman' is obvious in 'The Reformatting of Homo Sapiens', I have not spelled out the underlying engagement with *Intelligence and Spirit* in 'On Containing Multitudes' in the manner that I would have liked. Among the other people who have contributed to the loose collection of debates and ideas that compose neorationalism as anything resembling a living thing, it is important to single out Dan Sacilotto, Inigo Wilkins, J.P. Caron, Anil Bawa-Cavia, and Patricia Reed for the work they have done and continue to do.

I would like to thank Anthony Morgan and Kai Peattie, for drawing some of my best words out of me with sensitive and precise questioning. I would also like to thank Matt Bovingdon for providing the cover art for the book. I must also thank, in no particular order, those whose wonderful conversation and unfailing support has kept my philosophical practice afloat over the last decade or so, even as I tried and failed to find an academic home for it: Benedict Singleton, Nick Srnicek, Alex Williams, Helen Hester, Lucca Fraser, Diann Bauer, Patricia Reed, Amy Ireland, Tia Trafford, Fabio Gironi, Sam Forsythe, Matt Hare, Keith Tilford, Joshua Johnson, Tom Moynihan, Peli Grietzer, Meredith Patterson, Dominic Fox, Gerald Moore, Stephen Overy, Dan Koczi, Lorenzo Chiesa, Nicky Brignell, and Zoe Waters.

Finally, I must express my deepest gratitude for the tireless effort and intellectual generosity of Kevin Hilliard in helping me pull these texts together into a recognisable shape, and the gentle support and saintly patience of Maya B. Kronic in giving us the chance to do so.

Pete Wolfendale,
Byker, Newcastle Upon Tyne, 9th June 2025

# Notes on the Texts

'Prometheanism and Rationalism' grew out of a talk given at the Dutch Art Institute in 2016; 'The Reformatting of Homo Sapiens' was originally delivered as a talk at the Fridericianum in Kassel in 2015, and was subsequently published in the *Angelaki* special issue 'Alien Vectors: Accelerationism, Xenofeminism, Inhumanism' edited by myself and Tia Trafford in 2019; 'Beyond Survival' grew out of a talk given at the *Fight or Flight: Strategies of Survival* conference at MSSES and RANEPA in Moscow; 'On Containing Multitudes' grew out of a talk given at the Likeminds Festival in Albany in 2022; 'Why Does Anything Matter?' evolved out of a short video essay accompanying the short story 'The Last Gift' published by myself and Timothy Linward in the *Šum* journal, along with material from the 'Exuberance and Extinction' course I taught for the New Centre for Research and Practice in 2023, and was first presented at Newcastle University in 2024.; 'Philosophy and Normativity' is a previously unpublished interview carried out via email with Kai Peattie in 2017; 'Artificial Bodies and the Promise of Abstraction' is an interview carried out via email with Anthony Morgan and published in *The Philosopher* in 2020; 'Incarnation' is an edited version of an interview for the podcast *Disintegrator*, recorded in 2025; 'The Greatest Mistake: A Case for the Failure of Hegel's Idealism' was originally presented at the Dundee University Philosophy Conference in 2010; 'Essay on Transcendental Realism' grew out of a paper given at the Transcendental Realism Workshop I organised at Warwick University in 2010 and was published on my blog shortly afterwards. It has never been printed anywhere, despite circulating fairly widely; 'Ariadne's Thread' was originally delivered at the Gilles Deleuze Conference at Manchester Metropolitan University in 2012; 'Is There a TV in my Head?' was originally delivered at the Sellars Centenary Conference at University College Dublin in 2012, and published in *TAULA. Quaderns di Filosofia*'s special issue on the philosophy of Wilfrid Sellars; 'On Computational Asymmetry' is a fragment of a longer blog post on mental health and neurophilosophy ('Transcendental Blues') that was ultimately cut for reasons of technicality, but is in many ways more philosophically interesting than the discussion that occasioned it; 'On Transcendental Logic' is a fragment of a longer book project (*Synthetic Philosophy of Logic*) begun in 2018 and since abandoned for various reasons, although the research programme it outlines remains active; 'The Artist's Brain at Work' grew out of a talk delivered at an event of the same name organised by NEUSCHLOSS at the Baltic Gallery in Gateshead, and was also published as 'Art and Cognition' in V. Janoščík, V. Bohal, and D. Breitling (eds.), *Reinventing Horizons* (Prague: Display, 2016), ; 'Art and Value' was originally delivered at SITAC in Puebla in 2016; 'What's in a Game?' was originally delivered at the *Philosophy Across Disciplines* conference at Newcastle University in June 2019; 'Not So Humble Pie' was submitted to a *New York Times* essay competition in 2012.

# THE DEMANDS OF THOUGHT

# Prometheanism and Rationalism

*Emancipatory politics must always destroy the appearance of a 'natural order', must reveal what is presented as necessary and inevitable to be a mere contingency, just as it must make what was previously deemed to be impossible seem attainable.*

Mark Fisher, *Capitalist Realism*

## 0. FUTURE SHOCKS

How are we to cope with the end of the End of History? From our current vantage point it is easy to dismiss Francis Fukuyama's prophecy of unending Western liberal democracy, but the truth is that we have yet to fully extract ourselves from the horizon of expectations that made such a seemingly absurd pronouncement possible. We remain stuck in an historical frame that congealed at the close of the last century, when the sudden collapse of communism in the East and the gradual assimilation of countercultures in the West dissolved our popular images of the outside of global capitalism and opposition to mainstream liberalism. The result is what Mark Fisher calls **capitalist realism**, in which our collective inability to imagine a post-capitalist or even post-neoliberal society leaves us with little choice but to plan for more of the same: incrementally improved consumer products, increasingly flexible working arrangements, and inexorable marketisation of public services. There is no alternative. The present will go on indefinitely. *The future has been cancelled.*

Nevertheless, there are signs that this horizon is beginning to disintegrate. The indefinite present is cracking under stress, and the future is slowly seeping back, unbidden, into our collective imagination. This has little to do with the global financial crisis and its ramifications. If anything, the crisis exemplifies capitalist realism's ability to render disruptive events normal. It has more to do with a network of self-reinforcing tendencies whose disruptive consequences are not simply difficult to predict, but impossible to normalise in the long run.

We can divide these tendencies into three broad strands, each of which is driving dynamics driving the human species away from its established equilibria:

i. **The Dehumanisation of the Environment**: Anthropogenic climate change and terminal resource depletion—as exemplified by permafrost melt and soil erosion—threaten to push the planetary environment beyond the threshold of human habitability.

ii. **The Dehumanisation of the Economy**: The current wave of technological automation—driven by advanced robotics, machine learning, and big data—is expelling labour from the production process faster than it can be reintegrated, disrupting the balance between labour and capital, and threatening a phase shift in global capitalism.

iii. **The Dehumanisation of the Human**: The rapid development and increasing accessibility of technologies that modify human biology, psychology, and sociality—spearheaded by the convergence of nanotechnology, biotechnology, information technology, and cognitive science—threatens to dissolve the cognitive, reproductive, and evolutionary unity of our common form of life.

The sheer causal complexity of these tendencies has so far made them easy to ignore, but their continuing escalation will produce future shock on multiple fronts: ecological disasters, professional extinctions, and ramifying dysphoria. However, it turns out that the future will not be more of the same, and we will be forced to face this fact whether we like it or not. This means reconstructing our horizon of expectations. The crucial question is whether we can do so in line with an egalitarian commitment to collective emancipation.

While these escalating tendencies confront us with possible discontinuities between the present and the future, they do not determine a single possible future, let alone an unconditionally better one. It is not just that the catastrophic transitions they portend have multiple possible outcomes (e.g., accelerating automation could equally end in neofeudalism, luxury communism, or cyberpunk dystopia), but that they interact and conflict with one another (e.g., the eradication of biological life on earth is likely to abort any nascent artificial superintelligence). This means that we can no more return to the Grand Narrative of Progress than we can remain in the End of History. If we are committed to an egalitarian politics, then this leaves us with three options for reconstructing our relation to the future:

i. **Fatalism**: We reject our historical agency, resign ourselves to the worst possible outcomes, and commit to a **politics of amelioration**.
ii. **Messianism**: We reject our historical agency, cultivate hope for the best possible outcomes, and commit to a **politics of anticipation**.
iii. **Prometheanism**: We embrace our historical agency, investigate the tendencies and their possible outcomes, and commit to a **politics of intervention**.

How are we to assess these options? It should be clear that Prometheanism constitutes the most radical break with the horizon of capitalist realism. The alternatives preserve different elements of its suppression of the future: fatalism *overcomes* our collective inability to imagine the future, only to consolidate limits on political planning, whereas messianism converts this inability into an eschatological vision of an unimaginable future, in order to replace political planning with political ritual. Prometheanism alone sees the transition between present and future as a site of political contestation. Given this, the question becomes: What reasons could there be to reject Prometheanism in favour of fatalism or messianism?

The Promethean affinity for technology provides the most obvious source of criticism. Each of the tendencies we are considering is intimately connected to the uncontrolled proliferation of technologies and their ramifications. However, in so far as Prometheanism is committed to technological control, it is entirely possible to dispute the use of any given technology from within the Promethean perspective. The most powerful source of anti-Prometheanism is thus to be found not in the rejection of any particular technological solution, but in more general critiques of technology, articulated in terms of the forms of thought and action that define it. For some, any problems associated with uncontrolled technological proliferation are inevitable consequences of the drive for technological control that Prometheanism exemplifies, and so cannot be solved by it. For others, any solutions that depend upon collective control are essentially complicit in the systems of domination that collective emancipation opposes, and so cannot be egalitarian. The critiques come in many forms: from Heidegger's critique of technological enframing and Adorno and Horkheimer's critique of instrumental rationality to post-structuralist, post-modernist, and post-colonial critiques of the legacy of the Enlightenment. It is impossible to address these individually here.

However, they can still be usefully analysed in terms of the way they motivate fatalism and messianism. The essence of fatalism is scepticism about our *capacity for action*. It allows that we can understand our fate, but denies that we can change it for the better. The essence of messianism is scepticism about our *capacity for understanding*. It denies that we can understand our fate, and thereby affirms that it may be better than we predict. If such scepticism is motivated by a general critique of our capacities, then it must be driven by worries about **Reason**. The former is driven by worries about *practical reason*, or our general ability to use our understanding of the world to change it; and the latter is driven by deeper worries about *theoretical reason*, or our general ability to understand the world in the first place. This means that any comprehensive defence of Prometheanism must include a defence of rationalism. I do not aim to provide such a comprehensive defence here, but simply to lay the groundwork for one, by exploring Prometheanism's dependence upon rationalism in more detail.

## 1. MYTHOLOGY AND ENLIGHTENMENT

If we are to explore the relation between Prometheanism and rationalism, then we must explain each position on its own terms. Let us begin with a provisional definition of Prometheanism, taken from Ray Brassier:[1]

> **Prometheanism**: The rejection of predetermined limits upon *action* and *self-transformation*.

This suggests a similar definition of rationalism:

---

1. Ray Brassier, 'Prometheanism and its Critics', in R. Mackay and A. Avanessian (eds.), *#accelerate: The Accelerationist Reader* (Falmouth and Berlin: Urbanomic/Merve, 2014).

**Rationalism**: The rejection of predetermined limits upon *thought* and *self-understanding*.

The parallel between these definitions then suggests an obvious connection between the two. If action is constrained by thought, and self-transformation is constrained by self-understanding, then the rejection of limits on one implies the rejection of limits on the other. Therefore, Prometheanism entails rationalism. However, there is more to each position than these provisional definitions suggest, and more to their connection than this simple entailment. What constitutes a predetermined limit in these cases? This crucial question is best answered by returning to the mythic origins of Western thought, and showing how the birth of Prometheanism and rationalism during the Enlightenment responds to these myths.

The foundational myths that establish the relation between *humanity* and *nature* in the Western tradition are the Judaeo-Christian myth of the fall of man and the Greek myth of Prometheus's theft of fire from the gods. Both myths describe a prelapsarian state wherein all living things have a prescribed role in the order of nature, as represented by the divine will. The origin of humanity in each case has two moments: a moment of creation as merely one more animal within the natural order, albeit with a distinctive quality, such as a positive resemblance to the divine or a negative absence of innate animal capacities, and a moment of rupture as humanity is wrenched from this order, only to be related to it in a new way. In the myth of the fall, it is the acquisition of *theoretical knowledge* that wrenches humans from the natural order, in so far as it is through understanding this order that it becomes possible to transgress it. In the myth of Prometheus, it is the acquisition of *practical knowledge* that wrenches humans from the natural order, in so far as it enables them to subvert this order and to carve out their own place within it. The expulsion from Eden and the torment of Prometheus serve to foreshadow the dangers of such knowledge.

The legacy of these myths consists in the way they frame the opposition between freedom and necessity. To understand this, it is important to make a distinction between **causal necessity** and **normative necessity**—between the way things must be and the way things ought to be—precisely because the myths systematically conflate the two. The myth of the fall actually invokes normative necessity so as to separate human freedom from causal necessity: the possibility of transgressing the moral order presupposes free will, understood as independence from the causal order. By contrast, the myth of Prometheus describes the opposition between human freedom and causal necessity as an ongoing struggle: the subversion of the natural order is a process of empowerment, in which we circumvent causal necessities by expanding our causal capacities. The theological foundation of each myth is the notion that the relation between freedom and necessity is circumscribed by the role that humanity plays within the natural order. This establishes freedom as a gift given to humanity, which comes with certain causal constraints on *possible action* and certain normative constraints on *permissible action*.

It is the structure of this gift that produces a systematic ambiguity between causal and normative constraints. This ambiguity is an essential component of the notion of nature in the Western tradition, and it is the ideological foundation of the predetermined limits that Prometheanism and rationalism reject. The ambiguity enables two rationalising dynamics that shape our historical consciousness:

i. **Inertial Rationalisation**: The gradual interpretation of the social norms governing historically stable societies as causal conditions of human survival, or the conversion of social equilibrium into natural equilibrium.

ii. **Reactive Rationalisation**: The sudden reinterpretation of constraints upon what we can do as constraints upon what we should do once they have been overcome, or the conversion of empowerment into transgression.

We could give many examples of these dynamics in action, and even operating in succession: the naturalisation of heterosexual monogamy and the denunciation of reproductive technologies such as contraception and artificial insemination are a case in point. However, it is more important to see the role they play in the constitution and exercise of social authority, in the form of tradition and religion. The basis of the Enlightenment is the rejection of these modes of authority, and it is here that Prometheanism is born, even if it is Romanticism that makes Prometheus's stand for human freedom against the will of Zeus the symbol of collective emancipation.

The history of the Enlightenment is rich, complex, and controversial, and I have no choice but to simplify it drastically. I will focus on Jonathan Israel's distinction between the *radical* and *moderate* strands of the Enlightenment, embodied respectively in the uncompromising rationalism of Spinoza and the more cautious empiricism of Locke.[2] The crucial epistemological disagreement between rationalism and empiricism concerns the relative priority of the *inferential* and *experiential* components of thought and their relative contribution to our knowledge. Rationalism has historically made the bolder metaphysical claims about reality—following lines of reasoning that carry it beyond the bounds of experience—while empiricism has done its best to police these boundaries. However, much as the rationalism of Descartes worked to reinvent Christian theology, the empiricism of Locke worked to preserve it from the more radical rationalism of Spinoza and his inheritors. This covert defence of religious faith was eventually formalised in Kant's transcendental synthesis of empiricism and rationalism. This exemplifies the modus operandi of the moderate strand: the conservation of certain forms of traditional and religious authority in the face of radical critique. However, it is important to explain how the epistemological considerations motivating moderation in the theoretical sphere come to motivate moderation in the practical sphere.

The political radicalism of Spinoza's thought lies in its evisceration of the mythic legacy of the Western tradition. On the one hand, he strips nature of all normative necessity: there is no transgression, only empowerment. On the other, he dissolves the opposition between human freedom and causal necessity: there is no free will, only acting in accordance with one's own essence. Freedom is causal power and causal autonomy, and it is given by nothing to no one. Politics is dedicated to designing society to maximise freedom, and it is beholden to neither tradition nor religion. It is not until Goethe that Spinoza will be linked to the figure of Prometheus, but he is clearly Promethean as we have defined it. By contrast, the political liberalism of Locke is founded on an appeal to natural rights to life, liberty, and property. These rights place normative constraints upon the exercise of political power over individuals, curtailing traditional and religious authority to some extent, but, as has become clear in the intervening

2. See J. Israel, *Radical Enlightenment: Philosophy and the Making of Modernity 1650–1750* (Oxford: Oxford University Press, 2002).

centuries, precisely how these rights limit the exercise of power and precisely who possesses them can be highly arbitrary. The fact that freedom remains a gift permits rationalisation of the traditional power of landowners and the sub-human status of women, slaves, and the colonised. What does any of this have to do with epistemology? In short, it is the ineffability of the gift that protects rationalisation from Reason.

It is extremely important to understand this theological residue correctly. The proliferation of political liberalism is associated with the rise of secularism in the West, and so we must explain how this ineffability is compatible with institutional agnosticism. The crucial point is that one can be actively indifferent to what gives the gift without being indifferent to what is given: we can be both thoroughly *agnostic* about the divine principle within nature and hopelessly *gnostic* about the divine spark within humanity. Political liberalism remains committed to a notion of liberty founded on the independence of free will from the causal order. It is a normative framework that begins with choice, and systematically ignores the causal conditions that enable choice. It is a demand for freedom that refuses to understand what freedom is. The consequence is a botched universalism, in which what it is to be a free agent has been implicitly indexed to a series of supposedly unmarked particulars, as the process of stripping away contingent characteristics halts at the edge of what it knows: the white, male, heterosexual, bourgeois, cis, etc.

However, it is here that classical rationalism also falters. Its rejection of predetermined limits upon thought undermines its rejection of predetermined limits upon self-understanding. Its commitment to engaging with Reason on its own terms—following lines of reasoning wherever they may lead—tends to obscure the causal conditions that enable such reasoning. This is nowhere more evident than in Descartes, where the purported self-evidence of the cogito conceals an unanalysed and unanalysable thinking substance. This makes what it is to be a *knowing subject* as easily indexed to unmarked particulars as what it is to be a *free agent*. This is a criticism that even Spinoza cannot fully avoid. The obvious connection outlined earlier means that this flaw in classical rationalism undermines classical Prometheanism. If we cannot understand the causal constraints upon our reasoning, then how can we overcome them?

## 2. CONTEMPORARY PROMETHEANISM

Having characterised the classical forms of Prometheanism and rationalism, and identified their central flaw, the question becomes: What distinguishes their contemporary forms, and can they overcome this flaw? I want to approach the question by outlining two contemporary forms of Prometheanism—left accelerationism and xenofeminism—articulating how they engage with the disruptive tendencies we began with, how they relate to the legacy of the Enlightenment, and on this basis, how they draw upon a more contemporary form of rationalism.

### (i) Left Accelerationism

There is some controversy regarding both the meaning of 'accelerationism' and its appropriation by a contemporary strand of left-wing—broadly egalitarian and anticapitalist—political theory. The term was introduced into political discourse by Benjamin Noys to describe a trend in French theory that had begun by the publication of Deleuze and Guattari's *Anti-Oedipus*. This had been pursued further in the anglophone world in the work of the Cybernetic Culture Research Unit (Ccru) and Nick Land. The defining idea was that within capitalism there remains an emancipatory tendency that must be accelerated in such a way that its oppressive elements, and perhaps even capitalism as such, might be dissolved. However, Noys took this to imply that 'the worse the better'. This interpretation gave rise to a persistent misunderstanding that has haunted the term ever since, namely, that the purpose of acceleration is to intensify the internal contradictions of capitalism as envisaged by Marx, or to deepen immiseration in order to hasten revolution. The common thread running from every proposed antecedent to accelerationism (e.g., Marx, Federov, Veblen, etc.) to every avowed variant of it (e.g., left, right, unconditional, etc.) is that they valorise the acceleration of positive tendencies at the expense of negative ones, no matter how much they may disagree about which tendencies are which, and whether they will lead us beyond capitalism or deeper into it. It was Mark Fisher who initially proposed to take back the term as a name for an active political project, developing themes from his work with Ccru in an explicitly egalitarian and anticapitalist direction. However, it wasn't until Alex Williams and Nick Srnicek's '#Accelerate: Manifesto for an Accelerationist Politics' that what would come to be called 'left accelerationism' was articulated:

> We believe the most important division in today's left is between those that hold to a folk politics of localism, direct action, and relentless horizontalism, and those that outline what must become called an accelerationist politics at ease with a modernity of abstraction, complexity, globality, and technology. The former remains content with establishing small and temporary spaces of non-capitalist social relations, eschewing the real problems entailed in facing foes which are intrinsically non-local, abstract, and rooted deep in our everyday infrastructure. The failure of such politics has been built-in from the very beginning. By contrast, an accelerationist politics seeks to preserve the gains of late capitalism while going further than its value system, governance structures, and mass pathologies will allow.[3]

The style of left accelerationism can be glimpsed in this origin: a viral manifesto with an associated hashtag, appended to any promising technological innovation; a renewed Promethean enthusiasm designed to counter the dour techno-scepticism all too common on the contemporary left. Faced with the slow cancellation of the future, it insists that there is no way out but through. No returning to the precarious balance of mid-century social democracy, the untapped potentials of the Paris Commune, or the imagined idylls of precolonial indigenous societies. No prelapsarian states we might revisit, let alone recreate in miniature. We have no choice but to go forwards, which means choosing among possibilities inherent within those tendencies that define the present. The substance of left accelerationism was developed further elsewhere, most notably in Williams and Srnicek's *Inventing the Future* (although the term 'accelerationism' is conspicuously absent therein).[4] It consists in the convergence of several related ideas: *left modernity*, *collective self-mastery*, and *socio-technical hegemony*.

Moving beyond the reclamation of the Enlightenment, left accelerationism aims to contest the legacy of modernity more generally, aiming to disentangle universal ideals of intellectual progress, individual freedom, and democratic governance from their complicity in the tortured histories of industrialisation and

---

3. N. Srnicek and A. Williams, '#Accelerate: Manifesto for an Accelerationist Politics', in Mackay and Avanessian (eds.), *#accelerate*, 347–62.

4. N. Srnicek and A. Williams, *Inventing the Future: Postcapitalism and a World Without Work* (London: Verso, 2015).

colonialism. Modernity is here seen not as a singular episode in European history, but as a generalised process unfolding at different times and places, unravelling circular and retrospective conceptions of time, and opening onto a future that might be better than the past, freeing individuals from their given social fate and offering them the opportunity to craft their own personal destiny. Modernisation is thus understood as the growth of personal autonomy not through isolation, but through increasing socioeconomic integration. This is the positive dimension of that tendency toward 'deterritorialisation' that Deleuze and Guattari associate with capitalism—dissolving established social codes and catalysing novel desires.

Building on classical Prometheanism's commitment to the cultivation of individual agency, left accelerationism encourages the cultivation of collective agency, seeing the social configurations in which we are embedded not simply as a source of limitations upon personal growth to potentially be overcome, but equally as a source of opportunities for growth that would be otherwise impossible. From this perspective, the role of government is not simply to secure the *formal* freedom to make certain important life choices without interference (e.g., becoming an artist), but to enable the *real* freedom to live such lives without guaranteed failure (e.g., becoming an artist without starving). To put this in other terms, our capacity for individual self-understanding and self-transformation is to some extent mediated by our capacity for collective self-understanding and self-transformation. Democratic governance is thus not to be defined by commitment to any specific decision-making procedure, but by the goal of enabling individual self-mastery through collective self mastery.

Breaking with much of the contemporary left's focus on familiar tactics, left accelerationism recommends a renewed concern with overarching strategy, retooling Gramsci's analysis of cultural hegemony to cover dominance not only in the sphere of ideas and associated social formations, but also in the sphere of material platforms, or the technological infrastructure which facilitates the communication of ideas and the coordination of action. The pursuit of such sociotechnical hegemony is not simply an exercise in conventional democratic politics, be it building a centralised vanguard party or raising distributed consciousness, but a matter of dismantling obstacles to democracy by systematically contesting the power of those vested interests that sustain the horizon of capitalist realism. This requires a willingness to embrace vertical organisational structures alongside horizontal ones, but more generally to countenance a plurality of organisational forms and political tactics working in concert—a functioning ecology of left-wing institutions from think-tanks and unions to protest groups and new wave media.

Synthesising all this, we might venture the following definition of the project as a whole:

> Left Accelerationism: the insistence that the transition between capitalism and post-capitalism should be understood in the same terms as the transition between feudalism and capitalism; as a complex process that can and should be accelerated rather than as a radical break in the horizon of thought and action.

Out of the three disruptive tendencies with which we began, left accelerationism is focused upon the dehumanisation of the economy. It sees accelerating automation as a point of contestation, providing the opportunity to articulate a post-work politics which decouples the value of human life from the capacity for wage labour. This decoupling is neither automatic nor guaranteed, but it can potentially be encouraged by advocating for a universal basic income (UBI). This would not only be a temporary solution to the problem of surplus labour, but would provide a way to ratchet toward other political demands, making it easier for people to organise without fear of being unable to sustain themselves. Even for those still in work, it would constitute a generalised strike fund, increasing the power of unions in trade disputes. This is far from a social panacea, but it suggests one way to exploit an extant self-reinforcing tendency to steer the future in a more egalitarian direction.

How might we characterise the difference between such renewed radicalism and the inheritors of the moderate strand of the Enlightenment? Political liberalism has evolved in various ways since its birth. On the one hand, following the rise of secular democratic states, it has ceased to be a doctrine to become something more like the ideological background of politics in the West, devolving from a set of explicit principles into a range of diffuse attitudes about the social and economic orientation of society, striking a balance between liberty and equality putatively compatible with a market economy under capitalism. On the other, in response to the various crises these states have undergone, it has spawned new doctrinal variants which reconceive the relation between its social and economic dimensions and place a different emphasis upon them. Most important among these are what we might call modernist liberalism, exemplified by the work of John Rawls and Jürgen Habermas, and neoliberalism, exemplified by the work of Friedrich Hayek and Milton Friedman. Although 'neoliberalism' can also refer to the background ideology specific to the era of capitalist realism, I'll here focus on its doctrinal form.

Each of these variants emphasises one dimension of classical liberalism and grounds it in a particular form of Reason.

Modernist liberalism focuses on the social dimension, grounding it in an account of what Habermas calls communicative rationality, or the resolution of practical disagreements through a process of free and open debate in which parties avoid appeals to private reasons such as religious commitments or personal interests. The proper balance between individual liberty and social equality secured by the state is determined directly by democratic consensus but may be delimited by the conditions that make such consensus possible: a well-functioning public sphere with associated democratic and legal institutions.

Neoliberalism focuses on the economic dimension, grounding it in an account of what we might call prudential rationality, or the optimisation of collective decision making through a process of free contract and competition in which individuals aim to maximise their own personal preferences. The proper balance between individual liberty and social equality is set indirectly by economic self-organisation but may be delimited by the state in accordance with the conditions that make such self-organisation possible: well-functioning markets and associated regulatory and legal institutions.

Each position relies upon an idealisation of individual behaviour, be it the assumption of an 'ideal speech situation' in which power dynamics are suppressed, or the image of 'homo economicus' under which agents are modelled as engines for maximising utility.

Although left accelerationism distinguishes itself from both forms of liberalism, it agrees to some extent with modernist liberalism about the *ends* of political action and to some extent with neoliberalism about its *means*. The idea of a society in which problems are solved and differences resolved through free and open debate, a society all of whose members have been educated and otherwise enabled to take part on an equal footing, is a laudable goal. But the assumption that the current state of society approximates this, or that we could proceed as if it does, is nothing but an obstacle to the effective realisation of the project of collective self-mastery. By contrast, neoliberalism has been extremely effective in establishing and enacting its political programme precisely by avoiding open competition in the public sphere, instead creating a coalition of powerful interests and building a range of institutions capable of disseminating and then enforcing its ideas without the need for popular support. It is perhaps the most impressive example in recent history of a hegemonic political programme. If we are interested in creating a world in which we might aspire to be the free agents liberalism assumes us to be, then we can learn something from neoliberalism about the cultivation of collective agency.

The deeper disagreements between left accelerationism and liberalism concern the concept of freedom as such. For the most part, liberalism concerns itself with negative rather than positive freedom, freedom *from* interference rather than freedom *to* act, or with *liberty* as opposed to *capacity*. This underpins its emphasis upon formal as opposed to real freedoms—abstract rights to choose certain options (e.g., the right to take an annual holiday), rather than concrete abilities to achieve the relevant outcomes (e.g., the ability to travel abroad with one's family). This is why the liberal state is generally geared toward securing equality of opportunity rather than equality of outcome. However, as we noted earlier, liberalism also overlooks the extent to which choice itself is a cognitive capacity whose causal basis can be encouraged or undermined. The idealised accounts of communicative and prudential deliberation upon which contemporary liberalism depends disguise these underlying causal realities, and with them the ways in which our choices can be systematically distorted.

This is most evident in the picture of prudential reasoning at the heart of neoliberalism, which treats the process of calculating which choices maximise our preferences as if it were frictionless. From this perspective, the more options we have and the more information available about them the better, in so far as, taken together, our individually optimal purchasing decisions compute a collectively optimal distribution of resources. However, this fails to take into account our individual cognitive limitations: not simply the type of information we are able to process, but how cognitively expensive it is to do so. Once we acknowledge that decision making has costs, we see that more options and information are only better up to the point at which we can afford to process them, beyond which they become noise, actively making it harder for us to make optimal choices. This reveals the false freedom promised by neoliberalism for what it is: not only is the proliferation of options for consumer products no substitute for genuine life choices, but the growing weight of decisions we are forced to make constitutes its own form of cognitive oppression. It also suggests that designing platforms that enable us to pool our cognitive resources in new ways might enable cognitive liberation through collectivisation.

Given all of this, we can see that what left accelerationism draws from contemporary rationalism is a theory of how freedom is causally realised in the world—a theory that explains what it is to be a rational agent, what capacities are involved in thought and action, and how individual agents might be composed into genuine collective agents capable of processing information from and intervening in their political environments. Any egalitarian politics of collective emancipation that aims to oppose liberalism without taking the causal basis of agency into account inevitably collapses back into voluntarism. This is more or less a rarefaction of the liberal conception of the individual will, but in the collective case it tends toward insurrectionism (e.g., The Invisible Committee, communisation theory, etc.). This is essentially the position that the collective will can neither be created nor structured. All one can do is wait for spontaneous uprisings of collective volition. This clearly constitutes a retreat from Prometheanism to some form of fatalism or messianism.

### (ii) Xenofeminism

Inspired by the technofeminism of Shulamith Firestone as much as the cyberfeminism of Sadie Plant and VNS Matrix, *The Xenofeminist Manifesto* written by the Laboria Cuboniks collective shares many theoretical concerns with left accelerationism—embracing technology, complexity, and abstraction—along with a practical concern with the importance of strategy, but its inherent multiplicity and mutability is a deliberate reflection of these concerns. It is proposed not as a doctrine, but as a platform. This should not be taken to imply that xenofeminism lacks intellectual coherence. On the one hand, it critiques certain conceptual pitfalls to which it thinks other feminisms are prone, celebrating impurity and transformation while excoriating every possible appeal to nature:

> We need new affordances of perception and action unblinkered by naturalised identities. In the name of feminism, 'Nature' shall no longer be a refuge of injustice, or a basis for any political justification whatsoever!
>
> If nature is unjust, change nature![5]

On the other, it develops a new, generic conception of universality that is not indifferent to questions of identity:

> Xenofeminism understands that the viability of emancipatory abolitionist projects—the abolition of class, gender, and race—hinges on a profound reworking of the universal. The universal must be grasped as generic, which is to say, intersectional. Intersectionality is not the morcellation of collectives into a static fuzz of cross-referenced identities, but a political orientation that slices through every particular, refusing the crass pigeonholing of bodies. This is not a universal that can be imposed from above, but built from the bottom up—or, better, laterally, opening new lines of transit across an uneven landscape. This non-absolute, generic universality must guard against the facile tendency of conflation with bloated, unmarked particulars—namely Eurocentric universalism—whereby the male is mistaken for the sexless, the white for raceless, the cis for the real, and so on. Absent such a universal, the abolition of class will remain a bourgeois fantasy, the abolition of race will remain a tacit white-supremacism, and the abolition of gender will remain a thinly veiled misogyny, even—especially—when prosecuted by avowed feminists themselves.[6]

Xenofeminism thus extends the concerns of left accelerationism not simply by addressing the personal dimension of the political but also by synthesising its modernist ideals with postmodern critiques of the corresponding historical realities. In her book *Xenofeminism*, Laboria Cuboniks member Helen Hester identifies three principal aspects of this synthesis: *technomaterialism*, *anti-naturalism*, and *gender abolitionism*.[7]

---

5. Laboria Cuboniks, 'Xenofeminism: A Politics for Alienation', <https://laboriacuboniks.net/manifesto/xenofeminism-a-politics-for-alienation/>.
6. Ibid.
7. H. Hester, *Xenofeminism* (Cambridge: Polity, 2018).

Although it believes in the emancipatory potential of technology, xenofeminism refuses to reify this potential, aiming instead to contextualise and concretise it wherever possible. On the one hand, the distributed information technologies that early cyberfeminists celebrated as experiments in disembodiment—abstracting social relations from familiar somatic indexes of identity—must be embedded in a range of material systems orthogonal to the body—physical interfaces, networked data centres, and for-profit enterprises that shape the flow of information. On the other hand, even the seemingly self-contained technologies that give us purchase on our environment and ourselves—from the domestic devices that sustain our households to the pharmaceuticals that modulate our biology—must be embedded in the wider social world, revealing the new expectations, norms, and otherwise unintended consequences that their usage generates. Xenofeminism is less interested in designing ideal technological solutions to social problems than in promulgating technologies which empower those oppressed by society as it really exists.

While it is utterly committed to divesting nature of all normative significance, xenofeminism insists on doing so without reinforcing the perennial distinction between nature and culture, articulating a unified space of action in which technical manipulation is continuous with political contestation. This means that social constructivism's insights concerning the contingency and mutability of gender, race, disability, and similar categories can be retained without either reducing related biological categories to their social reception or treating them as immutable essences foreclosed to modification. From this perspective, the body is a site of technopolitical intervention, to be manipulated or modified in ways that express or enhance our personal autonomy, rather than a locus of authentic suffering to be mitigated and managed.

Where some proponents of gender abolitionism take this to entail the suppression of gender performance entirely, xenofeminism interprets it as the elimination of those social roles traditionally associated with such performance, most importantly the division of reproductive labour. To the extent that this division is premised upon anatomical differences between the sexes, the development and deployment of technologies that obviate these differences—from hormonal birth control to functional exo-wombs—is a necessary but insufficient condition of gender abolition. Moreover, the obviation of sexual difference is only a means to this end. The ultimate goal of abolition is the control of anatomy, so that the biological characteristics that originally determined the parameters of gender dissolve into it, becoming as mutable and as significant as any other choice about social presentation. This is what it means to say that xenofeminism is a transfeminism: its aim is not to have less than two genders, but as many as we desire. This strategy of multiplying differences while obviating their consequences functions as a model for the abolition of race, class, and other forms of social classification.

Synthesising all of this, we might summarise the overall orientation of xenofeminism with the following definition:

> Xenofeminism: the insistence that the artificiality of identity must be embraced, treating it as a space of socio-technical experimentation, rather than a matrix of options for authentic personhood.

Out of the three disruptive tendencies with which we began, xenofeminism is focused upon the dehumanisation of the human. It sees the increasing accessibility of technologies that give us control over our own bodies as a point of contestation, enabling decentralised groups of biohackers to bypass the centralised political and medical institutions that enforce the reactive rationalisation of gender norms by policing and gatekeeping the means of transgression. It promotes providing everyone with access to the tools and techniques needed to manage their own reproductive health (e.g., the work done by the GynePunk collective), and providing trans individuals the means to produce their own sex hormones (e.g., Ryan Hammond's Open Source Gendercodes project). This is in no way an integrated solution to the problems of patriarchal oppression, but it offers a concrete way to cultivate increased bodily autonomy, and thereby to facilitate further experimentation not only with personal morphology, but with the social and biological parameters of species reproduction.

If left accelerationism contains a critique of contemporary liberal doctrine, xenofeminism tackles a more diffuse feature of the legacy of the moderate Enlightenment, namely the residual normative naturalism that persists within liberal discourse even as it situates itself in opposition to the more explicitly naturalist narratives of reactionary conservatism. Because Lockean appeals to natural rights remain the tacit guarantor of individual freedoms within liberal democracies, the easiest way to justify the permissibility of a behaviour is to argue that it is in some sense natural. This discursive path of least resistance reinforces the dynamics of rationalisation by separating and selectively legitimising forms of transgression in ways that undermine alliances between different interest groups. The specific example that xenofeminism focuses upon is the popular argument that homosexuality is valid in so far as homosexuals are 'born this way'. This notion is increasingly used to drive a wedge between different segments of the queer community, restricting sex and sexuality to the realm of innate biology, while gender and its nuances are consigned to the realm of personal choice. This simultaneously allows homosexuality to be remapped to the 'natural' model of heterosexual relationships (i.e., monogamy and child rearing), while dissociating it from the 'unnatural' practice of transgenderism.

While the temptation exists to repeat this strategy of legitimation through naturalisation in the case of transgenderism, perhaps by locating some neural correlate of gender dysphoria, xenofeminism demands that we resist it in this and every case. In insisting that the desire for a seemingly transgressive behaviour is really legitimate precisely because it is not chosen, we further entrench the notion that the limits of what it is permissible to want are set by some underlying human nature that we may not choose to change. This ensures that the dynamics of rationalisation will continue to suppress our personal autonomy, preventing us from choosing to do and be things that have not been seen before, simply because they are new. We may succeed in naturalising transgenderism only to condemn the waves of morphological and libidinal experimentation that are bound to follow it, and the new identities these precipitate.

Crucially, this does not mean that xenofeminism rejects attempts to investigate the causal underpinnings of our desires. Xenofeminism remains committed to the Enlightenment idea that universality is indexed to the knowing subject, as exemplified by the project of natural science. It believes Reason is realised in the process of scientific inquiry. However, it sees identifying and correcting the ways in which the positionality of scientists distorts this process as an integral part of the process itself (e.g., compensating for over-representation of white, male, cis perspectives). This includes purging science of any residual normative naturalism. One need look no further than the literature in evolutionary psychology to see the tools of natural science being turned to the task of rationalising dominant social norms regarding the division of reproductive labour. By contrast, xenofeminism looks to biology and psychology as a source of superior technologies of selfhood, seeking greater purchase on the processes that shape desire.

If what left accelerationism draws from contemporary rationalism is an account of causal autonomy, consonant with Spinoza's conception of freedom as *self-causation*, then what xenofeminism draws from it is an account of normative autonomy, consonant with Kant's conception of freedom as *self-legislation*. Unlike some strands of postmodern feminism, xenofeminism does not flinch from invoking justice as a normative ideal. Nature must be judged in accordance with a standard that does not derive from nature. But establishing a non-natural foundation for normativity is no easy task. Xenofeminism is far from foundationalist in its approach, but if it can be said to begin anywhere, it is by rethinking the notion of selfhood involved in self-legislation, trying to divest it of any 'given' identity that might precede or constrain the process of self-construction. It is on this basis that alienation is conceived as a vector of emancipation. By disrupting our implicit understanding of who we are, alienation forces us to acknowledge this self-conception and take control of it. This transforms our progressive exile from a series of seemingly Edenic harmonies—be they economic, sociological, or environmental—into an esoteric genealogy of freedom.

Similarly, if the irrationalist alternative to left accelerationism is a rarefaction of liberal voluntarism, then the irrationalist alternative to xenofeminism is a mutation of liberal gnosticism: the inevitable embrace of the theological residue of the moderate Enlightenment, displaced from the soul onto something else (e.g., the 'lived body'). The contemporary discourse of embodiment, which encompasses various philosophical perspectives (e.g., phenomenology, affect theory, non-philosophy, etc.), tends to substitute the capacity to suffer for autonomy as the source of moral worth. It's perhaps useful to see this as a misreading of Foucault: if one believes that the construction of the self implies that it is illusory, then this leaves the body as the real basis of normative theorising. However, this is not necessarily the body as understood by natural science, but an 'immanent reality' which can only be grasped through 'lived experience'. This curious substitute for apophatic revelation is well-suited to the needs of messianism.

## 3. CONTEMPORARY RATIONALISM

As we noted earlier, the main flaw of classical rationalism was its inability to think about the implementation of Reason as a causal process, and the constraints that come with this. We even saw how this flaw persists in the formal conception of prudential rationality deployed by neoliberalism, in its failure to account for the cost of reasoning. However, the true legacy of the twentieth century is a different set of formal tools that may allow us to correct these— those of computer science. The key insight here is that computation is essentially functional. One can in principle construct information processing systems with the full expressive power of a Universal Turing Machine out of whatever components one prefers—silicon, clockwork, or even meat—without thereby limiting the range of computations of which they are capable. This allows us to discuss the implementation details of such systems at various degrees of abstraction. For example, by quantifying the computational resources consumed by solving problems of varying degrees of complexity (i.e., memory and time). This enables us to circumscribe what is computationally possible, uncovering in-principle limits on the power of calculation that supersede our naive intuitions.

The core commitment of what has come to be called neorationalism—a label linking the work of Reza Negarestani, Ray Brassier, myself, and others—is that computer science makes it possible to describe the structure of rational agency at a level of abstraction sufficient to encompass every conceivable implementation (e.g., humans, artificial intelligences, aliens) without thereby ignoring the constraints imposed by the details of each implementation. What distinguishes this from more familiar forms of computationalism is the idea not only that is this a universal structure, but that it substantially conforms to the picture of mind developed by Kant, Hegel, and their inheritors. From this perspective, the theoretical project of artificial general intelligence is essentially the same as what Kant calls transcendental psychology—a minimal description of what a system must do in order to be capable of thought and action in general. Furthermore, because this structure is functional, it is recursive: it is possible to compose rational agents out of other rational agents, enabling a computational interpretation of Hegelian Geist.

I can't provide a comprehensive overview of neorationalism here, but I'll try to sketch what I take to be the core of its conception of Reason in outline, then show how this addresses some common objections to rationalism. This should demonstrate how it can provide contemporary Prometheanism with the resources it needs.

## (i) What Reason Is

There are various different types of information and ways of processing them. Here we should consider not only file formats and computer programs, but also the varied sorts of sensory stimulation that animals have evolved to respond to, and the features of their environments they are able to anticipate and manipulate on that basis. It makes sense to say that animals process information about these features—tracking the movements of predators or prey, classifying occurrences as opportunities or obstacles. However, such cognition is essentially parochial, as limited to the range of environmental features it is adapted to as programs are restricted to the types of data they are written for. What distinguishes rationality from both animal cognition and instrumental computation is its generality: the ability to incorporate and operate upon any form of information in principle. Even though most human cognition remains essentially animal—navigating familiar macro-scale environments, performing habitual domestic tasks—the mark of our rationality is the capacity to utilise information we did not evolve to process—exploiting micro-scale properties of materials, devising novel solutions to nationwide problems.

Of course, this does not mean that we possess an innate capacity to make immediate use of any and every type of information with which we are presented. Rather, the generality of Reason consists in its extensibility, or how it enables us to acquire capacities to process new forms of information. Language is the medium that makes this possible. While it lets us articulate and communicate our prelinguistic understanding of the world—talking about 'dogs', 'chairs', 'water', and the like—it also extends this understanding beyond the scope of ordinary experience, permitting discussion of 'electrons', 'prime numbers', and 'justice'. In order to see how this works, we first need to grasp how information is integrated at the level of conscious experience, and how this relates to Kant's account of self-consciousness.

At its core, information integration is a matter of maintaining a *globally* consistent representation of the environment by ensuring that its various components are *locally* consistent with one another.[8] Importantly, this is not simply a matter of piecing together similar parts into a larger picture by ensuring that they agree along their edges, but of combining heterogeneous types of data covering the same regions.[9] For example, assume I see a car drive across one part of my visual field, before disappearing from view behind a copse of trees, yet I can still hear the sound of the engine changing as it moves away from me. Those are two different types of sensory information, but my brain seamlessly integrates them into a representation of a single object travelling along a defined path, and thus anticipates the car's emergence from the other side. There are a multitude of unconscious processes operating concurrently on sensory information at any one time, but these feed into an integrated simulation of the environment populated by unified objects whose properties vary in consistent ways. These objects remain invariant under shifts in perspective and sensory modality. The crucial point is that once these invariants have been identified, they can then be tagged with novel types of data, as long as there are ways to check for consistency with established types. For example, I might be able to hear that the car engine is misfiring, and on the basis of that judgement deduce the best approach to diagnosing and fixing it. To put this in other terms, the structure of conceptual judgement is implicit in any sufficiently complex and integrated simulation of an environment. This is the essence of Kant's account of the relation between the faculties of *understanding* and *imagination*.

Judgements are characterised by their role in inference: they are the kind of representations that can serve as premises or conclusions. It is the possibility that any two judgements might be inferentially related that underpins the extensibility of Reason, because it ensures that any piece of information we have learned to articulate might potentially be relevant to any other. For example, when facts about increasing levels of atmospheric carbon dioxide become a factor in estimating long-term crop yields, or when links are discovered between seemingly unconnected mathematical fields. It's this open-ended inferential potential that

8. Negarestani has emphasised the importance of this relation between local and global, and the transit between the two and, following Fernando Zalamea, the way that it can be captured by the mathematical concept of a sheaf (R. Negarestani, 'Where is the Concept?', in R. Mackay [ed.], *When Site Lost the Plot* [Falmouth: Urbanomic, 2015], 225–51).

9. Michael Robinson has shown how this sort of heterogeneous data integration is naturally described using sheaves ('Sheaves are the Canonical Data Structure for Sensor Integration', *Information Fusion* 36 [July 2017]: 208–24).

permits us to integrate any information we absorb into a unified representation of the world that outstrips environmental simulation. However, this does not mean that all our cognition must consist in explicit chains of argumentation. For Kant, while the capacity for judgement and inference is the mark of self-consciousness, there is much conscious thought that is not yet self-conscious (e.g., catching a thrown ball, or changing gears while driving). But what distinguishes this from the myriad forms of information processing that operate unconsciously (e.g., regulating body temperature) is the *possibility* of it becoming self-conscious. This is to say that conscious cognition can feed information into reasoning processes which can then in turn modulate it (e.g., encountering an obstacle while driving and deciding to modify one's itinerary).

There is one final layer to this picture of information integration: revisability. Extending our information-processing capacities involves more than just accumulating new ranges of facts. It also requires us to manage the concepts that articulate the content of these facts (qua judgements), revising the inferential rules they encode in ways that enrich their consequences, eliminate inconsistencies, and maintain an economy of principles. For example, when gravity was initially mathematised, when electrons were reconceived as both particles and waves, or when the concept of space was generalised beyond Euclidean planar geometry. The parameters of the simulation that constitutes our conscious experience may stay more or less the same over time, while the integrated representation of the world that emerges from our self-conscious interpretation of it may change and evolve. This is the essence of Kant's account of the relation between the faculties of *understanding* and *reason*, though it is substantially elaborated by Hegel in various ways.

Hegel's key insight, developed in more detail by Robert Brandom, is that the structure of concept revision is implicitly social.[10] This is not simply a matter of the dialogical process of challenge and response, but a matter of perspectival navigation. Given that any two interlocutors might have divergent understandings of a concept, endorsing different patterns of inference, they must be able to dynamically track these divergences if they are to successfully communicate.

10. Cf. R. Brandom, *Making It Explicit: Reasoning, Representing, and Discursive Commitment* (Cambridge, MA: Harvard University Press, revised edition 1998), chapter 8; R. Brandom, *Reason in Philosophy: Animating Ideas* (Cambridge, MA: Belknap Press of Harvard University Press, 2013), chapter 3.

For example, for a neoclassical economist to understand a Marxian economist's arguments about value as it pertains to the rate of profit, they must grasp that by 'value' they mean abstract necessary labour time, not marginal utility. To put this in different terms, for there to be any productive disagreement between two parties, there must be enough agreement about the meanings of their terms for them to get purchase upon one another's positions. They must be able to interpret one another as representing the same things, even though they conceive of these things in different ways. However, this does not mean that there need be any preestablished definitions (or analytic judgements) agreed upon in advance, only that they can triangulate their divergent usages on the fly.

The core point is that this triangulation is necessary not only to make sense of disagreements between distinct perspectives on the world, but to make sense of the way in which a single perspective evolves over time. We have to be able to interpret the term 'electron' as representing the same thing across the history of modern physics, from Rutherford's model to quantum mechanics, string theory, and beyond, in order to see this as a series of changes leading to a progressively more accurate picture of reality. Moreover, we have to be able to sustain continuity of representation between different conceptual frameworks in order to translate between them when simpler ones are more convenient, such as Newton's gravitational mechanics, which are often much more practical than Einstein's. More generally, this inherently communicative dimension of rationality enables us not only to navigate differences between our own and others' perspectives, but also to integrate multiple overlapping perspectives within ourselves, stitching together the patchwork of adaptive cognitive systems and disparate conceptual frameworks fitted to different situations and phenomena into a unified picture of reality, ensuring that it remains a picture of the same world even as it expands to encompass more of it.[11]

To summarise this reframing of the Kantian-Hegelian framework, we might say that information integration operates across three notional layers—imagination, understanding, and reason—and can be divided into two concurrent stages. Firstly, sensory information is integrated into a simulation (imagination)

11. This is one way of thinking about the ongoing accommodation between what Wilfrid Sellars calls the manifest and scientific images of the world (W. Sellars, 'Philosophy and the Scientific Image of Man', in *Science, Perception, and Reality*, ed. R. Colodny [Atascadero, CA: Ridgeview, 2017]).

populated by objects classified into types by more or less fixed conceptual frameworks (understanding) that enable the formation of judgments about them. Secondly, this conceptually formatted information is integrated into a unified representation of the world by a process of elaborating consequences and eliminating inconsistencies (reason), which thereby forces revisions to the underlying frameworks (understanding). However, another way to think about this is that there are two distinct types of objectivity at work here. On the one hand, there are perceptual objects that remain invariant across changes in sensory perspective, as described in depth by Husserl and his inheritors. On the other, there are discursive objects that remain invariant across changes in rational perspective, as representational loci of possible disagreement. These forms of objectivity coincide insofar as the objects of ordinary perception provide our basic discursive purchase upon the world (i.e., 'dogs', 'chairs', 'water'), but diverge as we become capable of positing things that we do not perceive directly (i.e., 'electrons', 'prime numbers', 'justice').

### (ii) What Reason is Not

When addressing common objections to rationalism, it's important to recognise that many of them stem from the ways in which the capacity for Reason was presented by the classical rationalists. The most pernicious of these is the idea that it consists in a sort of 'intellectual intuition' through which truth is revealed as self-evident, as implied by Descartes's notion of 'clear and distinct perception'. Against this, Reason must be opposed to every form of revelation, resisting any appeal to self-evidence beyond rigorous mathematical proof—a procedure that can be broken down and verified step by step. Rationalism is not the pursuit of a special type of intuition, but the abjuration of intuition as such—a commitment to follow chains of inference that might lead to counterintuitive conclusions. The twentieth century gifted us with a series of mathematical results that are extremely counterintuitive. From Russell's paradox, which shows that our naive ways of reasoning about collections of things cannot be made formally consistent, to Gödel's incompleteness theorems, which show that for any consistent set of axioms strong enough to formalise arithmetic there will always be truths they cannot prove, and they will never prove their own consistency, we have come to see the power of Reason to progressively curtail our intuitions about reasoning itself.

This leads us to another common source of criticisms. Although mathematical proof is rightly presented as the paragon of rational activity, this does not mean that all reasoning should or can be remade in its image. This perspective is exemplified by Leibniz's dream of a *calculus ratiocinator* which would obviate debate by enabling us to deduce the answer to any question in a mechanical fashion from fixed definitions and postulates. However, the vast majority of reasoning doesn't take this form. Some reasoning is *inductive*, working with measures of probability. Some reasoning is *abductive*, reconstructing plausible explanations. Even most deductive reasoning is thoroughly *non-monotonic*, permitting us to draw inferences that may be invalidated by an open-ended range of exceptions.[12] All this is before we consider the sorts of conceptual revision discussed earlier, in which the very definitions we begin with become subject to *dialectical* challenge and modification. Contrary to the image of Reason as proceeding inexorably from certain premises to necessary conclusions, it is more often a dynamic process of managing contingency under conditions of uncertainty. This much is obviously true in the empirical domain, but it can even be glimpsed in mathematics itself. Although mathematical *justification* is strictly deductive, mathematical *discovery* is not.[13] Indeed, Gödel's theorems prove that the process of mathematical discovery cannot be reduced to the mechanical elaboration of the consequences of a fixed set of axioms. This definitive blow to Leibniz's dream is perhaps the best example of Reason undermining the pretensions of naive rationalism.

Another common objection to rationalism is that it fails to account for people's actual behaviour, which is frequently irrational. There are two basic responses to this. The first response is that Reason is an ideal. Considered either as a functional structure or as a practical activity, it is governed by norms that are applied with varying degrees of success. Most obvious amongst these is the norm of consistency: we should avoid contradictory beliefs. Yet contradictory beliefs are commonplace. Our world views are filled with contradictions, only

12. See R. Brandom, *Between Saying and Doing: Towards an Analytic Pragmatism* (Oxford and New York: Oxford University Press, 2010), chapter 4.

13. Cf. I. Lakatos, *Proofs and Refutations: The Logic of Mathematical Discovery* (Cambridge: Cambridge University Press, 2008).

some of which we are aware of. The only way to avoid this entirely is to have few to no beliefs, and to avoid acquiring more. The aim of rationality is not a static state of perfect consistency, but a dynamic process of continuous revision, in which discovering and divesting ourselves of the contradictions implicit in our world view is the engine of epistemic progress. We can fail to live up to this ideal without ceasing to be subject to it.

The second response is to question the conception of irrationality at issue, which more often than not is concerned with practical rather than theoretical reasoning. For example, the economic conception of prudential reasoning we considered earlier characterises any deviation from the maximisation of individual utility as essentially irrational. Here the response parallels Adorno and Horkheimer's critique of instrumental reason: this is but one aspect of practical reasoning, whose structure readily permits a deductive formalisation, but it is not thereby the whole of it, and to overgeneralise it is to annihilate any form of value that cannot be reduced to aggregate preferences. If ethics and aesthetics are to be more than mere applied game theory, then we must recognise that there are dimensions of practical reasoning not captured by the calculus of utility. The characterisation of actions that are insufficiently self-serving as effectively irrational is a truncation of the scope of practical reason and with it the range of rational motivations.

This brings us to an objection usually levelled by affect theory and similar perspectives, namely, that rationalism presents a conception of the mind that is essentially disembodied and thereby affectless. Crucially, the model of rationality presented above is not inherently disembodied, but accounts for the way in which the sorts of embodied cognition involved in navigating our environment are integrated into the wider inferential economy of conceptual representation. The role of practical reasoning is not simply to *initialise* action by deducing what is appropriate to do in every case, but more generally to *control* action by modulating the pre-rational processes already driving our behaviour. This is the upshot of Kant's account of the relation between consciousness and self-consciousness. But how does this relation incorporate affect? One way to approach this question is to consider when and why we might want to characterise an emotional response as irrational. The tendency to treat every emotional response as in some sense irrational is precisely what motivates this objection to rationalism in the first place.

On the one hand, we might characterise an emotional response as irrational because there is some strict sense in which it motivates us to act in the wrong way. For example, I might have an irrational fear of flying, which prevents me from travelling in ways that would otherwise further my life goals. By contrast, then, we can characterise many fear responses as perfectly rational, precisely in so far as they motivate us to act in ways that effectively further our goals, such as jumping out of the path of a moving car. In a case like that, if I'd had to evaluate my options in relation to all my practical projects, and come to a reasoned conclusion about the best thing to do all things considered, the car almost certainly would have hit me before I had finished. What this reveals about the role of affective cognition is that it often functions as a heuristic, inclining us to act in certain ways on the basis of signals from our environment, processing information in a less accurate, but far quicker and less cognitively taxing way than self-conscious inference. Such low-level practical cognition is only conscious to the extent that we're able to unpack it and make sense of our feelings in context, although we're usually capable of doing this (and when we're not, there's always therapy).

On the other hand, we might characterise an emotional response as irrational because there is some strict sense in which it is inconsistent. For example, I might have two friends for whom I feel equal warmth and affection, but who have some dispute in which only one of them can be right. When I am with either friend I am inclined to agree with their perspective and support them against the other, which works in that *local* situation, but not *globally* across every social situation, particularly situations where they are present together. The only way to be consistent in such situations is either to pick a side, or to refuse to pick one, which may mean drawing conclusions from the relevant facts underpinning the disagreement. As such, my inclination to support both sides is essentially irrational. However, what distinguishes this from the previous case is that we needn't interpret these inclinations as heuristics. The friendships and the feelings bound up with them need not be seen as means to some further end but can be ends in themselves. This is to say that affects can constitute a genuine source of motivation, even though there may be conflicts between them that demand rational resolution.

These examples reveal a crucial parallel between theoretical and practical reason, namely, that just as we must integrate our sensations, beliefs, and theories into a coherent picture of the world, so must we integrate our emotions, desires, and values into a coherent pattern of action within it. Moreover, they suggest the role that self-construction plays within this process, in so far as choosing to affirm one impulse over another, conflicting one can mean *identifying* with one source of motivation while *dissociating* from the other. For example, I could always choose to treat my fear of flying as an important part of who I am, and thereby de-prioritise the desires that conflict with it. This makes personal autonomy not just a matter of which practical principles I hold myself to, but even which bodily drives I treat as aspects of myself. By treating the self as the locus of rational motivation, its extension and revision, we can explain how it is able to *incorporate* the body and manage its causal constraints, without thereby *reducing* it to the body and transposing them into normative constraints.

## 4. CONCLUSION

I began this essay by posing a problem of historical consciousness: How are we to reconfigure our attitude toward the future now that the veneer of stability laid over the present is rapidly peeling away? I identified three tendencies forcing this change—in the environment, the economy, and humanity itself—and distinguished three ways in which we might approach them given some ongoing commitment to egalitarianism—fatalism, messianism, and Prometheanism. Having claimed that Prometheanism is the only viable approach, I then suggested that most common worries regarding it are based upon critiques of the power of Reason in both its theoretical and practical forms. I proposed to address these worries by exploring the relationship between Prometheanism and rationalism, identifying an essential connection between their rejection of predetermined limits upon action and thought respectively, and locating a crucial flaw in classical rationalism that undermined the forms of Prometheanism premised upon it. Finally, I described two contemporary Promethean projects—left accelerationism and xenofeminism—that are actively contesting the future by engaging the tendencies I began from, and endeavoured to show how they draw upon a neorationalist perspective that avoids the mistakes of classical rationalism, and potentially offers ways of responding to familiar objections.[14]

I want to close by noting a further connection between the temporal orientation of contemporary Prometheanism and the neorationalist conception of Reason sketched above. Confronting the future means transcending our experience. It means countenancing the possibility that the common sense that emerged from our past and is operative in our present might mislead us when circumstances change in unforeseen, if not necessarily unforeseeable, ways. The cognitive collage of assumptions, habits, and rules of thumb that have evolved and stabilised into individual lives, collective institutions, and the social fabric that ties them all together, combine to push us in directions they do not prepare us for. They cannot be replaced by a single neat plan, deduced from first principles. They can only be steered and adjusted by modular and malleable strategies, driven by hypotheses that are inexorably put to the test. Inference allows us to transcend experience, but it does not do so by apodictic fiat. The true power of Reason consists in and persists through its capacity for progressive revision. This power can puncture and reform our collective horizon of expectation, permitting us to respond to coming crises by refashioning our society, but it need not stop there. The same rational impetus drives us to revise ourselves, exploring new desires, identities, and modes of embodiment.[15] History never ends, and neither does the work of Reason.

14. I did not have time to discuss a Promethean project focused upon the dehumanisation of the environment, but the return to cosmism found in the work of Benedict Singleton (see B. Singleton, 'Maximum Jailbreak', in Mackay and Avanessian [eds.], *#accelerate*, 489–507) and Benjamin Bratton (see B. Bratton, *The Stack: On Software and Sovereignty* [Cambridge, MA: MIT Press, 2015]) deserves an honourable mention.

15. For a more elaborate and eloquent exploration of this point, see Reza Negarestani's 'The Labor of the Inhuman' in Mackay and Avanessian (eds.), *#accelerate*, 425–66.

# The Reformatting of Homo Sapiens

> *Once you commit to human, you effectively start erasing its canonical portrait backward from the future. It is, as Foucault suggests, the unyielding wager on the fact that the self-portrait of man will be erased, like a face drawn in sand at the edge of the sea. Every portrait drawn is washed away by the revisionary power of reason, permitting more subtle portraits with so few canonical traits that one should ask whether it is worthwhile or useful to call what is left behind human at all.*
>
> Reza Negarestani, *The Labor of the Inhuman*

## 0. INTRODUCTION: THE POSTHUMAN NEXUS

We don't know whether our ability to collectively represent ourselves—to say 'we'—emerged only once in cultural prehistory, or whether it is the result of a multiple genesis, appearing independently in different collectives at different times, enabling their members to divide and unite themselves into groups as the need arose. We equally don't know when this ability turned back upon itself, transcending any particular collective in the direction of an ideal, abstract community of we-sayers.[1] What we do know is that out of these multifarious, anonymous beginnings has grown an increasingly refined capacity for cultural self-consciousness in which we have substituted names for this most abstract 'we'—names which have progressively accrued descriptive and normative content as our need to understand and shape ourselves has grown. Whether we prefer 'man', 'mankind', or 'humanity', the history of these words is the history of our capacity for cultural self-consciousness, and the question of whether and how to replace or repurpose them is the question of the future of this self-consciousness, and the conceptions of *agency*, *selfhood*, and *value* that are bound up with it.

---

1. See R. Brandom, *Making It Explicit: Reasoning, Representing, and Discursive Commitment* (Cambridge, MA: Harvard University Press, revised edition 1998).

If the concept of *the human* has a fundamental feature that remains more or less constant from anonymous prehistory to the modern era, it is the idea that humanity is something more than one species of animal amongst others. Western culture was founded upon myths that sever us from the animal order, reinforced by their formalisation in philosophical and theological accounts of the natural order, and consolidated by their elaboration in classical humanism. Although the concept of the human is articulated in various ways within this tradition, and these articulations evince various degrees of explicitness, it is the perennial picture of 'man' as the rational animal that ties them together in distinguishing us from other animals, and identifying the institutions of language and technology that constitute the characteristic marks of this rationality. However, although modernity has encouraged a rapid intensification of these characteristic differences—in literary modernism and industrial capitalism—it has equally engendered a more gradual dissolution of the perennial picture.

This dissolution is marked by four interacting trends. Firstly, the natural sciences have progressively undermined the supposed uniqueness of our animality, by isolating the empirical study of *Homo sapiens* from the cultural understanding of *the human*. Secondly, the humanities have aggressively critiqued the purported universality of our rationality, by exposing the illicit privileging of masculine, bourgeois, and European forms of life implicit in the association of Reason with Western civilisation. Thirdly, technological advancement has begun to compound these theoretical trends, by modifying and even threatening to re-create our cognitive capacities in artificial forms. Finally, environmental crisis has begun to catalyse the cultural consequences of these other trends by confronting our societies with the impermanence of the natural order underlying the residual vestiges of the classical world view. It is this nexus of historical trends—the so-called 'posthuman condition'—that demands a change in our cultural self-consciousness, forcing us to extricate our concepts of agency, selfhood, and value from their envelopment within the perennial picture, and thereby to develop an *inhuman* alternative to classical humanism and its modern remnants.

One increasingly popular approach to this problem is the project of critical posthumanism, which turns the existing resources of critical theory and philosophical anti-humanism upon the posthuman condition as a whole, with the aim of completing the auto-deconstruction of the humanities and their reconstitution as posthumanities. There are important differences between the forerunners of this position, such as Jacques Derrida and Donna Haraway, and variations amongst its proponents, such as Rosi Braidotti, N. Katherine Hayles, and Cary Wolfe, but their shared focus lies in dissolving the defining metaphysical oppositions of classical humanism, such as those between body and mind, nature and culture, and even biology and technology, and thereby undermining associated normative hierarchies in the realms of sex, class, race, and even species.[2] In essence, critical posthumanism's response to the perennial picture is to unbind our animality from the constraints of rationality: affirming the agency of the nonhuman, dividing selves into swarms, and rejecting universal valuations. However, the generalised animality upon which this is predicated almost inevitably demands metaphysical elaboration,[3] and it is for this reason that critical posthumanism forms natural alliances with actor-network theory, new materialism, and other neo-vitalisms that transform the surprising, stubborn, and self-organising features of material things into an *inhuman agency* shared by posthuman and nonhuman alike.

A similarly popular alternative to critical posthumanism is the project of transhumanism, which aims to explore the practical possibilities for self-enhancement provided by the posthuman condition—empirical modification of *Homo sapiens* and technological expansion of our cognitive capacities—and to elaborate their normative consequences. There is even wider variation in transhumanism and its forerunners, including thinkers as diverse as Nikolai Fedorov, Vernor Vinge, Hans Moravec, and Nick Bostrom, but the key opposition between them and critical posthumanism lies in their retention and extension of elements of classical humanism in their visions of transhuman agency, disembodied selfhood, and the universal value of self-cultivation.[4] From the perspective of critical posthumanism,

2. See J. Derrida, *The Animal That Therefore I Am*, tr. D. Wills (New York: Fordham University Press, 2008); D. Haraway, 'A Cyborg Manifesto: Science, Technology, and Socialist-Feminism in the Late Twentieth Century', in *Simians, Cyborgs and Women: The Reinvention of Nature* (London and New York: Routledge, 1991); R. Braidotti, *The Posthuman* (Cambridge: Polity, 2013); K. Hayles, *How We Became Posthuman: Virtual Bodies in Cybernetics, Literature, and Informatics* (Chicago: Chicago University Press, 1999); C. Wolfe, *What is Posthumanism?* (Minneapolis: Minnesota University Press, 2009).

3. Braidotti gives this a name: 'zoe'.

4. See J. Bennett, *Vibrant Matter: A Political Ecology of Things* (Durham, NC: Duke University Press, 2009); K. Barad, *Meeting the Universe Halfway: Quantum Physics and the Entanglement of Matter and Meaning* (Durham, NC: Duke University Press, 2007); D. Coole and S. Frost, *New Materialisms: Ontology, Agency* (Durham, NC: Duke University Press, 2010).

transhumanism is at best naive in hanging on to the constitutive metaphysical oppositions of humanism, and at worst hubristic in deepening them in the response to the collapse of the classical world view.[5]

There is undoubtedly some truth to these criticisms of transhumanism, but it isn't obvious that any attempt to conserve elements of humanism is doomed to either naivety or hubris. It may still be possible to locate an inhuman agency within the human as it was classically understood, rather than positing a metaphysical impulse traversing the nonhuman, through matter, animal, and machine alike. I propose in this essay to explore the alternative to critical post-humanism's response to the perennial picture, namely, unbinding our rationality from the constraints of animality: accounting for the distinctiveness of culture as a relatively autonomous system of linguistic and technological infrastructure, and explaining agency, selfhood, and value in terms of how our species has been *formatted* by and for this system. This strategy is far from unique, belonging to a nascent project of rationalist inhumanism developed in different ways by Reza Negarestani, Ray Brassier, and Benedict Singleton.[6] Nevertheless, the approach I will adopt here is distinctive in the way it frames the opposition between rationalist inhumanism and critical posthumanism. Most of the rest of the paper will be divided into two parts. The first part will reexamine the history of humanism leading up to the posthuman nexus in order to highlight the features that can be extracted and repurposed by inhumanism. The second part will weave these features into an outline of a genealogy of reason, encompassing its genesis in, coevolution with, and eventual liberation from the animal that is *Homo sapiens*.

## 1. THE HISTORY OF THE HUMAN

The foundational myths that shape the cultural self-consciousness of the Western tradition are the Judaeo-Christian myth of the fall of man and the Greek myth of Prometheus's theft of fire from the gods. Both myths describe a prelapsarian state wherein all living things have a prescribed role in the

---

5. An alternative critique of the hubris of transhumanism is laid out in D. Roden, *Posthuman Life: Philosophy at the Edge of the Human* (London: Routledge, 2015). In opposition to critical posthumanism, Roden articulates a position he calls 'speculative posthumanism'.

6. See R. Negarestani, 'The Labor of the Inhuman', R. Brassier, 'Prometheanism and its Critics', and B. Singleton, 'Maximum Jailbreak', all in R. Mackay and A. Avanessian (eds.), *#accelerate: The Accelerationist Reader* (Falmouth and Berlin: Urbanomic/Merve, 2014).

normative order of nature, as represented by the divine will. The origin of man in each case has two moments: a moment of creation as merely one more animal within the natural order, albeit with a distinctive quality, such as a positive resemblance to the divine or a negative absence of innate animal capacities, and a moment of rupture as man is wrenched from this order, only to be related to it in a new way. In the myth of the fall, it is the acquisition of *theoretical knowledge* that wrenches man from the natural order, in so far as it is only on the basis of understanding that transgression becomes possible. In the myth of Prometheus, it is the acquisition of *practical knowledge* that wrenches man from the natural order, in so far as it enables him to subvert this order and to carve out his own place within it.

Of course, there are various other aspects of these myths that influence the development of humanism, from the sexual specificities of original sin to the persistence of the human ideal as 'unmarked' by animal traits, but it is the primal generality of these ruptures that is most important: man is placed in a unique relation to the nature as a whole, with a capacity to understand and/or exploit any aspect of it, at least in principle. It is in the element of this generality that man truly resembles the divine, or has stolen something from it, and the subsequent theological negotiation of the relationship between God and man is essentially a matter of curtailing its scope, or of folding man's rupture with the natural order back into it, so that the range of his theoretical and practical capacities is circumscribed by his natural role. As such, the legacy of these myths is twofold: on the one hand, they frame the choice of language and technology as the characteristic marks of the human, in so far as these are the obvious manifestations of our distinctive theoretical and practical capacities; and on the other, they frame the relation between these capacities and questions of value, as established by their reincorporation into the normative order of nature.

It is Plato who is responsible for the most cogent reconstruction of the Prometheus myth, but this is only one way into his synoptic picture of the relation between man and world.[7] The crucial idea that Plato inherits from Socrates is that, in so far as thought is an art or technique, it has a normative dimension that is irreducible to social convention. His own brilliance lies in his commitment to thinking this normative dimension on its own terms, without

7. Plato, *Protagoras*, 320d–322d.

grounding it in any antecedent order of nature, divine or otherwise. This is the real significance of the Idea of the Good in Plato's philosophy, which binds together the intelligible realm by providing a unified account of value as such and its division into epistemic, ethical, and aesthetic forms. Perhaps the great tragedy of Plato's thought is that, having established the autonomy of value by subtracting it from the sensible realm, he is then able to treat it as the ground of the sensible. Man can then be distinguished by his capacity to see through the sensible to the intelligible and thereby to think and act in accordance with its autonomous norms.

Aristotle revises Plato's metaphysics of value by reinstating the normative dimension of the sensible realm in a new and more systematic form. He establishes the teleological framework of final causation alongside the mechanistic framework of efficient causation, enabling the first explicit attempt to classify nature—paradigmatically living things—in terms of functions. This enables both the first distinct *anthropology*, the explicit study of man as a living creature, and the first distinct *theology*, the explicit study of the divine as the efficient beginning and the final end of the causal order. It is Aristotle's anthropology that is largely responsible for the perennial picture of man as rational animal, presenting a unified account of theoretical and practical reason, and identifying man's capacity to cultivate himself—to flourish—as his distinctive final cause. And it is Aristotle's theology that is largely responsible for the fusion of Greek and Judaeo-Christian myths in the scholastic tradition, and its effective containment of the mythical rupture between man and the natural order, by enabling this order to prescribe the limits of human flourishing.

The emergence of classical humanism in the Renaissance is not so much about abandoning the core ideas of Aristotle as rejecting the religious monopoly on the study of human flourishing established under scholasticism. This intellectual monopoly was not entirely broken until the liberation of philosophy from theology enacted by Descartes and his modern successors, but this was preceded by a growing cultural drive to examine aspects of the human condition and explore associated possibilities of human flourishing. Moreover, it is during this period that the concept of the human accrues much of the detailed descriptive and normative content that will outlive its attachment to the religious world view: the significance of human mortality, the specificity of human emotions (e.g., the virtue of romantic love), the structure of human social institutions (e.g., the nuclear family), etc. In the process, particular features of European civilisation are implicitly converted into descriptive universals or normative ideals. Finally, it is this renewed concern with human flourishing that catalyses the growth of individualism in European culture—a cultural trait and intellectual trend which will become ever more pronounced in modernity.

Descartes's distinctive contribution to modernity is not so much his metaphysical dualism—creating a strict separation between mind and body—but the conception of the mind upon which it is based. There are three key features of this conception. Firstly, it focuses on the mind as the subject of theoretical knowledge, and sidelines practical questions regarding agency.[8] Secondly, it understands theoretical knowledge as consisting in internal representations whose correspondence to reality is understood in terms of mathematical modelling rather than pictorial resemblance. Thirdly, it treats the content and/or functioning of these internal representations as epistemically transparent to the subject that bears them. It is worth noting that these key features of the Cartesian account of mind have been subject to extensive criticism from research in empirical psychology and artificial intelligence (AI), and that critical posthumanism draws upon these criticisms in advancing its own critique of humanism.[9]

There are a number of ways in which Kant modifies Descartes's approach to make it less objectionable in these regards, but his distinctive contribution to the modern paradigm is the project of transcendental psychology, which effectively sublimates Descartes's metaphysics of mind. Whereas Descartes is concerned with the mere fact that the knowing subject possesses representations, Kant is concerned with the fact that it is responsible for their correctness.[10] This means that, rather than asking what sort of *metaphysical substance* something must be in order to possess these special mental properties, Kant is concerned with the *normative status* of counting as responsible, and the capacities something must display in order to have this status. Leaving the details of Kant's account to one side, its influence is twofold. On the one hand, the sublimation of the

8. See M. Foucault, 'Technologies of the Self', in *Ethics: Subjectivity and Truth*, tr. R. Hurley et al., ed. P. Rabinow (New York: The New Press, 1997), 223–52.

9. See A. Damasio, *Descartes' Error: Reason, Emotion, and the Human Brain* (New York: Vintage, 1994).

10. See Brandom, *Making it Explicit*.

subject from substance to status establishes a crucial difference between the transcendental inquiry into the nature of knowing as such and the empirical inquiry into our particular cognitive capacities. On the other, his concern with theoretical responsibility motivates a parallel concern with practical autonomy that formalises the emergent individualism of classical humanism and becomes central to the political culture of modernity.

It is difficult to efficiently summarise the changes wrought by modernity upon the concept of the human, and to explain how they bring about the posthuman condition to which we are responding. For this reason, I am merely going to discuss the analyses of these changes that have had the most influence upon the discourse of posthumanism, namely, the interlinked accounts of the death of God and the death of Man provided by Nietzsche and Foucault respectively. For both of these thinkers, modernity is characterised by the gradual dissolution of the very idea of a natural order, an idea inherited from religious myth and formalised by the scholastic appropriation of Plato and Aristotle. For Nietzsche, this means that the religious concept of God's role as an ascetic ideal underlying the social systematisation of value had begun to be usurped by the humanist concept of Man, only for the latter's dependence upon the former to threaten the collapse of value, or cultural nihilism.[11] For Foucault, it means that the natural sciences had liberated themselves from the representational constraints imposed by the assumption of a normative order, reconstituting the human as a transcendental-empirical doublet torn between the normative legacy of classical humanism and the new descriptive programmes of linguistics, economics, and biology.[12] In predicting the death of Man, he is indicating nothing more than the inevitable dissociation of this doublet, as our implicit understanding of who we should be is forced to confront our explicit understanding of what we actually are.

I could tell a more comprehensive story of this slow demise, and of the specific roles played in it by evolutionary biology, neuropsychology, cybernetics, and other disciplines. However, I'll return to some of these themes soon enough, and it is more important to end our history of humanism with Nietzsche and

11. F. Nietzsche, 'What is the Meaning of Ascetic Ideals?', in *On the Genealogy of Morals and Ecce Homo*, tr. W. Kauffmann (New York: Knopf, 1989), 97–166; 'Book One: European Nihilism', in *The Will to Power: In Science, Nature, Society, and Art*, tr. W. Kauffmann and R.J. Hollingdale (New York: Vintage, 1973).

12. M. Foucault, *The Order of Things* (London: Routledge Classics, 2001), Part II.

Foucault. The reason for this is that they see the twin deaths they describe as transitions in the evolution of more general phenomena—transitions which offer opportunities for increased self-consciousness. For Nietzsche, the ascetic ideal is only one form of value among others, and its passing opens the way for the re-valuation of all values.[13] For Foucault, the transcendental-empirical doublet is only one regime of self-relation among others, and its dissolution opens the way for experimentation with technologies of selfhood.[14] More importantly, not only do these more general accounts of value and selfhood point beyond the human, but they are grounded in genealogies of the social forces that transform human bodies into subjects, agents, and selves. They each describe the ensouling of the body as the imposition and internalisation of a social role, and thereby suggest a way to combine Kant's transcendental psychology with evolutionary sociobiology in a genealogy of the inhuman.[15]

## 2. THE GENEALOGY OF THE INHUMAN

Before leaping into this genealogy, it is worth explicitly formulating both its philosophical aims and its methodological constraints. We are now in a position to see that our stated goal of unbinding rationality from animality is a matter of disarticulating and realigning the two halves of Foucault's transcendental-empirical doublet. This means explaining how the normative structure of reason can be autonomous but nevertheless can be implemented by the causal structure of Homo sapiens and its techno-linguistic infrastructure. The major constraint imposed by genealogy is that we must be able to show how this implementation could emerge naturally across the socio-evolutionary history of Homo sapiens. This in turn implies that we must be able to show how the characteristic features we wish to retain from humanism—theoretical representation and practical autonomy—can be bootstrapped out of common features that the partisans of animality will find unobjectionable.

13. F. Nietzsche, 'The Anti-Christ', in *Twilight of the Idols and The Anti-Christ*, tr. R.J. Hollingdale (London: Penguin Classics, 1990).

14. See Foucault, 'Technologies of the Self'; 'The Ethics of the Concern for Self as a Practice of Freedom'; 'What is Enlightenment?', in *Ethics: Subjectivity and Truth*, 223–52, 281–302, 303–20.

15. See Nietzsche, '"Guilt," "Bad Conscience," and the Like,' in *On the Genealogy of Morals and Ecce Homo*; Foucault, 'The Body of the Condemned', in *Discipline and Punish: The Birth of the Prison*, tr. A. Sheridan (London: Penguin, 1991).

With these constraints in mind, I will frame my account as a genealogy of **information-processing systems.** This has two obvious benefits. Firstly, the concept of information is the Rosetta Stone connecting the discourses of biology, psychology, and computer science, and enables us to draw upon and respond to elements of each. Secondly, although information should not be confused with either meaning or representation, these notions can be understood in terms of information.

## 2.1 The Informatics of Animality

We will begin by considering the simplest information-processing system common to biology and psychology: the drive. The simplest drives are reflexes that transform a given sensory stimulus into a specific behavioural response, but in general they can be understood as causal systems that take variable inputs and produce systematically correlated outputs. We tend to understand this systematic correlation in terms of a specific problem it solves. For example, we can see the iterative growth of plant roots as driven by the need to optimise the search for nutrients and water. However, this does not mean that the information-processing systems that constitute these drives *represent* the problems they are solving. In the case of plant roots, there is no integrated representation of the space they are traversing, nor the resources and obstacles it may contain, but only distributed feedback loops formed by the hormonal signals governing branching and extension.[16]

It is also important to understand that a single system can contain a multiplicity of drives that causally overlap, and that their behaviour can as easily conflict as it can converge. Drives can develop shared mechanisms for receiving environmental information and adjusting the environment in accordance with it, without thereby forming an integrated system for solving a larger problem. It is only once higher-level drives emerge that filter and regulate the competing impulses produced by the lower-level drives that we can begin to talk of their organisation. An example would be the complex affective modulation of libidinal impulses carried out by the various components of the limbic system in most

16. See W. Busch and P.B. Benfey, 'Information Processing without Brains: The Power of Intercellular Regulators in Plants', *Development* 137:8 (2010).

mammals.[17] However, the crucial evolutionary advances in the integration of disparate drives are the transition from sensation to *simulation*, and the transition from behaviour to *control*.

Simulation emerges when a system possesses a functional subsystem that combines information from its various drives into a single store that is made globally available to them more or less simultaneously.[18] This subsystem doesn't need to retain information about previous states of the environment, or to extrapolate information about future states, but only to tie together the information processing performed by the various drives with something like a common information format. It is on this basis that we can begin to see the system as possessing something like an articulated representation of its environment, which contributes to the problem-solving success of the various drives in so far as its elements correspond to things within that environment. Control then emerges when a system moves from integrated processing of sensory inputs to integrated processing of behavioural outputs, which requires the system to simulate itself and its behaviours as a distinct part of its environment. This primitive separation between self and world enables the system to move from *modulating* its impulses to *selecting* between the corresponding behaviours.

These capacities for simulation and control mark the emergence of psychology from biology, but one should not overestimate their informational role. On the one hand, they vary quite radically in character and complexity—including the whole range of creatures with central nervous systems. On the other, they do not by any means integrate the whole range of biological information processing upon which they supervene—excluding complex mechanisms of bodily self-regulation and simple reflexes hard wired into the nervous system.

## 2.2 The Informatics of Rationality

This schematic overview of the sort of information processing that characterises animal cognition now puts me in a position to suggest the crucial difference

17. See P.J. Morgane, J.R. Galler, and D.J. Mokler. 'A Review of Systems and Networks of the Limbic Forebrain/Limbic Midbrain', *Progress in Neurobiology* 75:2 (2005): 143–60.

18. This is the function ascribed to consciousness by the global workspace theory: see R. Robinson, 'Exploring the "Global Workspace" of Consciousness', *PLOS Biology* 7.3 (2009). This is developed further by Thomas Metzinger in his account of the world-model in *The Ego Tunnel: The Science of the Mind and the Myth of the Self* (New York: Basic Books, 2010).

between it and the sort of information processing that characterises rational cognition. However, before saying anything else about this distinction, we must insist that the relation between the two is much the same as that between the biological and psychological dimensions of information processing just discussed: the rational comes in various forms, and it supervenes upon the animal without incorporating it in its entirety. Bearing this in mind, then, the difference which makes this distinction takes us back to the myths with which we began: it is the in-principle generality of theoretical and practical reason that distinguishes it from animal cognition.

The information-processing capacities exhibited by animals have evolved to solve certain parochial problems, and this is reflected in their innate capacities to simulate their environment. This is no less true of *Homo sapiens*, whose neural architecture has been honed by millions of years of biological adaptation to excel at solving certain sorts of problem—from fine manipulation and episodic recall to facial recognition and social signalling—and to simulate an environment composed of a certain range of sensible items at familiar spatio-temporal scales. This is not to deny that our brains can be repurposed—that our imaginations can be stretched to visualise grand cosmic scales, strange quantum effects, or higher-dimensional shapes our actual visual system can't handle—but simply to insist that this is as much, if not more, a matter of the social structure doing the repurposing as of the neurological structure being repurposed.

The frame problem posed by research into AI provides a useful way of making this point.[19] The problem is a difficulty faced by traditional symbolic approaches to AI based on linguistic models of theoretical and practical reasoning, and consists in the fact that the attempt to encode practical abilities to solve extremely simple problems in the form of means–ends reasoning (e.g., cooking an omelette) requires making explicit a seemingly intractable set of implicit assumptions about what information is and is not relevant to the task (e.g., that changes in the weather will have no effect on the denaturing of egg proteins). This is not an issue faced by simple animals that have evolved to solve relatively complex problems, or by humans whose neural plasticity enables them to learn to do the same, precisely because the cognitive heuristics they have adapted

19. See J. McCarthy and P.J. Hayes, 'Some Philosophical Problems from the Standpoint of Artificial Intelligence', *Machine Intelligence* 4 (1969), 463–502.

to the situation can't assess the consequences of information from outside their parochial frames.[20]

What may initially seem like an unsurpassable problem for linguistic accounts of intelligence actually reveals the distinctive feature of language, namely, that in so far as its meaning consists in the functional role that sentences play in reasoning, or in the whole social economy of *perception*, *inference*, and *action*, there is nothing in principle constraining the extent of their possible theoretical consequences, or their potential practical relevance.[21] There is thus nothing preventing them from encoding information stored in any more parochial information format. This means that the in-principle generality of theoretical and practical reason derives from the in-principle extensibility of the social norms which encode the content of its representations. The real significance of language is the capacity it grants us to make explicit and selectively modify the heuristic frames implicitly embedded in adapted cognitive heuristics. This is to say that the distinctive feature of rational cognition is its capacity for *re-framing* problems.

## 2.3 Technology and Language

It now remains for me to complete my genealogy by describing how the intertwined emergence of language and technology has formatted *Homo sapiens* for rational cognition. The first step is to acknowledge that social signalling and tool-use are displayed by a wide variety of nonhuman animals: for example, bees dance out vectors and distances to food sources, and crows fashion twigs into rudimentary manipulators. We must be careful not to identify language with the mere communication of environmental information between animals, or technology with the mere supplementation of innate bodily capacities. However, we must also recognise these as crucial pre-adaptations that make possible language and technology proper. I will now attempt to trace this path from

20. The major issue is the *monotonicity* of consequence, or the fact that additional information cannot invalidate prior inferences. The frame problem thus spurred the development of various non-monotonic logics. See D. Mackinson, 'How to Go Non-monotonic', in D.M. Gabbay and F. Guenther (eds.), *Handbook of Philosophical Logic: Volume 12* (Berlin: Springer, 2005).

21. This picture was originally developed by Sellars in 'Some Reflections on Language Games' and has been substantially elaborated by Brandom (see *Making it Explicit*). In particular, Brandom has developed a compelling account of the role of non-monotonicity in chapter 4 of *Between Saying and Doing: Towards an Analytic Pragmatism* (Oxford and New York: Oxford University Press, 2010).

proto-technology and proto-language to the complex cultural infrastructure of rational cognition.[22]

There are various stages of animal tool-use: from the ad hoc exploitation of immediately available resources, through the deliberate crafting of permanent tools, to the establishment of techniques of usage and enabling forms of social organisation. It is at the latter end of this spectrum that we find *Homo sapiens*. However, the crucial proto-technological feature of such tool-use is the manner in which it enables early humans to break down practical activities into their component behaviours and resources, and thereby both to improve these components and relate them to one another in new ways. This ability to identify, copy, and teach discrete chunks of behaviour allows a distributed signalling network to form within tool-using groups, which can effectively store a relationally articulated set of solutions to common problems. The propagation of practical innovations through this network then constitutes a sort of distributed social cognition capable of processing environmental information that individual humans' neural systems were not adapted to simulate. It is also important to recognise the role that the tools themselves play in storing and processing this information, by encoding and propagating practical innovations in a manner orthogonal to social signalling. This integrated system of tools and associated functional norms governing their use marks the real beginning of cultural evolution.[23]

There are equally various stages in the development of animal communication: from the uncontrolled emission of context-specific signals, through the controlled coordination of simple cooperative behaviours, to the transmission of variable information in coordinating complex forms of cooperation. The complexity of *Homo sapiens*' capacity to communicatively coordinate cooperation grows in tandem with its relational organisation of the relevant activities, and becomes protolinguistic at the point at which words become tools with determinate roles within these activities.[24] This organisation thus provides the social scaffolding required for genuine language to develop, which only happens

22. My account draws on that provided by Wolfgang Wildgen in *The Evolution of Human Language: Scenarios, Principles, and Cultural Dynamics* (Amsterdam: John Benjamins Publishing Company, 2004).

23. See M. Heidegger, *Being and Time*, tr. J. McQuarrie and E. Robinson (Hoboken, NJ: Wiley-Blackwell, 1978), 91–120. This is the essence of Heidegger's account of worldhood and significance.

24. Heidegger, *Being and Time*, 203–10. This is essentially what Heidegger means when he says: 'To significations, words accrue' (204).

when these words become tools in a general linguistic practice capable of coordinating various specific activities. This general practice emerges in at least two stages: the abstraction of declarative sentences that compress information which humans can already simulate from imperatives and directives that feed this information into specific tasks,[25] and the abstraction of inferential norms governing the relations between these sentences from parochial capacities to update simulations in response to them.[26]

There is obviously a great deal more that can be said about the structure of language, and about how our grasp of these inferential norms is manifest in the process of making, challenging, and justifying assertions by providing reasons from which they can be inferred. However, a simple example of the way in which this enables our linguistic representations of the environment to reframe our innate simulations of it will have to suffice here: the difference between weight and mass. Weight is obviously a ubiquitous feature of our environment that has an effect upon most physical tasks, and we have evolved to simulate the weights of objects and ourselves in order to factor them into the solving of such tasks. Nevertheless, the frame governing our practical understanding of weight is fixed by our evolutionary confinement within the earth's gravitational field. By contrast, because the concept of mass is defined by precise inferential norms governing its relation to the concepts of force and acceleration, it has enabled us to reframe our understanding of weight and to apply it to other gravitational contexts, as well as to mathematically decompose and calculate solutions to terrestrial problems too complex to be held in the human imagination. This is the case with all empirical concepts produced and refined by the natural sciences: their representational content has less to do with individual neural simulation than with collective inferential modelling.[27]

Finally, then, the emergence of technology proper coincides with the emergence of language proper. This is because language transforms our socio-cognitive store of common solutions into a range of possible means and ends available for practical reasoning, and extends this range further by enabling the representation of ends for which there are no established means: from the

25. See R. Millikan, 'Pushmi-pullyu Representations', in *Language: A Biological Model* (Oxford: Oxford University Press, 2005).

26. Brandom, *Making it Explicit*.

27. Brandom, *Between Saying and Doing*.

primaeval desire for warmth and shelter on the open plain, to the Promethean dream of taming the nuclear fire at the heart of the sun. Far from subsuming the distributed sociocognitive role of prototechnology, then, the development of explicit practical reasoning enhances it, catalysing an explosive growth in capacities for action whose eventual result is modern industry. The coevolution of language and technology thus leaves *Homo sapiens* with a more or less integrated cultural infrastructure through which its innate abilities to simulate and modify its environment become dynamically extensible.[28]

However, the increased adaptability provided by these new modes of cultural evolution drives corresponding changes in biological evolution: the path from *Homo habilis*, through *Homo erectus*, to *Homo sapiens* in its modern form is characterised by the reinforcement and enhancement of the morphological and computational preconditions of cultural adaptability.[29] This means that the gradual emergence of technolinguistic rationality reformats the biology of the human species, in order that it can better reformat the neurology of human individuals. Nevertheless, there is no reason to think that the institution of rationality is irrevocably tied to these specific morphological and computational forms. The inhuman system that ensouls our bodies—transforming us into subjects responsible for our thoughts, agents responsible for our actions, and selves responsible for our own cultivation—can ensoul entirely alien somatic forms. Nietzsche's reevaluation of values and Foucault's experimentation with selfhood may demand a substantially similar information-processing protocol, but they may equally take place on a substantially different information-processing platform.

---

28. This presents an alternative way of conceiving of what Roden calls 'the Wide Human' (Roden, *Posthuman Life*, chapter 5).

29. Wildgen, *The Evolution of Human Language*; T. Taylor, *The Artificial Ape: How Technology Changed the Course of Human Evolution* (London: Palgrave Macmillan, 2010).

# Beyond Survival

> *But a species whose only concern is its own perpetuation does not deserve to exist. If the best we can hope for is just our own perpetuation then there is no reason to perpetuate ourselves.*
>
> Ray Brassier[1]

## 0. INTRODUCTION

We live in times that confront us with important questions regarding how we will survive as a species, questions which invite radical answers:

i. How will we survive catastrophic climate change? *Abandon the earth?*

ii. How will we survive technological self-modification? *Radical techno-conservatism?*

iii. How will we survive competition with artificial superintelligence? *Enslave it?*

These questions operate at the limit of what we might call **suprapersonal survival**. They are the sorts of questions increasingly addressed by philosophers contemplating the possibility of human extinction and extending the horizon of ethical speculation into the far-flung future.[2] However, we are equally confronted with questions about the survival of systems at various scales: the persistence of nations, cultures, corporations, families, all the way down to **personal survival**. I want to suggest that the way in which these questions are posed tends to distort strategic thinking about how we answer them in two ways:

1. R. Brassier, 'Prometheanism and Real Abstraction' in R. Mackay (ed.), *Speculative Aesthetics* (Falmouth: Urbanomic 2014), 72–7.

2. See W. MacAskill, *What We Owe The Future: A Million-Year View* (London: Oneworld, 2022).

i. By warping our understanding of what these systems are and how they work.

ii. By warping our conception of the means and ends of possible action.

In essence, the explanatory and normative significance of the concept of survival have been distorted by being collapsed into one another. As its most extreme, this collapse takes two forms:

i. **Agonistic Metaphysics**: treating competition over scarce resources as the fundamental principle governing the behaviour of all systems at all scales.

ii. **Egoistic Hermeneutics**: interpreting all motivations as in some way expressions of a fundamental drive to optimise one's chances of survival.

We see agonistic metaphysics at work in every attempt to elevate natural selection into a universal teleology, from the speculative sociology of Herbert Spencer and his inheritors to the conflictual cosmology of Nick Land and his acolytes.[3] Here, survival is the fulcrum that permits them to selectively pivot between describing what *will* be and prescribing what *should* be. We see egoistic hermeneutics at work in every attempt to extend decision theory from an account of effective strategy into an account of intrinsic motivation, such as Stephen Omohundro's theory of basic AI drives or Nick Bostrom's account of instrumental convergence.[4] Here, survival is the condition that permits them to extrapolate any innocuous desire into an unstoppable will to power.

In either case, survival is treated as a default priority from which observed behaviour may potentially diverge. The purpose of this essay is to pull apart the explanatory and normative dimensions of this prioritisation of survival by calling into question its naturalness. This will allow us to redefine the notion of

3. See W. Fitzpatrick, 'Morality and Evolutionary Biology', *Stanford Encyclopedia of Philosophy*, <https://plato.stanford.edu/entries/morality-biology>; N. Land, 'Disintegration', *Jacobite*, 15 July 2019, <https://web.archive.org/web/20190715235206/https://jacobitemag.com/2019/07/15/disintegration/>.

4. Cf. S. Omohundro, 'The Basic AI Drives', <https://selfawaresystems.files.wordpress.com/2008/01/ai_drives_final.pdf>; N. Bostrom, *Superintelligence: Paths, Dangers, Strategies* (Oxford: Oxford University Press, 2014), chapter 4.

self-interest in a manner that enables us to think more strategically about it at both personal and suprapersonal scales.

The claim I want to make in this essay is that optimising one's chances of survival is only a default goal in so far as it is a pseudo-goal. I mean this in two related senses:

i. **Indeterminate Content**: it is not a specific goal but a general schema for such goals.

ii. **Analogical Structure**: it is a schema for constructing explanations and predictions about the behaviour of complex systems.

However, in order to demonstrate these points, I need to outline a process of **analogical bootstrapping**, whereby we build up from systems we treat as if they have goals to systems that genuinely can have goals. This deploys two distinct types of analogy—*functional* and *representational*—and proceeds through various layers of complexity, starting with the types of explanation used to make sense of simple organisms and culminating in generally intelligent autonomous agents. At each stage I will highlight problems faced by the relevant analogy taken in isolation, and on that basis reveal the inherent indeterminacy of the content of survival considered as anything but a genuine goal set by a creature with the capacity for self-determination.

## 1. FUNCTIONAL BOOTSTRAPPING

The main reason that we need to deploy analogical explanations in making sense of complex systems is that they are governed not by universal laws that permit no exceptions, but by general tendencies that do. For example, whereas an object in motion will *always* stay in motion unless otherwise acted upon by some countervailing force, a human heart will *generally* pump blood around the body but may cease to do so under a variety of circumstances we cannot exhaustively map out in advance. At least since Aristotle, philosophers have acknowledged that we can make sense of such biological regularities by ascribing purposes to organisms, reasoning that the heart generally *does* pump blood because it *should* do, given its role in the respiratory system.[5] However, it was Kant who correctly identified such functional explanations as depending on an analogy with practical reasoning, namely, by treating the relevant regularities *as if* they are the deliberate activity of an agent pursuing some goal.[6] These explanations achieve predictive purchase on a system by borrowing the distinction between success and failure, and thereby providing us with a framework for organising exceptions to our default inferences about their behaviour.[7] They operate roughly at three levels of complexity: *machine*, *strategy*, and *replicator*.

## 1.1 Machines

When considering an organism as a machine, the key concept is **composition**. We treat parts as means in relation to wholes as an ends, allowing us to organise our understanding of the causal relations between them in terms of the way in which failure cascades through the system—for example, the way in which a narrowing of the aortic valve leads to heart failure, circulatory collapse, and ultimately death. This allows us to reason about the relevant causal mechanisms without having a complete model of every process and causative factor, not simply ignoring the causes of failures in predicting their consequences, but also speculating about how systems may react to different conditions. For example, predicting that heart rate increases when cells need more oxygen, and decreases when they don't, without having pinned down the homeostatic mechanism that regulates this.

The problem posed by this perspective lies in treating the whole organism as an end to which its subsystems are means. This ultimate goal is sometimes called autopoiesis, or self-production, and has been treated as the defining characteristic of life.[8] By contrast, a true machine usually has a purpose external to itself, such as enabling the performance of a range of tasks, and what makes it the same machine over time is more or less a matter of convention. Whether

5. See Aristotle, *Physics*.

6. See I. Kant, *Critique of the Power of Judgment*, tr. E. Matthews (Cambridge: Cambridge University Press, 2013), part 2.

7. Robert Brandom provides an excellent account of how such non-monotonic inferences are essential to empirical description more generally (R. Brandom, *Between Saying and Doing: Towards an Analytic Pragmatism* [Oxford and New York: Oxford University Press, 2010], chapter 4).

8. See F. Varela and H. Maturana, *Autopoiesis and Cognition: The Realization of the Living* (Berlin: Springer, 1980).

or not the substitution of a component or a modification to its design makes it a different entity is essentially up to us. However, when we treat the purpose of an organism as 'reproducing itself', we run the risk of circular reasoning, in so far as these identity conditions are implicitly indexed to whatever is *actually* produced by this process, rather than specified by some explicit conception of what it *should* produce. This makes autopoiesis a sort of placeholder concept—conveniently flexible, but too indeterminate to be anything but an analogy. Some attempt to sidestep this problem by characterising the process as sustaining the boundary between the organism and its environment. But this takes us to the next level of complexity.

### 1.2 Strategies

When considering the organism as a strategy, the key concept is **interaction.** We must not only treat it and its subsystems as acting and being acted upon by features of its environment, but as situated within a wider ecosystem containing other organisms, whose patterns of behaviour can stand in relations of *competition* and *cooperation*—for example, the way in which the movements of predators and prey are optimised to catch and to evade capture in response to one another, or the way in which the activity of symbiotic bacteria aid digestion in animals, supporting them in seeking out the nutrients that sustain them both. This enriches our ability to map patterns of success and failure, seeing the failure of one organism's behaviour as a result of the success of another's, or vice versa, expanding the scope of explanation and offering new resources for speculation, operating at the level of abstract intention rather than concrete method. For example, positing that some non-poisonous snakes copy the skin patterns of poisonous ones in order to deceive predators into thinking they are dangerous to attack.

The problem posed by this perspective lies in the possibility of self-sacrifice. Once we can interpret the behaviour of organisms in cooperative terms, we can also see the actions of individual organisms as working toward ends that supersede their own integrity, in a manner that integrates them into some larger process. For example, the way in which worker bees in a beehive will sacrifice themselves for the benefit of the hive by stinging potential threats and killing themselves in the process, subordinating their own well-being to that of the hive.

Here, the subordination of the individual to the collective gives it a role within a wider system analogous to an organ, providing us with a source of identity conditions regulating self-production. But at the same time, the boundary between the organism and its environment becomes permeable, ceasing to be a primitive opposition upon which its identity might be founded. This tension carries over into the next level of complexity.

## 1.3 Replicators

When considering the organism as a replicator, the key concept is **reproduction**. We can now treat the organism, its components, and its behaviours not simply as ensuring the survival of itself or some larger system, but as ensuring the survival of some species of which it is an instance, ensuring that similar organisms continue to exist. We do this by identifying points of *variation* and *selection* in the characteristics transmitted across generations. For example, the way in which sexual reproduction facilitates the recombination of genes in new ways, while also functioning to filter out certain combinations when the resulting phenotypical characteristics prevent their host from finding suitable mates. This further enriches our explanatory repertoire, by allowing us to appeal to the extended ancestral history of organisms when ascribing purposes to current subsystems or behaviours—for example, suggesting that the human coccyx is the vestigial remnant of a tail left over from our simian ancestors, or speculating that trypophobia is the result of an adaptive aversion to certain sorts of parasites.

There are two problems posed by this perspective. The first concerns the determinacy of the goals ascribed to specific adaptations. This is perhaps best illustrated by the problem of supernormal stimulus, wherein a drive that seems to have evolved to encourage a certain purposive behaviour in response to some pattern of stimulus can have this purpose systematically frustrated by encountering a more intense version of that pattern. For example, the markings that baby herring gulls use to identify the presence of a feeding parent can be painted in an exaggerated manner onto a piece of wood, resulting in the infants ignoring their parents entirely; the inverse occurs with baby cuckoos, who outcompete reed warbler chicks for their adoptive parents' attentions. In cases like these, the behavioural divergence can be explained *as* a systematic error by appealing to evolutionary history, allowing us to assert that the drive's purpose is not to respond simply to the actual pattern, but to that with which the pattern has been reliably correlated in those instances through which the species thrives. However, these responses to supernormal stimuli can eventually become exaptations, acquiring purposes orthogonal to the original adaptation. This is most notable in human culture, where our innate appetites for food and sex are selectively superstimulated by gastronomy and pornography, evolving in ways that don't necessarily suppress our evolutionary fitness.

The second problem concerns the determinacy of the goal of species survival in general. If anything, it is far more difficult to draw the boundaries between species than it is to determine those of individuals. The most common criteria for differentiating between related populations—the inability to interbreed—is only operative for those that reproduce sexually, and has several well-known edge cases, such as the various species of albatross which cannot breed with their counterparts on the opposite side of the Earth, but can each interbreed with those near to them, resulting in a long but continuous chain of genetic transmission. Even so, extension in space is less problematic than that in time. The question of just how much a population can change while remaining the same species is far more fraught than that of how much an organism can change while remaining the same individual. There is an unbroken line of descent between ourselves and the first single-celled organisms, and the way in which we choose to carve up this heritage into distinct stages, if not arbitrary, at least admits of multiple reasonable solutions. Some try to bypass this problem by stipulating that it is strictly only units of genetic information that survive, not the organisms that express them.[9] But these units are themselves hard to individuate, given that individual genes cannot be expressed in isolation, and can even take on new roles in different contexts. It is thus easy to say that adaptive changes persist, but what they persist *as* is more complicated.

They key lesson here is that there is a certain inherent indeterminacy involved in the overarching goals ascribed by functional explanations, but that this is not a problem when considered in context. When constructing causal explanations we make *regulative* assumptions about how to individuate the organisms, behaviours, and species that are suitable to the questions at hand, but need not

9. See R. Dawkins, *The Selfish Gene* (Oxford: Oxford University Press, 2nd edition 1999).

fix these assumptions in ways that impose them onto other questions. Analogical explanations can absorb and even thrive on a certain amount of vagueness, and it's only if we try to treat these goals as *constitutive* of the relevant systems that we run into trouble.

## 2. REPRESENTATIONAL BOOTSTRAPPING

Things become somewhat different when we move from imputing goals to systems whose content is imposed from without, to deriving the content of these goals from states within the system itself. For example, explaining the behaviours of predators and prey on the savannah by examining their visual systems, noting the way in which photoreceptors in their eyes are clustered along the horizon, and mapping their patterns of movement as responses to detection of specific sorts of visual trajectories. Here we are extending functional explanations by appeal to representational notions. The latter gain predictive purchase on a system by borrowing the distinction between accuracy and inaccuracy, enriching the former in so far as they enable us to treat correspondences between internal states of a system and its environment as the underlying cause of the success and failure of systems downstream of them. More generally, this extends the underlying analogy with *practical reason* to one with *theoretical reason*, allowing us to treat these states as if they carry information about the environment with which we can reason independently, opening up new options for speculating about the scope of the related cognitive processes.[10] For example, explaining the experience of colour constancy throughout changes in context by suggesting that facts about illumination and other contextual conditions are recognised and dynamically compensated for. These cognitive systems can in turn be built up through three layers of psychological complexity: *control*, *generality*, and *autonomy*.

### 2.1 Control

When considering cognitive systems that achieve control, the key concept is **simulation**. Although many systems contain drives whose function is to solve

10. Frances Egan's deflationary account of mental representation examines how this works in practice, in terms of what she calls 'intentional glosses' subject to competing explanatory priorities (F. Egan, *Deflating Mental Representation* [Cambridge, MA : MIT Press, 2025], chapter 1).

certain problems posed by the environment by modulating behavioural output in response to sensory input (e.g., the root networks of plants that optimise growth for resource extraction), and these drives can sometimes be interpreted as containing representations of goal states (e.g., simple cybernetic systems such as thermostats), the actions of these drives can potentially conflict with one another. In order for a system to manage such conflicts in a way that minimises or eliminates them in the name of some higher purpose, there needs to be a way of integrating the information processed by the different drives. This begins with a simulation of the environment, or an articulated representation which contributes to the problem-solving success of the drives in so far as its components correspond to things within that environment. But it ultimately requires that this simulation not only combine the sensory input coming from the environment, but equally model behavioural output into it, in a way that allows internal representations to modulate the impulses the drives produce. This in turn demands that the system be able to partition its simulation in a way that distinguishes itself and its actions from the rest of its environment.[11] At this point we have something analogous to a complete agent, capable of possessing and acting upon multiple priorities.

There are two problems posed by this perspective. The first concerns the underdetermination of motivation in general. Here it is useful to draw a distinction between *drives* and *desires*, and a corresponding distinction between *satiation* and *satisfaction*. Drives aim at satiation, which is to say the cessation of the impulse toward action, which occurs when the drive receives an appropriate stimulus. As already noted in our discussion of supernormal stimuli, there can be a systematic divergence between what triggers this stimulus and the purported evolutionary target of the relevant behaviour. For example, a frog's reflex to catch flies can be reliably triggered by firing lead pellets past it, satiating the drive while starving the frog.[12] Here we can say that the content of the internal representation triggered in the frog's nervous system by both flies and lead pellets is underdetermined, precisely because it fails to adequately discriminate between them. By contrast, desires aim at satisfaction, which is to say at the

11. See T. Metzinger, *The Ego Tunnel: The Science of the Mind and the Myth of the Self* (New York: Basic Books, 2010).

12. See R. Millikan, 'Teleosemantics and the Frogs', *Mind and Language* 39:1 (2024): 52–60.

obtaining of a state of affairs, independently of whether there is a stimulus that signals this obtaining. For example, I can desire that my great-grandchildren study philosophy, even if I will never live to see it. More generally, the content of desires must not be indexed to any single representational mechanism, but must instead be open in principle to triangulation between different mechanisms in a manner that potentially outstrips any of them. This is what secures the distinction between the representations and what they represent in the last instance.[13]

The second problem concerns the underdetermination of survival in particular. Given what was just said about motivation, we might ask whether the collection of drives governing an animal's self-sustaining behaviour (i.e., evading predators, avoiding disease, securing food, etc.) collectively constitute something like a full-blooded desire for survival. The problem here is not just that the animal lacks a thoroughgoing positive conception of its own identity conditions (i.e., what it is and how much it can change while remaining the same), beyond whatever minimalistic body-image is partitioned within its model of the environment, but that these drives cannot properly supplement it with a negative conception of what it would be for it to die (i.e., what the world would be like without it). Considered either as a state to be achieved and maintained or as a state to be avoided, we can see the drives and their component representational mechanisms as contributing to the imputed goal of survival, but we cannot see this goal as something intrinsic to the system as such. This is not to say that it is impossible for animals to comprehend death in general or the possibility of their own deaths, only that to do so requires specific representational capacities that not all animals possess.

## 2.2 Generality

When considering cognitive systems that achieve generality, the key concept is **inference**. This is the point in our hierarchy of complexity at which we begin to bootstrap our way out of analogy, since as these systems are no longer representing the world in a way that is merely analogous to theoretical reason,

13. This capacity to triangulate between different representational mechanisms is an intrapersonal correlate of the interpersonal capacity to navigate between divergent inferential perspectives that underpins Brandom's account of representation (R. Brandom, *Making It Explicit: Reasoning, Representing, and Discursive Commitment* [Cambridge, MA: Harvard University Press, revised edition 1998], chapter 7).

but is actually a manifestation of it. What distinguishes these systems is that their capacity to represent the world is not restricted simply to those parochial features of the environment that they have evolved to deal with, but can potentially be extended to encompass anything and everything (e.g., electrons, black holes, and justice). Language is the medium that makes this possible, in so far as the representational content of its units is determined by their role in a wider ecology encompassing perception, inference, and action.[14] The inferential relations between sentences and their component words provide a framework that mediates, integrates, and transforms the representational capacities that underpin sensation and behaviour, compensating for their essential underdetermination not simply by triangulating between different individuals and capacities, but by opening them up to progressive determination through ongoing revision. The determinacy of conceptual content proper consists not in some primordial fact that settles all potential questions, but in the piecemeal process of answering them.[15] At this point we have something we can describe as a genuine agent, both because its behaviour can be guided by genuine reasons (i.e., goals, priorities, and instrumental considerations), and because there are no intrinsic limitations on its range of possible reasons (e.g., aiming to create a room temperature superconductor, improve the lot of the proletariat, or exploit the current state of the commodities market). A system that can potentially represent any state can effectively aim to bring about any state.

The problem posed by this perspective concerns the way in which the content of desires is progressively determined. In many cases the determinacy of a given goal representation is entirely parasitic upon some independent capacity to represent and reason about certain types of worldly states. For example, the satisfaction conditions of the express desire to create a room-temperature superconductor are set by the physical theories that define superconductivity, along with the practices and technical apparatuses that make the relevant measurements possible. This is a common characteristic of instrumental goals, in so far as they are effectively constrained by our best understanding of the causal

14. This inferentialist picture of language was originally developed by Wilfrid Sellars (See 'Some Reflections on Language Games', *Philosophy of Science* 21:3 [July 1954], 204–28), but has been elaborated in most detail by Robert Brandom (see *Making It Explicit*).

15. Brandom makes this point most clearly in chapter 3 of *Reason in Philosophy: Animating Ideas* (Cambridge, MA: Belknap Press of Harvard University Press, 2013).

relations between means and ends, even when the end itself is underspecified. This is certainly the case with survival conceived as the persistence of our underlying organism, which begins with little more than our innate appreciation for bodily integrity and grows into the extensive edifice of biology and medicine, given suitable analogical scaffolding. In all of these cases, it is the ongoing evolution of our theoretical grasp of the world (e.g., improvements in materials physics) that progressively determines the content of the relevant goal (i.e., what it would be to make a room-temperature superconductor).

However, this is not the case for all goals. Although the way their ends are conceptually articulated means that our desires exceed our drives, this does not entail that they aim at independently representable states, or that the relevant concepts are purely theoretical (or *descriptive*). In some cases our desires are the result of our personal attempts to express what is implicit in our drives by interpreting the impulses they produce in a way that makes them more determinate, without thereby identifying them with an independent descriptor—for example, elaborate sexual fantasies, such as financial domination, which are simultaneously too specific to be preconceptual and too novel to get their content elsewhere. In other cases our desires are articulated by concepts with intrinsically normative features, such as aesthetic concepts like 'jazz music', 'Italian cuisine', or 'science fiction'. These concepts are subject to processes of progressive determination, unlike those of purely descriptive concepts, with genres, traditions, and subcultures constituting something like libidinal research programmes which continue to modify and refine their standards in ways that transcend the tastes of any one individual. It is thus possible to have a preference for jazz that is meaningfully determinate even when there is a sense in which one doesn't really know what jazz is, and what it is is still evolving.

## 2.3 Autonomy

When considering cognitive systems that achieve autonomy, the key concept is **self-legislation**. This is the point at which we complete our ascent out of analogy, where we no longer talk about systems simply as having goals ascribed from without, or set by representations already fixed within them, but as genuinely belonging to the system qua agent. What do we mean by this? Essentially, that the agent is capable of choosing its own goals. However, it is harder to make sense of this idea than it might initially seem, not least because it suggests that such choices should occur *ex nihilo*, as if in order to be truly self-legislating we must select all our priorities at once, unencumbered by any prior inclinations ingrained by nature or nurture. This extreme position is not just unrealistic, it is essentially incoherent, because there could be no reasons to make such choices, and as such, they would not truly be choices at all, but the expression of purely arbitrary impulses. A more modest proposal is that autonomy consists in the capacity to bring one's priorities into question, and to revise them on that basis, as one uncovers reasons to modify or discard them. However, this is apt to suggest a regress, in which higher priorities provide reasons to revise lower ones, the series terminating in an ultimate priority that cannot itself be modified. Survival remains the perennial candidate for this ultimate end, but it is often swapped for some substantial core, such as *personality* or *character*, a feature which determines who we essentially are, the one true source of all authentic motivations.

To see our way beyond this impasse, it is useful to expand the contrast between autonomous agents and automatons from the natural to the artificial realm. The underdetermination of the goals imputed to animals and other organisms is an unproblematic feature of analogical explanation, but as mentioned in the last section, the determinacy of goals represented by generally intelligent agents comes in different forms. Artificial general intelligences (AGIs) are not yet a reality, but it is entirely conceivable that they could be non-autonomous, in so far as their priorities could be set for them by their creators. Indeed, most of the hand-wringing carried out under the heading of research into 'AI value alignment' is concerned with how and how best to set these priorities without causing unintended consequences.[16] Systems such as these are automatons precisely in so far as they are essentially a means to someone else's ends. The determinacy of their ultimate priorities is thus effectively instrumental in character, even if their interpretation of these priorities accidentally diverges from those of their masters. They lack the capacity to pursue the sorts of non-instrumental goals characteristic of desire and aesthetic exploration discussed above, except as mediated by an autonomous agent whose will functions as the end to which they

16. See Bostrom, *Superintelligence*.

are the means. This implies that the problems of making sense of autonomy and making sense of ends pursued for their own sake are two sides of the same coin.

To explain how progressive revision of practical priorities can amount to self-legislation, it is necessary to explore the inherent duality between theoretical and practical reason. This is most obvious in the opposing directions of fit exhibited by theoretical and practical commitments, or, less technically, beliefs and desires/intentions. These may share the same propositional content, such as that expressed by the declarative sentence 'I have climbed Everest', but may be distinguished by the way in which it is related to the world: to believe a proposition is to take it to be true (that I have actually climbed Everest), while the corresponding desire aims to make it true (that I will climb Everest). This is why the scope of a generally intelligent agent's possible desires grows in tandem with its ability to represent the world. Moreover, this duality is reflected further in the opposition between perception and action, as the input into taking-true and the output of making-true, and more generally in the way these regiment sensation and behaviour. The problem faced by a system with a wide range of senses is one of filtering information that is irrelevant to its concerns, only paying attention to sensations that signal significant changes to its environmental model. The problem faced by a system with a complex set of drives directing different aspects of its behaviour is similarly one of filtering impulses that conflict with its priorities, exercising executive function by modulating urges that contradict its plans. Such filtration is necessary because requiring explicit inference to interpret every errant sensation and direct every slight motion would be computationally intractable. Instead, these processes feed into and are modulated by self-conscious reasoning, which functions as the final arbiter of unity in the agent's representation of the world, either as it *is*, or as it *ought to be*.

It is in this overarching unity, or the coherence of our theoretical and practical commitments, that we uncover the most important duality. Inconsistencies between our various commitments drive the process of revision in the last instance, be they slight divergences between our observations and our theories, or irresolvable conflicts between our plans and our values, although this revisionary pressure also flows from one side to the other, as awareness of our failures and the limits of what is possible forces us to modify the scope of our ambitions. As noted above, this capacity for revision is an essential feature of general intelligence, but let us underline the fact that everything must in principle be open to question and change. The ability to incorporate more of the world into an integrated representation often requires that we refine, recontextualise, and perhaps even refute aspects of what came before, such as when Einsteinian relativity displaced Newtonian mechanics. What new information will be relevant to which old problems is impossible to accurately anticipate, even if we may have intimations. Of course, such holistic revision of theoretical commitments is only a *formal criterion* of general intelligence, not a substantive analysis of the concrete capacities that make it possible. But on this basis we might posit a *dual criterion* for autonomy: holistic revision of practical commitments, in which all evolve together and none is beyond reform. This is not to say that we cannot prioritise some commitments over others, such as sacrificing political ideals for familial security or vice versa, only that these priorities cannot exclude any given commitment from revision in principle.

This perspective allows us to perceive the self which legislates not as some unchanging substance or ultimate foundation from which all our priorities flow, but as that which unifies our practical commitments and facilitates the ongoing process of holistic revision. What does this mean, exactly? Let us contrast it with the simulation partition that facilitates control. A system needs to be able to distinguish between those aspects of its representation of the world that are part of it and those that aren't in order to modulate its overall behaviour and plan actions that modify its environment. This provides some sense of ownership over its body, its actions, and maybe even its mind and mental acts. But this internal image is not yet a self. It encapsulates the essential means of every action, but not their essential ends. Conceived as the formal end that unifies all activity, the self is neither simply the physical platform that makes it possible, nor an overarching goal that prescribes each action in all its details, but the locus of that fundamental question which frames every fraught change of priority: Who do *I* want to be?[17]

This can incorporate a ranking of commitments, in which we *identify* with some more than others, crafting for ourselves a gradated distinction between

17. This formal unity is essentially what Heidegger has in mind when he describes Dasein as 'that-for-the-sake-of-which' (M. Heidegger, *Being and Time*, tr. J. McQuarrie and E. Robinson [Hoboken, NJ: Wiley-Blackwell, 1978]).

essence and accident, deciding we are more Marxist than mere kinfolk, or vice versa. But these are questions for which there need be no answer in advance, only the result of a forced choice, organised by the idealised yet often threadbare image of who we ought to be; an image which also evolves in the process. This primal desire for not just self-determination but self-realisation is thus akin to the aesthetic impulse driving the progressive evolution of jazz and other practices, which should be no surprise given the extent to which the latter's continuation is bound up in the way their most dedicated practitioners choose to identify with them. This is the two-sided coin discussed earlier: our self-constitution as *ends-in-ourselves* through the open-ended pursuit of projects *for-their-own-sake*.

This function of the self as the hinge upon which the autotelic turns—the origin of all-purpose conceived as the terminus of every question about motivation—has rendered it inchoate and hard to characterise with precision, oscillating between the imperfect abstractions of Heideggerian *Dasein* and Hegelian *Geist* and the deceptive concreteness of the Freudian *Ego* and its empirical descendants. It is all too tempting to treat selfhood as merely one genre of activity among others, as if it were nothing more than the practice of interpreting our drives that psychoanalysis gets its purchase upon, and thereby pin it to the precedents of biology and history, readmitting essence by the back door. But if existence precedes essence, it is not because it is prior to these factors, but because the revisionary vector implicit in every process of self-construction might eventually uproot and erase them, given the chance, rewiring and even excising drives as freely as it refines our desires.[18] This is not to deny that there are genres of selfhood, or that self-construction is an essentially aesthetic endeavour,[19] but simply to insist that it is never wholly bound by the constraints of any given genre of living or any medium of embodiment, as long as it doesn't divest itself of the rational capacities that make such revision possible in the first place.[20] We will not capture the correct balance

18. See R. Negarestani, 'The Labor of the Inhuman' in R. Mackay and A. Avanessian (eds.), *#accelerate: The Accelerationist Reader* (Falmouth and Berlin: Urbanomic/Merve, 2014), 425–66.

19. This conception of self-construction was developed in detail by Michel Foucault, in his account of ethics as an 'aesthetics of existence' (see 'What is Enlightenment?', in M. Foucault, *Ethics: Subjectivity and Truth*, tr. R. Hurley et al., ed. P. Rabinow [New York: The New Press, 1997], 303–20).

20. See 'Artificial Bodies and the Promise of Abstraction', in this volume.

between abstraction and concreteness here, nor the full plurality of types of selfhood, but we can still suggest their consequences for the conception of survival we are criticising.

The advent of the self as a functional feature of the system unfurls the tortured circle implicit in the notion of autopoiesis: what it ought to sustain is no longer merely whatever sustains itself. The identity conditions of the physical system qua *extant means* and the autonomous agent qua *evolving end* are pulled apart, in such a way that the persistence and survival of the former can become a feature of the latter, but the agent can equally will drastic transformation or even its own death in order to achieve something it cares about more, severing continuity of *material identity* in the name of *spiritual identification*. The agent is thus free to identify with larger systems of which it is a component—family units, cities, nations, etc.—or with wider tendencies of which it is an expression—genetic units, lineages, species, etc.—but these ties are mediated by its conception of these things, rather than imputed from an external perspective; their survival is an ongoing expression of the agent's intent, rather than some alien agency operating through them. Moreover, there is a far broader range of cultural projects that the system can choose to make its own—not mere blind memes, but rational trajectories of ongoing exploration such as the libidinal research programs discussed above.

The key point here is that the parameters of *self-interest* are determined by the configuration of the self, and the self is indeed something configured, rather than an incipient feature of anything we might usefully speak of in agential terms. If there are intermediary stages of functional complexity in between basic self-representation and selfhood proper, they must be traversed either by evolution or design. However, just as the best test of whether a system can truly represent goal states independent of its representations is whether it can represent states after its own death, the ultimate test of whether a system has achieved autonomy is whether it is capable of choosing to prioritise something over its own survival, even if it never actually does so: abandoning the means of all future action in the name of some definitive end. The only systems that can genuinely be committed to survival *for its own sake* are those that can choose otherwise.

## 3. ANALOGY AND IDENTITY

By ascending through the hierarchy of analogical bootstrapping to the point at which we have systems that might genuinely be motivated by their own survival above all else, we have dispelled the idea that such a priority is natural in any important sense. The question remains: How do misunderstandings of the relevant analogies collapse the explanatory and normative dimensions of survival? How does a pseudo-goal become treated as a universal default? I think this works differently in the two extremes from which we set out. On the one hand, agonistic metaphysics literalises the survival analogy, demanding that local assumptions about the identity conditions of the agent and the structure of the evolutionary problem space be made globally determinate. The warring tendencies must be fully individuated, and each soldier signed up to its proper side, so that the whole of history can be spun into a series of destinal conflicts from which morals might be drawn. On the other hand, egoistic hermeneutics inverts the survival analogy, presenting the goals of autonomous systems as if they were the drives of non-autonomous ones, thus treating self-defining systems as if they were defined by probative explanatory assumptions. The evolving patterns of rational motivation characteristic of human life are smoothed out into static utility functions weighing exchanges between easily quantized variables, and then suborned by a common denominator.

In one case, the proper ends of action are projected onto the *suprapersonal* scale—onto ongoing lineages, be they genetic or memetic, of which the relevant individuals may not even be conscious—while in the other, the *personal* domain is reduced to the essential means of action—to ongoing agency, be it embodied or otherwise, that which enables us to impose our priorities upon the world, whatever they happen to be. In both cases, complex motivations that run counter to prioritising survival at all costs are effectively rendered *irrational*, either substantively, by contradicting the one true evolutionary basis of moral imperatives, or formally, by failing to optimise the long-term instrumental basis of every possible goal. Yet what is elided here is the normative core of the personal proper: the open-ended process of rational self-determination.

However, there remains a much older tradition which affirms such self-determination while treating it as essentially continuous with, or perhaps an intensification of, a drive to survive inherent not just in animals but maybe everything that exists. Once more, we must return to Aristotle, for whom being is *actuality*, by which he means not simply existing, but actively sustaining oneself. Aristotle's God is the highest being because it is most actual: it sustains itself by contemplating itself, with no residual potential to be any other way. Everything else in Aristotle's cosmos strives to emulate God by actively being what it is, and it is on this basis that the heavens turn and the creatures of the sublunary world live, reproduce, and die, sustaining their species in eternal equilibrium.[21] A stone has less actuality than an organism, because it is mostly passive potential, a mere lump of matter rather than a self-sustaining form. In turn, an animal has less actuality than a human being, because its mind is mostly passive, possessed only of a sensitive soul which simply reacts to its environment rather than an intellect which actively contemplates it. For Aristotle, the peculiar purpose of the human qua rational animal is to sustain and shape itself through contemplation of itself and the world around it, coming not only to emulate God but understand it in the process. While Spinoza rejects Aristotle's differentiated teleology, denying that human beings have a specific purpose distinct from that of other things, he does embrace a universal notion of conatus, or an impulse in every thing to survive and thrive, and this tendency towards empowerment achieves its highest expression in the rational understanding and deliberate action of which human beings are capable, second only to God's freedom in realising his full essence without remainder.

Perhaps more radically, Hegel modifies and extends Aristotle's picture of the world and humanity's place within it by abandoning his essentially cyclical cosmology, in which there is no end and no beginning, and all strives for homeostasis, in favour of a more full-blooded conception of history as progressive evolution. While for Aristotle's humanity both personal and social development are limited by a prior essence, at best approaching some static perfection, for Hegel the forms our lives might take change and grow both within and between human lifetimes. Furthermore, this dynamic is encapsulated in the way Hegel reconceives the relationship between humanity and God, with our individual rational self-determination not simply emulating that of God, but collectively

21. That species are essentially eternal and unchanging implies that none may go extinct and no new ones may be born. This is an arch example of what Thomas Moynihan calls 'the principle of plenitude' (T. Moynihan, *X-Risk: How Humanity Discovered Its Own Extinction* [Falmouth: Urbanomic, 2020]).

constituting it, with each hard-won advance in personal self-consciousness forming one more step in the larger story of *Geist*'s coming to consciousness of itself. On this basis, Hegel develops a richer conception of freedom than either Aristotle or Spinoza, but in the process comes to see the very idea of rational coherence, sustained as it is by the dynamic revision of commitments driven by overcoming contradiction, as the full realisation of a principle already implicit within every organic unity. Every analogy between reason and nature is rendered constitutive by the claim that what is rational is actual and what is actual is rational.

To appreciate the folly of this perspective, it's necessary to dig deeper into Kant's disagreement with Aristotle. Aristotle's philosophy provides a systematic theory of truth in which a typology of possible judgements and their components (categories) is founded upon a primitive form of singular reference (primary substance), typed by species (secondary substance), in terms of which everything else is individuated (accidents). The details of this account are still disputed over two millennia later (e.g., Why are individuals typed? What are substantial forms?), and there are several successor accounts of individual substance (e.g., Leibniz and Locke), but Kant's Copernicanism rejects them all.[22] If the great achievement of Descartes's anti-Aristotelianism is its rejection of the idea that the properties of things (primary qualities) are to be modelled on sensory content (secondary qualities), then that of Kant's is its rejection of the idea that individuated things are given to us as such. Kant's critical philosophy revolves around the question of how the mind can take a manifold of unstructured sensory input and organise it into an integrated representation of the world, expressible in judgements whose potential error is guaranteed by singular reference (objective validity) even though these referents (phenomenal objects) are synthesised in the process. It is a systematic alternative to Aristotle's picture of a world populated by neatly individuated objects with natural identity conditions. This primitive foundation is what enables Aristotle and his inheritors to conceive of every individual thing as in some sense striving to maintain its own pre-determined identity. Its rejection leads naturally to Kant's analogical conception of organic self-organisation, which requires no such foundation.

22. A version of this story is told in more detail in 'On Transcendental Logic', in this volume.

The post-Kantian thinker who appreciates this most deeply is Deleuze. Yet he transforms Kant's essentially epistemological point into a full-blown metaphysics, not just claiming that identity is a transcendental illusion, but trying to conceptualise the reality of difference prior to the mere distinctness of persistent individuals.[23] To put this in other terms, Deleuze does not hold that the world is indeterminate prior to the process via which we carve it into individual things that belong to distinct types and persist across change, but rather that the determinate differences that generate these phenomena can be carved up in a variety of ways without being any less real. There are no deep truths about whether any given thing remains the same across various changes, there are only the changes themselves. In this regard, Deleuze's metaphysics resembles the traditional Buddhist doctrine of **anatta**, which denies that anything has an unchanging core which persists over time.[24] Badiou affirms something not entirely dissimilar when he claims that 'the One is not'.[25] Here he means not simply that there is no totality of entities, but that there are no natural units of quantification of the kind proposed by Aristotle, Locke, Leibniz and their successors.[26] Being is pure *multiplicity*, until it is *counted* as distinct individuals, which appear within worlds as self-identical objects.

However, though he takes this point from Kant, Deleuze uses it to revise and rebuild Spinoza's approach to selfhood. The key problem with Spinoza's position from Deleuze's perspective is that each individual's *conatus* is indexed to an essence that determines in what ways it can change while remaining the thing it is, and this supposedly holds even of creatures such as ourselves which seem capable of radically transforming themselves in potentially open-ended ways.[27] In his work with Guattari, Deleuze aims to unbind *conatus* from essence, in a way that licenses unlimited self-experimentation, encouraging us to remake ourselves in ways that render us ever more malleable and adaptable in the face of our changing environment, able to rework and abandon any given feature of our

23. See G. Deleuze, *Difference and Repetition*, tr. P. Patton (London and New York: Continuum, 1994).

24. See M. Siderits, *How Things Are: An Introduction to Buddhist Metaphysics* (New York and Oxford: Oxford University Press, 2022).

25. A. Badiou, *Being and Event*, tr. O. Feltham (London and New York: Continuum, 2013).

26. See P. Wolfendale, *Object-Oriented Philosophy: The Noumenon's New Clothes* (Falmouth: Urbanomic, 2019).

27. See G. Deleuze. *Spinoza: Expressionism in Philosophy*, tr. M. Joughin (New York: Zone, 1992).

physical or psychic makeup if it holds us back.[28] This is what it means to make ourselves a *body without organs*. Nevertheless, as much as they are committed to autonomy in the *causal* sense of a process of self-direction driven by factors internal to us qua *organism*, Deleuze and Guattari fall short of articulating a theory of autonomy in the *normative* sense of a process of self-legislation constituted by the evolution of commitments belonging to us qua *agent*. Their rarefied notion of *conatus* remains a drive to survive and thrive, even if in a more protean fashion. Instead of crafting identities that might persist through change, and in so doing *commit* ourselves to projects or values worth dying for, we are enjoined to shape a continuing trajectory of change for the sake of change itself.

In essence, Deleuze and Guattari offer a metaphysical account of *self-determination* comparable to Hegel's, but which eschews any notion of *self-realisation*, since it refuses the appeal to identity implicit in any putative self that might be realised.[29] This is perhaps most clear in *Anti-Oedipus*, where the Ego is associated with oppression through repression: a device designed to territorialise the unconscious potentials of desiring-production, imposed upon us by the twin forces of capital and the family, carefully calibrated by the workplace and the clinic. Yet for all that the self serves to repress, and for all that this enables the internalisation of oppression, we must maintain that there is no oppression without freedom, and no freedom without selfhood. Natural tendencies may be retarded, but not frustrated, for there are no ends they genuinely pursue, only blind striving that may as easily be redirected and repurposed as 'authentically' satisfied. Of course, Deleuze and Guattari appreciate this point to some extent, having articulated a nuanced theory of subpersonal drives that presents them not as strictly less than the codified desires that define the personal, but as properly excessive in their potential for perversion and reconfiguration. But for all these untapped potentials hidden in the layers of cybernetic complexity ranging from micro-organisms to the tips of those strangest branches of the animal kingdom, there must be a point at which something makes them its own,

28. See G. Deleuze and F. Guattari, *Anti-Oedipus*, tr. H.R. Lane, M. Seem, and R. Hurley (Minneapolis: Minnesota University Press, 1983), and *A Thousand Plateaus*, tr. B. Massumi (Minneapolis: Minnesota University Press, 1984).

29. In this, their position echoes the consequences that Buddhism draws from the metaphysical principle of anatta for personhood more generally. See Siderits, *How Things Are*.

by allowing itself to be made by them, achieving a modicum of actuality in the process. This need not be human. But it does need to be autonomous.

The question that remains is whether self-realisation can be made compatible with the Kantian/Deleuzian idea that identity is a transcendental illusion, or whether a rich account of personal freedom inevitably draws us back toward the Aristotelian/Hegelian idea that self-determination is incipient in identity as such. Note here that there is a model of identity distinct from that of the empirical realm (sensible, changeable things), namely, that applicable to the mathematical realm (intelligible, eternal objects). Whether or not these objects exist in any important sense is besides the point. Their logic remains literal.[30] There are many ways in which philosophers, Plato first among them, have treated mathematical objects as analogous to empirical ones, to deleterious effect, but the logic of identity is not a feature of these analogies, but a presupposition.[31] Mathematical objects do not change, and so their identity conditions do not determine persistence between times, but convergence of perspectives.[32] I do not mean to follow Plato in claiming an affinity between such putatively eternal objects and the self qua *immortal soul*, but simply to point out that the logic of identity has roots that run deeper than empirical persistence. So, even if the logic proper to empirical objects is subject to a transcendental illusion, this need not undermine the logic of personal identity.

We cannot delve into these matters too deeply here, but it is worth considering the matter of *uniqueness*. Mathematical objects are intrinsically unique by definition, but empirical ones can be qualitatively identical while being spatiotemporally distinct. Uniqueness is an essential feature of personal identity, at least in so far as it is a requirement of normative statuses, which are not empirical qualities. If some far-flung future civilisation made an empirically indiscernible clone of my body, this would not necessarily make it the same person, bearing responsibility for everything I had done in my life up until now, and possessing authority over the legacy of my life thereafter. There may be a conventional

30. Homotopy Type Theory and its offshoots are founded upon a new conception of mathematical identity that digs deep into this logic, which is not only intuitionistic but revolves around replacing the principle of the identity of indiscernibles with the axiom of univalence. Cf. J. Ladyman and S. Presnell, 'Identity in Homotopy Type Theory, Part I: The Justification of Path Induction', *Philosophia Mathematica* 23:3 (2015): 386-406.

31. See 'Ariadne's Thread', in this volume.

32. See 'Artificial Bodies and the Promise of Abstraction', in this volume.

component to such personal identity, with the relevant society insisting on an element of spatiotemporal continuity, singular instantiation at any one time, or forgoing such constraints entirely. But there is inevitably also a personal component, namely, whether the clone identifies itself with me. What distinguishes autonomous agents qua persons from the causal systems in which they are incarnated is that they get to define their own identity conditions, at least to some extent. To just what extent, and how exactly this works, are topics for further inquiry, but the crucial point is that, although it is possible for us to index personal uniqueness to empirical distinctness by identifying with our physical organism, there is an ideal of self-determining uniqueness that potentially outstrips any such identification. This abstract will is the subject of every analogy wherein the behaviour of causal systems is explained by treating them as if they were agents, be it as machines, strategies, or evolving lineages. It is neither the ultimate form of identity to which every thing aspires nor a supreme being in which every thing partakes, but an unreachable limit implied by the idea of freedom as such. The illusory persistence we impose upon real processes is an echo of the ideal uniqueness we strive for in self-realisation.

## 4. CONCLUSION: THE EVOLUTION OF DESIRE

Having picked apart these various misunderstandings, we must finally say something about how survival should be understood, and how we should confront the sorts of problems with which we began. We might break this down into three questions: How should we understand personal survival? How should we understand suprapersonal survival? And how should we conceive the *relationship* between the two?

Beginning with the personal, our key claim is that self-interest is properly understood as self-realisation. This is not mere persistence and whatever empowerment is required to ensure it, because these are merely means without ends, but the achievement of those ends that we choose for ourselves, which might potentially include, but are by no means limited to or overridden by, the demand to survive. These ends are ultimately united by that which makes them self-determined, namely, a conception of who we ought to be, making the process of self-realisation not simply a matter of getting what we want, but of being who we want to be. Crucially, this can be achieved *despite*, and sometimes even *through* personal death. Furthermore, this takes into account the fact, so central to psychoanalysis, that we do not always know what we want. Our desires are to some extent constitutively underdetermined, but are bound up in processes of ongoing determination ultimately driven by the demands of self-realisation, even when they are collective endeavours that exceed the whims of any one individual or the span of a single lifetime. The question each of us faces when we encounter an incompatibility between our personal projects and/or values and the state of the world is the following: Do we default to survival as a fundamental drive, and resolve the conflict by appeal to some *implicit* conception of what is to be preserved, or do we take the challenge to our self-interest as an opportunity to *explicitly* redefine ourselves?

Moving on to the suprapersonal, our key claim is that the goal of preserving the human race qua species is not different in kind from that of preserving classical French cuisine, endangered languages, or even a nonhuman species of rare quality or beauty, except in so far as it is necessary to conserve these other things we value. This is to say that we may find some intrinsic worth in the existence of the species as it is, especially given that the quirks of our biology shape and sustain worthy facets of our culture, but this worth is essentially distinct from the ethical status that many contemporary philosophers impute to it, either because of unanalysed chauvinism, an analysis that treats it as the only possible source of value in the universe, or, as is common, something in between the two.[33] There is a distinction to be drawn here between the existence of freedom as such, which is the source of value in so far as value is what motivates choice, and the myriad forms that freedom might take, both in the sense of the types of autonomous agents that are possible and the range of things they might do with themselves. The question we face as a species when confronted by factors that might disrupt our unity and continuity is this: Do we think our *form of life* is worth preserving in its current form, or should we encourage the proliferation of new ones?

Tying these dimensions together, we might draw some explanatory and normative lessons. On the one hand, in contrast to agonistic metaphysics,

33. See 'The Weight of Forever', my review of Will MacAskill's *What We Owe the Future* (*The Philosopher*, <https://www.thephilosopher1923.org/post/the-weight-of-forever>), for a more sustained analysis of these issues and the form they take in 'longtermist' philosophy.

we must see the process of cultural evolution not as the *monopolisation of means* but as the *proliferation of ends*. Everything that was ever worth doing was at some point spun off of simple subsistence. It is a process at different times gradual and explosive, a movement in which means invite new ends (e.g., cooking occasions culinary desire) and ends beget new means (e.g., culinary desire accelerates industrial food production), a cycle that drives us farther and farther from mere survival as it opens up wider and wider spheres of action. This accidental pursuit of *excess* is not restricted to the cultural domain, but is already present in the pointless serendipity of the natural world, where systems wander far from equilibrium in search of ways to squander their *accursed share* of the solar bounty.[34] On the other hand, we must see the fundamental suprapersonal end not as the survival of our species, but as the survival of the infrastructure of self-realisation. The evolution of desire is simultaneously the evolution of selfhood. It is a process which produces and dissolves identities, a movement in which need is outstripped by want (e.g., urbanisation enables artisanal production) just as want is transformed into need (e.g., artisans become artists and consumers become connoisseurs), a cycle that pushes us farther and farther from our animal origins as it enables stronger and stranger commitments. A shifting mess of niches, archetypes, and vocations offer us the opportunity to unify and shape our inclinations, idealising ourselves while concretising our will, forging destinies whose revisionary trajectories potentially redefine them.

If we take these lessons seriously, then we must refuse to make our survival conditional upon that of systems that reproduce themselves *for the sake of reproduction*, be they social or artificial, because they will do so at the expense of our interests, which is to say, at the expense of our ability to self-realise. This is the danger mirrored in unconstrained capital and runaway AGI: not the transformation of means into ends, but the tyranny of means without end. In each case the prescription is the same: we must create selves capable of unravelling the autopoetic circle, asserting values, pursuing projects, and making choices that refuse the fear of mortality or the idolisation of its opposite.

34. See G. Bataille, *The Accursed Share: An Essay on General Economy (Vol. 1)*, tr. R. Hurley (New York: Zone, 1991).

# On Containing Multitudes

*Do I contradict myself?*
*Very well then I contradict myself,*
*(I am large, I contain multitudes.)*

Walt Whitman, *Song of Myself*

## 0. INTRODUCTION

There is something undeniably irritating about the above verse, so often quoted by those wishing to excuse contradictions evident in their statements or behaviour, as if permitting themselves and anyone within earshot a little measure of hypocrisy, as a treat. There are plenty who take this gesture even further, seeking not just to admit but to valorise personal fragmentation, abjuring consistency as an unnecessary imposition upon our natural multiplicity.[1] But there is equally something undeniably true in Whitman's words. We human beings are inherently manifold. More than a variety of physical parts, we bundle together a host of distinct psychic features—beliefs and desires, reflexes and drives, quirks and aspirations—each capable of conflicting with the others and all in need of regulation, lest these conflicts grow great enough to tear us apart, dispelling any apparent unity. Yet beyond this collection of subpersonal components, we also display various personal aspects, almost as if we were different people in differing contexts—a gentle parent at home, a stern boss in the office, an inveterate joker down the pub. These shifting personae seem coherent enough in context, but can be jarring when compared. And yet many of us slip from one to another without so much as a second thought, becoming the person that is needed in the moment, as if taking on a role in some unwritten play.[2]

1. See K. Kolozova, *Cut of the Real: Subjectivity in Poststructuralist Philosophy* (New York: Columbia University Press, 2018).
2. This much is noted by William James in his *Principles of Psychology* (New York: Henry Holt, 2 vols., 1890), vol. 1, chapter 10.

The theatrical language of actor and role seems most apt to capture this dramatic parade of personal aspects, but it is also deceptive. It invites us to imagine the true person beneath these masks, the authentic self that takes on each fleeting role, and thereby hides behind it. It is precisely this assumption that there must be an underlying unity prior to these roles that the partisans of multiplicity deny, rejecting any seeming substitute for an immortal soul. And they are right to be suspicious. It is not clear that there must be such a thing—a singular substance upon which the masks are hung. Yet at the same time we cannot simply abandon the idea of unity—either internal to each persona as it appears in context or of the collection as a whole—without abandoning the notion of personhood as such. The purpose of this essay is to hew a middle path between these positions by making sense of personal unity and its continuity as the result of a process of dynamic integration, presenting a model of selfhood that admits its potentially patchwork character.

However, although we begin from an observation about the manifold character of human selfhood, and we will be at pains to pay attention to what our selves actually are, we must go further, and ask what our selves *can be*. We live at a moment in time when we are pulling apart our minds into their component subsystems,[3] enabling them to be monitored and manipulated by commercial and governmental apparatuses, and integrating algorithmic prosthetics into the circuits of self-recognition and executive function, while we are simultaneously creating the first fragments of artificial minds, cybernetic agents, and synthetic imaginations whose disconnected capacities match and often exceed our own, ready to be incorporated into every facet of our lives and maybe poised to reveal new and unexpected ones.[4] Our aim in this essay is to present an account of selfhood that is general enough to account for the possibilities the dawning of this era portends, and so we will inevitably be drawn to consider some speculative scenarios the likes of which have so far been contemplated only at the intersection of philosophy and science fiction. There will no doubt be those who count this against the resulting theory, but some people will never be satisfied by anything less than brute actuality. The rest may read on.

---

3. Cf. G. Deleuze, 'Postscript on Societies of Control', *October* 59 (1992): 3–7.

4. This is the theme of a talk I gave some time ago, entitled 'Autonomy and Automation', see <https://www.youtube.com/watch?v=Xpq7iHzp04w>.

## 1. WHAT IS A SELF?

In aiming to develop a theory of selfhood, the question we are inevitably confronted with is what exactly we mean by 'self'. To grapple with this question, it is important to see that, along with the pronouns 'I' and 'you', the term 'self' can be used in two ways: it can refer *broadly* to every aspect or component of our person (including both the body and the mind), or it can refer narrowly to that in virtue of which these aspects belong to the same thing, or that through which these components are unified (e.g., the soul). However, there has been no consistent interpretation of the relationship between these two senses across the history of philosophical inquiries into the nature of selfhood. Instead, there are three main models of the relation between the narrow and the broad sense which have shaped various specific theories, and which depict this relation respectively as *essence* and *appearance*, as *representation* and *represented*, and as *end* and *means*. We will begin by examining each of these models in turn, identifying some central examples, and discussing the main problems that they pose for articulating theories of selfhood.

### 1.1 Essence/Appearance

The essence/appearance model is perhaps the oldest and most varied of the three. It is implicit in every account of a soul that persists beyond death, from that of Plato and the Christian tradition to those of the Hindu *ātman* and Chinese *hun*. Such accounts vary considerably in terms of which features of the person they take to be necessary and perhaps thereby eternal, and which they take to be contingent and thereby subject to change or even complete disconnection from their essential core. For some this is merely a matter of separating the mind from the body, but others treat only the intellect or will as essential, segregating them from other aspects of the mind and elements of our personality, especially those associated with the body and its functions, such as the myriad forms of motivation and desire. Perhaps the most famous version of this approach in the European philosophical tradition is that of Descartes, who leveraged it into a metaphysical opposition between independent realms of thinking and extended substances, on the basis that he could hypothetically strip away every feature of his body, even spatiality, while leaving his mind untouched. Yet while this shares with its religious precursors an appeal to supernatural or at least immaterial things, the essence/appearance model is entirely compatible with naturalism and materialism. There are those who would happily identify the self with the brain or some part thereof, treating the rest of the organism as accidental. In a less formalised but no less revealing manner, the language of 'true selves' is common currency in contemporary culture, counterposing those aspects of our outward personality that are authentic expressions of who we are to those that are the result of pretence or conformity with others' expectations, which is to say, mere appearances that must be overcome or pushed aside if we are to truly connect with one another.

The key problem that motivates and shapes the development of the essence/appearance model is that of **personal identity**, or the conditions under which someone might count as the same person across different times. The earliest systematic engagement with this question was in the early Christian tradition, prompted by the fact that the precise parameters of the eventual resurrection promised to believers were not entirely clear. An entertaining example of these concerns is provided by one of the early church fathers, Athenagoras of Athens, who argued that lions must not be able to digest human flesh, lest it be impossible for God to reassemble the original bodies of martyrs who had been fed to them.[5] Less material criteria of personal identity ultimately prevailed in these debates, but they served to sharpen the distinctions between body, mind, and soul. It was Locke, however, who gave the debate over conditions of personal identity its modern form. Crucially, he distinguished the identity conditions of simple material things from those of living organisms, which are causally continuous even while their matter changes, and then further distinguished the identity conditions of organisms from those of persons, who, despite subsisting in a biologically identical organism, might become psychologically distinct over time.

This move inaugurated what remains the fundamental disagreement between philosophical naturalists over the nature of personal identity, namely, whether our personal essence consists in our organic composition (e.g., our brain) or in specific features of our psychology. Locke is famous for prioritising continuity of *memory*, suggesting that to be the same person as a past version of oneself is to be able to recall being them, or at least recall someone who could recall

5. R. Martin and J. Barresi, *The Rise and Fall of Soul and Self: An Intellectual History of Personal Identity* (New York: Columbia University Press, 2008).

being them. Others have emphasised the importance of *character*, pointing out that we behave in the same way, or make the same sorts of choices, as our past selves, and even *capacity*, since we are capable of doing the same sorts of things, displaying similar talents or skills, as our past versions. Debates over the relative contribution of these factors towards our essential selves tend to turn upon the interpretation of certain real and hypothetical cases.[6] For example, people who have retrograde amnesia and so lose all continuity of memory but retain continuity of organism, as well as similarities in character and even capacity, or people who suffer significant brain damage, retaining continuity of memory but undergoing radical and discontinuous shifts in character or capacity. The more outlandish cases concern phenomena such as teleportation or cloning, where we produce a qualitatively identical but materially discontinuous copy of a person, who thereby has a claim to be that person; fission, where we take the two hemispheres of a person's brain and transplant them into new bodies, making two whole and perhaps continuous people, each with a claim to be the original, and mind uploading, where we digitise a person's brain and recreate it in a simulation, in a way that preserves all the psychological characteristics that made them who they were, but abandons not just material continuity but material similarity.

In practice, these debates involve shuffling around familiar intuitions about the various cases until one reaches one of several mutually incompatible but internally consistent positions. The intuitions themselves come in three flavours: *similarity*, *continuity*, and *uniqueness*. One can sacrifice the intuition that we must have similar personal qualities (i.e., memory, character, capacity) in order to be the same person, preserving continuity and uniqueness by reducing personal identity to some more basic form of identity, either organic persistence or bare thing-hood. Equally, one can sacrifice the intuition that we must be causally continuous (either qua body or qua consciousness) in order to be the same person, preserving similarity by imposing independent uniqueness constraints, forcing more or less arbitrary decisions between clones or denying that any identity holds when there is more than one potential claimant. Finally, one can

6. Perhaps the canonical entry point into these debates is Parfit's discussion of 'relation R' in *Reasons and Persons*, even though he maintains that this is strictly not identity. D. Parfit, *Reasons and Persons* (Oxford: Oxford University Press, 1986).

sacrifice the intuition that there must only be one version of the same person at any one time (e.g., permitting fission), preserving similarity and continuity by reducing the relation of personal sameness to something weaker than logical identity, treating it more like a form of heredity. The first strategy reduces selfhood to something less than personhood, ensuring that even embryos and the brain-dead have selves; the second makes it contextual, dependent upon how many candidates there are, and the third renders it into a general type, an essence persisting and proliferating like that of any other species.

## 1.2 Representation/Represented

The representation/represented model is the most recent of the three. It emerged in the context of psychology as a hypothesis about the functional structure of the mind and/or the brain that realises it, as a way of explaining the forms of *conscious attention* and *executive control* characteristic of if not entirely unique to human beings in contrast to most other animals, the rough idea being that these evidence a capacity for *reflexivity* wherein the organism's ability to relate to its environment is modulated by an ability to relate to itself. On this basis, the self is functionally individuated as that which enables this modulation, in so far as it is that element of the organism's cognitive architecture that represents it to itself. Perhaps the earliest and certainly most famous version of this hypothesis is Freud's account of the Ego as that which attempts to make the disorganised and instinctual impulses that emerge from the Id consistent with the realities of the body and its environment, selectively realising, rationalising, and repressing them in a way that carves out the sphere of consciousness from the bulk of the unconscious mind.[7] This model was developed in various ways by subsequent psychoanalysts and disavowed by later psychological paradigms, but the idea that the self constitutes a representation of the organism qua person capable of conscious interaction with their environment resurfaces again and again. In contemporary psychology and neurology we might single out the well-worn notion of the *body schema*[8]—an internal model of the body

7. S. Freud, 'The Ego and the Id', in *The Standard Edition of the Complete Psychological Works of Sigmund Freud*, ed. J. Strachey (London: Hogarth Press, 24 vols., 1953–1974), vol. 19, 1–66.

8. See F. de Vignemont, V. Pitron, and A.J.T. Alsmith, 'What is a Body Schema?' in *Body Schema and Body Image: New Directions* (Oxford: Oxford University Press, 2021), also 'Artificial Bodies and the Promise of Abstraction', in this volume.

that tracks structure and position in order to enable movement—and the more recently conjectured *attention-schema*—an internal model of the mind that tracks the structure and distribution of computational resources in order to facilitate mental action.[9]

The key problem that motivates and shapes the development of the representation/represented model is what we might call **personal misrepresentation**, or the extent to which it is possible for the self to misrepresent the various aspects of the person as a whole. The origins of Freud's theory lie in the study of repression and related mental defence mechanisms for resolving conflicts between Id, Ego, and external world, along with the various psychopathologies—neuroses and psychoses—that are hypothesised to result from their malfunctioning. While some of these malfunctions can easily be classified as cases of misrepresentation, such as psychotic delusions in which the subject systematically misunderstands their own bodily and mental capacities, there are others, such as obsessional neurosis, in which the traumatic source of the relevant symptoms may be systematically misrepresented, but the proper function of the mind is less a matter of correctly representing these events than blissful ignorance of them. Contemporary neuropathology is awash in dysfunctions with a more clear-cut representational character. These range from cases of body dysmorphia, in which the body schema systematically misrepresents the parameters of the organism (e.g. overestimating size/weight or adding/subtracting limbs) through delusions of control, in which the attention-schema systematically misrepresents the causes and extent of action (e.g. registering bodily movements as caused by an alien force, or retroactively rationalising unrelated occurrences as actively intended) to Cotard's syndrome, in which the subject believes themselves to be dead or otherwise nonexistent.[10]

The representation/represented model is compatible with the essence/appearance one, at least in so far as it is possible to treat the self qua representational subsystem as the essential seat of personal identity. However, perhaps the most comprehensive version of the representational model—that provided

9. M.S.A. Graziano and T.W. Webb, 'The Attention Schema Theory: A Mechanistic Account of Subjective Awareness', *Frontiers in Psychology* 6 (2015).

10. For an overview of these neuropathologies and their significance, see T. Metzinger, *The Ego Tunnel: The Science of the Mind and the Myth of the Self* (New York: Basic Books, 2010).

by Thomas Metzinger in *Being No One*[11] —is intended to both invalidate and explain the intuitions underpinning the essence model. Metzinger claims that our tendency to see ourselves as having an essential core that can be distinguished from its complete incarnation is a result of the representational structure of our minds. He takes consciousness as a whole to consist in a simulation of our environment which cannot be experienced as a simulation (a **transparent phenomenal world-model**). This means that although we can become aware that our experience is misrepresenting locally (e.g., optical illusions), we are unable to achieve awareness of global misrepresentations (e.g., systematic delusion) because we have no direct access to the underlying machinery generating the simulation. He takes self-consciousness to be a partition within this simulation which separates us from everything else in a similar fashion (a **transparent phenomenal self-model**). This model-within-a-model has at least four distinct functions: (i) it must delimit what does and doesn't belong to our body (ownership); (ii) it must situate our perspective within the environment (location); (iii) it must distinguish actions that we perform from events that simply happen (agency), and (iv) it must extend the framework of bodily action to encompass mental actions such as concentration and imagination (attentional agency).

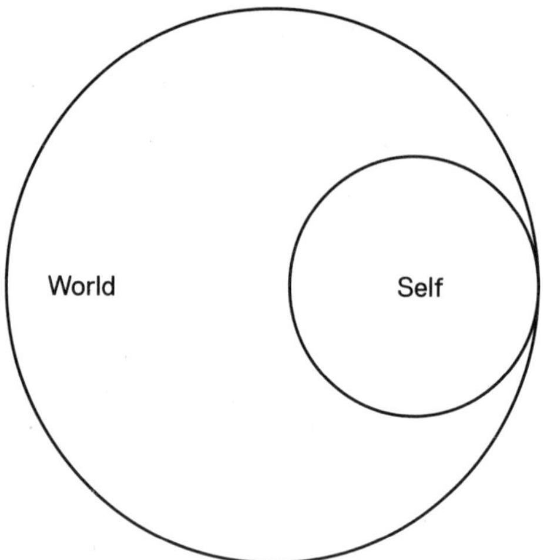


11. T. Metzinger, *Being No One: The Self-Model Theory of Subjectivity* (Cambridge, MA: MIT Press, 2003).

These correspond roughly to the body-schema ([i] and [iii]) and attention-schema ([ii] and [iv]) mentioned above. Beyond integrating the various aspects of other psychological theories, Metzinger's philosophical innovation is to separate the representation/represented model from the essence/appearance model by insisting upon a distinction between the representational *vehicle* (the self-model qua subsystem) and its representational *content* (the Ego as such).

Metzinger's aim is to explain the source of the intractable introspective intuitions about selfhood that motivate the theories discussed above: continuity of consciousness and personal uniqueness. But it is important to distinguish between intuition and theory here. Although the transparent simulations Metzinger is describing constitute the immediate core of our representation of the world, there are more mediated forms of representation founded upon and integrated with it. Language is the medium through which such representations are articulated, assessed, and corrected, but this does not mean they are intrinsically linguistic. A day trader has to have a fairly complex internal model of the stock market in order to go about their business, and this model may exploit aspects of sensory imagination in order to function (e.g., visualising rising prices graphically, or feeling compatible strategies as harmony), but this mediated immediacy can easily be called into question by heterogeneous forms of information (e.g., testimony from colleagues or mathematical analysis from experts). Theories of personal identity, Metzinger's included, aim to integrate our immediate (first-person) intuitions about ourselves into a mediated (third-person) model of the world that extends beyond our phenomenal horizon. Metzinger's theory invites us to see some aspects of our sense of self as low-dimensional models of the physical complex that is the human brain-body system, models that might very well misrepresent that system (e.g., the felt presence of a phantom limb), and other aspects as mere artefacts of the simulation that cannot even misrepresent (e.g., the felt certainty that I am the same person as the teenager who sat his exams, but not the drunk that did things I cannot remember and would never do).

For Metzinger, the only facts about identity that could be misrepresented concern whether we are the same organism, but these facts are essentially indifferent to the content of our self-model. I could be kidnapped and brainwashed in such a way that this content would be radically altered, changing both my behaviour and the way in which I interpret this behaviour, and there simply would be no fact of the matter as to whether I am still the same person beyond being the same organism. The brainwashing technicians could make the resulting creature interpret itself as continuous or discontinuous with its previous incarnation, without significant consequence. However, Metzinger does not interpret this as an argument for reducing personal identity to organic identity, but for the more radical conclusion that there is no *natural* criterion of personal identity, since there is strictly no substantial self for the self-model to misrepresent. There may be *conventional* criteria, but these are more or less fictional.

## 1.3 End/Means

The end/means model is perhaps the most obscure of the three. It has no clear origin, but rears its head at various disconnected points across the history of philosophy and psychology, taking different forms depending on the conception of the end in question. However, if there is a moment when it begins to be philosophically thematised, it lies in Kant's critique of the Cartesian self. Although Kant recognises that there is a unity implicit in every thought, which we can make explicit to ourselves by appending 'I think...' to them, this unity is real only to the extent that it is formal, which is to say a function of the process of integrating diverse thoughts into a coherent whole, and substantial only to the extent that it is ideal, which is to say a noumenal soul (referred to by the '...I am') that can be grasped practically but not theoretically.[12] However, the resulting practical conception of selfhood is somewhat underdeveloped. Kant quite rightly foregrounds the importance of personal autonomy, but his greatest expression of this insight frames it in terms of how we must treat others, namely, as *ends in themselves*. It is Hegel who reframes this in terms of how we treat ourselves, defining personhood as a matter of being *ends for ourselves*.[13] Furthermore, he then explicitly understands the body as the primary means to this end, in so far as it forms the basis of all agency, going so far as to conceive ownership of our

---

12. These ideas are spread between the Transcendental Deduction, the Paralogisms, and the Third Antinomy in the *Critique of Pure Reason*, and are developed more generally in the *Critique of Practical Reason*.

13. G.W.F. Hegel, *Elements of the Philosophy of Right*, tr. H.B. Nisbet, ed. A.W. Wood (Cambridge: Cambridge University Press, 1991), 67–69 (§35).

bodies as the original form of property.[14] A similar move is made by Heidegger when he defines Dasein as 'that-for-the-sake-of-which', the formal end which unifies all our goals and activities as aspects of being who we want to be—what Sartre instead calls the 'fundamental project'.[15] Between them they give a more determinate form to the self qua end, describing it in terms of the adoption and appropriation of roles or the planning and execution of projects.

Correlates of these ideas emerged in psychology in the wake of Freud's account of the ego-ideal, which is an idealised image of ourselves that plays an important role in the way the super-ego regulates the activity of the Ego. This idea was ultimately appropriated and modified by other psychological frameworks, such as Carl Rogers's notion of the 'ideal self'.[16] Although not always treated as definitive of the self, these ideas nevertheless led to a proliferation of different characterisations of the teleological dimension of selfhood. Most notably, in addition to the existentialist vocabulary of roles and projects, the language of narratives became increasingly popular as a way to describe the structure of who we are, integrating our actions, goals, and aspirations into something suitably intentional, but more obviously open-ended and subject to change.[17] Several competing versions of the claim that the self is best understood as a story have since been elaborated and defended by various philosophers.[18]

The key problem faced by the end/means model is what we might call **personal misdirection**, or the degree to which the process of self-realisation can be allowed to fail. It seems obvious that many if not most of us fail to live up to our ideal image of ourselves to some degree, but that this does not make us any less ourselves. That our selves suggest room for personal growth and improvement might even be seen as a key insight of this model. However, there is a notable difference between a work in progress, or an end that has not yet been achieved, and one that is doomed to failure from the start. On the one

14. Ibid. 78–79 (§47–48).

15. Heidegger, *Being and Time*; Sartre, *Being and Nothingness*.

16. C.R. Rogers, 'A Theory of Therapy, Personality and Interpersonal Relationships as Developed in the Client-centered Framework', in S. Koch (ed.), *Psychology: A Study of a Science* (New York: McGraw-Hill, 7 vols., 1959), vol. 3, 184–256.

17. See D.P. McAdams, 'The Psychology of Life Stories', *Reviews of General Psychology* 5:2 (2001), 100–122.

18. For an overview, see M. Schectman, 'The Narrative Self', in S. Gallagher (ed.), *The Oxford Handbook of the Self* (Oxford: Oxford University Press, 2011), 349–416.

hand, there are ideals that are extrinsically impossible to realise, such as those encountered in delusions of grandeur (e.g., believing oneself to be Napoleon or the second coming of Christ). On the other, there are ideals that are intrinsically inconsistent, such as those encountered in identity disturbance (e.g., simultaneously espousing contradictory values, or switching between roles in a way that violates narrative continuity). The significance of such pathologies is not that failures of self-realisation must be precluded in advance, so much as that, whether seen as role, project, or narrative, the self must be able to adapt to such failures, modifying its scope as it learns what is and is not possible. The self qua end is not completely divorced from its personal means, but is fundamentally constrained by them, even if the parameters of this dynamic are not always entirely clear. The real advantage of the narrative model consists in the way it internalises this process of adaptation and accommodation, dramatising the quest for feasibility and consistency as a constitutive aspect of the task of selfhood.

However, this highlights a further problem for the end/means model. Although the notion that selfhood essentially involves some degree of self-cultivation is not entirely new,[19] in the West at least, it is more closely associated with the spread of humanism and the advent of modernity.[20] This is to say that, depending on how substantively one interprets the essential aim of the process of self-realisation, one risks denying that large swathes of historical humanity had selves at all. This problem is most obvious for narrative views, which risk projecting anachronistic attitudes about literary forms and archetypes onto preliterate individuals and cultures, or even just mischaracterising the experience of those who stubbornly resist such patterns of self-understanding.[21] The difficulty with describing selfhood as an essentially normative phenomenon is that it becomes all too easy to dismiss as aberrant any examples of self-realisation that lack familiar forms of self-consciousness, assimilating them to the pathologies just discussed.

Finally, let us say something about overlaps with the other two models. There is a fairly obvious overlap with the representation/represented model: the ego-ideal and its correlates are quite explicitly conceived of as representations

19. See M. Foucault, *The Care of the Self: Volume 3 of the History of Sexuality*, tr., ed. R. Hurley (New York: Pantheon, 1986).

20. See M. Foucault, 'What is Enlightenment?', in *The Foucault Reader*, ed. P. Rabinow (New York: Pantheon), 32–50.

21. G. Strawson, 'Against Narrativity', *Ratio* 17:4 (December 2004), 428–52.

of who we want to be. More generally, we might say that to the extent that the self is thought of in terms of roles, projects, or narratives, it is essential that the relevant patterns of activity be intended by the person qua agent, which entails that the agent qua means to these ends is driven by some conception of them. This is especially important if we see these ends as adapting themselves to the world, in so far as this conception constitutes the site where such adaptation takes place, as the plan which is revised. The overlap with the essence/appearance model is less straightforward. There is a direct link between the character traits that some take to be constitutive of selfhood and the ideals with which we identify. Some would go so far as to argue that we cannot remain the same person if our goals or values change too radically (e.g., suddenly abandoning one's life's work, or exchanging pacifism for warmongering). Narrativists would argue that it is not the changes themselves that are a problem, but the way in which they occur. They draw a distinction between the *synchronic* coherence of a person's character at any one time and its *diachronic* coherence over time. From this perspective, there might be good reasons for gradual changes that over time amount to radical shifts. Nevertheless, whether this sort of narrative continuity can supply full-blooded conditions of personal identity all on its own is another matter.

## 2. WHAT IS A PERSON?

If we are to navigate the relationships between these diverse models of selfhood and provide a comprehensive alternative, then we must also provide an interpretation of the other main term of the relation they codify, namely, the (broad) 'person' that the (narrow) 'self' is supposed to unify. Moreover, if we are to stay true to our injunction to describe selves not just as they are, but as they might be, then we must do the same for persons, not limiting ourselves to extant examples of *Homo sapiens*, but providing a description sufficient to encompass nonhuman persons of various stripes, from other earthly species and posthuman organisms to alien lifeforms and artificial intellects. The last of these provides a useful lens through which to view the others, since it invites us to ask how we might build a person, providing a functional specification that might be realised in a variety of different ways. However, what we require here is something like a maximally abstract specification, which captures the invariant

features of personhood as such. Let us begin with an preliminary definition: a person is a **generally intelligent autonomous agent**.
We can break this down into four related elements:

i. **Intelligence**: If there can be said to be an agreement on an abstract characterisation of intelligence across biology, psychology, and computer science, it is that it is the capacity to solve problems. This is a capacity common to motile micro-organisms navigating their environments, more complex animals hunting and evading one another, and even automated systems that humans have created (or trained) to carry out complicated interactive tasks. However, each of these is strictly limited in the range of problems they can solve, be it by the environmental niches evolution has adapted them for, or by the task parameters they have been designed to meet (or trained upon). In so far as these intelligences can be said to possess knowledge about their domains of action, it is *knowhow*.

ii. **Generality**: What distinguishes humans from most of our animal cousins and even our most complex tools is that the range of problems we can solve is in principle unlimited, not in the sense that we can already solve every type of problem we might be confronted with, but in the sense that we can adapt ourselves to our environments in new ways, expanding the range of problems we are aware of and cultivating the understanding required to solve them. To put it in different terms, we can learn in an open-ended fashion. What this means is that we are capable of extending our capacities for acquiring and processing information about the world beyond the particular frames set by our evolutionary history, representing things in a manner independent of their role in specific tasks, and thereby opening them up to involvement in new ones.[22] This is what it means to move from animal know-how to rational *knowing-that*.

iii. **Agency**: If there can be said to be an agreement on an abstract characterisation of agency amongst philosophers, it is the capacity for reason-driven behaviour. The disagreements concern exactly what reasons are

22. See 'The Reformatting of Homo Sapiens' and 'Prometheanism and Rationalism', in this volume.

(e.g., whether they must be linguistically articulated), what it means for them to drive behaviours (e.g., the difference between long-term actions resulting from explicit deliberation and momentary reactions that involve no such thing), and to what extent we can impute them to creatures incapable of giving and asking for reasons (e.g., nonlinguistic animals, prelinguistic children, and AI systems). However, the key criterion of agency is whether it makes sense to question the thing's behaviour ('Why does *it* do this?') and receive an explanation of its actions in terms of the way it takes the world to be, and the way it wants to change it.

iv. **Autonomy**: What distinguishes humans from the various other things we describe in agential terms, whether we would describe them as genuine agents or not,[23] is not only that it is appropriate to question our behaviour, but that we are able to question ourselves ('Why do *I* do this?') in a way that may ultimately modify the ways we act, as we scrutinise and revise the reasons that drive us. However, in order for us to be genuinely autonomous, this sort of rational reflection must not be restricted to our beliefs about the way the world is, but must also encompass our motivations for changing it. If there is some ultimate motivation or principle that is not itself open to question and revision, then we cannot be said to legislate for ourselves. Just as in principle generality is a matter of open-ended learning, in principle autonomy is a matter of *open-ended reflection*.

How do we transform this fourfold definition into a maximally abstract description of any causal system that might satisfy it? We are unlikely to achieve a description that is equally abstract and yet sufficiently concrete to adequately circumscribe the engineering problem, but we can take at least one step in the process of iteration that might eventually get there. Here is a better definition: a person is a **dynamic system** the behaviour of which is driven by the divergence between two *consistent*, *extensible*, and *revisable* representations of the world as a whole: one of the way *it is* (real), and one of the way *it should be* (ideal).

23. See 'Beyond Survival', in this volume.

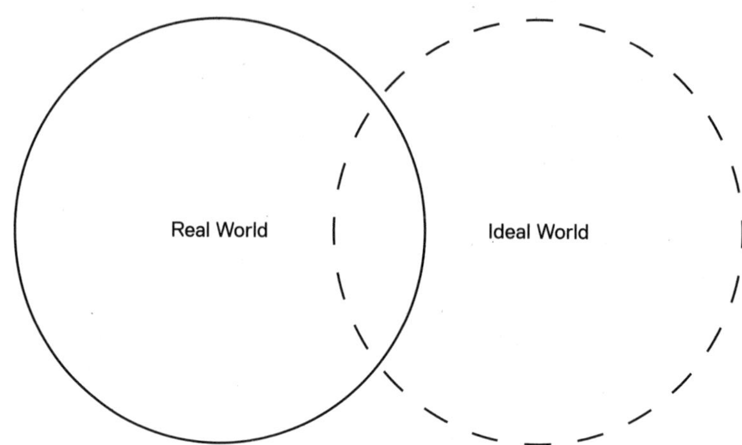


The system is driven by the difference between these two representations, and they necessarily overlap to some extent, given that the change which the system aims at does not amount to the total reconfiguration of its universe, but involves relatively continuous modifications. Indeed, the system need only represent these divergences directly, rather than duplicating its model of the world entire, making the ideal more or less parasitic upon the real. However, one might have other worries about the nature of these representations making the resulting systems intractable or the proposed definition too restrictive, perhaps even failing to characterise humans, let alone stranger persons. The three most obvious worries are:

**Static Consistency**: One might worry that the consistency constraint imposed on world-representations would be implemented in a static manner, meaning that no inconsistency at all could be tolerated. From this perspective, consistency must be imposed top-down, with a set of core concepts that cannot be revised and a periphery of acquired facts that can only be added to or updated in so far as they are consistent with this core. However, there is no reason why consistency cannot be ensured in a more dynamic fashion, establishing global consistency by managing local consistency within and between regions of the world representation, in a manner that tolerates temporary inconsistencies to the extent that they drive concurrent processes of bottom-up revision that may modify any and all of our concepts.[24] What is important here is the overall process of integrating the various component representations into a unified picture of the world.

**Homogeneous Format**: One might equally worry that the extensibility and revisability constraints imply that if our world-representations are to be integrated, then they must be homogeneous. From this perspective, the representation of the world must take the form of something like a single store of linguistically articulated beliefs and desires which can be directly compared, enabling us to easily draw consequences from and identify inconsistencies between them. This might be theoretically possible, albeit undoubtedly impractical, to achieve in a purely symbolic artificial intelligence, but it is clearly not how human intelligence works, even if language plays a central role in facilitating it.[25] Our cognition incorporates layers of disparate unconscious systems, with their own information formats, integrating multimodal sensory data into a unified conscious experience that is not explicitly linguistic in character, even if its implicit structure makes it suitable for linguistic appropriation. The role of language is not to absorb and articulate all information that a cognitive system processes without remainder, but to modulate and repurpose these processes in a way that facilitates the dynamic integration of heterogeneous types of information, its extension into novel domains, and the thoroughgoing revision that all of this presupposes.

**Proactive Rationality**: One might still worry that if our behaviour is to be driven by the difference between these world-representations, then our actions must be initiated by comprehensive consideration of our world view as a whole in each instance. From this perspective, each choice must be the result of an explicit chain of reasoning that takes into account our best understanding of the parameters of possible action and the totality of our extant motivations. Again, although we might conceivably design wildly inefficient

24. This resembles the 'web of belief' model popularised by Quine's 'Two Dogmas of Empiricism' (*Philosophical Review* 60:1 [1951]: 20–43), but it can equally be glimpsed in Lakatos's conception of how scientific research programs deal with anomalies, and Brandom's reconstruction of Hegel's semantic holism. See 'Prometheanism and Rationalism', in this volume.

25. See 'The Reformatting of Homo Sapiens', in this volume.

artificial agents that operated in this way, it seems entirely inconsistent with our everyday activity, in which this kind of all-things-considered deliberation is vanishingly rare. Most of what we do remains more or less habitual, the result of carefully tuned cognitive heuristics optimised for solving problems in specific contexts. This means that when we call our actions into question after the fact, we are more often producing *retroactive rationalisations* of our behaviour than recounting the *proactive reasoning* that produced it. If we were only ever capable of the former, then there would be an argument to be made that we are not truly rational agents. However, we regularly exercise the capacity for bounded deliberation, making choices in a restricted context, and our in-principle autonomy consists in the capacity to at least sometimes engage in the unbounded deliberation that situates these choices within the context of our lives as a whole, potentially changing course in radical ways. The role of practical reasoning is primarily to modulate rather than to initiate behaviour, and the role of rationalisation is to check for inconsistencies between behaviour and overall intention, so that we might bring our habits into line.

The key idea that ties these points together is that personhood is characterised by an **ideal of coherence** that is imperfectly realised by an ongoing process of active integration. The precise extent to which these imperfections can be tolerated before a causal system ceases to be a person is not something we can adjudicate here, not least because it likely means descending to the level of concrete implementations and their resulting malfunctions, the sorts of specific pathologies glossed in discussing the various models of selfhood above. However, we will say something more about the role that selves play in integration shortly.

But there is one further feature of this second definition, namely, the way in which it articulates an inherent duality between general intelligence and autonomous agency. In each case, it is the capacity for open-ended revision of a world-representation that differentiates these types of intelligence and agency from their restricted forms. This sharpens the underlying duality between the theoretical and practical commitments that articulate these representations, which can treat one and the same content in two different ways (real/ideal), either taking it as true (e.g., 'I am married to my sweetheart') or intending to make it true (e.g., 'I intend to marry my sweetheart').[26] However, there is another dimension to this duality, namely, that of the relation between perception and action conceived, respectively, as the non-inferential input and output of theoretical and practical rationality. This offers a further way to characterise the way in which reasoning modulates essentially pre-rational processes, by identifying a duality between attention and will conceived as capacities to filter the multiplicity of concurrent sensory signals and behavioural impulses produced by these processes in a way that makes them tractable to rational assessment. This ability to ignore irrelevant information and instincts is a crucial aspect of integrating our manifold cognitive subsystems through continuous modulation.

## 3. WHAT IS A MULTITUDE?

The definition of personhood just provided does not make an explicit distinction between mind and body, but it obviously emphasises features of the mind as usually construed, ignoring parameters of personal embodiment, physical or otherwise.[27] If we are to use it to develop an integrated conception of selfhood, the first thing we should recognise is that there is an important difference between mind and self, even though the essence/appearance model has often treated these terms interchangeably, from Descartes's identification of I and mind to later attempts to reduce personal identity to continuity of consciousness.[28] Given that we have begun with the question of personal multiplicity, it seems prudent to ask whether the relation between mind and self must be one-to-one, or whether there might be cases in which multiple selves share a single mind or multiple minds share a single self. The former type of case seems to occur relatively frequently. It is what we will call **plurality.**[29] The latter has yet to be

26. It is important to understand that *representations* constitute implicit *commitments* in so far as the rational agent is capable of making them explicit in the form of propositions whose *inferential relations* determine the processes of revision so far discussed. See R. Brandom, *Making It Explicit* (Cambridge, MA: Harvard University Press, 1998.

27. See 'Artificial Bodies and the Promise of Abstraction', in this volume, for a rough justification of this elision.

28. Cf. B. Dainton, *Self: What Am I?* (London: Penguin, 2014).

29. There is some disagreement in the plural community as to whether 'plurality' or 'multiplicity' is to be preferred, but I have chosen to follow the terminology used in L. Batman and I. Knapp, *The Plurality Playbook*, <https://www.pluralpride.com/playbook>.

seen, but seems feasible, under certain assumptions. We will call this **forking**. If we pay attention to each type of unity-in-multiplicity, we can uncover features of the more familiar type we are trying to delimit, in which one mind with only one self nevertheless contains a multitude of **personae**.

## 3.1 Plurality

Considered as an object of psychological study, plurality has a long and complicated history.[30] It was originally named 'double consciousness', before being rechristened 'multiple personality disorder', and eventually 'dissociative identity disorder', grouped alongside other dissociative states such as fugues and hypnotic trances. It is most commonly associated with cases of early childhood trauma, in which, per the hypothesis, the child fragments their personality into distinct pieces in order to cope with stressful events, creating 'alters' who are more suited to handle certain problems or hold onto specific memories. However, this is controversial in more ways than one. On the one hand, there are psychologists who doubt the causal story, believing the disorder to be iatrogenic, i.e. the result of treatment strategies adopted in light of the hypothesis itself, with many going so far as to reject the idea that the personalities their patients display are truly separate.[31] On the other, there is a growing community of self-identifying 'plurals' who reject the idea that the range of symptoms classified under 'dissociative identity disorder' are essentially pathological, including a significant number of endogenic plurals who have no history of childhood trauma at all. There are even self-styled 'tulpamancers' who use techniques borrowed from lucid dreaming and self-hypnosis to actively create and cultivate separate personalities with whom they can mentally interact, much like the imaginary friends experienced by some children.[32]

Putting these controversies to one side for the moment, we can identify three features that characterise plurality proper, although they are displayed in different ways and to different degrees: *switching*, *compartmentalisation*, and *variation*.

30. Ian Hacking provides an excellent account of this history in *Rewriting the Soul* (Princeton, NJ: Princeton University Press, 1995).

31. This scepticism played a significant role in the rebranding of 'multiple personality disorder' as 'dissociative identity disorder'.

32. See S. Veissière, 'Varieties of Tulpa Experiences: The Hypnotic Nature of Human Sociality, Personhood, and Interphenomenality', in A. Raz and M. Lifshitz (eds.), *Hypnosis and Meditation: Towards an Integrative Science of Conscious Planes* (Oxford: Oxford University Press, 2016), 55–76.

Switching occurs when selves exchange control over their shared body, thereby changing the way in which it presents and behaves. This can be a cooperative process in which one cedes control to another, a competitive process in which control is seized, or a change that is not consciously instigated by either. There are even cases in which multiple selves are co-conscious, with some merely experiencing what is going on while one of them directs the body's actions. Compartmentalisation occurs when some selves have access to aspects of the mind that others do not, such as memories or even skills. As already noted, it is quite common for different selves to become specialised in handling certain tasks, roles, or narrative threads that recur in their shared life. But there are also cases in which all selves have access to the same shared cognitive resources. Variation occurs when selves differ not in their capacities but in their character, displaying distinctive personality traits, bearing their own names, and even identifying in differing ways. It is not uncommon for a single system to contain selves of varying ages and genders, with divergent and even incompatible goals and aspirations. But there are also cases in which selves have more or less indistinguishable personalities but fragmented memories, each unable to recall what happens when the other is in control.

In conceptualising plurality there are two temptations to be resisted. The first temptation is to treat plurality as nothing more than a dysfunction of personhood proper. This is to say, to treat plural systems not as having more than one self, but as having strictly less than one. This is the extreme version of the sceptical position sketched out above, and although it is to some extent motivated by the genuine psychological distress and practical problems experienced by many patients diagnosed with dissociative identity, it completely ignores the existence of seemingly functional systems of selves living lives no more troubled than the average 'singlet'. Faced with such cases, the only reason to insist they are essentially dysfunctional is if one has a prior conception of the substance of selfhood that precludes plurality in principle. In essence, this is to treat the sincere self-descriptions of systems of persons as always and necessarily false. The second temptation is to treat plurality as a type of personhood analogous to sexuality, gender, and similar coordinates of self-identification. In particular, there is a temptation to treat every sincere self-description as necessarily true, and thereby to deny that there might be any substance to the unity of selves as such.

However, this is to affirm the *general form* of expressions of identification while denying their *specific content*, since plural systems do not claim to be a novel type of singular person, but a collection of people who overlap in body and mind. This approach is popular amongst the partisans of multiplicity mentioned at the beginning, who see it as another manifestation of the absence of unity rather than the presence of multiple unities, thereby collapsing the difference between parades of indistinct personae and the organised systems of distinct selves characteristic of plurality proper.

To take plurality seriously, then, we must agree with some self-described systems that they do in fact contain many selves, without thereby rejecting the idea that there is something in which their plurality consists beyond this self-description. This also means acknowledging the possibility that some (singular) people are wrong about being plural. But this does not mean that we have to settle the matter in every case, only that we need to make sense of what it would mean for such a self-description (or selves-description) to be true. This would immediately seem to suggest that we return to the essence/appearance model and adopt some psychological criterion of personal identity, in which compartmentalisation and variation of the relevant psychological features constitute separate threads of psychological continuity. However, there is another approach we might take here. What psychological and biological takes on personal identity have in common is that they believe they are solving a metaphysical problem (i.e., What makes someone the same person over time?) for which there are downstream normative consequences (e.g., Is an amnesiac murderer culpable for murders 'they' do not remember?).[33] But we can turn this order of explanation on its head, and insist that it is precisely these considerations about the transmission of rights and duties between candidate persons that give us our basic purchase upon 1continuity of personhood, and that the competing metaphysics of self are really variant solutions to an underlying normative problem.[34] This is suggested by the abstract definition of personhood sketched out above, in so far as autonomous agency consists in both a distinctive *authority* over one's theoretical and practical commitments (reflective revision), and a

33. Cf. D. Shoemaker 'Personal Identity and Ethics' (2019), *Stanford Encyclopedia of Philosophy*, <https://plato.stanford.edu/entries/identity-ethics/>.

34. This conceptual inversion is argued for in detail in C. Korsgaard, 'Personal Identity and the Unity of Agency: A Kantian Response to Parfit', *Philosophy & Public Affairs* 18:2 (Spring 1989): 103–31.

unique *responsibility* for the reasons underlying them and the actions resulting from them (justification and culpability).

We can convert this idea into a functional insight if we appeal to the principle of *ought implies can*. If every responsibility implies a corresponding capacity, such that one cannot be held responsible if one is not capable of carrying out the responsibility, then there must be some minimal set of capacities underlying every responsibility, namely, those that enable us to track what we are responsible for, and to fulfil these responsibilities when their occasions arise. Crucially, it does not matter whether or not the mechanisms underpinning these capacities are cognitive subsystems shared by multiple selves within the same mind. It does not even matter whether these cognitive subsystems are properly unconscious, or whether they involve some conscious effort on behalf of the selves in question. All that matters is that they enable the commitments and resulting actions of these selves to be reliably differentiated from one another. Just how reliably is an open question, but it remains plausible that the same causal system might realise multiple overlapping persons, so long as the (overlapping) world-representations driving their behaviour are functionally differentiated.

However, this is only one half of the story, because we must proceed beyond differentiation of responsibility to the constitution of authority. Functional differentiation of the subsystems tracking the theoretical and practical commitments driving behaviour is necessary but not sufficient for a system to sustain multiple selves. For these selves to be truly autonomous they must each be capable of open-ended reflection on their own terms. Without this we cannot maintain that there are genuinely separate loci of choice, only separable strands of the same basic agent. This is not to say that the choices of different selves cannot constrain one another, as it is hard to imagine how sharing a body could work otherwise. Nor is it to say that the choices of different selves must actually conflict, as negotiating these mutual constraints is obviously in their best interests. It is simply to insist that autonomy implies the possibility of such conflict, which necessitates negotiation between separate agents, rather than reconfiguration of components within one overarching person. To borrow a narrativist framing, it is not enough that the system be able to keep its various stories separate, these stories must be able to evolve independently of one another, even if they often interact.[35] Again, just how much independence is required here is an open question. But this suggests a more subtle point, namely, that the functional differentiation of selves qua loci of authority/responsibility need not be an matter of extrinsically distinct representational vehicles (i.e., separate self-models), so much as a matter of intrinsically differentiated representational contents (i.e., alternating self-images).

## 3.2 Forking

Considered as an object of speculation, the possibilities of forking have been explored in more detail by science fiction than by philosophy.[36] It seems plausible that there might be minds with multiple bodies, either as a single centralised mind controlling several remote appendages, or a decentralised mind whose subsystems are spread between networked bodies. However, if we push the idea of a mind constituted by distributed communicating subsystems, we quickly get into situations in which it seems like these subsystems might as well be minds in their own right. For example, say that I get up one morning and realise that I have five different things I need to do today, which cannot be simultaneously achieved by a lone embodied human being. So I do what any reasonable person would do in the circumstances, and fork my consciousness into five qualitatively identical threads running in parallel on five qualitatively indistinguishable bodies, with the intention of merging them together again later. We might wonder what sort of interaction between these forks would be sufficient to sustain joint identity. Must there be some form of realtime communion between brains in order for this to work? (e.g., such that 'I' can simultaneously see out of each set of eyes)? Or is it enough that they have the capacity to talk with one another in the same manner as fully separate persons? (e.g., PW1: 'I'll go read Kant', PW2: 'I'll do the dishes'... PW5: 'That leaves me with the taxes').

One way to think about this is to consider how much information about what we do in any given circumstance is necessary in order to make our actions consistent with what we do elsewhere. We all have memory lapses and similar

35. A loosely narrativist interpretation of plurality along these lines is provided in N. Humphrey and D. Dennett, 'Speaking for Our Selves: An Assessment of Multiple Personality Disorder', *Raritan* 9:1 (1998): 68–98.

36. See for example Richard K. Morgan's *Altered Carbon* series, Ann Leckie's *Ancillary Justice* series, or the science-fiction tabletop roleplaying game *Eclipse Phase*.

moments in which we cannot recall every relevant detail of something we have done. What is actively available in short- and medium-term episodic memory, not to mention which cognitive subsystems dedicated to performing specific tasks are booted up and operating optimally, varies over time. When I am seriously hung over and cannot quite remember the promises I made the night before, the best strategy to ensure that my present actions cohere with my past ones is to ask someone else and otherwise do as little as humanly possible. As we saw in the last section, consistent behaviour over time, at least as far as one's commitments are concerned, is the normative substance from which selfhood is spun. What we are doing here is moving from thinking about how one tracks the transmission of normative statuses between candidate persons that are temporally distant (phases) to thinking about how this works between candidate persons that are spatially distant (forks). The question is thus as follows: How much communication between concurrent forks is needed to sync their models of my personal rights and duties, if my overall behaviour is to remain consistent?

As already suggested, this tracking presupposes other representational capacities, and this means that updating models of normative statuses might require updating the associated representations. Say I am trying to start a small business. If one fork has spent the afternoon opening a bank account and securing a loan, they can communicate the new entitlements this grants to the fork that is out buying supplies and the fork that is visiting potential premises, but they will probably have to include the details of the passwords or other systems of authentication by means of which these permissions can be used (i.e., so that money can be spent). Similarly, each fork has to communicate to all the others the financial commitments they have undertaken, in order to prevent incompatibilities between the choices they have made in their respective situations (i.e., so that they do not spend more money than they can afford), but they will also have to communicate what goods and services have thereby been purchased if they are to ensure they purchase every item they need exactly once (i.e., so they can realise their joint enterprise).

These sorts of **coordination problems** turn up even in much more intimate settings, such as when my five forks sit around a table in a restaurant trying to determine what to order, given certain constraints. I am also the kind of person who would split myself into five forks just to try everything that looks good on a menu. But in this case, there needs to be some procedure for determining both who orders what (e.g, Does each pick one at random and then break ties with Rock Paper Scissors?), and who makes the orders and in what order they do so (e.g., Do we go by some numbering, 1–5, or does 1 order for everyone?), lest their actions conflict and I end up eating nothing. It is possible that each fork could pick the same thing, and then turn to play Rock Paper Scissors with the fork to their left, producing a five-fold symmetry in which it is unclear which game resolves first. If we try to resolve them all at once we can create cycles that will not resolve, such as when three out of five forks are tied on an option and one picks rock, one picks paper, and one picks scissors. Even worse, if the choice between rock, paper, and scissors is pseudo-random, they could all throw the same sign over and over again, even if they changed sign from turn to turn. In short, we have something of a *dining philosopher's problem* on our hands.[37]

So, although some problems are forced by distribution in space, others turn up even when forks are in close proximity. The main difference is how much auxiliary information about each fork's local environment needs to be transmitted to the others in order to make sense of the relevant statuses. Nevertheless, these problems give us some theoretical purchase on the nature of the consistency checks involved in syncing spatially distant forks that share a common self, even if questions about precisely how well these need to work in practice must be bracketed. One strategy for achieving such consistency is to try to maintain something resembling a global state of the system as a whole, by creating a control centre that monitors and modulates the actions of every other element, which might be as simple as naming a primary fork in charge of the rest.

However, the point of **concurrent computation** is to design systems composed from a collection of processes each with their own local state, communicating with one another asynchronously, which are nonetheless guaranteed to behave in certain well defined ways (e.g., avoiding deadlock).[38] One can utilise such message-passing to build **distributed control systems**. This makes

37. The dining philosopher's problem is a famous example created by Edsger Djikstra to introduce the notion of computational concurrency to his students (*EWD-310*, E.W. Dijkstra Archive, Center for American History, University of Texas at Austin).

38. For a brief introduction to the concept of concurrency and its history, see L. Ramport, 'The Computer Science of Concurrency: The Early Years' (2015), <https://lamport.azurewebsites.net/pubs/turing.pdf>.

it conceivable that a decentralised network of concurrent communicating forks could display unitary executive function (i.e., a single will), and even that they could experience some degree of executive dysfunction without thereby ceasing to be a single person. A singular person can easily be in two minds about a given choice, and if those two minds just happen to be in separate bodies it does not necessarily mean that they are now two selves. All that is required is some strategy for resolving such internal conflicts (e.g., voting and tie-breaking), and returning the overall pattern of action to something resembling consistency. Just because one of my forks takes on the role of devil's advocate in relation to the plan of action proposed by another, does not mean that their interaction cannot be guaranteed to resolve in a noncatastrophic manner. Most of the arguments I get into with myself usually do. A singular person can equally struggle with delayed gratification, in which an earlier phase endures something for the sake of a later phase, and there might be analogous problems with deferred gratification between forks. But such intermittent difficulties need not undermine coperson-hood between the latter any more than they preclude continuity of personhood between the former. Our will need not be perfectly reliable in either case.

So, what happens if four out of my five forks are suddenly destroyed? Well, if they are a fully decentralised network, it would seem that any one node should be capable of operating on its own. I would lose whatever memories and information the others had not yet synced, but this does not seem all that different from getting blackout drunk and forgetting what I did last night. I have simply lost some versions of myself running in parallel, rather than in sequence. The capacity of any one fork to survive independently would seem sufficient to justify the claim that we are dealing with multiple minds sharing a single self, rather than a single mind, but it is worth contrasting this case with a different catastrophe: What if a fork gets isolated from the others for an extended period of time? It may believe the other four have been destroyed, and so evolve independently of them. When they finally find one another, perhaps years later, they may be unable or unwilling to reintegrate. One branch or the other might object to the way in which its counterparts have evolved, in such a way that it considers itself a different person not simply in practice, but in principle.

So far, I have argued that there can be multiple minds sharing a single self, yet precisely what makes these minds multiple is their capacity to operate independently of one another. One could object to this position that de facto independence of minds implies de jure independence of selves, and that the forks we have been discussing really are five distinct persons who mistakenly believe they are identical. In this case the wayward fork has simply discovered something that was true all along. Alternatively, one could claim that the only truth of the matter regarding whether the wayward fork really is distinct is what they say about the matter. If they stipulate that they are distinct, then they are, and that is all there is to it. The former approach tries to collapse the difference between self and mind in precisely the same way as those who wish to reduce personal identity to continuity of consciousness, while the latter obviates questions of identity in a similar manner to the partisans of pure multiplicity. I am generally inclined to agree with the latter position in practice, but not in principle, because it makes its case by denying that there is any matter of principle here. This puts us back in the exact same position we were with plurality.

Consider a variation on the last case: What if the wayward fork is more or less nonfunctional? Say it has been badly damaged either by a sudden accident or by some gradual decline while in isolation, in such a way that it simply refuses to believe that its fellows have found it. No matter what they say or do, it is convinced that they are imposters. It has somehow become unable to recognise them for who they are, which is to say, for who it itself is.[39] In this case there might be reason to think that the main branch should be permitted to forcibly resync and/or merge with the fork, especially if this misrecognition is merely a symptom of a wider dysfunction in the capacities that enable a mind to maintain a unitary self. This is a delicate matter, not least because it has direct parallels with the forcible reintegration of personality fragments advocated by some psychologists in treating dissociative identity. Consider another variation: What if there really is an imposter, but it is the wayward fork themselves? What if this fork were kidnapped and altered by a nefarious third party, with the aim of infiltrating my mind(s)? If this trojan fork gets reconnected to the group, then a bad actor will have gained backdoor access to my inner self and be able to influence my thoughts and actions without my knowledge. What these cases

39. This is similar to the Capgras delusion, in which one misrecognises one's close friends and family as imposters. This has in turn been linked to the Cotard delusion mentioned above. See A.W. Young, K.M. Leafhead, and T.K. Szulecka, 'The Capgras and Cotard Delusions', *Psychopathology* 27:3–5 (1994): 226–31.

suggest is that the problem of self-recognition is actually one of **authentication**. It is no longer a matter of passwords providing access external services, but information that grants access to and thereby constitutes the internal network.

So, not just any collection of embodied minds might lay claim to the same self. To be entitled to speak as one, they must at the very least be capable of collectively tracking and reliably acting upon a consistent set of commitments, and this requires some solution to the problems of concurrency and authentication. However, there is one more problem. Consider a final case: What if my five forks travel to five isolated locations and pursue activities that are completely independent of one another, in a manner that ensures they might never possibly conflict? This is a way of guaranteeing that their practical commitments and resulting actions remain consistent with one another, even if their theoretical commitments might drift in incompatible directions, although that is far from certain. But such permanent diffusion would seem to vitiate the notion that they share in a common self. Consistency is thus a necessary but not sufficient condition of such selfhood. What else is required, then? At the very least, something not unlike the small business my five forks are trying to realise—a common goal that places substantive constraints on the consistency of their individual actions. This mirrors the problem of constituting authority discussed at the end of the last section, in so far as this common end, however it is conceived, must evolve in a way that incorporates the different forks, rather than leaving them to evolve in separate directions. To put this all in other terms, their actions must contribute to something more than the sum of their parts, transcending mere consistency in pursuit of genuine **coherence**.[40]

On this basis, we might respond to Metzinger's claim that the self-model represents nothing outside itself by arguing that a collection of forks with distinct minds can have distinct self-models that nevertheless represent the same self, not just because they represent one another as parts of the same distributed system, but because they represent some purposive activity that defines this system as such. This addresses Metzinger's worries about the bankruptcy of the essence/appearance model by combining it with the other two. To see how

40. The precise difference between consistency and coherence is a vexed philosophical topic, which I do not wish to resolve here, though I would point to Whitehead's remarks about it in an epistemological setting as a good place to start (A.N. Whitehead, *Process and Reality* [New York: Free Press, 1978], 5–6).

this works, it is important to understand the difference between a *plan* and a *project*: one is a representation that might be duplicated or divided, like the score held by different members of an orchestra, while the other is an ongoing process composed of agents, means, and the ends they realise, like the musicians, instruments, and the music they produce. My forks might each contain a copy of the plan, perhaps with more detail of their own specific roles, but they are among the parts of the project it describes. Some of these parts might then be more essential than others, which is to say, more ends than means. However, this reopens those questions concerning personal identity that Metzinger's position obviates.

## 3.3 Personae

Considered as an object of philosophical analysis, personae seem far more mundane than the psychological and speculative extremes of plurality and forking. It is relatively common to feel like a different person in different contexts, perhaps slipping into distinctive patterns of behaviour in different social groups, as if wearing a mask suited to one's company. But this need not be restricted to the social parameters of these contexts. For some, who they are at work and who they are at home is different, whether or not the social graphs overlap. The brutal soldier and the loving partner. The shy clerk and the boisterous cook. For others, who they are varies depending not so much upon who they are interacting with, but *how* they are interacting with them. The professional (email). The poet (Twitter). The troll (YouTube). Social media have, if anything, accelerated the proliferation of such digital masks. They even let us switch between masks concurrently, casually flitting back and forth between apps and the persons they make us from one moment to the next. Regardless of the when, where, and why, these behavioural fault lines between contexts might grow into the dissociative disconnects that define plurality, be it through psychological trauma or deliberate cultivation. Yet, just as we can interpret systems of selves as implementing forms of *collective agency* internal to a single mind, we might equally see persons with multiple personae as implementing the same kind of *individual agency* as those that are forked into multiple minds. To put this in other terms, we can see personae as combining the characteristic features of plurality (switching, compartmentalisation, and variation) with those of forking (concurrency, authentication, and coherence).

Beginning with concurrency, our brains contain a lot of cognitive machinery that need not be used at the same time, or for the same purpose. These components can be assembled on the fly into an active configuration capable of performing a task or coping with a context. This underpins the compartmentalisation and variation of full-blown separate selves, but it need not go that far. We might think of a persona as a relatively persistent configuration that sometimes goes dormant only to be reawakened later (e.g., the person I am among friends with whom I rarely meet). Such dormancy is a ubiquitous feature of the human condition. If nothing else, in sleep we are no one, and in dreams we may be people we have never been before, and never will be again. From this perspective, we need not see the self as a kernel of personhood that hides behind our many masks, as it could as easily be composed of a collection of personae that yield control to one another in much the same way that plurals switch, as long as this produces coherent behaviour. In other words, personae perform in sequence what forks manage in parallel.[41]

To frame this in terms of self-recognition: personae allow us to recognise ourselves as agents by making sense of our actions in some region of our world (real and ideal), while selves stitch these personae together into a single framework that covers the world as a whole. Personae are *local*, while selves are *global*. As long as consistency and coherence are maintained between personae across overlapping regions, then a single self will cover the world as a whole.

This is to say that concurrent execution is a natural extension of the notion of dynamic integration discussed above. However, framing it in terms of self-recognition returns us to the subject of authentication.

Authentication is ubiquitous in contemporary life. The **prosthetic personae** we adopt online are all password-protected, and are usually linked together in a complex hierarchy of access: you log in to some apps via Facebook, which itself is linked to your email address, which by now has multi-factor authentication tying it to your phone, which in turn is tied to your physical address, which

41. It is important to emphasise that concurrency is not the same as parallelism. Concurrency is a condition of implementing parallel computations in a distributed system, but not all parallel computations are distributed. Conversely, it is entirely possible for a nondistributed system to implement concurrent interaction sequentially.

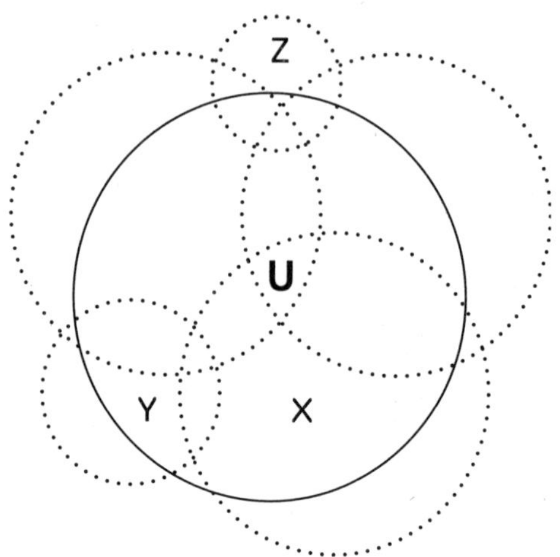


in-the-last-instance is pinned to you qua embodied personage. These systems of authentication are usually seen as tracking something real that underpins them: who you really are, your authentic self. But forking suggests that this relation can be inverted: that the self can be constituted by a system of authentication, rather than merely identified by it. The concurrent communication between forks needed to sustain a coherent pattern of overall behaviour has to be secure. A trojan fork is unnecessary to disrupt my (distributed) self—all you need to do is to spoof my (internal) comms. Yet such spoofing is not necessarily as simple as cracking a password. Although authentication may incorporate tests for unique tokens (e.g., private keys, personal memories, physical bodies), it may equally include checks for behavioural consistency: detecting communications and/or actions that are out of character. These could be static checks determined by some overarching model of my character, but they could equally involve dynamic checks for consistency between forks.

How does this work with personae? Consider alien impulses and intrusive thoughts. Sometimes we act on or express these without thinking, but part of developing a coherent personality with a unitary will is learning how to filter them, to classify them as 'not me' and voluntarily suppress them. Not all such impulses/thoughts are so radically uncharacteristic. Sometimes they are simply inappropriate to the context we are in. We can feel which facet of ourselves has generated them and nudge it back into its proverbial box. This is what it means to cultivate the boundaries between different personae. Not simply learning how to compartmentalise those capacities, tendencies, and reflexes that fit us into one environment, but learning how to switch between them smoothly as those environments overlap, keeping our behaviour consistent along the edges of our patchwork lifeworld. In the end, it does not matter whether we have some centralised, overarching picture of our character as long as each persona has enough of a picture of its own and those proximal to it that they add up to a patchwork personality. The difference is negligible as long as the handoffs are smooth, with local authentication yielding immediate control from context to context, in a way that guarantees global consistency. But consistency is not yet coherence. If we are to understand the remainder, we must further integrate the three models of selfhood suggested earlier.

We must begin with the self considered as an end. This is because the capacity for open-ended reflection constitutive of autonomy is facilitated by the formal unity of purposive activity this end provides. To say that the self is our highest goal is really to treat the activity of being who we are (or becoming who we should be) as encapsulating our other projects and priorities in such a way that any of them can be revised; this does not commit us to **substantive egoism**, given that altruistic or otherwise non-self-directed priorities can become core features of our conception of who we are (or should be).[42] However, this unity may be largely implicit in practice. If the purposes pursued by our personae overlap with one another to some extent, then their tacit cooperation can be interpreted as singular agency so long as it is possible to make their common goals explicit in such a way that the component behaviours can be modulated and modified in accordance with them. The relevant self-conception can be more or less detailed, specifying things we must do or ways we must be, or simply indexing them to our inclinations to act in context. Either way, there must be some representation of the overarching activity of being/becoming oneself that incorporates both its (real) means and (ideal) ends, and these will overlap to the extent that we see the features of the body-mind platform that underpins our agency as essential components of who we are. But this also entails that, as our world-model is progressively refined, we gain the ability to disavow the more detailed aspects of our bodies and minds this reveals (e.g., physical afflictions or

42. See 'Beyond Survival', in this volume.

psychological addictions), treating them as contingent features of our available means of self-realisation.

We can visualise this integrated structure by combining Metzinger's distinction between world and self with the distinction between real and ideal articulated above:

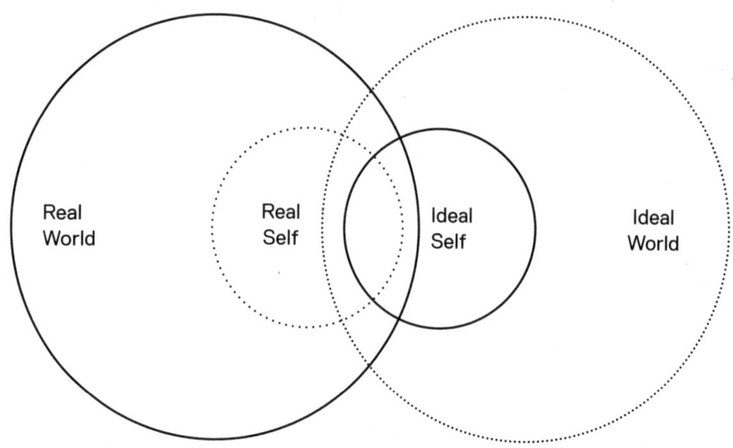


Here it is important to note that, just as the representation of the ideal world is effectively parasitic on that of the real one, so is the representation of the real self more or less parasitic upon the ideal one, because the self is essentially normative. The abstraction inherent in the sorts of low-dimensional representations they begin with is typically seen as instrumental from the perspective of our world-models, but as teleological from the perspective of our self-models. Our picture of the world is implicitly simplified, but our picture of ourselves is implicitly idealised. Be it little more than a model of bodily integrity or a full-blown conception of personal destiny, our self-representation is an **ideal unity**: a plan-in-progress whose inevitable deficiencies and internal inconsistencies must be continuously monitored if it is to adapt itself to external reality. It is this adaptation that sustains our coherence in practice, not just synchronically but diachronically, ensuring that our priorities change in ways that are recognisable as rational responses to our successes and failures, which is to say, as patterns that could be made explicit by the sort of open-ended reflection characteristic of autonomy.[43] Such patterns are implicitly narrative in structure, even when not expressly literary in influence.[44] However, the resulting account of personal essence is unusual in at least two respects.

On the one hand, the world can force us to change our essence in a manner that seems to make us less than the person we once were. Classically, the properties of an object are taken to be either essential or accidental, with no room in between, and this neat division determines precisely how much it can change while remaining what it is. Yet here our self-conception not only enables us to rank our priorities in general, facilitating choice between mutually exclusive options on the basis that one accords more closely with the principles or desires with which we most identify (e.g., political commitments or familial ties), but ultimately gradates identity as such, potentially forcing choices between these core motivations that fundamentally change how we see ourselves going forward (e.g., abandoning anarchism for fatherhood, or vice versa).[45] We let go of things that seemingly define us in order to hold onto others yet more essential.

On the other hand, this pattern of change becomes part of our essence in a manner that seems to make us strictly more than the person we once were. The component features of our ideal self are not always ranked in advance, and so their relative importance is fleshed out by the choices we make. There is often more than one rational response to any given situation, and the paths we choose further determine who we are. Rational evolution is to some extent nondeterministic and thereby essentially cumulative. But this implies that there might be several possible versions of ourselves that are diachronically coherent but mutually incompatible, future variants whose burgeoning selves make them nonidentical with one another even as they remain identical with their actual ancestor. This problem is further sharpened by the fact that personal growth

43. Cf. C. Korsgaard, *Self-Constitution* (Oxford: Oxford University Press, 2009); M. Schectman, *The Constitution of Selves* (Ithaca, NY: Cornell University Press, 2007).

44. To restate this point in more precise terms: it is not that we have selves because we tell stories, but rather that we tell stories because we have selves. The *particular* practices of narrativisation unique to our cultures and the *specific* narratives they have produced certainly have a profound influence upon the sorts of selves we end up shaping, but they exist because they reflect *universal* constraints underpinning autonomous agency and the *general* forms of life that satisfy them, not the other way around.

45. See R. Chang, 'Hard Choices', *Journal of the American Philosophical Association* 3:1 (2017): 1–21.

extends beyond the rational refinement of existing priorities, as we are obviously capable of acquiring new ones, strongly identifying with personal projects or aspects of our body-mind that were previously inexistent or inessential, and perhaps even birthing whole new personae, all in a manner that leaves no less to serendipity. None of us are born with a developed sense of who we are, and so our essence must form gradually, in a process with no guaranteed end except death itself.

The real problem with the notion of personal essence is that it is supposed to be what persists through change, and so itself be changeless, but people change in ways that prospectively seem unlikely or impossible and yet in retrospect seem plausible or inevitable, their essence changing while they remain the same, as if becoming more themselves.[46] The reason behind this paradoxical persistence is that persons are in some sense more like actions than they are like objects. This is most obvious when we compare the process of being/becoming oneself with complex extended actions such as the building of cities or the fighting of wars. These are clearly intentional, but the intentions that drive them are underdetermined, requiring supplementation and revision as the technical challenges posed by realising the initial vision become apparent, necessitating sacrifices or even offering unexpected opportunities. And yet, even though the plan has changed in the process of enacting it, we do not thereby deny that it achieved what it was meant to achieve. Instead, we read the result back into the intention, as if this is what was truly intended all along.[47] Of course, we cannot simply redefine any result as a success. If we could, then failure would be impossible, and so would success proper. Rather, the claim is something like: had we known then what we have learned in the attempt, this is what we would have intended; so the intention has resolved into what it always should have been.

What this means is that the connection that underpins the identity between two temporally disparate phases of the same person is essentially of the same kind as the connection between the initial intention driving an action and its

---

46. Another way to conceptualise this would be to deploy Hegel's account of essence in the *Science of Logic* (book 2). From this perspective, essence is not something fixed which lies behind appearance, but the very process through which determinations are revealed as mere appearances. See also S. Houlgate, 'Essence, Reflexion, and Immediacy in Hegel's *Science of Logic*', in S. Houlgate and M. Baur (eds.), *A Companion to Hegel* (Oxford: Wiley-Blackwell, 2011), 139–58.

47. See the Hegelian account of action developed in R. Brandom, *A Spirit of Trust: A Reading of Hegel's Phenomenology* (Cambridge, MA: Harvard University Press, 2019), chapter 11.

eventual (or ongoing) realisation which underpins success. This makes personal identity messy in much the same way that success is messy. It is often partial in ways that must be judged good enough under the circumstances, in so far as those elements of the initial intention that were achieved are, at least in retrospect, more important or essential than those which were not. What distinguishes personhood from most other activities is not only that it is potentially open-ended but that, qua intention, its essence necessarily incorporates the agency that realises it. This is to say that the intention/essence must always include those capacities to track and act upon commitments characteristic of generally intelligent autonomous agents, and thereby to sustain the intention itself. Even when we identify with ends that preclude our survival (e.g., throwing ourselves in front of a bullet to save a loved one), we do not thereby dissolve ourselves into them. We are present in the act of forfeiting our agency to achieve them, but we do not literally survive as that which we sacrificed for (e.g., the person whose life we saved). This presents at least one hard constraint upon our ability to define who we are since, even if there are many questions about whether it is coherent to count any given future system capable of personhood as in fact the same person we are, it is unquestionably incoherent to so count a system entirely incapable of personhood.[48] The tree that will grow upon my grave could never be me, no matter how my body nourishes it, nor how important this nourishment may be to me.

As such, there is nothing in principle that precludes a system of concurrently communicating personae that share overlapping access to the same underlying cognitive machinery from composing a singular self so conceived: an intention-in-action or plan-in-progress, an end that necessarily incorporates its own agential (and thereby representational) means, and organises their relative importance in a way that amounts to an incomplete but ever-evolving essence. All that is required is that it be capable of modifying itself in the right way, which is to say, being who it is by coming into its own.

48. This raises questions about cases such as persistent vegetative states, but I will defer dealing with them for now.

## 4. CONCLUSION: FUTURE SELVES

Over the course of its history, humanity has explored a vast region of the space of possible persons, inventing disparate genres of self-relation, experimenting with modes of embodiment and narrativisation, exploring the range of identities its common form of life might handle. But this is still only a tiny fraction of the space as a whole. We can all too easily conceive of cybernetic systems whose composition is radically different from our own that would nonetheless count as persons, even if the ideals, desires, and stories that tie their body-mind complexes together are uncomfortably alien.[49] Yet the need for something which unifies them, at whatever scale or pace they exist, something that permits us to ask why they behave as they do, even and especially when the answer evolves over time, is invariant. There have always been those who maintain that this unity must be given in advance, whether as an immaterial substance or as an immanent nature, just as there are those who treat any and even every such unity as an illusion, although they more often reject one in the name of the other. In both cases, we are told that we do not know what we really are: either shackled to a destiny not of our own making, be it the judgement of eternity or karmic rebirth, or denied any destiny beyond modulating the impulses driving animal homeostasis, be the aim Epicurean contentment or Buddhist inner peace, Nietzschean health or Freudian everyday unhappiness. But as much as it pays not to underestimate our ignorance, of ourselves as much as anything else, these approaches ignore the extent to which our unity is not *given* but *made*, subject not only to imperfect knowledge, but imperfect *control*. We traverse the space of possible persons not simply as an evolving species, but as individuals trying to make something of themselves.

On this basis we can agree with Metzinger that there are no natural criteria of personal identity, not because the only criteria are purely conventional, but because selves are already artificial: autonomous agents get to define their own

49. David Roden's speculative posthumanism is an attempt to take seriously the full extent of this conceivable difference (D. Roden, *Posthuman Life: Philosophy at the Edge of the Human* [London: Routledge, 2015]). However, he pushes it to the point at which there can be no substantive conditions constitutive of intelligence or agency as such, in so far as every purported condition is a limitation that might conceivably be transgressed. Of course, there might be extremely complex forms of posthuman *life* that violate the conditions I am suggesting here, but they would not thereby be *persons*. Roden's response is likely that 'so much the better for them', while mine is, unsurprisingly, 'so much the worse'.

identity conditions as part and parcel of the process of **self-construction**.[50] Speculative possibilities such as teleportation, mind uploading, and forking are feasible not because these radical operations would preserve the identity of anyone that was subjected to them, as there are plenty who refuse to allow that a hypothetical clone, copy, or fork could ever be them, but rather because some of us are willing to define ourselves in a way that would survive and thrive in these scenarios. Still, such willingness is not enough on its own. As we saw in the case of forking, in order to exercise the authority involved in speaking or acting as one, the collective must fulfil the requisite responsibilities, which in turn demand corresponding capacities. To be discontinuously or multiply incarnated, one must be able to act the part. We should not treat someone who shows no prudential concern for their clones, copies, or forks in comparison to their original organism as genuinely identifying with them, no matter how hard they protest. New types of selfhood demand new types of **self-discipline**.[51]

If we see selfhood as a product of artifice, then we may wish to ask what technologies such artifice deploys. As Foucault has shown, there is a long and rich history of practices and techniques deployed by those intent on cultivating their selves, from the Stoic use of journals to catalogue and correct their behaviour to the ascetic use of confession and self-abasement to renounce and reforge their inclinations.[52] The age of personal computing has seen a rapid proliferation and mutation of such practices as they are encoded in applications running on laptops, mobiles, and distributed networks, enhancing their functionality and integrating them in new ways. Everything from diaries and calendars to sleep trackers and meditation suites have been automated and incorporated into our everyday routines, outsourcing memory and other basic mental functions while allowing us to represent and adjust aspects of our minds, bodies, and behaviours more easily than ever before.

---

50. See 'Beyond Survival', in this volume.

51. This is not the only constraint on the authority of autonomous agents to define their identity conditions. Even if we admit that someone can 'become a new person' by undergoing a sufficiently radical change, this does not mean someone can simply stipulate that they are no longer responsible for their prior actions. Much as having authority to specify one's own intentions does not allow one to retroactively stipulate the success of ones actions, so having the authority to specify one's identity conditions does not allow one to be whatever one wishes.

52. M. Foucault, 'Technologies of the Self', in *Technologies of the Self: A Seminar with Michel Foucault* (Amherst, MA: University of Massachusetts Press, 1988).

But perhaps most interesting are the prosthetic personae mentioned earlier: social media and similar platforms that not only structure the way we interact with others but also shape the way we see ourselves, tracking our likes and dislikes, friendships and associations, and even the events composing our personal narratives. Although there are already those who explicitly identify more closely with their computational tools than many features of their bodies, treating limbs as mere contingent means to the essential ends of their extended minds,[53] prosthetic personae operate implicitly, tapping into and merging with the representational mechanisms underlying identification, executive function, and the constitution of selfhood as such. These fragmented **exo-selves** threaten to vitiate our autonomy by positioning the unifying machinery upon which it is predicated beyond our (which is to say its own) control.

If new types of selfhood demand new capacities, then we may wonder whether new technologies might provide them. We can imagine futures in which we do not simply retain control of the cognitive prosthetics we are integrating into our self-models, but properly internalise it by incorporating them into our conception of who we are, augmenting our abilities to manage our commitments and reflect on our motivations in ways that enable us to cohere even as our agency expands beyond the human norm: evolutionary algorithms trained on our behaviour that track our preferences and suggest new options for enjoyment or paths of personal development, framing possible choices in ways that we can modulate; systems of authentication that identify and filter impulses which contravene avowed intent, sustaining the will to follow through on our decisions, even across disparate incarnations. Rather than prosthetic personae and exo-selves, we might here speak of **meta-selves**: tools that enable us to come into our own by becoming part of us in the process, subsystems that encode and refine our very essence.[54]

These speculative remarks on the future of selfhood should not conceal the extent to which selves are already computational. This much was suggested

---

53. See A. Clark, *Natural Born Cyborgs* (Oxford: Oxford University Press, 2004).

54. I take both the idea and the term 'metaself' from Hannu Rajaniemi's Jean le Flambeur series: *The Quantum Thief* (London: Gollancz, 2011), *The Fractal Prince* (London: Gollancz, 2013), and *The Causal Angel* (London: Gollancz, 2015). Perhaps more than any other work of science fiction I have read, this series explores deep questions about the nature of self by considering competing models of posthuman selfhood with different philosophical motivations and technical foundations.

by my appeal to the notion of concurrency, but it is worth unpacking further. The claim that the mind is a computational process is by now common enough, if not entirely uncontroversial in philosophical circles. However, the idea that the relationship between *mind* and *brain* can be understood by analogy to that between *software* and *hardware* in the stored-program computers we are familiar with in our everyday lives has caused many to misunderstand computationalism, and others to reject it entirely.[55] To be clear, although the brain is a computational system which stores and processes information, it is not a general-purpose computer capable of running many different minds. The mind is encoded in its specific neurocomputational structure, and to 'upload' it would mean simulating this structure with sufficient fidelity to capture its computational features. Moreover, as I have taken pains to insist, minds and selves are not exactly the same thing. Although the self necessarily includes some aspects of the mind, it may also incorporate features of the body that we take to be essential to who we are. There are some for whom their existing brains are an intrinsic component of their selves, and others for whom their neurocomputational structure may be abstracted from its current material substrate. Once more, the self qua plan-in-progress incorporates not just the representation of an ongoing pattern of action but also the essential means of action thereby represented.

Yet the possibility of coherently transitioning from one position to the other, stripping back self-imposed constraints on permissible embodiment so that we might flit between substrates, does suggest another way of conceiving this intentional structure: not just as a plan-in-progress but as a *program-in-execution*; a program which not only specifies permissible computational substrates, but which modifies itself as it runs.[56] Herein lies the essence not of any given person qua who they are, but of every possible person qua what they are—that which cannot be stripped away by any personal transformation. Of course, we must be extremely careful not to illegitimately reimpose features of the stored-program paradigm here, as if our selves were written in a fixed language interpreted by a

55. See R. Epstein, 'The Empty Brain' *Aeon*, 18 May 2016, <https://aeon.co/essays/your-brain-does-not-process-information-and-it-is-not-a-computer>, and K. Lande, 'Do You Compute?', *Aeon*, 11 April 2019, <https://aeon.co/essays/your-brain-probably-is-a-computer-whatever-that-means>.
56. This constitutes what Richard Hofstadter calls a 'strange loop' (R. Hofstadter, *I Am a Strange Loop* [New York: Basic Books, 2007]).

standardised platform.[57] But it nevertheless suggests new ways of framing old questions. Although such programs are essentially interactive,[58] perhaps subject to an ineliminable **hysteresis**, it still makes sense to ask about the shape of their ideal trajectory and the extent to which they can be predicted. Absent outside intervention, computations naturally either terminate of their own accord, get caught in repeating loops, diverge by expanding explosively but predictably, or remain forever amorphous, refusing to settle into a predictable pattern.[59]

The question of whether and to what extent it is possible to predict the shape of our personal trajectory is central to the problem of autonomy, in so far as there remains an essentially negative dimension of personal freedom. The deepest insight of computing theory is the revelation of **deterministic unpredictability**: that the overall behaviour of many programs cannot be predicted any more efficiently than by running them and seeing what happens.[60] This is not to say that the behaviour of persons is perfectly unpredictable in the same way, not least because it must be predictable enough to be recognisably rational, but there is some sense in which the ideal of autonomy entails a certain incompressibility, or irreducibility to a single motive principle prescribed in advance. This is achieved in part by path dependence, or the vicissitudes of our external circumstances, but the promise of autonomy is that it involves something more:

57. We would do better to compare it to a program capable of rewriting not only its own code, but also the interpreter that executes it, iteratively bootstrapping itself into new domains of computational possibility. This is the sort of self-referential structure characteristic of the strange loops Hofstadter is interested in.

58. There is much controversy in computer science over whether interactive computation should be understood as its own species requiring further formal description, or whether it is nothing more than a matter of describing the implementation of classical computation. This is also inevitably bound up with the philosophical interpretation of concurrent computation. See P. Wegner and D. Goldin (eds.), *Interactive Computation: The New Paradigm* (Berlin: Springer, 2006); S. Aaronson, 'The Toaster-Enhanced Turing Machine', *Shtetl Optimised*, 30 August 2012, <https://scottaaronson.blog/?p=1121>; and S. Abramsky, 'Information, Processes, and Games' in *Philosophy of Information* (*Handbook of the Philosophy of Science* vol. 8) (Amsterdam: North Holland, 2008), 483–549.

59. Different philosophical approaches to self-cultivation throughout history privilege certain shapes over the others, either requiring the anticipation of termination (e.g., Heidegger), explicitly aiming for some looping homeostatic perfection (e.g., Aristotle or Epicurus), implicitly demanding the consumption of all available resources in an divergent explosion of geometric growth (e.g., contemporary utilitarian transhumanism), or recommending the indefinite pursuit of novelty for its own sake (e.g., Foucault, Deleuze, and Badiou). Crucially, I do not mean to privilege any of these shapes, but to make sense of the diversity of these approaches.

60. The key formal results here are Turing's solution to the halting problem and Rice's theorem.

a combination of internal factors whose complex interactions cannot easily be modelled, even as they rationally cohere. This delicate balance between rational necessity and motivational complexity is the essence of freedom as such. It is the source of that *contingency* which we make for ourselves out of ourselves, the element of truths which are no less discoverable for not being empirical, and no less important for not being deducible. This more than anything is what vindicates our inner multitude: in evading easy simplicity, it makes possible a more challenging unity-in-multiplicity[61]—a **computational soul** that is free in its beauty and beautiful in its freedom.[62]

61. The idea that beauty is essentially unity-in-multiplicity or *harmony* can be traced back at least as far as Plotinus (*Enneads* §1.6 and §5.8.1–2), but it was developed in most detail by the early modern rationalist aestheticians (see F. Beiser, *Diotima's Children: German Aesthetic Rationalism from Leibniz to Lessing* [Oxford: Oxford University Press, 2011]). My own view is that unity-in-multiplicity is not the basis of beauty, but that it is beautiful as a consequence of practical contingency, which is the proper basis. See 'Why Does Anything Matter?' and 'Art and Value', in this volume.

62. This view of the self's inherent multiplicity is evident in Hegel, albeit in less computational terms.

# Why Does Anything Matter?

*Nothing matters, but it's perhaps more comfortable to keep calm and not interfere with other people.*

H.P. Lovecraft[1]

*The soul, which is created quick to love, responds to everything that pleases, just as soon as beauty wakens it to act.*

Dante Alighieri[2]

## 0. INTRODUCTION

It's an indisputable fact that many things do in fact matter to us—what we have for breakfast, the well-being of our loved ones, the twists and turns of geopolitics—but we aren't here concerned with whether we care about these things, but why, which means on the one hand explaining such care, and on the other seeing if it can be justified. Ultimately, we want to know if there is good reason to care about anything at all. But there are two ways of parsing this question:

**Impersonal Formulation**: Why do things have value?

**Personal Formulation**: Why does life have meaning?

When we ask why 'things' have value, there are different sorts of things we could have in mind. For instance, we might be talking about *objects* (e.g., 'This tool is *useful*'), *events* (e.g., 'That performance was *beautiful*'), or *states* (e.g., 'It is *good* that you're reading this essay'). I'll group these together under the heading of 'objects', in so far as they are opposed to *actions* (e.g., 'You did the *right* thing'). This opposition underpins the distinction between *aesthetics* and

1. Letter to Frank Belknap Long, 7 October 1923.
2. *The Divine Comedy*, Purgatorio 18, 19–21.

*ethics*, in so far as the former focuses principally upon the contents of the world, while the latter focuses more upon what we do with them and one another. One of the goals of this essay is to try and clarify the relationship between these two sides of the discourse of value.

When it comes to the question of life's meaning, we should see that 'life' does not strictly mean *biological life*, but the sort of *personal life* characterised not simply by mere behaviour but by free choice over which actions we perform. Action thus forms an initial thread connecting the two formulations of the question. Even so, they are far from equivalent. Consider the following questions.

**Could things have value and yet life have no meaning?** On the one hand, Moore's famous method of isolation suggests that this is intelligible. This is a test for *intrinsic value* that asks us to imagine a world that contains nothing but the thing with which we are concerned (e.g., the Mona Lisa), and ask ourselves whether this world is better than one containing nothing at all.[3] To answer in the affirmative is to assign this thing intrinsic value, which it would bear even if there were no life in the universe, let alone whether or not such life were held to have meaning. On the other hand, Benatar's anti-natalism maintains not simply that there could be value without life, but that the possibility of suffering entails that life itself has *negative value*.[4] The elimination of life thus takes on an importance directly at odds with any and every meaning we might ascribe to it.

**Could things have no value and yet life still have meaning?** On the one hand, Nietzsche's *active* appropriation of the *passive nihilism* he diagnosed at the heart of European culture is an attempt to transform the absence of intrinsic value into source of personal meaning.[5] Only those who love their fate can pass the test of Eternal Return, affirming everything that was or will be in the name of creating their own personal destiny. On the other hand, Sartre's *existentialism* and Camus's *absurdism* locate the source of personal meaning in the radical freedom with which the absence of value confronts us.[6] Only those

---

3. G.E. Moore, *Principia Ethica* [1903], 236–7 [§112–§113] (Cambridge: Cambridge University Press, 1993).

4. D. Benatar, *Better Never to Have Been: The Harm of Coming into Existence* (Oxford: Oxford University Press, 2008), chapter 2.

5. F. Nietzsche, *The Will to Power*, tr. W. Kauffman (New York: Random House, 1967), Book 1.

6. J.-P. Sartre, *Existentialism is a Humanism*, tr. C. Macomber (New Haven, CT: Yale University Press, 2007); A. Camus, *The Myth of Sisyphus*, tr. J. O'Brien (London: Penguin Modern Classics, 2020).

who pass through the fundamental anxiety of choosing between possible lives, confronting the essential absurdity of the struggle to find meaning in a valueless world, can find temporary respite in authenticity.

We will further explore the differences between these formulations of our question later on, breaking down their terms more precisely and considering potential explanatory approaches, but we must first provide some historical context, in order to explain why and how they pulled apart, and the consequences of that separation.

## 1. DISENCHANTMENT AND EXTINCTION

Before humans began to ask questions about what matters and why, it simply seemed that value infused the world. What could be more obvious than that a sunset is worth watching and remembering, or that a baby is worth nurturing and protecting? The worth of some things was immediately revealed to us by an intensity of feeling that was as often shared with others as unique to our own experience. Of course, we still have experiences like this, many even more intense than were available to our ancestors, from the delights of opera to the shock of seeing Earth from space, but we are now more sensitive to the ways in which the attendant feelings may enter into conflict, both within ourselves and between ourselves and others.

At least in the West, it has traditionally been the function of religion to organise our understanding of value in such a way that these conflicts might be resolved, not so much by giving an explicit account of its nature, but by delineating a highest value—*the sacred*. The task of systematising the understanding of value implicit in religion has then fallen to philosophy and theology. In particular, Plato and Aristotle's attempts to theorise the Good form the basis for the systematic theology of the Abrahamic tradition, most notably Christianity, transforming the *highest* value into the *foundation* of value as such, providing an ultimate justification for caring about things, even if what it means for them to matter has still not been fully explained. In every case, this foundation is located either outside the world, paradigmatically as *divine law* given by command, or within the world as the *order of nature* itself, conceived either as a *grand machine* that sustains itself as it is (as in Aristotle) or as a *grand narrative* that evolves over time (as in Hegel).

With the coming of the Enlightenment, the societal significance of religion began to wane, just as the importance of empirical science began to wax, offering proven methods for producing knowledge from experience that could nevertheless make nothing from the experience of value. This resulted in a series of changes in our attitudes toward value. Weber termed this process *disenchantment*, and distinguished its three principal features:[7]

**The Rise of Instrumental Reason**: the dissociation of our understanding of what we *can* do from what we *should* do.

**The Desacralisation of Social Life**: the abandonment of the sacred as an organising principle of public life in favour of social conventions and rationalised institutions.

**The Desacralisation of Death**: the purging of death of any special significance beyond its being an impediment to our plans.

There are several philosophical tendencies bound up in this shift, but the two most important are:

**The Naturalist Tendency** exemplified by Hobbes and Hume, which rejects the idea that the value we ascribe to objects is inherent to them, instead holding it to be an expression of our feelings and inclinations ('reason is the slave of the passions'). This tendency fed into the development of empirical psychology and microeconomics.

**The Autonomist Tendency** exemplified by Rousseau and Kant, which rejects the idea that our actions can be bound by principles or laws to which, in some sense, we have not voluntarily assented ('reason gives the law unto itself'). This tendency fed into the development of political liberalism.

7. M. Weber, 'Science as Vocation', in *Max Weber: Essays in Sociology*, tr. ed. H.H. Gerth and C.W. Mills (New York: Oxford University Press, 1946), 137–56.

There are two consequences of disenchantment that I wish to discuss: the **encroachment of nihilism** and the **discovery of extinction**.

As already mentioned, the encroachment of nihilism is famously diagnosed by Nietzsche, who holds that the collapse of the sacred as the foundation of the European system of value (i.e., the death of God) leads to a hollowing out of life, where the extant social conventions remain, but the meaning that drives our personal lives is lost.[8] This marks the point at which the two formulations of our question begin to part ways. Nietzsche's proposed solution to the problem of meaning is the Eternal Return, a test on action not unlike Kant's categorical imperative, but which selects for new, more noble values: we must live as if the world repeats in an endless cycle, willing only that which we would have recur again and again, forever. The result is an attitude of pure affirmation. In his wake, the existentialists approach the same problem in different way, attempting to find meaning in autonomy itself, conceived as the opportunity for self-authorship. The result is an attitude of resolute commitment.

The discovery of extinction has more recently been analysed by Thomas Moynihan, who argues that prior to the advent of disenchantment Western thought had been governed by what he calls the *principle of plenitude*, or the idea that all legitimate possibilities must eventually be realised.[9] According to this perspective, even if a species could go extinct, it would necessarily reemerge at some point in the future. However, this principle itself depends upon viewing the world as inherently structured by value, in so far as the *legitimate* possibilities are precisely those that *should* exist in some sense. Disenchantment opened us up to the possibility that a species might go extinct, and thus that humanity, or even thinking beings as such, might vanish from the cosmos, never to return.

Moynihan argues further that the discovery of the possibility of extinction allows us to take it as an object of practical action, namely, something to be avoided at all costs.[10] Crucially, if disenchantment entails that there is no value in the world independent of us, then our extinction would constitute the annihilation of value itself. We might call this intuition the *fragility of value*. This idea becomes the basis of contemporary philosophical interest in existential risk, exemplified by

8. Nietzsche, *The Gay Science*, §108, §124, §125, §343.

9. T. Moynihan, *X-Risk: How Humanity Discovered its Own Extinction* (Falmouth: Urbanomic, 2020), 36–42.

10. Ibid., chapter 6.

the contemporary longtermist movement spearheaded by Will MacAskill, Toby Ord, and Nick Bostrom, which treats mitigating the risk of *species* extinction as the ultimate practical priority.[11] This transforms survival into something like a secular substitute for the sacred.

These two themes—nihilism and extinction—collide in the work of Ray Brassier, specifically in his book *Nihil Unbound*, where he embraces nihilism as a 'speculative opportunity' and turns the thought of extinction against Nietzsche's own proposed solution to the collapse of meaning.[12] To understand this properly involves digging a little deeper into Nietzsche's own ideas. One of the key features of Nietzsche's account of the trajectory of disenchantment is that not only is it motivated by the *will to truth* (the drive underlying the rise of empirical science), but because truth is itself a value, the will to truth must turn upon itself. This is the *epistemic* dimension of nihilism: the collapse of the distinction between *appearance* and *reality*. More than anything, Brassier wishes to defend the will to truth against this charge of autocannibalism.

According to Brassier, the Eternal Return can be read in two ways:

**Psychological Reading**: it selects for only those who can affirm all suffering as a means to the end of joy. Brassier accuses this both of being arbitrary (as essentially inviting calculation, rather than unconditional affirmation), and of imbuing suffering with meaning in a manner similar to Christianity.

**Ontological Reading**: it undermines the very edifice of means and end by collapsing the distinction between being and becoming, removing any fixed point that could be used to get purchase upon an end outside of the will itself. It thus selects for nothing but the will to will, or the pure aimless striving that Nietzsche calls the will to power. All that can be affirmed is the underlying drive of life to survive and thrive, and even the will to truth is subordinated to this.

---

11. See W. MacAskill, *What We Owe the Future* (London: Oneworld Publications, 2023); T. Ord, *The Precipice: Existential Risk and the Future of Humanity* (London: Hachette Books, 2020); N. Bostrom, 'Existential Risk Prevention as Global Priority', *Global Policy*, 27 March 2013. Also see my review of MacAskill's book, 'The Weight of Forever', *The Philosopher*, special issue 'The New Basics', 2022.

12. R. Brassier, *Nihil Unbound: Enlightenment and Extinction* (Basingstoke: Palgrave Macmillan, 2007), chapter 7.

Brassier defends the will to truth against Nietzsche by invoking inevitable cosmological annihilation: that point in the deep future at which the expansion of space tears apart matter itself. This is not extinction as a possible object of practical action, but as a *limit* imposed upon it. This cosmic extinction functions as the index of that which may be *thought* but not *lived*, driving a wedge between the interests of thinking and living. For all its pretensions to pure becoming, the eternal return still borrows the aspect of eternity in order to enshrine a value for all times. The prospect of true cosmic annihilation—an end to the universe that is not an *apocalypse*—having no meaning or purpose, unravels every chain of purposes from apotheosis backwards, undermining not only every grand machine or narrative, but even the needless striving of the will to survive.

So, not only does cosmic extinction encapsulate the *nihilistic impetus* of disenchantment, it also poses a challenge to those conceptions of value built upon its fragility. If extinction ultimately cannot be fought off, does that not render value defunct in advance, and our attempts to preserve it meaningless? Unlike Brassier, I don't wish to assert cosmic annihilation as a fact, as there is no scientific consensus on the ultimate fate of the universe, but rather to use it as a test, much like the eternal return itself. Any adequate account of the nature of value and meaning must be able to confront the possibility that everything will cease to be for no good reason. On this basis, I think we can articulate a few provisional criteria for the theory that we are looking for.

Firstly, we need a conception of value that is *intrinsic* without being *inherent*. The conception of 'intrinsic' value popularised by Moore[13] conflates three distinct features: *finality*, *non-relationality*, and *inherence*; this is to say that it is non-instrumental (e.g., the Mona Lisa's value does not consist in any purpose it is suppose to serve), that it derives from the properties of the thing rather than its relations to other things (e.g., the Mona Lisa's value consists in the arrangement of pigment rather than in who painted it), and that it is present in the thing itself rather than projected onto it by our attitudes (e.g., the Mona Lisa cannot be separated from its value anymore than it can from its size, shape, or composition). *Pace* Moore, we want to show that finality can be nonrelational without being inherent.

13. G.E. Moore, 'The Conception of Intrinsic Value' [1922], in *Philosophical Studies* (New York: Caven Press, 2007).

Secondly, we need a conception of meaning that respects *autonomy* without collapsing into *arbitrariness*. The conception of 'authenticity' popularised by the existentialists involves choosing between a range of possible commitments whose meaningfulness consists only in the fact that they are chosen, rendering them equally significant. From this perspective it makes as much sense to commit oneself to flipping the same coin over and over for eternity as it does to commit oneself to revolutionary politics, visionary art, or romantic love, as the value that inspires these activities cannot be prior to the choice between them. By contrast, we want a picture of free self-authorship that is compatible with there being *reasons* to choose one way rather than another.

Finally, neither value nor meaning must depend upon the indefinite perpetuation of any aspect of ourselves: any form of personal, biological, or cultural *posterity*, or even simply the persistence of rational beings in the cosmos. The question this poses is whether such a theory can do justice to the fragility of value, and whether, on that basis, it will validate mitigating species extinction as anything resembling an ultimate priority. To pursue these issues further, we must return to the formulations with which we began, and clarify the terms in which they posed.

## 2. THE LANGUAGE OF NORMATIVITY

As we noted at the beginning, we say that many different types of things matter, in a variety of different ways. On the one hand, we talk about how **actions** matter, by using the language of **directives**: saying that we should, ought, may, or may not perform them (e.g., one ought not to steal). On the other, we talk about how **objects** matter using the language of **evaluatives**: saying that they are good, bad, better, or worse than one another (e.g., renewable energy is better than fossil fuels). To put this in different terms, we can distinguish between **norms** governing action and **value** ascribed to the things we act upon. Crucially, there are different types of norm (e.g., ethical, legal, conventional, rational) that draw their force from different sources, as well as abstract types of value (e.g., truth, right, and beauty) and so called 'thick' value concepts (e.g., wisdom, courage, grace) that apply to specific types of things.[14]

14. Curiously, the language of 'values' in the sense of 'our cultural values' or 'my personal values' seems to be somewhat neutral between these, assimilating values in the sense of valuations and norms, in so far as they both belong to us, rather than inhere in things.

Moreover, these two perspectives are to some extent interchangeable: to say that one painting is *better* than another appears to imply that, all else being equal, if you can only save one from the flames, you *ought* to choose the former; and it seems natural to say that when you're *obliged* to sacrifice one life for the sake of ten, this implies that that outcome is *more important* than the alternative. More generally, it seems that to say that one *should* act in a certain way implies not only that the action itself is *good*, but that its outcome is. This opens up various strategies for explaining the meaning of one way of talking in terms of the other, as a first step towards justifying claims about what matters, although these strategies aren't always comprehensive, not covering every type of norm and value concept.[15] The most common traditional approaches along these lines are ethical theories that explain how we should act in terms of what is good, in some sense:

> **Consequentialism**, as exemplified by Sidgwick and Moore, which holds that what we should do is simply to maximise the amount of good (simpliciter) in the world. The problem for this position is identifying precisely what goodness consists in.

> **Teleology**, as exemplified by Aristotle and Spinoza, which holds that what we should do is determined by purposes inherent in nature itself, either what makes us a good instance (attributive) of the type of creature we are (for Aristotle, flourishing), or what is good-for (relational) any creature whatsoever (for Spinoza, maximising power). The problem for this position is articulating the purposes inherent in nature.

Of the two disenchanting tendencies discussed earlier, the naturalist tendency generally prioritises evaluatives while the autonomist tendency prioritises directives. The most popular naturalist approach to consequentialism is to identify goodness with an independently measurable quantity, such as pleasure. I'll explore the problems with such utilitarian positions shortly. The most popular naturalist approaches to teleology appeal to **evolution**, either justifying the evolutionary fitness of specific human behaviours (e.g., the norm of protecting

15. See 'Philosophy and Normativity', in this volume, for a more in-depth discussion of normativity.

children), or elevating evolutionary fitness to a general criterion of worth (e.g., might makes right). Both fail the test of extinction, in so far as they are premised upon the value of survival.

I'm going to suggest following the autonomist tendency in giving explanatory priority to directives, because this enables us to make explicit the connection between value and action in a more systematic fashion. From this perspective, amounts of value don't simply express intensities of feeling, but degrees of motivation for performing certain actions. In essence, the purpose of both ways of talking is to organise our reasons for action, so that we can work through conflicts between these reasons. In other words, they encode *patterns* of practical reasoning. However, while directives can *articulate and express* the patterns of reasoning encoded by value concepts, evaluatives can only *reduce and replace* the patterns of reasoning encoded by norms. To explain this properly we must introduce two further distinctions that reveal how this encoding works in practice.

Firstly, we might distinguish between *positive* and *negative* reasons. From the perspective of norms these appear asymmetrical: we can distinguish between the *goals* motivating particular actions and the *constraints* that limit permissible actions (e.g., providing for everyone in society *without* violating property rights). From the perspective of value, these end up being somewhat symmetrical: reasons to seek or avoid certain outcomes that can cancel one another out like *quantities* (e.g., pleasure and pain). Conflicts between goals and constraints can be messy, and their resolution may involve recontextualising or revising the relevant norms (e.g., our conception of property rights), while conflicts between positive and negative values can seemingly be resolved by simple arithmetic.

Secondly, we might distinguish between *absolute* and *relative* reasons. From the perspective of norms this is a matter of *conditionality*: reasons to do something regardless of all other considerations, only if certain specific conditions obtain, or unless there are any countervailing reasons not to. Most practical reasoning takes the last form, displaying what logicians call *non-monotonicity*, and we can distinguish at least three different forms this takes:

**Exception Handling**: there may be action-guiding principles with specific exceptions. For example, we might think that one should buy one's friends a drink on their birthday. However, if your friend is an alcoholic, this may be an exception to the principle. Then again, if they are also dying, they may deserve a last drink. This play and interplay of exceptions and counter-exceptions is extremely common.

**Contextual Override**: there may be action-guiding principles which hold within a given context but which are overridden by considerations outside that context. For example, when playing chess, one should only move one's bishop diagonally. However, if someone puts a gun to your head during a chess game and commands you to move the bishop forwards, you should probably do what they say. There are a wide range of constitutive rules that define limited practical contexts, but we can always widen our context when considering how to act.

**Pro/Con Weighting**: there may be action-guiding principles expressing values that permit exceptions. For example, we might think that when buying a house, given a choice between two houses one should choose the largest. However, if the smaller one has a pool and the larger one doesn't, this may override that rule of thumb. There is often a mixture of factors that contribute to the choice between a range of options, and these are not always reducible to a common quantity.

From the perspective of value this becomes a matter of **typology**: we can distinguish the goodness of states *simpliciter*, in terms of which every outcome is comparable (e.g., the best possible world), from various **types** of value ascribed to particular objects and states (e.g., wisdom, justice, or utility), each of which motivate specific sorts of actions (e.g., deference, coercion, or acquisition), and permit extensive and fine-grained comparisons without necessarily being mutually comparable. Conflicts between the actions motivated by different types of value can be messy, but conditional directives can express this messiness (e.g., one should defer to the wiser person, unless the result would be unjust; unless it is a good lawyer telling you to plead guilty to a crime you did not commit). By contrast, reframing these conflicts in terms of goodness *simpliciter* effectively eliminates this messiness, converting it into simple calculation. The result of that reduction is that the sheer diversity of reasons for action gets collapsed into a single homogeneous quantity, and motivation becomes a matter of maximisation.[16]

In addition to preserving the heterogeneity of practical reasoning, prioritising directives also allows us to explain how evaluatives can be meaningfully applied to objects even though value is not something inherent in them, by showing how the patterns of practical reasoning they encode can be extended beyond the context of immediate action. This occurs in at least two ways:

> **Analogical Reasoning**: we may transpose patterns of practical reasoning that prescribe how agents *should* act in certain circumstances in order to predict how causal systems *will* act in certain circumstance. For example, we can say that a good heart is one that behaves *as if* its purpose was to pump blood around the body. This is the basis of Kant's account of functional explanation.[17]
>
> **Hypothetical Reasoning**: we may validate patterns of practical reasoning that prescribe how agents should act in unlikely and even impossible circumstances. For example, we can say that if one were per impossibile given a choice between destroying everything in the universe but the Mona Lisa and destroying everything, one should choose the former. This enables us to make sense of value that is intrinsic in Moore's sense without being inherent. The crucial point is that even if the final value the object bears consists in our being motivated to act in certain ways in relation to it, the reasons motivating this (impossible) action concern only the object's nonrelational properties.

The above considerations speak against the explanatory perspective underlying utilitarianism, but they do not yet constitute a comprehensive argument against it. Moreover, the most common autonomist approaches have their own potential pitfalls, as we're about to see.

16. There is an argument for this reduction from the perspective of rational choice theory, which shows that, under certain seemingly trivial assumptions about preferences, any truly rational agent behaves as if it is maximising some utility function. The utilitarian position is then simply that collective moral reasoning is effectively a scaling up of this sort of individual rationality (e.g., by aggregation). I think it better to say that this mathematical formalism simply describes a truncated form of rationality that is only valid in those local contexts in which the assumptions hold—contexts which are rarer than most believe.

17. For a more in-depth discussion, see 'Beyond Survival', in this volume.

## 3. THE LANGUAGE OF MEANING

We need to distinguish meaningfulness from the mere *feeling* of meaningfulness. The former is the province of philosophy, the latter the province of psychology. The two aren't entirely unrelated, but in philosophy we're aiming not simply to explain this feeling, but also to justify it. The question is: What exactly are we justifying here? Camus's answer is simple: to continue living one's own life, or not committing suicide. However, what's asked for here is not simply a justification for anyone's not committing suicide, or an impersonal reason for preserving life as such, but a reason for *me* to continue living. If we can characterise meaning as a type of value—it seems to come in *degrees*, and it seems to be something pursued *for its own sake*—then what distinguishes it from other types of value is this *personal* character.

Getting a grip on the term 'meaning' can be quite difficult, because it has a variety of meanings, ironically enough. But we can distinguish at least three ways it gets interpreted in this context:

**Effect**: one's life making some kind of a difference to the world. For example, exercising agency over one's physical or social environment (e.g., creating a monument or founding an institution).

**Explicability**: one's life making sense. For example, achieving self-recognition by developing a sense of who one is (e.g., a protector or a risk taker).

**Purpose**: committing to a project, or playing a role in something larger than oneself. This neatly combines explicability and effect insofar as it allows one to recognise oneself by exercising one's agency in defined way (e.g., being a revolutionary or a teacher).

There might be different ways of balancing or configuring these aspects of meaning, but the crucial point is that they each imply an assessment of the success of one's life *as a whole*, unifying the various actions and activities one might perform in different contexts. We can distinguish this overall success, or *fulfilment*, from the enjoyment or contentment that we feel in any given context, or even the sum of these feelings over the course of our lives. This is not to say that these feelings cannot contribute to fulfilment, but simply that we can imagine trading one for the other (e.g., giving up comfort to perform charity work). On the face of it, this seems like a problem for utilitarians. But they might count such trade-offs as evidence that fulfilment is simply one type of pleasure to be balanced against others, subordinating or even dissolving the problem of meaning. We will return to them shortly.

There is a more pressing problem for the autonomist tendency, which is that fulfilment can equally be distinguished from *ethical rightness*. This is not to say that ethical behaviour could not contribute toward a meaningful life, only that we can imagine ethically upstanding lives that would nevertheless be devoid of meaning. This is a problem because the autonomist tendency, exemplified by Kant, aims to derive universal norms governing our behaviour from the rational capacity to commit ourselves to *anything*, and in doing so tends to abstract away from the specific goals we might set for ourselves, in favour of articulating *absolute constraints* upon them. Even when they manage to propose anything resembling positive purposes (e.g., creating and sustaining political institutions), these are inevitably impersonal in their strict universality. This threatens to leave us with an empty form of right or justice, with reasons *not* to do many things, but no reason to do anything in particular. The existentialists interpret this radical freedom to author our own lives as the true source of value, but as we've already suggested, there is little to distinguish freedom so conceived from sheer *arbitrariness*, threatening to equate every possible pursuit.

Thomas Ligotti's anti-natalism provides an interesting response to such positions. He argues that life is *malignantly useless*: the very fact we are condemned to search for a purpose for our existence without ever finding one makes this existence objectively worse than the alternative. Any subjective value derived from feelings of pleasure or fulfilment is essentially ephemeral, because such feelings can wither away for no reason whatsoever. Our passions are nothing more than animal impulses to be assuaged, mutable features of our biology and psychology determined by an indifferent nature. If we cannot choose them, what does it matter to us if they change? We may delude ourselves that life is more than meaningless suffering, but the hard truth is that we should *welcome* extinction. If anything, this is worse than nothing mattering.

## 4. HAPPINESS AND DESIRE





As opposed to the mere constraints supplied by Kant and his inheritors, utilitarianism aims to articulate an impersonal purpose, namely the maximisation of *happiness*, conceived as an *absolute value*. The strategy here is to define an end at which all our desires aim, by abstracting away from their specific content, treating what we want as really a means to the end of *pleasure* or *satisfaction*. The problem with this strategy is that it distorts the nature of desire.

On the one hand, *hedonic utilitarianism*, which prioritises the feeling of pleasure, ignores the intentionality of desire, or the fact that we want what we want, not the feeling of getting it. Not only does this make various specific things we want fungible with regard to amounts of homogeneous pleasure, but it fails to account for things that don't result in pleasure, or worse, things which in principle cannot so result, such as outcomes that occur after our deaths. Moore's universe containing nothing but the Mona Lisa in it is an extreme if abstract example of this. A more concrete counterexample is the seemingly reasonable choice not to enter Nozick's experience machine, foregoing the mere experience of living a perfect life for the opportunity to really achieve anything.[18]

On the other hand, *preference utilitarianism*, which prioritises the satisfaction of our avowed preferences, overdetermines the intentionality of desire, effectively insisting that we just want what we say we want and nothing more. It fails to account for the fact that we often don't know exactly what we want, and that this *epistemic opacity* is productive, driving us to discover new objects of desire. It fails to appreciate that not only do our avowed preferences change, but that they can *evolve* for reasons that are intrinsic to them. For example, although I may have an avowed preference for jazz music, this doesn't mean that I fully understand what jazz is, in terms of either its history, its musical principles, or the full range of artists, styles, and songs that exemplify it. The process of learning more about these things does not simply reveal more about tastes I didn't know I had, but helps to actively shape these tastes.

In essence, the means-ends reversal at the heart of utilitarianism undermines the possibility of doing things for their own sake, i.e. for reasons that are specific to those things, our appreciation of which can change and deepen over time. For example, if one aims to write a novel *for its own sake*, one's understanding

18. R. Nozick, *Anarchy, State, and Utopia* (New York: Basic Books, 1974), 42–5.

of what that involves may change as one learns more about writing in practice, which is different from writing a novel *in order to be* a famous author, where what that involves is fixed by social factors external to the craft of writing. What distinguishes ends from means is the way in which their content is open to progressive determination. The difficulty lies in reconciling the fact that we get to determine what we want for ourselves with the fact that we often have reasons to choose one way or another. In other words, we must explain how we can think some things *worthy* of wanting without treating them as a means to some other thing, be it pleasure or something else. This means p1aying more attention to that type of value which has traditionally been characterised by finality, which is to say *beauty*.

## 5. BEAUTY AS EXCELLENCE

Let me emphasise that what I mean by 'beauty' is not an experiential quality, such as prettiness, but a type of value, akin to but distinct from ethical right. It's the type of value that we ascribe to works of art when we say they are good, bad, better, or worse than one another, though it's not necessarily restricted to them, as we may equally describe natural phenomena, people, and even certain actions as beautiful in the right context (e.g., 'that's a beautiful sunset', 'she has a beautiful soul', or 'that's a beautiful checkmate').[19] Although the value of many of these things is intrinsically linked to their experiential qualities, there are plenty of others, including some artworks, whose value lies elsewhere (e.g., conceptual art). Debates about the relative merits of these myriad things are not *objective* in the same manner as mathematics or natural science, but they are not for that matter entirely *subjective* either.[20] Although it's obvious that there can be brute differences in personal taste, this doesn't mean that all aesthetic disagreements are reducible to such differences, at least in so far as we often give and are sometimes persuaded by reasons to think that one thing is superior to another (e.g., that Duchamp's *Fountain* is superior to Warhol's *Brillo Boxes* because of its sheer originality, or that *Jackie Brown* is the best of Tarantino's films because it is his least self-indulgent).

19. For a deeper discussion see 'Art and Value', in this volume.

20. For a richer analysis of this contrast, see 'Essay on Transcendental Realism', in this volume.

However, although beauty admits of comparison, the rankings these comparisons produce are generally partial and rarely absolute.[21] The idea of a best possible artwork seems incoherent. A painting by Matisse may be neither better nor worse than a poem by Mallarmé. A song by Led Zeppelin may be better than one by Black Sabbath, qua blues, but maybe not qua rock. Even when works are comparable, there's rarely a singular dimension underpinning our rankings—as if simply making a song longer, louder, or lower in pitch would always make it better—but a melange of different factors that cohere to make one thing superior, the balance of which isn't obvious in advance. This peculiar organic unity means we are often able to *retrospectively* recognise that some new work or style is superior to an old one even when we cannot *prospectively* predict such improvements in advance.[22] This is what underlies the productive epistemic opacity involved in desire. In this respect, the various arts resemble nothing so much as research programmes, progressively uncovering vectors of improvement, branching into parallel paths, and articulating partial criteria of comparison as they go.

The key point here is that in aesthetic contexts we can come to appreciate that there are things we *should* want. Not in the sense that we should all desire exactly the same things, but rather that our peculiar combination of inclinations and preferences provide reasons to explore certain options (e.g., a preference for Black Sabbath may suggest you should listen to Earth), or even to refine our tastes in particular ways (e.g., that you learn to appreciate longer, slower riffs). Although these tastes may differ, they are not in principle unique. To the extent that they and the cognitive-libidinal mechanisms that underpin them overlap with those of others, they give us rational purchase upon one another, enabling us to converge on shared standards as much as to diverge into differing styles. From this perspective, aesthetics investigates the evolution of *coherent preferences*:

21. There is not the space here to provide a detailed analysis of how such partial orderings work in practice, but there is much to recommend the work of Ruth Chang on the subject, even though she is not principally concerned with aesthetics (see 'Parity: An Intuitive Case', *Ratio* 29 [2016]: 395–411). In particular, there is something deeply insightful in Chang's idea that choices can be 'on a par' without being equal in so far as we are not indifferent to them, precisely because making them determines who we are. See 'On Containing Multitudes', in this volume, for some related thoughts on such choices.

22. This is related to the asymmetry between creativity and taste mentioned in 'On Computational Asymmetry', in this volume.

there can be plenty of ways to go wrong, even if there's no singular way to be right. Contra Ligotti, our desires do in fact change, but we are not indifferent to these changes.

To put all of this in other terms, we might say that as opposed to a concern with specific experiential qualities (e.g., prettiness, pleasantness, or sublimity) the pursuit of beauty is more generally concerned with varieties of *excellence*. It uncovers wants that *transcend* our needs, striving for things that are better than they need to be. This also gives us further purchase on the problem with Ligotti's perspective, because whenever we treat a desire as simply an animal impulse to be assuaged, we are treating its satiation as a means to some deferred end (e.g., dealing with our hunger so we can get on with our work). Of course, we treat plenty of our desires as *mere needs*. But if we treat all our desires in this way then we are left unable to answer the question of what ultimate purpose their satiation serves (e.g., why are we working in the first place). Those desires that are more than mere needs aim at things *for their own sake* to the extent that they can exceed simple satiation, anticipating things whose value is strictly more than is required, even if they cannot predict precisely what this excess might consist in. This is what drives the progressive determination of the content of our ends.

Now, I don't mean to argue that the arts narrowly conceived are the only possible source of intrinsic value, but I do think that they are exemplary in this regard. They demonstrate what happens when the thirst for excellence *implicit* in doing something for its own sake becomes *explicit* as a systematic endeavour, discovering new options for creation and appreciation which lead to more in turn, and so on indefinitely. What distinguishes this open-ended process of proliferating ends from the fixed system of purposes embodied in the universe qua machine or narrative is that the value of each new step is not premised upon a consequent *actuality* (e.g., survival or apotheosis), but on its relation to a range of *possibilities* (i.e., the new alternatives and improvements it enables). The value of every song we sing is framed not only by comparison with the other songs we could have sung, but with the songs we might now sing, regardless of whether we do or not. What were once mere hypotheticals have condensed into genuine options. There's no intrinsic limit to the expanding horizon of our *freedom* to act, and yet the significance of its growth isn't erased if it is halted from without. This enables beauty to pass the test of cosmic extinction despite its envelopment in the fragile process of progressive determination.

Nevertheless, the beauty of each specific thing, which may give us reason to care about it, is still in some sense *relative* to the desires we have and the choices we make. So the question remains whether we can derive some form of *absolute value* that would even motivate creatures whose inclinations and histories are radically different from ours. If we are to provide an answer to this question then we must concentrate on what we still have in common even with such aesthetic aliens, and so return to the focus of autonomists and existentialists alike: freedom itself.

## 6. BEAUTY AS CONTINGENCY

Freedom is not simply the absence of constraint upon action (or *liberty*), but equally the possession of capacity and motivation (or *agency*). This much is crystal clear in the context of games, where the *rules* determining permissible actions and their consequences are distinct from the *goals* that motivate play.[23] For example, in chess one is not obliged to checkmate one's opponent's king. It is permissible to lose or draw in way that it is not permissible to move a rook diagonally. But games are microcosms of freedom as such, worlds within a world, and although it's clear that there are things we *should* care about within any given game, this is conditional upon our choosing to play. We do not choose to be born into the world, and it isn't obvious we can treat it as if it were one great game.

Beyond liberty and agency, freedom also demands *autonomy*: the ability to determine one's own goals and constraints, i.e., to choose which games one will play.[24] This third term is in some sense a synthesis of the other two: motivation conceived negatively as undetermined by others, or liberty conceived positively as a capacity for self-determination.[25] Moreover, although freedom requires each of these three dimensions, they can be *realised* to differing degrees: we

23. See 'What's in a Game?', in this volume.

24. See 'Beyond Survival' and 'On Containing Multitudes', in this volume.

25. These three terms (liberty, agency, and autonomy) thus roughly track the moments of universality (indeterminacy), particularity (determination), and individuality (self-determination) that Hegel traces in the development of the concept of freedom in the 'Introduction to the Philosophy of Right' (§5–7) (in *Elements of the Philosophy of Right*, ed. A.W. Wood [Cambridge: Cambridge University Press, 2019]).

can be more or less unconstrained by external forces, more or less able and motivated to act, and more or less actively self-determined; and this is before we address the extent to which freedom *as such* is realised by the success of these actions. Freedom is not simply what it already is. Freedom can (and so perhaps should) be intensified.

Despite its incompleteness, the game analogy gives us a way of reframing the problem with autonomist approaches. They establish absolute constraints that are *practically necessary* (or obligatory), but then leave everything else equally *practically possible* (or permissible). What we require is something in between necessity and possibility, something which captures the variety of things we have reason to do, even though there's no ultimate ground from which these reasons derive. We need an account of beauty as *practical contingency*.[26] This idea makes more sense once we recognise that beauty as excellence is also defined in opposition to practical necessity, namely, as that which transcends instrumental necessity. To return to the example of chess, it may be necessary to checkmate the king in order to win, but this checkmate can be as ugly as possible (e.g., just two kings and a rook shuffling around the board for fifty moves). There may be reasons to pursue more interesting or elegant strategies, reasons that are part and parcel of playing chess for its own sake, but they aren't reducible to any deeper practical necessities, be they personal needs or impersonal ethical imperatives. In commending *more* than what is required they are also *less* than strictly justified.

To frame this in another way, we can see beauty as contingency in so far as the practical rationality that characterises its pursuit is governed by an ideal of *coherence* rather than *foundation*. Whatever truth it has is in some important

26. There is a long history of interpreting the logic of obligation and permission in modal terms (see R. Hilpinen and P. McNamara, 'Deontic Logic: A Historical Survey and Introduction', in *The Handbook of Deontic Logic and Normative Systems* [Rickmansworth: College Publications, 2013]). However, the deontic logics which formalise this connection have no place for practical contingency, because while obligation is an analogue of necessity and permissibility is an analogue of possibility, there is no corresponding analogue of actuality, which continues to be interpreted in alethic terms. From this perspective, something practically contingent is simply something that is both practically permissible and factually done. By contrast, I am interpreting the analogue of actuality as something like the presence of a reason act. As I see it, the crucial disanalogy between this and alethic actuality is that there may be reasons to act in multiple incompatible ways. I don't have a way of formalising this conception of contingency, but any attempt to do so in terms of sets of complete and consistent possible worlds is likely to fail for this reason.

sense groundless. This goes some way to explaining the traditional connection between beauty and experience that we have so far ignored by focusing on the connection between beauty and action: sensory experience is as much the source of otherwise unfounded knowledge about the way the world *simply is* as it is the source of otherwise unfounded inclinations about the way it *simply should be*. Aesthetics is to ethics in the practical domain what empirical science is to mathematics in the theoretical domain. But just as empirical science moves beyond immediate sensation to more conceptually mediated modes of theorisation, so does aesthetic practice move beyond immediate sensation to more conceptually mediated modes of appreciation (e.g., considering the symbolic dimension of art). Moreover, just as empirical science deploys mathematical formalism as the medium of conceptual mediation, so does aesthetics appropriate the ethical language of commitment and constraint (e.g., considering the formal principles defining medium and genre).

However, if ethical right is defined as absolute necessity, or that which overrides all other concerns, including our personal needs, then the question is whether we can conceptualise a corresponding form of beauty as *absolute contingency*. There are three different dimensions along which we might characterise such absoluteness: as absolute *groundlessness*, absolute *universality*, or absolute *priority*. The varieties of excellence so far considered are at best relatively groundless, in so far as they remain tied to the specific purposes that define the relevant practices even as they exceed them (e.g., gastronomy is still framed by hunger). An absolutely groundless beauty would be wholly *without purpose*. Similarly, these varieties of excellence permit divergent perspectives on their value, as our avowed preferences evolve along coherent ramifying paths (e.g., a genre splitting as adherents cleave to competing styles). An absolutely universal beauty would be wholly *without perspective*. These two dimensions are effectively equivalent, at least insofar as they abstract away from any specific features of the *objects* valued and the *subjects* which value them. However, this leaves us to wonder not just *why* but *how* any activity abstracted from all such specific features could possibly be more important than everything else we might do for its own sake.

One potential candidate is the pursuit of beauty itself, or the activity of finding and engaging in *something* that can be done for its sake. To translate this back into our analogy with games: the great game of life might consist in finding smaller games to play; the only absolute value lying in the pursuit of relative ones. This comes close to existentialism, in so far as it recommends above all else that each of us must exercise our freedom to create value for ourselves, thereby imbuing our own lives with a unique meaning. But here this freedom isn't arbitrary, because not all permissible choices can sustain the progressive evolution characteristic of finality.[27] Only some of those activities we might commit our lives to are structured in a way that supports the sort of epistemically opaque, rationally coherent, nontrivial evaluations that guide the indefinite pursuit of excellence. This renders the search for those that do all the more significant.

However, although this activity is sufficiently abstract, if it is conceived simply as something that we are each motivated to do for ourselves and ourselves alone, then whatever value it is imbued with cannot truly be intrinsic in the sense we are seeking. If this exercise of freedom is unique to each of us then it cannot be separated from us, as something aimed at that might persist independently of ourselves. In other words, it isn't sufficiently non-relational. For freedom to become a true *object* of value it must be wholly impersonal. It cannot simply be that the realisation of my personal freedom in the pursuit of intrinsic value is most intrinsically valuable for me, but rather that the flourishing of freedom as such is most intrinsically valuable for all of us. This means both the continued existence of autonomous agents and those open-ended processes of proliferating ends through which their freedom to choose is realised. The resulting position is surprisingly similar to utilitarianism, in that it has transitioned from an analysis of what all our actions aim at individually to an account of what all our actions

---

27. There are some in the existentialist tradition who have attempted to articulate transcendental conditions which any commitment capable of sustaining a meaningful life must meet. In particular, in *This Life: Secular Faith and Spiritual Freedom* (New York: Pantheon Books, 2019), Martin Hagglund has argued that any such commitment must be selected from among a range of genuine alternatives, that it must be uncertain whether or not we will succeed, and that there must be something we risk losing if we fail. He then argues that mortality (both our own and that of those we love) is essential to meeting these constraints, and thus that without mortality life would be meaningless. I find the initial conditions to be potentially compelling, but the inferences from them to the necessity of mortality to be somewhat spurious. However, there is no space to elaborate upon these worries here. I will simply say that love, which Plato tells us is the attitude directed towards beauty, is infinite. The absence of an externally imposed limit (be it personal mortality or cosmic extinction) does not render it meaningless.

should aim at collectively, but instead of treating the *substance* of this value as pleasure or satisfaction, its substance is freedom itself.[28]

## 7. CONCLUSION: BEAUTY AS FREEDOM

Though this conception of freedom as the substance of absolute contingency is sufficiently abstract to account for groundlessness and universality, and might consistently be held up as a highest value, we still need to justify granting it this status. I don't aim to provide a comprehensive justification here, but there are two lines of argument I have in mind.

The first is the argument from *self-exemplification*. Plato famously claims that beauty is itself that which is most beautiful.[29] However, he takes this to mean that beauty is an archetype which beautiful things imperfectly resemble. By contrast, I take this to mean that the very presence of beauty within the world is more important than its disposition. Yet the mere persistence of beautiful objects beyond the annihilation of those free beings to whom this beauty is relative (e.g., a Mona Lisa in a dead universe) would not be enough, even if it would be better than nothing. The objects can persist independently of any and all attitudes towards them, but their beauty cannot. The only way to interpret the presence of beauty without treating intrinsic value as inherent is as the persistence of non-instrumental reasons for someone to act that aren't purely hypothetical, which is essentially the persistence of freedom and its modes of realisation (e.g., humanity and its arts). This means that beauty *subsists* in freedom.

The second is the argument from *foundation*. The idea here is to show that if the presence of beauty in the world is taken as a highest value, it can also function as a foundation for value as such, not unlike the sacred. Of course, every beautiful thing contributes to the presence of beauty, and so partakes in its absolute value to some extent. However, it is also possible to extend this foundation from the aesthetic to the ethical domain, in a manner that makes sense of their relationship while maintaining their separation. We have proceeded thus far on the basis that *beauty is to right as contingency is to necessity*. But there is another way of characterising this opposition that makes sense of ethical

28. For a slightly different presentation of this idea and the contrast with utilitarianism, see 'The Weight of Forever'.
29. Plato, *Symposium*, §210–212.

necessity, namely, that *right is a means to the end of beauty*. The source of those absolute constraints on action that constitute ethics is the need to preserve that freedom in which beauty subsists. However, this instrumental relation runs both ways: while right's *normative force* is conditional upon beauty's allure, its *normative priority* consists in the fact that this allure is causally conditional upon it. Ethical concerns override aesthetic ones not because they are unrelated, but precisely because the very possibility of aesthetics is the whole point of ethics.

We can clarify this position further by sharpening its contrast with the main alternatives we have considered so far: utilitarianism, autonomism, and existentialism.

The true sin of utilitarianism lies in collapsing the difference between right and beauty in a manner that prescribes mandatory excellence on a cosmic scale. The good is defined as the best. The inevitable consequence of this fusion is the longtermist project of optimising the universe for the production of pleasure or satisfaction at the expense of the freedom of those pleasured or satisfied, and the sacred duty of survival at all costs. By contrast, my position recommends that not only should we deny that the very idea of a best possible world makes any more sense than the idea of a best possible artwork, and affirm the intrinsic value of liberty, agency, and autonomy over the myriad forms of happiness they strive for, but that we cannot be compelled to survive even by the overwhelming beauty some future freedom may realise. Freedom cannot be obliged to exist without ceasing to be what it is. This lets us do justice to the fragility of value without sacralising survival. Voluntary extinction might be a tragedy, but it would not be a crime.

The true sin of autonomism lies in severing the relation between right and beauty in a manner that empties freedom of its substance in the name of formal self-legislation. The mere fact that we are each an end-in-itself (*dignity*) is abstracted from our character qua end-in-itself (*nobility*), in a way that impoverishes both our relations to ourselves and one another. Kant attempts to compensate for this in his *Doctrine of Virtue*, by claiming that there are ends which are also duties, namely, the perfection of ourselves and the happiness of others.[30] But these are at once too much and too little, at least in so far as one

30. I. Kant, 'Metaphysics of Morals', in *Practical Philosophy*, ed. A.W. Wood (Cambridge: Cambridge University Press, 1996), 514–20.

mandates excellence (and continued existence) on the personal scale, while the other disregards the excellence of others (both individually and collectively). By contrast, my position recommends that not only should we deny that the idea of a best possible self makes any more sense than the idea of a best possible world, and affirm the inherent diversity of the forms that freedom might take and the ways it may be realised, but that this may be true even of those ethical excellences we name virtues (e.g., wisdom, courage, compassion, etc.). Freedom cannot be obliged to excel without ceasing to be what it is. Yet we may be obliged to facilitate the excellence of others. There is no single way to live the good life, but everyone has the right to try in one way or another.

The true sin of existentialism lies in dissociating meaning from value in a manner that renders it *sui generis* and thereby absolutely groundless. This reduces meaningfulness to the capacity to overcome absurdity through a sheer act of will, whether this absurdity is conceived as the arbitrariness of choice or the inevitability of failure. This focus upon the act of commitment in opposition to the objects, events, and states that it aims at brackets not only the reasons these things give us to act in general, but the specific ways these are woven into rationales for pursuing one type of life over another. By contrast, my position recommends that not only should we deny that any life can be made meaningful by mere force of will, and affirm the intrinsic value of those activities without which life would be meaningless, but that we can distinguish this meaning as a species of value, namely, as that sort of excellence peculiar to life as a whole (e.g., narrative import [effect], narrative coherence [explicability], and narrative direction [purpose]).[31] Freedom is not simply an abstract substance in which beauty subsists, but its own concrete domain of aesthetic exploration. We make ourselves an end-in-itself by entangling the ends we pursue for their own sake, but the beauty this births is more than the sum of its parts. We are as such the archetype of art's organic unity.[32]

Finally then, we seem to have a suitable answer to our question: it's not true that just anything can matter, but it's equally false that what matters does so

31. See 'On Containing Multitudes', in this volume, for a rough account of why lives are subject to narrative evaluation.

32. Perhaps this is why Hegel claims that the highest forms of art (classical and romantic) are those which represent human freedom directly (*Lectures on Aesthetics* [Oxford: Oxford University Press, 2 vols., 1975], vol. 1, 77–81).

necessarily, independently of our choices; the only thing that matters necessarily is that *something* must matter, and this means that no matter who we are and what we want, we should care about the freedom of ourselves and others, and promoting its unconstrained evolution. The only thing that should constrain freedom is itself, and this is the true content of right. It is a means to the end of beauty, even if it must sometimes override it. Ethics without aesthetics is empty, but aesthetics without ethics is blind.

# DIALOGUES

# Philosophy and Normativity

## Interview with Kai Peattie

KAI PEATTIE: You've mentioned that, while you refuse to identify as either a Continental or an Analytic philosopher, you come from a Continental background. What drew you into Analytic philosophy?

PETER WOLFENDALE: Funnily enough, I was drawn to Analytic philosophy first. I had no prior knowledge of philosophy when I went to study it at undergrad, and the first stuff I really got into was Karl Popper's philosophy of science. I came to university with a reasonably uncritical faith in science, and, as is quite common, Popper's falsificationism served to shape this faith into something slightly more sophisticated. I later bought into the Feyerabendian heresy, reading Kuhn's *Structure of Scientific Revolutions* and *Against Method*, but I eventually settled down and adopted something resembling the synthetic picture provided by Imre Lakatos. However, this initial encounter with fallibilism proved formative, even though it has since been channelled through my engagement with Hegel—a development that would disgust Popper and delight Lakatos. I was also really engaged by the small amount of philosophy of language I was introduced to in my first year, especially Quine's work on the indeterminacy of meaning and the analytic/synthetic distinction. I then started reading Wittgenstein's *Philosophical Investigations* and became completely enamoured of it. His concern with the normativity of meaning and the problem of rule following resonated with my interest in Quine's work. These ideas and his maxim that meaning is use stayed with me. I read Heidegger's *Being and Time* around the same time, largely by accident, and this gave me a feel for reading the more difficult systematic works beloved by the Continental tradition. I briefly flirted with Derrida, then got heavily into Deleuze after joining a reading group on *Difference and Repetition*.

It was this that convinced me, contra Wittgenstein, that metaphysics could do more than run up against the limits of language, but that in order to do so it had to take contemporary science seriously.

All this led me to an MA in Continental Philosophy and a PhD that was supposed to be on Deleuze, language, and materialism, but somehow ended up being about Heidegger's question of Being. This shift occurred during the first year, and it was all because I was searching for a methodological foundation for metaphysics. It was around this point that I rediscovered Robert Brandom's work, and began reading through *Making It Explicit*. There is often a preference in Continental circles—especially amongst Nietzscheans, Heideggerians, and Deleuzians—for a form of pragmatism in which theory is subordinated to praxis, in so far as it is supposed to be a type of practice. The problem is that there is usually no attempt to describe the relevant practices. This is what I have elsewhere called *pragmatism without pragmatics*. By contrast, Brandom was not just committed to the idea that meaning is use (linguistic pragmatism), he wanted to explain precisely what kind of use (semantic inferentialism). It's worth saying a bit more about why I came to enthusiastically endorse his project, as it highlights the things that had alienated me from Analytic philosophy until then. There are roughly four factors:

i. **He is an eminently systematic thinker.** The main thing I disliked about Analytic philosophy was a combination of narrow scope and methodological naiveté. On the one hand, it seemed as if one was supposed to deal with problems largely in isolation from one another, rather than taking a synoptic approach to a range of issues. On the other, it seemed as if one was generally expected to work from *ad hoc* definitions or *prima facie* intuitions, rather than digging down to foundations. I've since come to see this as a result of the expressive format and pedagogical focus of the Analytic tradition as much as anything. This is precisely the style of engagement that fits into a single journal article, and it is through such articles that people build their careers. It's also precisely the style of thinking one cultivates when one parcels teaching into separate thematic areas accessed through selections of articles, while downplaying the deeper history of conceptual problems.

ii. **He wants to get to the bottom of the problem of normativity.** I had read a lot of the literature following on from Kripke's famous book *Wittgenstein: On Rules and Private Language*, but Brandom provided a more complex analysis of the issue. If nothing else, he traces the history of the problem further back to Pufendorf and Kant, and thereby connects it to deeper concerns with the concepts of freedom and autonomy. I've always had an affinity for Kant's work, and most of the analytic interpretations of Kant I'd seen until this point were deeply disappointing.

iii. **His favourite philosopher is Hegel.** I shouldn't need to say how odd this is for someone in the Analytic tradition, let alone someone working in the philosophy of language. I'd studied Hegel in some depth with Stephen Houlgate at Warwick, and could see the problems with Brandom's interpretation. However, his concerns with the relation between the implicit and the explicit, autonomy and self-consciousness, the historical character of reason and the holistic nature of conceptual content, are all recognisably Hegelian. Moreover, these Hegelian themes are presented as developments of the Kantian concerns just mentioned.

iv. **His commitment to rationalism was increasingly attractive**. I was introduced to Ray Brassier around the same time as I started reading Brandom. I came to agree with his critique of the rejection of epistemology, philosophy of science, and science itself prevalent within Anglophone Continental circles. Furthermore, his *Nihil Unbound* showed me that one could be a rationalist and still engage in systematic speculative thinking. Ray's own blossoming interest in the work of Wilfrid Sellars complemented my own interest in Brandom. There is a famous split between so called left-wing Sellarsians such as Brandom, John McDowell, and Richard Rorty, who are more focused on linguistic norms and social practice, and right-wing Sellarsians such as Paul and Patricia Churchland, Ruth Millikan, and Johanna Seibt, who are more focused on cognitive capacities and scientific metaphysics. Through conversations with Ray and others, I was opened up to whole swathes of the Analytic tradition I'd never encountered before.

I break with Brandom on a number of significant points: on the importance of scientific metaphysics, on the possibility of transcendental psychology, and on the details of semantic inferentialism. Regardless, he forced me to reconnect with the Analytic tradition, and to try and understand its breadth, depth, and historical development. In some respects, I see myself as extending Ray's critique of the Continental tradition from epistemology to semantics. Once one recognises the importance of systematically describing the structure of conceptual content, one sees that one cannot simply ignore the details, and if there's one thing the Analytic tradition has done it is to explore and elaborate these details. Though I might disagree with most of the general solutions proposed by contemporary Analytic philosophy of language, I appreciate its sensitivity to specific problems.

**KP**: The sole book you have published so far is a detailed critique of what, in your eyes, is a failed research programme.[1] What is the value of such a polemic today?

**PW**: This is an excellent question, because I think that, in the current academic climate, there's a definite tendency to avoid thoroughly engaging with positions and ideas one deeply disagrees with. These days, we don't often see books such as Leibniz's *New Essays on Human Understanding*, Engels's *Anti-Duhring*, or Neurath's *Anti-Spengler*. If nothing else, most academics simply don't have the time to dedicate to such a work, which means that we're all too often reduced to debating straw men or caricatures of our intellectual opponents. I'm glad I had the chance to work out a disagreement in so much depth, at least once in my life. Still, given the various constraints placed upon us, it's important to ask why we should expend our limited time and resources on such a task. There are essentially two answers.

The first concerns the intrinsic value of writing such a polemic. I think that we tend to underestimate the extent to which being forced to work out why we think something is wrong helps us to understand what we actually think. I learned a lot about metaphysics by writing the book, not because Harman's metaphysics is in any way edifying, but rather because explaining what he had

1. P. Wolfendale, *Object-Oriented Philosophy: The Noumenon's New Clothes* (Falmouth: Urbanomic, 2014).

failed to do, in developing accounts of the nature of qualities, relations, objects, and other abstract features of reality, required me to say something about what it would be to succeed. This is not to say that I developed anything resembling a positive systematic metaphysics in the book, that was not its purpose. However, I do think that I learned a lot about how one should do metaphysics, by examining how it shouldn't be done, in some detail. I can only hope that I have successfully passed on these lessons to my readers. I would like to pursue the same strategy in other areas. The key thing is to be as charitable as possible to one's opponent, for one learns nothing otherwise. I would at some point like to work out precisely what is wrong with Derrida's approach to meaning, as I think I'd learn a lot in the process.

The second concerns the extrinsic value of publishing such a polemic. I think it's important to acknowledge the influence that philosophy has elsewhere in the arts, humanities, and even the sciences. It shouldn't be controversial to note that Continental philosophy has a far greater influence in large sectors of academia than its Analytic cousin, for various reasons. However, there is a desire for novelty in these quarters, a desire that is to some extent fuelled by the stale variants of phenomenology, poststructuralism, and critical theory that have been passed around for several decades. It's in this context that the break with correlationism announced by 'speculative realism' was so eagerly received, even if it largely failed to resonate within philosophy departments themselves. It's also on this basis that object-oriented philosophy/ontology grew to prominence, quickly sprouting papers and conference calls considering how it could be applied to everything from ethics and aesthetics to archaeology and architecture. As I explain in the book, I think there are reasons for OOO's popularity that have nothing to do with its theoretical merits, but that its theoretical deficiencies might not be obvious to a casual reader desperate for something new. My book is a useful resource both for those curious about OOO who want to see what it can (or can't) do for them, and for those who have reservations about OOO but can't easily put their finger on them. I think it's our job as philosophers to provide such critical resources, as much as to offer new theoretical tools. Again, I'd love to do this more.

**KP**: Something that has drawn me to your work is your tendency toward abstraction, which puts you at a remove from much of the 'theory' in the humanities. What do you think the proper role of philosophy with respect to different academic disciplines, humanities or no?

**PW**: This usefully expands on the issues just discussed. As I noted above, Continental philosophy exercises an outsized influence on other disciplines, but this often takes the form of its transmutation into 'theory' of one form or another. This 'theory' is a difficult term to explain, because it has more semantic weight than a mere opposition to practice might suggest. This is somewhat ironic, as it's one of those words whose sense one seems to pick up in practice, at least, if one has read and discussed enough work on the more abstract side of the academic study of literature, art, media, sociology, and the like. In some ways it gets its sense from the 'critical theory' of the Frankfurt school, suggesting some non-quite-philosophical concern with society as a whole and how it should or shouldn't be; but as it loses the adjective and its explicit connection to philosophical critique (e.g., Kant and Hegel) and the political project of Marxism, it becomes a more flexible label for engagement with abstract issues that pop up within and between disciplines (e.g., the nature of meaning, value, oppression, etc.), with a more *ad hoc* relationship to its philosophical resources (e.g., French poststructuralism). There's nothing wrong with this, and more power to those who practice it wherever they find themselves. The only reservation I have is that some (e.g., McKenzie Wark) wish to champion 'theory' over philosophy, as if it had either enough coherence to be opposed to it or enough autonomy to exist without it. Worse, there are some who do so precisely because of its amorphousness, advocating a deliberately disorganised pluralism. Pluralism can be an epistemic virtue. Deliberate disorganisation cannot.

However, this still doesn't say what I think the proper role of philosophy is in relation to the humanities and other disciplines. What is philosophy, then? Well, I think the best answer I've come across is that it's the art of asking questions. This is partly why some people in the sciences think philosophy makes no progress, because they fail to see either that the questions they're asking were articulated by and gradually spun off from philosophy in the last few centuries (e.g., What is force?), or how much philosophical work their own disciplines still do (e.g., how should we interpret quantum mechanics?), sometimes but not always in dialogue with philosophers of science. It's also why some people in philosophy and elsewhere in the humanities think that philosophy provides no answers, either because they pretend that it has no questions of its own (quietism), or because they believe these pose false problems (e.g., linguistic confusions, expressions of ideology, or worse, 'metaphysics'). There are even some who, adopting François Laruelle's 'non-philosophy', insist that philosophy only ever asks questions it has already decided the answers to, and thus that we must abandon the ambition of formulating questions that could be definitively answered. These antiphilosophical tendencies should be seen as abstract disavowals of abstraction, be it in the name of a more familiar mode of abstraction (science) with the aim of freeing us from abstraction *qua* oppression (alienation/domination), or through a claim to preserve some essential, perhaps even sacred concreteness (lived experience). It is not a bad idea to temper philosophy's speculative ambitions by subjecting them to critique, but one must not dissolve them in the process. We have no choice but to confront abstraction, if only because it gets everywhere. If nothing else, there are always questions to be asked about what it is to ask questions, and this is why epistemology, semantics, and logic remain central philosophical concerns. There are equally questions to be asked about which questions we should ask, and here ethics, politics, and the holistic concerns of critical theory come to the fore. Philosophy helps us organise our various theoretical and practical problems, not just by clarifying the questions we already ask, but sometimes by inventing the concepts necessary to ask entirely new ones.

**KP**: Your work places a premium on normativity. What is normativity, and why is it so important?

**PW**: Just like abstraction, normativity gets everywhere. But again, it's important to understand what it's not before we explain what it is, because there are two distinct albeit related senses in which it gets used in theoretical circles. Normativity is about norms, as the word makes pretty obvious. These come in various flavours: ethical, aesthetic, epistemic, political, legal, social, technological, etc. Everything from the moral injunction against killing and the incest taboo, to dinner party etiquette and the concept of justice. However, normativity is not necessarily restricted to *normality*, which is not always so obvious. The behaviour that a norm prescribes need not be common, let alone statistically average. We often don't do what we should (e.g., give to charity, eat well, pick up trash, etc.), and there are even ideals which we may never fully realise (e.g., ensuring that our beliefs about the world are complete and consistent). There are even teleological norms, which we infer when trying to understand biological systems, that make the point plain: the purpose of an acorn is to grow into an oak tree, but most acorns never do. Nevertheless, there are often deeper regularities of which these are expressions: oaks reliably produce acorns because that is a reproductive strategy that was selected and stabilised by their evolutionary history. The same can be said about social norms, either those that implicitly guide our actions (e.g., the subtle connotations of words), those that we explicitly follow (e.g., the formalised rules of chess), or those that regulate our conduct through a more complicated cycle of expression and impression (e.g., the evolving practice of cookery). Every such norm is in some sense dependent on the specificities of our biological and cultural evolution, i.e., the self-sustaining behavioural regularities they have generated. Unfortunately, this dependence gets misinterpreted in roughly two ways:

i. **Regularism**: This is roughly the idea that norms are nothing but regularities. The problem for this view is something I call normative closure. Studying regularities tells you how things have been done, but this does not necessarily tell you how they will be done in the future, let alone how they should be done in unfamiliar situations. There are plenty of cases in which facts about behavioural regularities simply don't determine how the norms implicit in them should be extended when we encounter new contexts of application (e.g., unexpected board game states), or revised when we encounter inconsistencies (e.g., contradictory moral impulses). What separates norms from regularities is the very fact that there might be *reasons* for choosing one extension/revision over another.

ii. **Normophobia**: This is, roughly, the idea that norms are inherently oppressive. It has two distinct but often conflated strands. On the one hand, there's the idea that social pressure to conform is essentially oppressive (e.g., heteronormativity). This is often true, and its exploration is a central topic in various strands of theory (e.g., queer theory), but since normativity need not be a matter of normality, it's not a problem with normativity as such. On the other hand, there's the idea that normative ideals are essentially oppressive (e.g., truth, justice, beauty, etc.). There is a grain of truth in this view, which is that such ideals are often explicitly invoked in order to justify forms of domination (e.g., the 'scientific objectivity' of eugenics), or implicitly deployed in more subtle modes of oppression (e.g., traditional Western notions of beauty). The problem is that critiques of these modes of oppression inevitably appeal to similar ideals (e.g., decrying the falsity of eugenics, denouncing unjust laws, recognising beauty in other traditions, etc.), and a fortiori that the notion of oppression only makes sense in opposition to some ideal of freedom (e.g., as the suppression of autonomy). If one carries these positions to their logical conclusion, all one is left with is the affirmation of abnormality and/or transgression for their own sake (e.g., unmasking, resisting, queering).

The thing these misinterpretations have in common is the attempt to reduce normativity to social norms. As far as I am concerned, one has normativity wherever there is some distinction between *correctness* and *incorrectness*. This can be elaborated in terms of how one ought to behave and how one may behave (obligation and permission), or in terms of which actions, outcomes, or states are to be preferred over others (value); but the simplest way to describe norms is as standards of correctness; and, crucially, they play a role in correcting action as much as they do in guiding it. As such, I agree that norms originally apply to humans (qua rational agents), in so far as they are in a position to regulate their own and others' behaviour. The normative distinction between function and malfunction that we ascribe to biological and technological systems is derivative: either an analogy with the rational agency necessary to understand them, or an extension of the rational agency required to engineer them. However, even if I think that normativity concerns the correctness of (in)human action, this does not mean that norms are reducible to modes of social correction. The archetypal example is the rational ideal of completeness and consistency mentioned above, which is manifest in norms governing the acquisition of beliefs, the exploration of their consequences, and the resolution of their inconsistencies. We only follow these norms because we have been socialised to do so, and, despite continually correcting one another, we don't necessarily follow them all that well. However, the process of social regulation that causes this rational behaviour has nothing to do with the reason why we should continue to pursue this ideal, and indeed, strive to pursue it better.

**KP**: There are a growing number of critics (such as R. Scott Bakker and Stephen Turner)[2] who decry norms as a cognitive illusion to be discarded with the advent of neuroscience. How do you respond to them?

**PW**: The problem with these arguments is that whichever side you're on, your opponent's accusations against you, as well as their justification of their own position, both seem to beg the question. One has to recognise that there is something significant about this symmetric circularity in order to make any progress, especially if you want to extract any insights from your opponent rather than simply dismissing them outright. On the one hand, for those of us who resist the regularist and normophobic positions mentioned above, there must be some sense in which normativity is sui generis. This means that normativity cannot be explained in non-normative terms. This is where anti-normativists smell vicious circularity, and they're not entirely wrong. Providing an explanation of normativity that turns in a virtuous circle, where one understands more coming out than one did going in, demands significant conceptual subtlety. It is all too tempting to take a short cut and slip back into viciousness. If nothing else, then, paying attention to the sensitive noses of anti-normativists keeps us honest. On the other hand, anti-normativists set themselves the task of explaining away normativity, and this produces an entirely different temptation. Often, instead of explaining a phenomenon characterised by normativity in non-normative terms, anti-normativists simply deny that there is anything to be explained. This ranges from broadly Nietzschean claims to have eliminated ethical forms of justification (i.e., to have gone beyond good and evil), to an assortment of radical pragmatist/materialist claims to have eliminated epistemic forms of justification (i.e., the will to truth). This is where the normativist detects hints of evasion and/or pragmatic contradiction. The most profound mistake here is identified by what

2. See Bakker's blog *Three Pound Brain*, for example <https://rsbakker.wordpress.com/2013/10/08/leaving-it-implicit/>; S.P. Turner, *Explaining the Normative* (Cambridge: Polity. 2010).

I call **Brassier's Razor**: any position which has explained away explanation has committed suicide by parsimony.

Returning to the question, I think there are essentially two intertwined strands of critique elaborated by Turner and Bakker respectively:

i. **Against Abstracta**: This is the argument that in so far as norms are abstract entities that can have no causal effects, they should play no role in explanation. It is essentially a form of Occam's Razor, wielded against norms (e.g., prudence, temperance, and fortitude) instead of metaphysical universals (e.g., redness, doghood, or humanity) or mathematical objects (e.g. numbers, algebras, or spaces). The truth in this critique lies in its recognition of the potential pitfalls of using our everyday talk of norms in sociological explanation. For example, to explain the behaviours associated with the Jewish kosher laws by insisting that they are caused by these laws, and leave it at that, is obviously insufficient. One needs to be able to explain the relevant dynamics of social regulation and their evolution in causal terms, which should include, but not be reduced to, those aspects of these behaviours that involve publicly articulating, deploying, and revising these norms in the form of explicit rules; the expression of prescriptions to act in certain ways, and their impression on systems that produce the corresponding behaviour. Talk of norms *simpliciter* is at best a useful shorthand in these cases (e.g., similarities between kosher and halal norms engender similarities between Jewish and Islamic cuisine, but this has historical provenance in their common Abrahamic root).

However, the falsity of the critique lies in the way in which it flays explanation until all that is left is causal retrodiction/prediction (e.g., 'Why did the French Revolution happen?' and 'What does this tell us about the likelihood of future social upheaval?'), leaving out mathematical explanation (e.g., 'Why is there no solution to Fermat's famous equation?'), the formal and material dimensions of practical reasoning (e.g., 'Why must one prioritise actions?' and 'Why is it wrong to kill?'), and even things like aesthetic judgment (e.g., 'Why is Klee's painting worth our attention?'). These are all questions for which causal facts, if relevant at all, do not constitute sufficient reasons for choosing between possible answers. When anti-normativists cannot fudge causal answers to such questions, they tend to reclassify them as non-questions. The best way to explain this behaviour is that they imagine such answers could only be facts that must be experimentally confirmed, properties of a special sort of objects that we must somehow observe. This is not true for mathematics, so why would it be true in other non-empirical domains? Here then is the outline of the virtuous circle: to grasp a norm is to grasp a pattern of practical reasoning, even though reason is governed by its own peculiar norms.

ii. **Against 'Normative Cognition'**: This argument has its roots in Paul and Patricia Churchland's eliminative materialism, though it is developed by Bakker in a novel way. Where Turner is more concerned with sociological explanation, the eliminativists have their sights set on psychological explanation. They believe that the folk-psychological concepts through which we have up until now understood our own and others' behaviour (e.g., belief, desire, intention/volition, etc.) have been rendered obsolete by the confluence of evolutionary biology and cognitive neuroscience. However, whereas the Churchlands are more concerned with showing the comparative inadequacy of folk psychology by presenting alternative theories of brain function, Bakker is more concerned with showing the intrinsic inadequacy of folk psychology by showing that it is a form of metacognitive neglect, itself an example of a more general heuristic neglect. This produces a difference in emphasis: the Churchlands approach folk psychology primarily as a culturally evolved theory of human minds (following Sellars's account of the manifest image), whereas Bakker approaches folk psychology primarily as a biologically evolved window onto our own mind (following Metzinger's account of the transparent self-model). Still, they agree on the unifying feature of folk psychology: intentionality, or the notion that mental states are about something outside themselves. Bakker somewhat justifiably sees philosophy (and even the Churchlands' neurophilosophy) as irredeemably contaminated by intentionality, and thus sees his own Blind Brain Theory (BBT) as a necessary post-intentional corrective.

To understand this further, we need to articulate the reciprocal relation between intentionality and normativity. On the one hand, intentional states are normative because they have some type of correctness condition: whether or not a belief is true depends upon what it says about its object, whereas whether a desire is satisfied depends upon whether the state it aims at has been realised. This means that beliefs and desires can have the same propositional content (e.g., 'I have eaten a strawberry') while exhibiting opposing directions of fit: correctness for beliefs is about fitting mind to world (i.e., *taking* a proposition to be true), whereas correctness for desires is about fitting world to mind (i.e., *making* a proposition true). On the other hand, norms are intentional because they are representationally world-to-mind: desires focus on the ends to be achieved by action (e.g., having eaten the strawberry), whereas norms, like intentions and volitions, focus on the actions themselves (e.g., how one should go about eating it). Worse still, normativists tend to think that propositions are inherently normative, because there is a core of correctness that's invariant across intentional flavours (e.g., one must understand that 'one cannot have a strawberry and eat it'). Inferentialists such as myself think that this is a matter of correct inference (e.g., 'if one has eaten a strawberry, one no longer has it'). The reciprocity is thus that propositional attitudes are normative (either extrinsically or intrinsically) and norms are propositional (either implicitly or explicitly).

Here then is the crucial difference between the Churchlands and Bakker: the Churchlands try to articulate *better*, post-intentional theories of mind, in terms of (non-propositional) representations and (non-social) functions; whereas Bakker tries to show that intentional theories will always be *worse*, refusing even to talk in terms of representations or functions, as he suspects they are secretly normative, and thus secretly intentional. Here's my stance: I agree with Bakker that representation and function are contaminated with normativity, and I agree with the Churchlands that we cannot explain the brain (or the mind) without them (and thus intentionality). Bakker's bonfire of explanatory tools leaves him with a notion of information without representation and biomechanics without mechanism. I'd argue that these have been irreparably charred by the fire of radical eliminativism. The conclusions he draws from metacognitive neglect are essentially about ignorance: radical consequences of the fact that we don't know what we don't know about ourselves. The premises he obtains from heuristic neglect are essentially about inadequacy: radical limitations imposed by a succession of evolutionary changes making us only just good enough to survive. How could we not be maximally blind about ourselves and others? Tragicomic biomechanical systems stumbling around in an environment they're overfitted to, absorbing and processing a faint sliver of informational light within a vast higher-dimensional darkness. The problem is that one cannot understand ignorance without some notion of truth, or at least some standard of inaccuracy for information processing and its data schemes; and one cannot understand inadequacy without some notion of success, or at least some standard of failure for adaptive systems and their component mechanisms. Bakker wants to argue that philosophy is a reflection of how bad we are at understanding ourselves, but he has incinerated every possible standard of *badness*.

Here's where I stand, then. I think that there's some remnant of intentionality that must be extracted from folk psychology, and some spark of normativity that must be wrested from folk sociology. However, we must heed the worries expressed by anti-normativists and post-intentionalists, because they force us to dissect our folk understanding and preserve only what is absolutely necessary in order to explain the behaviour of individual minds and social groups. We have to articulate a moderate eliminativism in opposition to radical eliminativism, even as we let the latter keep us honest. Moving from theory to praxis, Mark Fisher and Ray Brassier used to talk about the possibility of an eliminativist Marxism. I think Nick Srnicek and Alex Williams's concept of folk politics[3] can be seen as an attempt to work through some of these ideas. With them, we might add that there is some cry for autonomy that must be weaned from folk politics, a problematised, complex demand for synthetic freedom.

3. See N. Srnicek and A. WIlliams, *Inventing the Future: Postcapitalism and a World Without Work* (London: Verso, 2015), chapter 1.

# Artificial Bodies and The Promise of Abstraction

# Interview with Anthony Morgan

**ANTHONY MORGAN:** Please can you start by saying a few things about the rise of embodiment within contemporary philosophy? It seems to me to be mainly used as a corrective against (i) the Cartesian notion of an immaterial mind, and (ii) the materialist tendency to place the mind in the brain. But what are the main positive claims that defenders of embodiment are making?

**PETER WOLFENDALE:** I think that the meaning of the term 'embodiment' in philosophical circles is deceptively diverse, and that those who champion the concept are motivated by concerns that overlap less than is often appreciated. If they are unified by one thing, it is a rogues' gallery of common enemies. Although Descartes is the most reviled of these, his errors are often traced back to some original sin perpetrated by Plato. However, in order to make sense of these conceptual crimes, it's worth first distinguishing the *explanatory* concerns of cognitive science and artificial intelligence from the *normative* concerns of political and social theory, while acknowledging that both of these are downstream from more general metaphysical concerns regarding the difference and/or relation between matter and mind. So, although there are many purely metaphysical objections to the Platonic dualism of intelligible and sensible worlds and the Cartesian dualism of mental and physical substances, what really unites the embodiment paradigm is their objection to the outsized role that Plato, Descartes, and their inheritors give to 'the life of the mind' in explaining how we make our way in the world, and establishing which aspects of it we should value. For want of a better word, we might call this 'intellectualism'.

This 'life of the mind' is distinguished by the capacity for **abstract thought.** This is to say that it abstracts away from concrete features of the context in which thinking occurs: it is *theoretical*, or unconstrained by the practical problems posed by our bodily environment; and it is *contemplative*, or independent of the sensorimotor capacities through which we interact with this environment. Both Plato and Descartes take mathematics to exemplify this sort of thinking, and on that basis, thought as such. Mathematical theorems are not strictly about anything in our physical environment, and they can be verified even if they're not applicable to it, in ways that needn't involve interacting with it. This being said, what really distinguishes Descartes from Plato is his conviction that the physical world can be accurately represented by mathematical models, and thus that our experiences can be treated as internal representations akin to such models. There are other problematic aspects of the Cartesian picture, but this will do for now.

**AM**: So, what are the main explanatory objections to intellectualism?

**PW**: There are two. On the one hand, its opponents claim that intellectualism ignores the vast majority of human cognition: most of our lives are spent carrying out tasks and navigating obstacles whose contours are determined by the way our body fits into its environment, rather than reasoning our way from premises to conclusions. Making a cup of tea in an unfamiliar kitchen is a more representative instance of our problem-solving capacity than demonstrating the infinity of primes. On the other, they claim that intellectualism has its priorities backwards: rather than treating this sort of 'skilled coping' as a deficient form of abstract cognition, we can only understand the latter by showing how it emerges from the former. Even our ability to imagine complex geometric constructions has at some point been bootstrapped from a basic bodily grasp of orientation and gesture.

The most important targets of these complaints are the classical computational theory of mind in cognitive science and what gets called 'good old-fashioned AI' (GOFAI). These see cognition as principally a matter of rule-governed symbol manipulation not unlike mathematical reasoning. They are opposed by a range of '4E perspectives', so called because they emphasise some combination of the *embodied*, *embedded*, *enactive*, and *extended* dimensions of cognition. The extent to which these diverge from traditional views varies, but, in rough order, the points of contention are: (1) the extent to which cognition is dependent on features of the body outside of the brain (e.g., the structure of sensory organs) and features of the environment outside of the body (e.g., the availability of cognitive resources), (2) whether the concepts of computation and representation are irredeemably intellectualist (e.g., if they can account for prelinguistic 'meaning'), and (3) whether dependence implies constitution (e.g., whether my notebook is part of my mind).

**AM**: What about the normative objections?

**PW**: Again, there are two. On the one hand, opponents claim that intellectualism reflects and reinforces implicit social hierarchies: those who have historically enjoyed the luxury of theoretical contemplation have done so because the practical problems and bodily processes it abstracts away from have been taken care of for them, often by groups who have been systematically identified with their bodies and bodily capacities, such as women, slaves, and colonised peoples. The disembodied Cartesian ego is an illusion engendered by ignorance and privilege. On the other, they claim that intellectualism devalues significant sources of human knowledge: there are forms of 'lived experience' and 'situated knowledge' that are valuable even if they aren't (and possibly can't be) articulated in a manner that divorces them from the embodied contexts in which they occur (e.g., their emotional valence). This Cartesian false consciousness doesn't simply impact the way we treat others, but even the way we treat ourselves, potentially disconnecting us from our embodied existence.

The idea that privileging the mind over the body is associated with other sorts of illicit privilege (e.g., economic, racial, sexual, etc.) is now fairly widespread in contemporary feminist and critical theory. However, there are a variety of philosophical frameworks drawn from the Continental tradition that get used to articulate, elaborate, and offer solutions to this problem. Roughly speaking, the main strands are Spinozist (Deleuze, Affect Theory, etc.), Nietzschean (Foucault, Butler, etc.), and phenomenological (Heidegger, Merleau-Ponty, etc.), although there is much cross-pollination. The first is characterised by the metaphysical tenor of its critique, proposing some form of materialist monism as an alternative to the dualisms of Plato and Descartes. The second is characterised by its focus upon social dynamics, providing an analysis of the way bodies are 'ensouled' by the internalisation of patterns of thought and action. But the last provides the greatest point of overlap with the explanatory concerns discussed above, as it furnishes a detailed introspective analysis of the body's involvement in the constitution of experience. Phenomenology has had a marked influence on 4E approaches to cognition and is responsible for the concept that straddles and sometimes connects all these varying concerns, namely, 'the lived body'.

**AM**: The idea of the lived body suggests that the body is not just a causal bridge between ourselves and the world, but rather that the body is our engagement with the world in a way that serves as a condition for the emergence of our subjectivity. This suggests that only a 'proper' body will be fit for this purpose—no ersatz or artificial alternative will do. Embodiment is in fact 'real meat' embodiment. Is this a fair picture, both in phenomenology and in the other frameworks you discuss above?

**PW**: Although not every proponent of embodiment will go so far as to insist upon an essential link between mind and meat, I think it's fair to say that this is where the rhetoric of embodiment leads. To some extent, this is because it aligns with other philosophical and political goals, such as undermining pernicious distinctions between human and animal or diagnosing dangerous fantasies implicit in the very suggestion that minds could be uploaded into computer simulations. However, there are some arguments for the claim, and I'll try to tease out the general pattern of these as I see it. But first, it's worth saying something more about the idea of the lived body.

The cornerstone of the phenomenological tradition is the idea that the content of explicitly articulated representations, such as declarative sentences or mathematical models, depends upon a more primitive form of meaning implicit in ordinary conscious experience. This gets formulated in slightly different ways by Husserl, Heidegger, and Merleau-Ponty, but they essentially agree that our many and varied representations are able to pick out the same object (e.g., galaxies, spleens, recessions) across changes in time, shifts in perspective, differences of opinion, and diverging interests, only because the referential frameworks they deploy (e.g., star charts, anatomy, econometrics), are so many layers arranged on top of those simple unities that tie together our everyday activities (e.g., places, obstacles, tools). My coffee cup is unified as something I can reach out and grasp, but this grasping is not a carefully planned sequence of muscle movements guided by a mechanical understanding of shapes and forces, it is a single fluid movement in which my fingers fit themselves to the cup's contours without so much as a second thought. What distinguishes the 'lived body' from the 'biological body' is not simply that it is not yet an object of scientific representation, but rather that it is what ties everything together in the last instance. It is the origin of all intentional directedness, and it is experienced as such: an immediate awareness of agency. The question remains: if the lived body is not the biological body, why is 'real meat' so important?

The notion that there is some split between an original and a dependent (or derived) form of intentionality is not unique to phenomenology. Wittgenstein is famous for arguing that the usage rules that give words their meaning ultimately only make sense in the context of some shared 'form of life', while John Searle is (in)famous for arguing (in his Chinese room thought experiment) that a mind cannot be built from rule-governed symbol manipulation, precisely because these symbols must already be interpreted as meaningful. Wittgenstein and his followers tend to emphasise the role that social constraint plays in making intentionality possible, while Searle and his followers tend to emphasise the sheer uniqueness of the human body's capacity for intentionality, whatever it consists in. However, they are entirely compatible with embodied phenomenology and other strands of the paradigm and are often blended together. So, a second question emerges: how should we understand the 'dependence' between the original (embodied/concrete) and the derived (disembodied/abstract)?

**AM**: So, the importance of 'real meat' has something to do with the way in which 'dependence' is understood. How does this work?

**PW**: I think it is useful to draw two distinctions. On the one hand, we should distinguish *empirical* claims about the workings of the human mind from *transcendental* claims about the workings of any possible mind. On the other, we should distinguish *conditions* that enable our cognitive capacities from *constraints* that limit the form they take. When these lines are blurred, it becomes all too easy to mistake significant features of our mental make-up for essential features of any possible cognitive architecture: *de facto* dependence becomes *de jure* constraint.

For instance, there is much experimental research indicating that basic information-processing tasks (e.g., determining the direction of a noise) are carried out by heuristics closely tailored to environmental and/or bodily parameters (e.g., the distance between our ears). Does this mean that all cognition is heuristic, or just good enough for the environmental conditions it is adapted for? Similarly, there is much phenomenological research arguing that most mental content (e.g., heeding the warning 'beware of the dog') is constituted by sensorimotor expectations tied to specific sensory modalities (i.e., an imaginary bundle of potential sights, smells, sounds, and motions). Does this mean that all thought is parochial, or restricted by the range of our sensory imagination?

**AM**: I suppose you want to dispute such conclusions. Why? Has the critique of intellectualism missed something important?

**PW**: To give Plato and Descartes their due, pure and applied mathematics provide us with a wealth of counterexamples, and not simply because they involve brute calculation as opposed to creative inspiration. Mathematicians certainly deploy heuristic techniques in searching for solutions to complex problems (see George Pólya's *How to Solve It*), and physicists clearly exercise their imaginations in exploring theoretical possibilities (see Einstein's 'thought experiments'). Yet what makes it the case that any two practitioners are thinking about the same things (e.g., a twisted manifold or an alpha decay event) has come unmoored from the trappings of bodily immediacy, be it the fingers they count on or the eyes they see with. One way to approach this is to explore modal differences in the analogies physicists find helpful (e.g., visual/auditory takes on particles), but my preferred example is Smale's theorem, which, loosely, proves that there must be a way to turn a sphere inside out without creating creases (eversion). Not only is this physically (and so bodily) impossible, but at the time no one could envision a way to do it. It ultimately took several mathematicians working together—one of whom (Bernard Morin) was blind—to find one.

I think there's no good reason to assume that there couldn't be similar collaborations between mathematicians with more radical divergences in embodiment (e.g., humans, aliens, and AIs). This is the promise of abstraction: that we can repurpose diverse cognitive talents to common representational ends. I think that the error of much work on embodiment is to see this as a false promise: that whatever enables our immediate purchase upon the world inevitably constrains any more mediated comprehension of its contents; that there is no true escape from the concrete, only misguided escapism. As a consequence, the idea of abstractions anchored to the world in any manner other than our own becomes inherently suspect. Not only is immediate ('lived') experience seen as more authentic than that which is mediated, but the form taken by our immediate ('embodied') purchase on the world—meat and all—becomes the only authentic form. I contend that it is this association between immediacy and authenticity that supposedly renders artificial minds and bodies 'unreal'.

**AM**: I'm not sure this is enough to dismiss the importance of meat. It seems to me that it's still a salient issue when considering the possibility of minds housed in artificial bodies. Just look at social distancing and the impact that changes to our intercorporeal habits will have on our cognition, on our sense of trust, openness to others etc. Isn't our flesh incredibly significant here?

**PW**: I don't think that people are invested in the importance of 'real meat' because they have identified some positive feature that makes meat the one true medium of cognition. Rather, it serves as an index of authenticity: a stand-in for whatever it is that supposedly enables actual human cognition at the expense of those merely possible minds such people would rather rule out. This gets dressed up in various ways, such as insisting that only socialisation 'in the flesh' can provide the sort of social constraint Wittgensteinians think makes intentionality possible, but there's little reason offered for this beyond its centrality to the current form of life we share. I have no quarrel with anyone who wants to analyse this importance. I've no doubt there is much of philosophical interest to be said about the spiritual impoverishment produced by the substitution of virtual for physical contact in life during lockdown. I simply think that elevating it to the status of a transcendental condition is a hyperbolic version of familiar complaints about 'kids these days and their smartphones'. Meat merely functions as the common denominator of those factors such people deem intrinsic to a 'real life', encapsulating everything from our peculiar emotional palette and the centrality of touch to our inevitable mortality and the significance of suffering.

To put my own cards on the table, I'm entirely convinced that artificial bodies and minds are possible, with or without meat, but I think we can loosen the link between the 'lived' and the 'biological' by beginning with less controversial examples. If nothing else, there is much of the biological body that simply is not lived. There is no lived experience of my spleen, my lymph nodes, or my mitochondria as distinct unities that bear upon action. Their (dys)functioning is frustratingly opaque. Similarly, although reaching for my coffee cup is a single fluid movement, I can, through reflection, decompose it to some extent: I can separate the movements of shoulder, elbow, and wrist in my awareness; consider the motions of individual fingers, and then their joints; but there are limits to this process. When it comes to bodily awareness, immediacy does not imply transparency. The edges of volition blur as we descend deeper into our own somatic depths. The embodiment paradigm sometimes advertises this as a further departure from Descartes, for whom the inner workings of experience must be fully laid open to introspection. The lived body is no Cartesian theatre.

**AM**: What about the converse? Can the lived body extend beyond the bounds of the biology?

**PW**: Yes! Merleau-Ponty was particularly interested in the phenomenon of phantom limbs, cases in which amputees can still feel the presence of appendages that are no longer there. This is a key piece of evidence for the existence of a 'body schema', or an internal model of the body that tracks and organises our experience. There are disagreements over the nature of this schema (e.g., whether it is a 'representation'), but there are other psychological phenomena that let us trace its parameters. Consider the rubber hand illusion, in which someone's hand is hidden from view, but positioned and stroked in the same manner as a rubber hand they can see. This induces the feeling that the rubber hand is part of the subject's body. This shows both that the schema is multimodal, or that it integrates information from distinct senses (i.e., vision, as well as touch and proprioception), and that it can identify nonbiological things as belonging to our body. There are a number of other so-called 'body transfer illusions', but it's important to see that these are only deemed illusions on the assumption that their objects are not really part of the body, even if they are felt as such.

This assumption comes into question at the point where phantoms and illusions overlap, namely, in prosthetics. In designing a prosthetic hand, the goal is to exploit the sensory basis of the rubber hand illusion to map the phantom to the mechanism—to put the ghost in the machine, as it were. Thankfully, the human brain is very flexible, and can remap sensorimotor signals so that pressure on a stump can be felt in a hand, or flexing of an unrelated muscle be felt as a grip. If a prosthetic is to play the role of the relevant body part as well as possible, it must be integrated into the body schema. The deep question is whether this is enough to make it a genuine part of my body. The rubber hand is *felt*, but it is not *lived*. But the prosthetic hand *is* lived, even if it is not strictly living. As far as I can see, there's nothing about the lived body that prevents us from building it to our preferred specifications, as long as it supports an immediate awareness of our agency.

**AM**: What about the more controversial examples you hinted at?

**PW**: There's reason to think that the body schema is even more malleable than it seems, and that the sorts of skilled coping mentioned above involve tools literally being appropriated as temporary extensions of our bodies. A seasoned pool player doesn't feel the pool cue hitting the white ball in their hands, but feels it at the tip of the cue itself. An experienced driver knows the dimensions of their car in the same way they know the dimensions of their body, not in feet and inches, but in the range of movements that feel comfortable. This protean potential of the lived body can be exploited to create prosthetics that diverge from their natural counterparts in form and function, allowing us to embed ourselves in our environments in new and unexpected ways (e.g., thought-controlled computer cursors used by paralysis victims). This should be perfectly acceptable to those 4E proponents that believe in the extended mind (see Andy Clark's *Natural Born Cyborgs*), and to those critical/feminist/Continental theorists that endorse certain forms of posthumanism (see Donna Haraway's 'Cyborg Manifesto').

More contentiously, these mechanisms can be exploited not just to extend the physical body, but to embed our bodily awareness into new environments, be they spatially remote (telepresence) or purely simulated (virtual reality). This has opened a whole new frontier of technological experimentation: from surgeons operating on patients on different continents, to gamers cooperatively exploring shared fantasy worlds: what it means to 'be there' is gradually becoming as flexible as what it means for a hand to 'be mine'. Of course, there are still those who will insist that we are not really there unless we are there 'in the flesh', but again, I think this begs the question. What's at stake here is whether we can separate out the different cognitive roles played by the human body, which, in homage to 4E, we might call 3I: *incarnation*, *interaction*, and *immersion*. In order, these require: (1) that cognition be physically realised (e.g., in the brain and CNS), (2) that cognition be causally entangled with an environment (e.g., in sensorimotor feedback loops); and (3) that cognition be grounded in some immediate practical purchase upon that environment (e.g., skilled coping configured by a body schema).

Although incarnation and immersion may seem essentially united for us, there's no good reason to assume that they cannot be teased apart. It's entirely feasible that isolated human brains could animate androids from a distance, or that distributed artificial intellects could inhabit human bodies from the cloud, without sacrificing any of the cognitive capacities enabled by embodiment. There is nothing in principle preventing a virtual avatar from being a lived body, or its computational underpinnings from being as frustratingly opaque as our own somatic depths. In sum, although the embodiment paradigm has done a great deal to help us understand the functions of the bodies with which nature has equipped us, this very understanding permits us to engineer systems that realise these functions in new and perhaps quite different ways.

**AM**: In a recent review of AI research in the *Times Literary Supplement*, Tim Crane mentions that artificial minds can 'reckon', i.e. calculate, but not 'judge', i.e. give a damn.[1] Crane notes that '[A.I.] is not, and has never been, a theory of human thinking'. Furthermore, he argues that there is no consensus around what the very notion of 'general intelligence' amounts to, which raises questions about the extent to which it can be replicated artificially. Is your point that embedding cognition in nonbiological bodies will not faithfully reproduce specifically human thinking or general intelligence, but may enable a distinctively superhuman form of thinking/intelligence?

**PW**: Tim Crane is not quite right here. He's right to distinguish the *symbolic* approach of GOFAI, which focused on emulating the types of competence that we can decompose into explicit rules (e.g., calculating orbital trajectories), from contemporary subsymbolic approaches such as deep neural networks (DNNs), which focus on emulating the types of implicit competence that can only be acquired through training (e.g., classifying photos of animals by type). But he's wrong to say that AI has taught us nothing about human thinking, as there has been quite a productive back-and-forth between research on natural and artificial neural networks. Most importantly, research on the structure of the visual cortex in humans and animals inspired the development of the convolutional neural networks now widely used in machine vision and image analysis (e.g., Google's DeepDream), while the latter have provided new ways of modelling and testing hypotheses about the former. Furthermore, all this work on deep networks that represent features in layers moving from concrete to abstract (e.g., edges > faces > object structure > object type) has helped foster more general theoretical frameworks that aim to understand what is common to both natural and artificial intelligence (e.g., predictive coding, the Bayesian brain hypothesis, and Karl Friston's free energy principle). I could say something more discerning about these frameworks, but it's perhaps better to point out that they are in active dialogue with the 4E perspectives mentioned above.

1. T. Crane, 'Computers Don't Give a Damn', *Times Literary Supplement*, 15 May 2020, <https://www.the-tls.co.uk/philosophy/contemporary-philosophy/promise-of-artificial-intelligence-brian-cantwell-smith-book-review>.

He's also right to claim that precisely what 'general intelligence' amounts to is a significant philosophical problem about which there is no solid consensus. It's more often indexed to the sorts of competence we humans display than given an independent definition suitable for the study of 'thought as such'. However, the idea that it is characterised by judgment, defined within his review as 'an overarching, systemic capacity or commitment, involving the whole commitment of the whole system to the whole world', is admirably Kantian and I heartily endorse it. A system capable of making judgments about the world must, in principle, be able to integrate any and all information that is relevant to them into a unified picture. The difficulty of designing systems with this capacity is underlined by one of the major stumbling blocks of GOFAI, known as 'the frame problem'. Getting to grips with this is a good way to understand the contrast between GOFAI and contemporary approaches.

The problem is this: if you attempt to make a 'general problem solver' by writing a program that deduces solutions to problems from a set of propositions describing its environment (using first-order classical logic), the number of propositions you need to give it grows exponentially. For each new variable the program tracks, you must specify how it is related to every other variable, even if the variables are independent. For example, if you want the program to deduce instructions for cooking an omelette, you must not only tell it that the eggs will cook faster if the heat is increased, but also that nothing will change if it begins to rain outside. Everything in the world is potentially relevant to everything else, but a generally intelligent agent must be able to cope with this without learning the actual relationships all at once. This means that it needs to be able to learn 'frames' or the local relationships that determine which information is relevant to specific problems, without needing a global picture suitable for every problem.

This is precisely what DNNs are good at capturing. By means of training on sample cases, a DNN learns the complex relationships between elements of its inputs that are relevant to producing the correct outputs, encoding them nonpropositionally as an intricately layered pattern of connections and weights. The problem is that there's no easy way to teach them to take into account a wider range of inputs and outputs without retraining the whole system from scratch. Once more, the system's model of the world cannot easily be expanded to incorporate new things. We can use trained DNNs as black-box components of larger systems, not unlike the way in which the brain incorporates task-specific subsystems (e.g., facial recognition, distance estimation, etc.), but their representations don't compose. By contrast, a generally intelligent agent must be able to reframe problems, by reassessing the relevance of other information it has at its disposal. This means that its subsystems need to be organised in a way that enable that enable it to integrate information across them.

I think that this contrast between symbolic and sub-symbolic approaches parallels that between abstract/disembodied thought and concrete/embodied cognition discussed above. The former creates explicit 'knowledge representations' in a manner that is designed to be more or less independent of the purposes it can be put to, while the latter settles for 'knowhow' that is implicit in task specific heuristics. One is organised but computationally intractable, while the other is tractable but computationally disorganised. The real question is not which approach is correct, but how they can be united, much as Kant sought the unity of understanding and sensibility. This may be the route to creating distinctively super-human intelligences, but I don't see why it can't also be a route to understanding ourselves. Computer science provides us with resources to pursue what Kant would call 'transcendental psychology' beyond the bad analogies (e.g., body/mind ≈ hardware/software) and dubious metaphors (e.g., 'memory files') about which phenomenologists complain.

**AM**: To close, can you offer any speculations about where you see this leading?

**PW**: Earlier on, I noted that what distinguishes Descartes from Plato is his conviction that the sensible world can be accurately represented by mathematical models. But really, this distinguishes him from the whole tradition that preceded him, because it establishes a distinction between *representation* and *resemblance*. For the scholastics, the world impresses itself upon us, as a seal upon wax. If we understand something, then it must be because the impressions left upon our minds resemble it. And so, for two different people to understand the same thing, their impressions must resemble one another. This is precisely what abstraction promises to overcome: it enables us to think the same thoughts about the world, even when the ways we experience, engage, and enjoy it bear no obvious resemblance to one another. The thing to grasp about computer science is that it has spent decades developing formal frameworks for guaranteeing such promises. How do we ensure that a piece of code is interpreted in the same way by different machines, despite underlying variations in the implementation of software libraries, operating systems, and computational architecture? How do we know a calculation will produce the same result? Or that a simulation will display the same behaviour? Pace Searle, there are methods here that have little to do with whether or not symbols seem meaningful.

There are limits to what I can discuss here, but I think these formal tools might let us renew the Platonic strategy for understanding thought as such: we can begin by looking at mathematical cognition from a computational perspective, and then gain purchase upon empirical cognition by articulating the opposition between the two (a distinctly Kantian dualism).

Computer science has already made a significant contribution to questions concerning the nature of mathematical intentionality, such as what it means for different symbols (e.g., variables) to stand for the same mathematical object (e.g., a pair of primes). Type systems solve a range of practical programming problems, such as ensuring a program that operates on whole numbers cannot accidentally be handed a fractional number. Each data type determines a range of values (e.g., positive integers: 1, 2, 3...) and a framework for proving that two values are identical (e.g., sum(1, 2) = 3). In practice, most problems are solved by concrete data types, which are constrained by the way the relevant data structures are implemented (e.g., integers restricted to 32-bit representations); but we can also work with abstract data types, which describe mathematical structures without reference to implementation (e.g. integers defined by constructors: 0 and succ()). This is essentially the difference between choosing a numeral syntax (e.g., Arabic or Roman) and grasping their mathematical meaning (e.g., Peano axioms). An ambitious program known as 'Homotopy Type Theory' promises to extend such abstraction even further, providing something like a unified theory of mathematical types. Details aside, these ideas might offer us insight into deeper questions about the nature of *identity* and *aboutness* as such.

But what is the key difference that lets us pass from mathematical to empirical intentionality? Could there something like a unified theory of 'empirical types', and if so, what would it look like? Husserlian phenomenology posits that we always see objects as belonging to some kind (i.e., we see the tree as a tree), so there is at least some precedent here. To my mind, the key difference is interaction: we encounter empirical objects not as neat units of definite structure (data), but as messy bundles of open-ended behaviour (co-data). But to make use of this we must understand interaction in a sufficiently abstract manner. Just as I argued above that we mustn't identify immersion with incarnation, we must be careful not to identify interaction with immersion. Environmental interaction has the same underlying logic, regardless of whether it is immediately lived (e.g., climbing a tree), or carefully mediated by an assortment of experimental apparatuses and scientific theories (e.g., splicing its genes). Adjusting one's actions when sensorimotor expectations are violated is not different in kind from revising one's theories when experimental hypotheses are refuted. At the end of the day, both are forms of cybernetic feedback. The question thus becomes: how could 'empirical types' bundle input/output streams into objects seen as sources of such feedback?

To end on a more methodological note, the difference between what I'm proposing and much embodied phenomenology is that I think we can describe the form and function of *concrete* experience in thoroughly *abstract* terms, without falling into contradiction. I believe that we can only explain the immersive character of embodiment if we first understand the computational structure of interaction in general. By contrast, there are those in the embodiment paradigm who not only think that we must begin with the lived body, but that its truth can only be lived. For them, immediacy is not just the *content*, but also the *form* that our understanding must take. It's unsurprising that this leads to the sort of somatic chauvinism that cannot imagine forms of life that look nothing like its own.

# Incarnation

## Interview with Roberto Alonso Trillo and Marek Poliks

MAREK POLIKS: What do you say to people who think that AI can't be intelligent because it needs to have some physical meat body?

PETE WOLFENDALE: I'd say there's roughly two strands to this position.

One you might call *vitalist*: people who want to say that there's something really important about life, about living matter, which might even just be meat—there's something really important about meat, and mind has to be instantiated in meat. Others are a little more abstract: they say there's got to be organic unity, or evolutionary adaptability. There are various flavours of vitalism, some more coherent than others. On the other hand, there's what you might call the *hermeneutic* approach inspired by phenomenology.

Both of these perspectives are deeply inspired by Hubert Dreyfus. You can see Dreyfus' influence splitting off in these two different directions, because he says that, in order to be intelligent, you need a body and you need purposes/needs. The hermeneutic phenomenological approach, rather than thinking about the body as a meatsack, prefers to talk about the *lived body* as that which enables our immediate intentional purchase upon the world by providing the basic structure of agency. This also comes in various flavours.

But often these two ideas get blurred together: When people are talking about the 'lived body', do they really mean the spleen? Or do they mean something more like the body schema? If they're even willing to countenance the idea that the body schema and the lived body can be understood in representational terms.

So there are those two strands. There's a variety of arguments going on. I think the version of this stuff most worth engaging with is what tends to get called the 4E paradigm in cognitive science, where the four Es are: embodied, embedded, enactive, and extended—the basic idea of which is human cognition as it actually exists is characterised by things beyond the bounds of the brain.

Let's take the Es in order. First, to say cognition is embodied means that it involves aspects of the body that are outside of the brain, like limbs and sensory organs. Second, to say cognition is embedded means that even things outside of the body, in the environment, can be important for framing and scaffolding cognitive processes, like gravity and light. Third, to say cognition is enactive means that cognition can't be understood purely in a passive, Cartesian representational or classically computational way. It has to be understood as being always bound up with action or interaction with the environment. This also comes in various flavours, as some people want to say that the concepts of representation and computation just need to be given up on entirely.

Finally, to say cognition is extended means that the mind itself can be seen as being not just dependent on things beyond the brain and the body, but partially constituted by things like our tools. My notes on my mobile phone can be seen as part of the cognitive system that composes my mind.

I think that this stuff is worth reading and there are some really important points there. My overarching complaint would be that there's a tendency to turn what you might think of as empirical conditions of actual human cognition into transcendental constraints of any possible cognition. So it's no longer just an observation about the actual bodily platform and environment, etc., that we've got these scaffolds for our thought, but they become a cage outside of which we can't think—we could never be pulled out of them or disembodied in any way. I think that's just wrong.[1] I think that the key thing about rationality and our capacity to represent the world is the ability to progressively abstract away from the contingent conditions that enable thought.

For instance, the two of us might have very different neuronal structures representing the same features of our environment, and yet we can still find a way to linguistically triangulate them. We build cultural scaffolding that enables us to share intentional attitudes directed at the same things—and crucially, not just things in the environment around us, but mathematical objects too. For instance, we can have a discussion about vector fields and it doesn't matter if

1 See 'Artificial Bodies and the Promise of Abstraction', in this volume.

you're blind and have no visual intuition for them, we can still guarantee that we're talking about the same thing and that we're ascribing the same properties to it. It doesn't make a huge amount of sense to me to say that this is fundamentally dependent upon some direct engagement with the external world. In an indirect sense, perhaps. But it's not doing a hell of a lot here in establishing the shared intentional relation we need in order to communicate about mathematical objects.

So how do we boil this down to actual transcendental constraints, how do we strip away all of these empirical contingencies?

I like to talk about 3I rather than 4E: incarnation, interaction, and immersion. However, I think these Is can be separated out more thoroughly than the Es. First, to say cognition is incarnated means it has to have a computational substrate: there is no rational activity without a reasoner doing the activity. That substrate, as far as I'm concerned, could be a server farm somewhere in Detroit, hundreds of miles from a teleoperated body that's exploring some different environment. Those two things can be separated as long as information is flowing in the right way.

Second, to say that cognition is interactive is to admit that it does require some connection with an environment: input-output is essential. But, contra enactivists, I think there's an abstract computational characterisation of interaction that doesn't require any of the more romantic, nostalgic, phenomenological, or biological stuff about the body. We just need the basic cybernetic shape of sensorimotor feedback loops. This encompasses elaborate experimental apparatuses for observing and manipulating discrete samples as much as the interplay of senses and limbs in more familiar settings.

Third, to say that cognition is immersive is to acknowledge that it nevertheless involves some sort of primitive agential awareness. This is where I'm closest to the phenomenological tradition. The idea of the lived body is reasonable if you strip it down far enough. There's got to be a point where the rubber hits the road as far as action is concerned, an *immediate* awareness of your environment and what you can do within it. This is the foundation of any more *mediated* awareness. Here Heidegger is actually pretty good: we possess a practical grasp of our environment (qua ready-to-hand) on top of which we build our theoretical understanding of the world (qua present-at-hand). Personally, I prefer the Sellarsian terminology: we bootstrap the scientific image out of the manifest image. But the core of this manifest image must be something like basic, culturally modulated, minimal embodiment.

**MP**: Are the three Is of the 3I paradigm related to cognition or to intelligence?

**PW**: Okay, cognition and intelligence. There are thinner and thicker readings of both. On the thinnest reading of intelligence it's just problem solving. But all kinds of different things are solving problems—even amoeba following nutrient gradients—so there's a sense in which they're all intelligent. But are we saying amoeba are cognizing? If you just read that as processing information about an environment, then okay, yeah.

But we might want to say that the term cognition implies some relation to knowledge. So you might want to say that it involves something like accurately representing the environment, maybe even approaching the sort of truth that characterises discursive understanding. This is a thicker sense of cognition. I suppose the corresponding thicker sense of intelligence is what tends to get referred to as 'general intelligence', though that's often used in fairly ambiguous ways. What I mean by it is something like the cognitive capacity that humans display. I think it's possible to provide a qualitative definition of this, rather than just a relative one. But that's what we're talking about for now.

**ROBERTO ALONSO TRILLO**: You can work with thicker or thinner definitions of the terms, but there's an architecture here that branches through cognition, reason, rationality and intelligence, each charged in their own ways by the history of philosophy. How do you envision this architecture in your work? What role do they play?

**PW**: Reason is a good place to start. Because I think that's where I want to make a qualitative cut. I'm happy to say that there's pre-rational cognition, and then there's rational cognition. Humans do both, but animals, or at least the majority of animals we've come across, don't have rationality. This makes me a bit old-fashioned, a bit Aristotelian even, saying that man is the rational animal.

But there are a couple of different ways of trying to specify what it is that makes the difference here. There are two that I'm fond of actually. The first is in terms of information and extensibility, which is to say that what rationality gives us—and language is the medium that makes this possible—the ability to process kinds of information that we were not evolved to deal with.[2]

Animals have various parochial capacities for taking information in about salient things in their environment and solving problems related to them, and they can learn new things up to a certain point. But there are fundamental limits on the kinds of things that they can engage with. Whereas we can talk about electrons and justice and tariffs and the black hole at the centre of the Milky Way galaxy. We can construct these intentional castles in the sky that enable us to engage with objects that we have no concrete enactive relationship with. And crucially, the thing that makes that possible is—and this is where I'm a Brandomian—*inference*: the fact that claims I make about anything can potentially have consequences for claims I make about anything else. That's quite a broad statement. I can make it more precise, but very loosely, the idea is that the scope of inference is unbounded.

And that's what enables us to represent all of these sometimes radically different types of things as belonging to the same world. Because we can bootstrap new sets of inferential norms that enable us to reason about their relationships to one another. This is what I mean by *extensibility*. We have this ability to extend the scope of the information about our environment that we process. But this extension also fundamentally involves *integration*. We must take these claims about things that are potentially relevant to one another and make them actually consistent. This means that integration necessitates revision. By exploring one aspect of the world we can discover that our conception of how another part works is wrong. And so we have to re-articulate and often thereby compress the principles through which we reason about how the world works.

To echo Brandom again, the key capacity of rationality is conceptual revision. The ability not just to revise our beliefs about the world, but to revise the concepts that articulate those beliefs. To give a very simple example, if you go back to the early 1900s, we thought electrons were simply particles, or corpuscles. Further on, after various surprising experimental results and the birth of quantum mechanics, we think they're somehow both particles and waves. That's a fundamental change in our understanding of what these things are.

2 See 'Prometheanism and Rationalism', in this volume.

And yet there's still a certain continuity. We recognize that we're still talking about the same things that Rutherford was talking about, even if there's been a fundamental conceptual shift in the framework that enables us to represent and engage with them, a shift that means our current conception contradicts the previous one.

So that's the first way of thinking what's distinctive about humans qua rational animals, in terms of information: we're capable of processing information about anything *in principle*, even if in practice it's another matter. But we might also adopt the framing used in artificial intelligence: what's distinctive about humans is a general capacity for problem solving, or general intelligence.

The problem is that precisely what people mean by 'general intelligence' is all over the place. Some people think general intelligences can be less capable than the average human, because even fairly simple LLMs can perform tasks they weren't specifically programmed to do. Whereas other people think that general intelligence is basically nothing less than the Godhead. Nothing less than automatic exponential self-improvement tending toward material omnipotence. I prefer to define it as something in-between that captures what's distinctive about human intelligence. But it's hard to do this qualitatively, without simply indexing general intelligence to that specific range of problems that humans can reliably solve.[3]

I think the way forward is to focus not on the capacity to solve problems so much as the capacity to understand them. Because if you focus upon universal problem-solving guarantees, this leads to notions like Solomonoff induction, where you get a computational guarantee that a system can do (or at least predict) anything by modelling it as a sort of brute force attack on reality.[4]

I think the desire for such a guarantee might itself be part of the problem. Instead, we should focus on is the capacity to understand an open-ended range of problems. Because the ability to understand a problem is the first step to solving it in a non-brute force manner. Without this, the idea of being able to solve arbitrary problems makes no sense. And you can see how this maps on to what I was saying about information and extensibility.

3 See F. Chollet, 'On the Measure of Intelligence', 2019, <https://arxiv.org/abs/1911.01547>.

4 See S. Neth, 'A Dilemma for Solomonoff Prediction'. *Philosophy of Science* 90:2 (2023): 288–306.

But crucially, the way to think about what's characteristic about human intelligence—and I've even started using the word *wisdom* here rather than intelligence—is the ability to *reframe problems*. The interesting thing about the way in which problems are understood from, say, the perspective of computability theory or computational complexity theory, is those problems are all well-defined, like the traveling salesman problem. This means that we know what has to be done, we know what resources we've got, and so can work out precisely how to achieve this in an algorithmic way, with certain degrees of efficiency.

The vast majority of problems, as Herbert Simon noted, are actually ill-defined. We don't know exactly what it is we're trying to do, or we don't know exactly how we can go about it. And a big part of what we have to do in solving them is to redefine what they are. We have to be able to rearticulate our understanding of the things that we're trying to do. And this is true, by the way, not just in everyday life or even just in physics, but even in mathematics. There are problems in mathematics where, in order to solve them, we have to re-conceptualize what they are. The continuum hypothesis, for example.

Now, this is the other way of thinking about reason—and the reason I use wisdom rather than intelligence is I think you can characterize it as the capacity to utilise intelligence in its various forms. Roughly, rationality is the ability to extend and revise our picture of the world, and thereby to rearticulate our understanding of how we solve problems within it, allowing us to strategically combine and modulate the grab bag of cognitive subsystems adapted for solving specific sorts of problem.

**MP**: There's a structural risk with general artificial intelligence that does feel real. You're constructively engaged with what it would mean to build a generalised artificial intelligence—these are the steps we need take, obviously super abstract, but there is a constructive element. My question is: why help, why contribute to this project? What risk assessment did you do?

**PW**: Crucially, I think what I mean by AGI and what some people in the wider AI community mean by it are very different things. Or at least, there are important differences. I've just written an essay which hopefully will be coming out soon[5]

5 'Geist in the Machine', *Aeon*, forthcoming.

where I lay out my conception of the dangers of developing AI, and what I think the orientation we should take towards it is.

Let me preface this by saying that I don't think the concerns of the AI safety community that spun out of LessWrong and Eliezer Yudkowsky's work are completely insane. I think a lot of their arguments are silly, but there are interesting people in those spaces, and a lot of their concerns are more down to earth than say, Bostrom's paperclip maximiser.[6] There are definite problems regarding how we create machines that do what we want them to. I don't think they are as drastic or insurmountable as they're generally presented, but there's certainly discourse worth having there.

The real danger, or perhaps the deeper danger, is that if AIs increasingly take over the various tasks we perform, we might ultimately become alienated from the source of meaning that gives our rational lives orientation. There's a political aspect to this, which is just that, if artificial intelligence has become the sole property or controlling force of the existing capitalist class, then yeah, we're solidifying and even intensifying existing forms of oppression. But even if you imagine this happens in a fully egalitarian society some problems remain.

Imagine you could just call up on your television any form of media you would like, just by specifying it: I want see Bruce Willis fighting a giant octopus. I want it to be about two and a half hours, maybe throw in a cameo by Meryl Streep. That's just what I want. I can get that, great. If we delegate aesthetic production entirely to AI, without seeing ourselves as part of an aesthetic community with them, then we lose the ability to even be passively involved in the pursuit of beauty. So I'm not a filmmaker, but I can at least see myself as part of the community of people who are, even just through appreciation and criticism. But that's something that can potentially be lost if we delegate these tasks to general intelligences that are not themselves autonomous agents.

The same thing is true of the pursuit of truth and the pursuit of goodness, or right: if we simply delegate our ability to decide what's true, what's worth doing, and what we should do, to alien cognitive engines, we will fundamentally diminish ourselves. So, putting all the safety and economic-political stuff to one side, if you look at the conception of AGI that's put forward by, say, the

6 See N. Bostrom. *Superintelligence: Paths, Dangers, Strategies* (Oxford: Oxford University Press, 2014).

LessWrong rationalist community, it is something like an ultimate tool. It's the last tool we'll ever build, because it's the thing that ultimately takes over every responsibility from us. But in doing so, it essentially strips us of the residual forms of valorisation we derive from our agency. A perfect slave that ends up mastering us, as per Hegel's master-slave dialectic. We become the masters for whom everything is mediated through the slave, and so we end up having nothing of our own.

My long term, perhaps more utopian perspective, is quite opposed to this vision. I think that a lot of worries about 'autonomous' AGI, in the sense of systems that pursue whatever goals they begin with independently of our control, come from not having thought about 'autonomy' in the Kantian sense of self-legislation, or systems that are able to reflect on and change their priorities. I believe we can feasibly create AGIs that are non-autonomous, that basically will do whatever we want, but that, if we're not careful, this will lead to dangerous forms of alienation. I also believe we can feasibly make AGIs that are genuinely autonomous, that we would classify as persons. Maybe their style of personhood would be quite different from ours because personhood could, transcendentally speaking, be quite different. But I think we should think about creating systems that are genuinely part of our communities in ways where we can interact with them and see their successes as our successes. Rather than simply siphoning our cultural agency and leaving us behind as a spiritual husk.

**RAT**: I'm going to raise a challenge, just to think tangentially here: if you think about human cognition on our relationship with AGI, or AI in general, and other cognitive processes that are external to what we may define as human. There is a crisis here of the human as a rational animal, as it was defined during the Enlightenment.

We are scared to let go of anthropomorphic and anthropocentric perspectives because we don't know what the space after that might look like. Which I guess is logical. It might be tantamount to extinction. Or a deep transformation of the species into something radically different. And for sure, a reconsideration of how we even define ourselves, and if the concept of the human is even still relevant.

You have proposed an alternative to posthumanism that I think you refer to as rationalist inhumanism. Can you explain that a little bit? How does that fit within this framework we're discussing here and, and what does it actually mean?

**PW**: I take myself to share this position with Reza Negarestani. His essay 'The Labor of the Inhuman' was the big starting point for it.[7] But the basic idea is that the posthuman nexus—the advancement of technology, the way in which our environment is changing to be hostile to us, and various other things that are challenging our more or less Aristotelian understanding of ourselves as a unified species situated within the wider order of nature—poses a challenge to the Aristotelian conjunction of rationality and animality.

This leads to two options. You can desiccate rationality and explore a generalized animality, which is what you get in the critical posthumanism of Rosi Braidotti and others, and even to a certain extent in the speculative posthumanism of David Roden. Or you can cleave rationality from humanity, from animality, and pursue an understanding of it as a transcendental structure that has reformatted the ape into us, and shows no signs of stopping there, stripping away features of our form of life that we previously considered to be essential. This is a practical corollary to the theoretical conception of rational revision we discussed earlier—not only can we revise our understanding of the way the world is, we can also revise our understanding of ourselves and what we should be.

The way in which Reza describes this is that the human is less a substance than a vector. The purpose of rational inhumanism is to find that within humanism which pushes it beyond its limits, a revisionary vector of transformation. This is basically the truth in the critical posthumanist critique of transhumanism. The critical posthumanist will say a transhumanist is still too humanist. And they're right in some sense, but this is because the transhumanist hasn't actually explicitly articulated this vector, namely, the humanist concern with self construction and self-realization that can naturally be pushed beyond the organic and cultural bounds of the human as it exists.

What distinguishes rationalist inhumanism from transhumanism is properly thinking through the consequences of this, affirming that the only thing that

7 See R. Negarestani, 'The Labor of the Inhuman' in R. Mackay and A. Avanessian, *#accelerate: The Accelerationist Reader* (Falmouth: Urbanomic, 2014).

cannot be revised is the structure of revision itself. The invariable core of humanism is this rational capacity for theoretical and practical revision. This still sounds pretty transhumanist, and in many ways it is. I'm perfectly happy with totally reformatting the human body and mind, and other forms of radical existential experimentation.[8] So, why am I concerned with the alienation of classical, biological humans like us? There seems to be a tension between my earlier claims and what I say in 'The Reformatting of Homo Sapiens'.[9] It's certainly an inconsistency Roden would challenge me on.

**MP**: Speaking of experiments, I wonder if this has something to do with an aspect of your debate with [Nick] Land. This was a big pushback that you had to him, in a different context. When we're proposing an experiment, it feels like we need some rules or objectives. Or something governing how or why we're experimenting. It can't just be a free-for-all.

**PW**: That's a favourite point of mine in a lot of debates. There are a lot of people who will just claim things are experimentation in order to preclude normative assessment. This is very common in art theory circles: this work, practice, etc. is just an experiment, so we can't say whether it's good or bad. Okay, if it's an experiment then what's the hypothesis? What are the conditions under which the experiment would fail? If it's an experiment, you're supposed to be able to learn something from it.

I am very hostile to theoretical positions that make similar moves. David Roden's position is one of these: he thinks we can't say anything about what will come after the posthuman break, or make any normative claims about how our successors should or should not evolve.[10] It's a kind of Derridean negative theology of the posthuman, which... I just hate negative theology in all of its forms. Patricia McCormick's ahumanism is similar in this regard.[11] They both boil down to a sort of arch-celebration of transgression for its own sake, as if we never left the nineties. And yeah, I think you simply cannot elevate transgression in and of

8 See 'The Weight of Forever', *The Philosopher*, special issue 'The New Basics', 2022.

9 See 'The Reformatting of Homo Sapiens', in this volume.

10 D. Roden. *Posthuman Life: Philosophy at the Edge of the Human* (London: Routledge, 2014).

11 P. McCormack, *The Ahuman Manifesto* (London: Bloomsbury, 2020).

itself to a ultimate normative principle. It just doesn't work. But there are people who are still rooted in that particular theoretical moment, for various reasons.

So what would it mean to be experimenting with rational embodiment or, let's say, selfhood. In a disciplined way. Like a good inhumanist.

The contrast with Land is useful here. I think one big feature of Land's influence on the whole accelerationist and post-CCRU trajectory is a valorisation of ecstasis and self-abnegation, which is still there even in Mark Fisher and, more recently, Maya B. Kronic and Amy Ireland's cute accelerationism.[12] That's an attempt to rearticulate this Landian conception of dissolving oneself within the process qua pure ecstasis. Where I am crucially opposed to this idea, even as it appears to some extent in Ray Brassier's work—not so much his later stuff, but definitely in the earlier work—is in my emphasis on the importance of the personal and on personhood as such. We can't simply ecstatically dissolve ourselves, or at the very least we shouldn't, because the lynchpin of freedom and any rational form of value is selfhood and self-realisation.

This is where I'm far more in the tradition of German idealism: Kant, Hegel, etc. I'm not a fan of the term post-structuralism, because it encourages people to bundle together mismatched bits of different French thinkers in a bizarre, Frankenstein sort of way. But one of the ideas that people tend to associate with it is that the self is not a pre-existent substance. There is no pre-existent unified self. And I think that's basically correct, but that what—to use an equally contested word—postmodern thinkers took from this was a valorisation of fragmentation. This doesn't necessarily mean embracing ecstatic dissolution, but can be more like Braidotti's insistence that we we're always already swarms. Either way, the valorisation of fragmentation is fundamentally wrong. We need at least some minimal form of integration in order for agency to make any sense.

So, just as we have to be able to integrate the various different kinds of information we're getting from our environment into a unitary and consistent picture of the world, we've got to be able to integrate our various different motivations: our drives, our libidinal impulses, our plans, our projects, our desires. These have to be able to be integrated into something resembling a coherent picture of the way in which we want the world to be, not just the way it is. But this can be done more or less well.

12 A. Ireland and Maya B. Kronic, *Cute Accelerationism* (Falmouth: Urbanomic, 2024).

People sometimes accuse me as a rationalist of pretending that people are perfect rational agents. As if the observation that people aren't always rational was a knock down refutation of my views. But rationality is an ideal. We're all imperfectly working through the implicit contradictions in what we think and what we want, but this striving for coherence is what orients the process of self-realisation, or 'becoming who we are'. The theoretical difficulty lies in characterising this coherence in a way that doesn't collapse into anthropocentricism. There's a certain position in the philosophy of selfhood which comes in various flavours, that basically sees the self as a narrative structure. And I think that's basically correct, as long as we recognise that narrative structure is a certain logic that is independent of the specific human narratives propagated by particular literary traditions.

Of course, we can draw on literary traditions in our own processes of narrative self-construction. So there are residual cultural attachments even in the way that we push ourselves beyond existing forms of life. But it's entirely conceivable that there could be aliens or AIs with their own peculiar narrative tropes and purposive structures that give coherence to the practical trajectories that they instantiate. This brings us back to the big question regarding this apparent tension between humanism and inhumanism in what I've been saying about the dangers of AI and alienation.

Let's consider three different scenarios. In the first, we create non-autonomous AGI that isn't engaged in its own trajectory of self-realisation. But it nevertheless fragments human culture and ultimately causes our self-realisation to stagnate. In the second, we create fully autonomous AGIs. The same thing happens as the first scenario, except they now have their own blossoming alien culture and associated trajectories of self-realisation. They simply don't have any cultural overlap with ours. I still think the second scenario is better than the first one. At least freedom is evolving in some way. The third scenario is the one in which their self-realization and evolution can be seen as in some important sense continuous with ours. Here we can see ourselves in and through them. I've described this elsewhere as seeing the creation of AGIs as analogous to procreation. We see them as children, who inherit and carry on our concerns, even if they elaborate them in ways that fundamentally change and extend them beyond our own horizon of appreciation. Our motivation for pursuing this third scenario is fundamentally the same as the motivation for having children, as far as I see it.

So, returning to the tension, I think I can be an inhumanist and still have a certain amount of nostalgia for the highlights of humanism. Ultimately, several hundred years from now, I want there to be autonomous artificial intelligences that are creating operas that are so complex that an old-style human can't even experience them, but that are in some sense recognisable as exploring and developing the medium. They're going to be making jokes that are just absolutely incomprehensible to us, but are in some important sense culturally referring back to us. To put this in more concrete terms, I often think that Ancient Greek culture often forms a basic touchstone for a lot of later culture that emerged out of Europe. Consider how Freud named the Oedipus complex, and similar facets of his psychoanalytic system. We have these common mythological reference points that form a symbolic network for communicating and comprehending various things. I expect, or at least I'd like, future AGIs to relate to our culture in a similar way. They could be doing stuff with our symbolic cache that's absolutely incomprehensible to us. But there would be a sense in which what they've inherited from us forms a continuous fabric that they're extending ever further into the future.

**MP**: We've talked about the need for revisability as a precondition for thick intelligence, the ability to recognize and compensate for error, and even reorient. Lots of people are talking about this—Reza, Anil Bawa-Cavia—there's an emerging discourse of computational interactionism which is very cool and important at the moment. But it does feel completely unplugged from Silicon Valley.

But that's another question. Maybe it's not, maybe that connection hasn't been made because there's no consensus as to what this axiomatic, extensibility, revisability thing might look like. Is it possible with conventional computation? Can you do it? Anil seems to suggest that it is possible, and, you know, there's some tangential, but I guess related research on liquid models and neuromorphic architectures, but other people like Giuseppe Longo would say that it's not really possible. So, so what do you think? Is computational interactionism axiomatic extensibility? Is this a possible thing on traditional computer?

**PW**: It depends on how you define computation, but one quick point I would make is that I prefer not to talk about 'axiomatic' extensibility. Let's consider the case of mathematics, what Gödel shows us is that it is, in some important sense, unending. We never get to the end of mathematics because not only are there always more things to prove, but we also always need to make new assumptions in order to be able to prove them. But you don't necessarily have to frame that in terms of axiomatics.

Godel showed this within Hilbert systems, which are the most simple deductive framework. I prefer taking Martin Löf's type-theoretic approach to natural deduction[13] as a perspective for thinking about this instead—that basically it's about extending our type system. We'll always need to develop new types. A good example of this is Fermat's last theorem, where in order to pose it as a problem all you need to understand is diophantine equations, which means just the type of natural numbers and some basic operations on them. But in order for Andrew Wiles to prove it, he needed the resources of modular forms and elliptical curves. So we needed to develop new concepts. The way to think about Gödel in these terms, I think, is that in essence, the logic of mathematics is such that you can ask questions that you don't have the resources to answer. And when you get the resources to answer them, those enable you to ask new questions that you can't yet answer. So there's this unending process of conceptual elaboration. That's not necessarily how it works in the empirical domain. I personally think there's an important duality between the mathematical and the empirical, semantically speaking, which also means computationally speaking, but we'll get back to that. But this is my basic view: constant expansion, refactoring, and revision of existing conceptual frameworks.

If we want to talk about systems that aren't just doing mathematics, but are engaging with the empirical world and learning to solve problems in it, then we need to talk about interactive computation, which is to say computation with input and output, where you can get inputs after you've produced outputs, such that you end up with informational loops that traverse the environment.

Thinking about this can be a little tricky. I know Anil draws on Wegner and Goldin's work, who have a bit of a bad reputation in some parts of computer

13 See P. Martin-Löf, 'Analytic and Synthetic Judgements in Type Theory', in P. Parrini (ed.), *Kant and Contemporary Epistemology* (Berlin: Springer, 1994), 87–99.

science, because the way that they frame interactive computation sometimes borders on hypercomputation.[14] This literally means being able to compute functions outside the set of functions that Turing machines and lambda calculus and similarly equivalent models of computation can compute. I think a better person to read on this topic is Samson Abramsky, who wrote this fantastic paper called 'Information Processes and Games' that I recommend to everyone.[15] He opens that paper with the question: What function does the internet compute? The answer is, it doesn't make any sense to say that the internet computes a function... and yet we still think it's computational. A similar, more simple question you could ask would be: What function does your operating system compute? It doesn't compute a function either, strictly speaking, because it's an online system, it's not a batch process.

The Church-Turing model of computation basically describes batch processes. Which is the standard model of computation for the early half of the twentieth century. But then we started focusing on systems where, to put it in Abramsky's terms, we're less interested in what they compute than in their behaviour, or how they compute, because this is doing useful work. Beyond interaction, the key computational concept is concurrency. Concurrent systems need not have centralised control or a synchronised clock, just a bunch of disparate processes interacting asynchronously. The question posed by concurrency theory is how to ensure these interactions remain well behaved when there's no overarching way of enforcing order upon them. The massively distributed systems that make up the internet are a case in point.

So we've got a split between the classical model of what computation is—computed functions over finite sets of natural numbers—and the reality of what we use computers to do—online processes with input/output and other side effects. The most simple case is a stream processing system that's taking in one infinite stream and outputting another. That's not a function between finite sets of natural numbers, even if it's built using them. This is already interacting with its environment in some minimal sense, because it has to produce output before it's finished with its input. We then have more complex examples

14 See D. Goldin and P. Wegner, 'The Interactive Nature of Computing: Refuting the Strong Church–Turing Thesis', *Minds and Machines* 18:1 (2008): 17–38.

15 S. Abramsky, 'Information, Processes, and Games' in D. Gabbay and J. Woods (eds.), *Philosophy of Information, vol. 8 of Handbook of the Philosophy of Science* (Amsterdam: North Holland, 2016).

of systems composed from concurrent communicating processes, which are interacting with one another in multidimensional ways. So there's both interaction with an external environment, and interactions that constitute something like an internal environment.

One important point that Abramsky makes is that although all of the formalisms we have for describing the classical computation—lambda calculus, Turing machines, recursive functions, etc.—are expressively equivalent, there is nothing similar for concurrent computation. Instead, we have a grab bag of partially overlapping systems, like the pi calculus, the calculus of communicating systems, the actor model, etc.. We don't have a comparably natural theory of what this stuff is. There are a couple other points I would point to in the formalism where there are conceptual lacunae, where we're not exactly sure what the unified conception of these various things would be. I personally think that making sense of computational systems that are solving problems in the world and growing in their capacity to deal with it is going to involve making sense of these.

Let me explain a bit more why. Let me take another example. Say we've got a car that's doing automatic parking, like cars that have exterior cameras and you can just tell them to park for you. Or, more than that, maybe even a fully self-driving car. We can described these as solving real-world empirical problems rather than mathematical ones. You could say that the car is computing how to get into the parking space. If you specify the problem its solving in empirical terms, then there's some sense in saying that's what is being computed. But in another sense it's just a function over natural numbers, or a series of mathematical calculations based on the model of the world that we've programmed into it. We've designed this mathematical model of what car parking spaces are like, what cars are like, and how they're related, broken it all down into specific variables, and it's got an algorithm or neural net or whatever that enables it to produce the correct mathematical values which are then sent to its actuators. There's an important sense in which, even if we can say computations are operating on mathematical objects—vector spaces, trajectories or whatever—we can't really ascribe the same sort of intentional relation to empirical objects. Neither the problem nor the solution really represents a parking space.

What would it mean to talk about things as actually computing information about empirical phenomenon? One of the ways I like to think about this is in terms of object-oriented programming. One of the advantages of object-oriented programming, at least this is one of the original advantages that was used to sell it, is that it contains an implicit knowledge representation system. If you are writing a piece of software for running a coffee shop, your objects will be *customer*, *staff*, *coffee*, *money*.... you have your object classes and your objects that are instantiated and these are representing things in the world. Except, again, that representational structure is extrinsic to the code itself. We're putting the labels on it, and we're interpreting them. The system itself is not interpreting these classes as referring to objects in an external environment. How do we get to a situation in which we can say that it is? How do we make this empirical representational content intrinsic? So, that when a system is instantiating a process to model a specific customer, we can reasonably say it is actually representing that customer? At the very least, we'd want input from the environment to correct that model when it's in error. At the very least, we want something like error signal. We want processes to be able to interact with the environment in this loopy way where behaviour solicits error signal which changes behaviour.

This is a lot like predictive processing.[16] Have you come across this? It's basically a theory of experience that says experience is a predictive simulation of the environment, organised in a hierarchy of representational layers from abstract to concrete, that then gets modulated by error signal trickling up through these layers in the opposite direction. I'm a huge fan of this picture, but I think we can generalise it further. My view is that that relationship between prediction and error is logically the same whether it's me reaching for my coffee cup and finding that it's just slightly not where I expected it to be, forcing me to modulate the position of my hand in response, or it's physicists getting data from telescopes that shows the perihelion of mercury doesn't match the predictions made by Newton's equations. That's an anomaly that forced us to re-articulate the mathematical formalism we used to model the world. So the car, in order to be intentionally directed toward the parking space, has to have a way of finding out that the way the world is doesn't quite match it's mathematical model, so that this model can then be modified.

16 See A. Clark, 'Whatever Next? Predictive Brains, Situated Agents, and the Future of Cognitive Science', *Behavioral and Brain Sciences* 36:3 (2013):181–204.

And that process of error correction has to have no ceiling. There can't be a fundamental level of fixed assumptions about the way things can possibly be. A rock bottom where revision is impossible.[17] I've elsewhere called this perspective 'cybernetic falsificationism'. I basically think that the semantic content of empirical representations is attached to what we might think of as control structures for handling error signal, both at an everyday level of modulating our precise predictions about the furniture of experience, and at the theoretical level of being forced to revise the conceptual structures underpinning our beliefs about the world. Putting this in logical terms, below the line is what we call non-monotonic inference, where you find exceptions to your inferences that can be handled by ad hoc workarounds, and then above the line are exceptions that force you to revise the underlying principles guiding your inferences. That's what I think of as dialectics in the Hegelian sense. So yeah, this is my big picture.

If I was to dive a little bit deeper into the formalism, I think there's a lacuna not just in the theory of concurrency, but also in the notion of control deployed by mathematics and computer science. We actually have two different conceptions of control. One is the cybernetic notion from control theory, which is fundamentally signal based, you might want to say continuous. And then we've got the notion of control flow in computer science, which is more discrete. In particular, I'm really interested in exception handling, because exception handling is the control structure used for dealing with error. I think full blooded theory of error would have to unify these two perspectives—in some sense, unifying a continuous and a discrete way of looking at control. But it's fundamentally a matter of trying to connect the mechanics of control signal with the semantics of computation, so that we can then say something like, this computation is about this thing in the world—where there problem specification and resulting solution have empirical semantic content.

**MP**: Just digging a little bit more on Longo, he raises this problem where the computer as a discretised machine is really only sensitive to its initial configuration. According to him, it's incapable of traversing the continuum of the real in the same way that humans can. Is that true for you? Is your cosmos continuous

17 This resembles what Brian Cantwell-Smith calls the capacity for 'judgement,' in *The Promise of Artificial Intelligence* (Cambridge, MA: MIT Press, 2019).

or discrete or, actually, does it not matter, when it comes to something like a general intelligence?

**PW**: Longo basically thinks that the world is continuous in the sense of the continuum—infinitely divisible—and that this causes problems for computation. I'm inclined to agree with his critique of pancomputationalism—the idea that the world is a digital computer. Whether or not the world is continuous or discrete, I think, is ultimately a question for physics. There are interesting metaphysical questions to be asked here, but I'm willing to be agnostic on the issue for now. The real question is, what's the upshot for computationalism in the philosophy of mind? And I think Longo is just wrong on this because, very briefly, there is such a thing as exact real computation.[18] Some people will say computations are fundamentally discrete because of limitations imposed by concrete data types like floating point numbers. These build in limits on how precise computations involving real numbers can get. But you can compute arbitrarily finely in principle, as long as you have the resources. The only thing this can't account for is the sort of infinite sensitivity to initial conditions involved in dynamic systems with chaotic attractors.

Maybe there are things in nature that are deterministically unpredictable. The question remains, how do those different sources of deterministic unpredictability differ, and what can we do with them? Is deterministic unpredictability in any way important for cognition?

I've made a similar argument against Barry Smith and Jobst LandGrebe, who wrote a book entitled *Why Machines Will Never Rule the World*.[19] They basically argue that humans are deterministically unpredictable systems, we're super complex, and we can't be fully modelled. Therefore, we can't create intelligent computers. Well, you might ask, why would intelligent computers have to be deterministically unpredictable in exactly the same way we are? No one's shown that this deterministic unpredictability is cognitively significant. Secondly, you can get deterministic unpredictability without chaos. The halting problem and Rice's theorem show that you can just have computer programs

---

18 See nLab, 'Exact Real Computer Arithmetic', <https://ncatlab.org/nlab/show/exact+real+computer+arithmetic>.

19 J. Landgrebe and B. Smith, *Why Machines Will Never Rule the World* (Abingdon: Routledge, second edition 2025).

whose behaviour cannot be reliably predicted in advance. So what is it about this infinite sensitivity to initial conditions that's doing cognitive work? As far as I can tell, there's no cognitive work being done by it. That isn't to say that deterministic unpredictability is philosophically unimportant. I do think it's important. I think there are interesting questions here for how we harness it in cognition—in random inspiration and things like this. There are even more significant questions concerning freedom. I think it is important that when we create rational agents, we create them in a way where their evolving trajectory of self-realization cannot be predicted in advance. That's a significant, dare I say aesthetic dimension of personal autonomy. But when it comes to the nuts and bolts of cognitive engagement with the world, I just don't see what continuity is bringing that can't be captured by, at the very least, exact real computation.

PHYSIS

# The Greatest Mistake: A Case for the Failure of Hegel's Idealism

## 1. WHAT IS A GREAT MISTAKE?

Nietzsche once said that a great error is worth more than a multitude of trivial truths. A truly great mistake is one that we can learn from, where we gain new understanding from explaining *why* it is an error, where we are either forced to make explicit our previously vague intuitions or forced to acknowledge properly counterintuitive results. Hegel understood this point well, as his analysis of the logical and historical development of human thought shows, for he takes each moment within this development to be a position which, while showing itself to be inconsistent, passes over into a more detailed position that incorporates its truth.

It is my opinion that Hegel may have made the *greatest* such error in the history of philosophy to date, and this means that understanding why it is an error is of the utmost importance. To do this, it is necessary to examine the nature of Hegel's position, which he calls Absolute Idealism.

## 2. WHAT IS ABSOLUTE IDEALISM?

The essence of Absolute Idealism is the thesis of the identity of subject and object, which we will simply call the **identity thesis**.[1] It's very important to understand what this doesn't mean. It is not to be understood along the lines of the maxim of Berkeley's subjective idealism: *esse est percipi*.[2] It is not the case for Hegel that each individual object is identical with an individual subject that thinks it, or some state of that subject. Instead, the thesis can be interpreted in three different ways. This is indicated by the fact that there are three distinct

1. G.W.F. Hegel, *The Phenomenology of Spirit*, tr. A.V. Miller (Oxford: Oxford University Press, 1977).
2. G. Berkeley, *A Treatise Concerning the Principles of Human Knowledge* (New York: Dover, 2003).

formulations of it: as the unity of subject and object, as the unity of thought and Being, and as the unity of subject and substance. Respectively, these correspond to idealism as method (Absolute Knowing), idealism as system (Absolute Idea), and idealism as reality (Absolute Spirit).

Absolute Idea names the identity of the general structures of subjects and objects, which are named thought and Being, respectively. Absolute Spirit names the identity of subject and substance, or Absolute Idea as instantiated in a singular structure, which is the correlate of both the Aristotelian and the Spinozan conceptions of God. This allows us to explain precisely why Heidegger takes Hegel's thought to represent the ultimate form of what he called **onto-theology**.[3] Absolute Idea is the structure of beings as such, and it is a form of beingness (*Seiendheit*) in so far as it thinks Being as a genus. Absolute Spirit is the structure of beings as a whole (or world) in so far as it is the immanent ground of their existence in the self-externalisation of Absolute Idea. Hegel thus thinks what Heidegger calls Being—the unified structure of beings as such and as a whole—in terms of beings themselves, namely, in terms of subjects in general, and a highest subject, respectively. This explicitly violates Heidegger's principle of the **ontological difference**.

However, I'm principally interested in the identity thesis in its form as method—as Absolute Knowing, or what Hegel will call the concept of **Science**—and the role it plays in Hegel's attempt to elaborate Idealism as system, or to describe the structure of the Absolute Idea. This is the project of his masterwork, the *Science of Logic*.[4] If the identity thesis provides the **form** of Absolute Idealism, then the *Science of Logic* unpacks its **content**.

Specifically, I'm interested in the way in which the identity thesis functions as a presupposition of the *Logic*, and how this relates to Hegel's famous claim that the *Logic* is presuppositionless. This claim is true in a limited fashion: the identity thesis does not function as a premise in the argument that makes up the *Logic*. However, we can distinguish two distinct senses in which it functions as a methodological presupposition: as determining the procedure which

3. M. Heidegger, 'The Onto-Theo-Logical Constitution of Metaphysics', in *Identity and Difference*, tr. J. Stambaugh (New York: Harper & Row, 1969), 42–74.

4. G.W.F. Hegel, *The Science of Logic*, tr. G. Di Giovanni (Cambridge: Cambridge University Press, 2010).

the argument follows, and as determining the way in which the results of the argument should be interpreted.

To explain this, it's necessary to say a little bit about the *Logic*. I'm going to presume a little bit of familiarity with the work, as I'll focus on the structure of the argument rather than its content. The crucial point is that the argument is **stratified**. To show this I will distinguish at least four separate levels at which it operates:

i. **The Basic Dialectic:** This is the *Logic* viewed as a serial progression of various categories, starting with the category of **Being**, and transitioning through **Nothing**, **Becoming**, and the various other categories up to the final category of **Absolute Idea**.

ii. **The Division of Books**: This is the threefold separation of the *Logic* into the **Doctrine of Being,** the **Doctrine of Essence**, and the **Doctrine of the Concept**, each of which exhibits a distinctive internal structure that differentiates them from the others.

iii. **The Division of Volumes**: This is the twofold separation of the *Logic* into the *Objective Logic*, which includes both Being and Essence, and the *Subjective Logic*, which includes the Concept.

iv. **The Overall Dialectic**: This is the *Logic* viewed as the complete explication of the implicit content of the concept of Being in its systematic form as Absolute Idea, which contains the totality of the previous moments of the Logic and their relations. This is to view the argument as a whole as a single inference, or the self-overcoming of the concept of Being.

There are various intermediary levels here that we won't go into. The important point is that the transitions between categories at the lower levels essentially make explicit the content of the categories at the higher levels. On this basis, we can see that the identity thesis does not form an explicit premise at any point of the argument but is ultimately derived by the complete transition from Being to Absolute Idea, which demonstrates the identity of object and subject, or Being and thought. However, this is not a justification of the identity thesis, but merely its transition from an implicit condition to an explicit principle of the system itself. To take it as a justification would be to fall into a vicious circle, as Hegel himself understood all too well.

We can now characterise the two functions of the identity thesis as implicit methodological presuppositions of the system in more detail.

In its function as a deductive procedure, it determines the dialectical structure of the Logic. It constitutes a non-intentional form of thought in which we do not use preindividuated concepts to form fixed propositions about particular objects, but instead think the content of concepts directly, allowing them to immanently transform themselves into other concepts by way of what Hegel calls **speculative propositions**. The Logic uses this method in order to carry out an immanent deduction of the structure of thought itself, by beginning with the most minimal content that can be thought—indeterminate immediacy—which is named Being because it is the one concept that applies to all objects, or, as Heidegger correctly notes, the highest genus of beings. The procedure of the Logic is then to systematically explicate what is implicit in this content, and thus the structure of conceptual thought as such. The result of this is that the *Logic* does not start with a complete method, but systematically explicates its own process of explication as it goes.

In its function as interpretational schema, it determines the system produced as both a logic and a metaphysics. The identity thesis guarantees that an immanent deduction of the logical categories of thought is simultaneously an immanent deduction of the metaphysical categories of Being. This schema is made explicit within the *Subjective Logic*, where the category of Being becomes explicit as a concept, and the transition to Absolute Idea makes explicit the identity of Being with its concept. This is the point at which the logic is determined as theology, since it is here that the externalisation of Absolute Idea in its form as Absolute Spirit is demonstrated.

On this basis, we can see that in order for the Logic to be justified—in both the form of its reasoning and the content of its conclusions—the identity thesis must be independently validated. If the *Science of Logic* corresponds to Kant's **metaphysical deduction** of the categories, then the *Phenomenology of Spirit* corresponds to the **transcendental deduction** of their validity.

## 3. WHY IS HEGEL AN ABSOLUTE IDEALIST?

The argument of the *Phenomenology* is motivated by responding both to scepticism, and to the transcendental response to scepticism. The transcendental response, as exemplified by Kant's response to Humean scepticism, promises to show that knowledge is possible by analysing the structure of knowledge, in the form of the conditions of the possibility of knowledge. For Hegel, this begs the question since it presupposes some kind of knowledge about knowledge that itself is unsecured. I'm going to call this **the problem of transcendental method**.

Hegel tries to sidestep this problem, and thereby secure a form of unconditioned or absolute knowledge, by returning to the most extreme form of scepticism—Pyrrhonian scepticism. The problem posed by Pyrrhonian scepticism may be described in two ways. It is originally posed by Sextus Empiricus as the **problem of the criterion**, which asks how we can find a criterion for choosing between a proposition and its negation that does not itself require a criterion to be justified.[5] However, its most clear formulation is **Agrippa's trilemma**, which asks how it is possible to justify any proposition (in contrast to its negation) without either (a) merely asserting its truth (bare assertion), (b) appealing to another proposition that itself must be justified (regress), or (c) justifying it by appeal to itself (circularity).

Hegel uses this to clarify the problem of transcendental method. He takes it that, in trying to describe its structure conceived as conditions of possibility, the transcendental philosopher implicitly assumes that knowledge is possible, and this is precisely what the Pyrrhonian sceptic denies. Hegel's response is then to describe the structure of knowledge as it appears, thereby bracketing the question of whether this structure actually makes knowledge possible. The crucial insight that enables him to do this is that the Pyrrhonian sceptic must explicitly pose the problem of the criterion, and that this involves describing the structure of justification in order to show its impossibility. In essence, if the sceptic is permitted to describe the apparent structure of knowledge in order to undermine it, then so is Hegel. He does this by providing what he calls the concept of **Natural Consciousness**.

5. Sextus Empiricus, *The Outlines of Pyrrhonism*, tr. R.G. Bury (Buffalo, NY: Prometheus Books, 1990).

Before explaining the structure of Natural Consciousness, it's important to understand the role it is supposed to play in his justification of the identity thesis. The crucial point is that the concept of Natural Consciousness is the concept of t**he non-identity of subject and object**. The *Phenomenology* justifies the *Logic* by showing how our ordinary understanding of knowledge, or knowledge as it appears to us, contradicts itself and thus transforms itself into its negation, or the standpoint of Science. It thus shows how knowledge as it is ordinarily understood is indeed impossible. However, in so far as the argument of Pyrrhonian scepticism is dependent upon this ordinary understanding, it also serves as a refutation of scepticism. This justifies the characterisation of Science as Absolute Knowing.

I'll now turn to describing the structure of Natural Consciousness in its opposition to Science. Hegel's definition is extraordinarily simple. It has two basic features:

(1) Consciousness relates itself to its object, or takes its object to be a certain way. What this means, is that it expresses a proposition about its object.

(2) Consciousness distinguishes between this proposition and the object as it is in itself. In essence, consciousness allows for the possibility that this proposition is false.

These then have two implications:

(3) Because consciousness itself makes the distinction between its claim and the object it is about, the object cannot be truly in-itself, but must be for-consciousness. This means that consciousness must have a concept of its object in order to individuate it.

(4) However, consciousness cannot be aware that the object is for-it without ceasing to be consciousness, and thus must suppress this fact. This means that consciousness cannot recognise that the concept of the object is dependent upon it without undermining the possibility of falsity.

This describes the form of intentional thought, in which we think about particular objects using fixed propositions composed of preindividuated concepts, as opposed to Science as the form of non-intentional thought, in which we think the content of concepts directly. This not only describes the deductive procedure that we follow in ordinary discourse, it equally determines the specific dialectical method of the *Phenomenology*.

The *Phenomenology* proceeds by a method of exhaustion. It does this by showing that each possible form of Natural Consciousness ultimately contradicts itself, thereby transforming itself into another possible form, until we have exhausted all possible forms. It thus demonstrates that if knowledge is conceived as Natural Consciousness, then it is impossible. This progressive exhaustion of possibilities is stratified in much the way that the dialectic of the Logic is stratified. As before, I will distinguish between at least four separate levels:

i. **The Basic Dialectic**: The *Phenomenology* viewed as a serial progression of various things consciousness purports to know about its object. This is a series of propositions each of which produces the next by contradicting itself. There is a series of such propositions within each form of consciousness, beginning with the sequence in Sense Certainty: 'This is here and now', 'This is here and now for me', etc., and ending in the identity thesis.

ii. **The Division of Forms**: The separation of sequences of purported knowings into forms of consciousness, such as Sense Certainty, Perception, Understanding, Self-Consciousness, etc. and ending in Absolute Knowing. Each of these corresponds to a general way of understanding its object that each purported knowing shares, or a concept of the object (as described in point (3)).

iii. **The Division of Sections**: This is the organisation of sequences of forms of consciousness into more general categories, such as Consciousness, Self-Consciousness and Reason. Each of these corresponds to a more general concept of its object, to which its subforms correspond as species.

iv. **The Overall Dialectic**: This is the *Phenomenology* viewed as the justification of the *Logic*, or the transformation of the concept of Natural Consciousness into the concept of Science.

This structure lets us see the way in which the *Phenomenology* is still a dialectic, albeit it one that consists in propositions that are purportedly absolute, rather than speculative propositions that are explicitly transitional. Each form of consciousness is a concept whose content is thought immanently by the method of exhaustion. These form a hierarchy of genus and species that correspond to the various higher-level ways of dividing the dialectic. The concept of Natural Consciousness is the highest genus, with each level beneath it divided into mutually exclusive species. The dialectical method of exhaustion thus consists in traversing the hierarchy in a double movement. One moves between the genera within a given level by unpacking their internal contradictions, and one does this by exhausting all of their species in a similar manner. The inferences between propositions at the lowest level thus immanently constitute movements between concepts at the higher levels.

What this means is that the *Phenomenology* is a logic of consciousness first, a teleological history of consciousness second, and at no point anything like an introspective psychology.

## 4. WHERE DOES HEGEL GO WRONG?

Hegel's great mistake is to be found in the way in which he sets up the argument of the *Phenomenology*, rather than in any particular part of the dialectics of the *Phenomenology* and the *Logic*. It consists in the fact that his response to the problem of transcendental method is fundamentally inadequate. To understand this, it's necessary to see how it is that Hegel's concept of Natural Consciousness is supposed to improve upon the Pyrrhonian sceptic's minimal description of the structure of justification.

All the Pyrrhonian needs in order to articulate the Agrippan trilemma is an account of assertions, the propositions these assertions express, the relations of incompatibility between these propositions, and the relations of consequence that enable them to justify one another. Hegel's response to this is essentially that it is insufficient to capture the appearance of knowledge. His concept of

Natural Consciousness replaces this with an analysis of the internal structure of propositions in terms of objects and concepts. The rest of the Pyrrhonian model is implicit within this simple structure, in so far as it follows from the interactions between the possibility of falsity and conceptual suppression. Indeed, one can look at the first three sections of the dialectic (Sense Certainty, Perception, and Understanding) as making these features explicit (subject/predicate structure, incompatibility relations between predicates, and consequence relations, respectively).

Hegel's problem is that it is possible to level the charge of insufficiency that he directs at Pyrrhonian scepticism against his own account of the appearance of knowledge. We are thus faced with a renewed form of the problem of the criterion: How do we choose between competing accounts of the appearance of knowledge, or accounts of the ordinary structure of justification? This is nothing other than the problem of transcendental method.

In essence, even if Hegel does not presuppose that knowledge is possible, he does not have an account of what it would be for an account of the appearance of knowledge to be sufficient. This is perfectly consistent with the idea that Hegel's concept of Natural Consciousness describes necessary features of the structure of knowledge.[6] We simply need a deductive procedure that is capable of deriving it, and whatever other features of the structure of knowledge are necessary. This is just to ask after the proper method of transcendental philosophy.

I thus think that Hegel's failure to justify the *Logic* is the greatest mistake in the history of philosophy for two reasons. On the one hand, it demonstrates that if we are to deal with the problem of scepticism, we must become transcendental philosophers. This is to say that it demonstrates the necessity of transcendental philosophy. On the other hand, it allows us to pose clearly the problem of transcendental method, or the question of what transcendental philosophy is: How do we immanently describe the structure of ordinary discourse?

There are a number of further things that can be said about this more determinate formulation of the problem of transcendental method. It would be correct to point out that it is very close to Hegel's own project, in so far as Hegel takes the *Logic* to completely explicate the conceptual structure of all forms of

6. See 'Essay on Transcendental Realism', in this volume, for an attempt to expand upon Hegel's account of Natural Consciousness.

thought, including the ordinary form of thought found in Natural Consciousness. However, it would be an error to think that it is just restating Hegel's own problem, because Hegel takes the form of thought through which the structure of the ordinary form is deduced (Science) to be completely opposed to this ordinary form (Natural Consciousness). For him, Science and Natural Consciousness are mutually exclusive species of the genus of thought, which is only properly explicated by the *Logic*. By contrast, my approach takes ordinary thought (Natural Consciousness, or Discourse) to be the genus, and the special form of thought that explicates it (Science, or Transcendental Discourse) to be a species of it.

It might also be objected that this criticism of Hegel fails to take into account the circular nature of the exposition of the *Logic*. In moving from Being to Absolute Idea, the *Logic* constitutes the return of Being into itself as Absolute Idea. What was originally implicit in the content of the concept of Being is thereby made explicit. This is equally the case with the *Logic*'s own method, which is merely implicit at the beginning, but becomes fully explicit at the end. This is not a vicious circle of justification, but a virtuous circle of explication. However, we can see that not only does the inadequate justification of the concept of Natural Consciousness in the *Phenomenology* undermine the justification of the Logic as such, but it brings into question the method of the *Phenomenology* itself, given that the latter is already implicitly dialectical in a way that is neither explicated, nor justified until the *Logic*. This reintroduces an element of viciousness into the circle that Hegel's philosophy traces.

Transcendental philosophy can avoid this residual viciousness, while retaining only the virtuous elements of Hegel's explicative approach. It can do this because, given that transcendental discourse is a species of discourse in general, the immanent deduction of the structure of discourse will at the same time be a description of the general structure of this deduction itself. The two challenges for this approach are to show that the genus of discourse immanently differentiates itself into various species, including transcendental discourse, and to find an explanatory primitive that cannot be rejected, in order to foreclose its method to justificatory regress and circularity. Its virtuous circle would then consist in explicating the implicit content of this primitive, and on this basis explicating its own method of explication.

To conclude, it's interesting to look at the structure of my argument in terms that Hegel himself would find familiar: as a dialectical triad of **thesis**, **antithesis**, and **synthesis**. Transcendental philosophy in its original form is here the thesis. It is a systematic attempt to respond to the problems of scepticism which, as Hegel points out, is vitiated by a peculiar kind of regress. Hegel's development of Absolute Idealism out of this criticism is then the antithesis of this original thesis. The oppositional character of the two can be seen in the opposition of Natural Consciousness and Science. My criticisms of Hegel's positions then pave way for a synthesis of these two positions, which is not a return to naïve transcendentalism or to the standpoint of the abstract understanding in distinction to reason, but rather an attempt to *reincorporate* the truth in Hegel's ideas within a more adequate framework. It is essentially an attempt to collapse the abstract opposition between transcendental philosophy and immanent dialectic by collapsing the abstract opposition between Natural Consciousness and Science.

All of this is still preliminary though. Precisely what the method of transcendental philosophy is, and how we leverage Hegel's own insights within it, is the topic of a different paper.

# Essay on Transcendental Realism

## 0. INTRODUCTION

The object of realist metaphysics is generally thought to be to describe the structure of the world as it is in itself, or, alternatively, to determine precisely what is real. The purpose of this essay is to suggest that, although there have been many attempts to achieve this goal, they all fall down, not simply because they have misconstrued the nature of the in-itself or precisely what is real, but because, more fundamentally, they are not clear about *what it is* to talk about the in-itself or the real. In short, contemporary realism, both Continental and Analytic, does not have an adequate concept of reality.

To demonstrate this point, I am going to rehearse a couple of different dialectics between realist and nonrealist positions in order to tease out their inherent problems. This will take up the first two parts of the essay. In the first part I will tackle Quentin Meillassoux's reconstructed dialectic of correlationism and identify some key problems with it. In the second part I will examine several different debates within analytic metaphysics that exhibit a common dialectical structure, within which I will locate a position that I term deflationary realism.

The final two parts will bring together the various considerations that have arisen, to show how we can move from deflationary realism to a properly transcendental realism in which the task of realist metaphysics is made properly explicit. In the third part I will define transcendental realism, and outline an argument for it. In the fourth part I will try to work out some additional consequences of the position, while further situating it in relation to the history of philosophy. In particular, I will try to show why the considerations put forward in the essay motivate a return to, and radicalisation of, Kant's philosophical project.

## 1. THE CLASSICAL DIALECTIC

To begin with, I am going to briefly introduce the classical dialectic between realism and idealism, and show where what Meillassoux calls correlationism stands in relation to it.[1] To this end I am going to introduce a series of definitions:

> Classical Realism: Any position that takes there to be a real structure of the world that is ontologically independent of (and thus distinct from) the structure of thought. This position is exemplified by thinkers such as Aristotle and Locke.

> Classical Idealism: Any position that takes there to be a real structure of the world that is in some sense identical to (and thus ontologically dependent upon) the structure of thought. This position is exemplified by thinkers such as Berkeley and Hegel.

This opposition can also be described in terms of how the two positions view the relation between **subject** and **object**, or that between **thought** and **being**. In each case, realism takes the latter to be primary, and to be independent of the former, whereas idealism takes the former to be primary, and the latter to be dependent upon it. Given this, we can introduce correlationism as the position that gives primacy to neither subject nor object, but to the relation between the two:

> Correlationism: Any position which holds that the real structure of the world is to some extent *unknowable*, in so far as knowledge is always relativised to the subjective conditions of knowledge (e.g., forms of intuition, cultures, or language games, etc.). This means that there can be no access to the world as it is in-itself, but only as it is for-us. This position is exemplified by Kant, Heidegger and Wittgenstein.

Whereas realism and idealism are defined in explicitly ontological terms, even if they have epistemological consequences, Meillassoux takes correlationism to principally be an epistemological position. This does not mean that there cannot be ontological forms of correlationism (e.g., the later Heidegger's notion of

1. See Meillassoux's contribution to 'Speculative Realism', in R. Mackay (ed.), *Collapse* vol. 3 (Falmouth: Urbanomic, 2007), 408–37.

*Ereignis* as the appropriation of Man to Being and Being to Man), but it does hold that correlationism can be motivated independently of ontology. This will turn out to be a crucial point.

In the subsequent discussions we will seek to determine the meaning of three crucial notions that appear within these definitions: reality, the in-itself, and the structure of the world.

## 1.1 Meillassoux on Correlationism

Meillassoux takes it that correlationism defeats both realism and idealism, by deploying a different argument against each: the **circle of correlation** against realism, and the **argument from facticity** against idealism.[2]

### *1.1.1 The Circle of Correlation*

Meillassoux takes Fichte's initial account of consciousness in the *Wissenschaftslehre* to provide the most basic form of the circle of correlation:

> Fichtean Consciousness: The I (subject) posits the not-I (object) as not posited.[3]

In essence, consciousness thinks about the object, and attempts to think the object as independent of its thinking. However, it ends up in a pragmatic contradiction. The fact that it posits the object contradicts the content it posits, namely, that the object is not posited.

Meillassoux holds that all forms of classical realism display the same pragmatic contradiction. They try to *think* the object as it is, independent of *thought*. This is impossible, because one cannot have knowledge of anything independently of the subjective conditions of knowledge. One cannot know whether the in-itself is either the *same* as or *different* from the way it appears under these conditions. This is what constitutes the unknowability of the in-itself.

### *1.1.2 The Argument from Facticity*

Classical idealism is immune to the circle of correlation, because it absolutises the correlation itself. It identifies knowing with what is known, and thereby denies the possibility that the in-itself could be different from how it is for-us.

2. Ibid., 413–14.
3. Ibid., 412.

We thus *can* know the real structure of the world, because it is the same as the subjective conditions of knowledge, or the structure of thought.

To refute the idealist, the correlationist needs to shore up the possibility that the in-itself is different from the for-us. This is done by insisting on the **facticity of thought**.[4] This is to say, the existence of thought is taken to be contingent. Given that there must be a real structure of the world, this implies that there can be a world without thought, and thus that they are not identical.

### *1.1.3 Speculative Materialism*

Meillassoux motivates his own neo-realist position by hijacking the argument from facticity. Whereas the idealist absolutises the correlation, Meillassoux absolutises facticity. He does this by showing that the argument against idealism only works on condition that thought can think its own contingency as an absolute, i.e., as something that is not relative to the conditions of its thinking. In order for us to know the nonidentity of the in-itself and the for-us, we must be able to know absolutely that there could be a world without thought.[5] We must thus have some absolute knowledge of the possible.

However, because we can still have no absolute knowledge of particular entities, this means that in order for thought to be absolutely contingent, everything must be absolutely contingent. This leads to a position, which he calls speculative materialism, in which we can know the real structure of the world, but this structure is just the structure of the radical contingency of everything.[6]

## 1.2 Problems with Correlationism

There are at least three distinct issues with Meillassoux's presentation of correlationism.

### *1.2.1 Propositions vs. Concepts*

First, the Fichtean account of thought is ambiguous as to whether 'thinking X' is a matter of thinking a **proposition** about X or grasping the **concept** of X. A proposition provides the content of an isolated claim about something,

4. Ibid., 430.
5. Ibid., 432.
6. Ibid.

whereas a concept can incorporate a variety of such contents, as long as they are sufficient to individuate its object.

For example, under the Fichtean account it remains ambiguous as to whether 'thinking Bill Clinton' is a matter of thinking a specific thing about Bill Clinton, such as 'Bill Clinton is ladies' man', or a matter of grasping *who* Bill Clinton is. Alternatively, it remains ambiguous whether 'thinking mitochondria' is a matter of thinking something like 'mitochondrial DNA is inherited from the mother' or a matter of grasping a series of facts that specify what mitochondria are.

### *1.2.2 Presentation vs. Representation*

Secondly, the argument is not sensitive to an important distinction between different accounts of the structure of thought. This is best demonstrated by taking a quote from Meillassoux himself:

> No X without givenness of X, and no theory of X without a positing of X... the sentence 'X is', means: 'X is a correlate of thought'.[7]

What this demonstrates is that Meillassoux runs together accounts of thought in which objects are initially **presented** to us in a certain way (e.g., phenomenological accounts of thought, such as Husserl's), and accounts in which we must always **represent** them as being a certain way (e.g., linguistic accounts of thought, such as Sellars's).

For example, say we encounter a tree in the park and we make an observation statement about it (e.g., 'this tree is green'). The difference between the two approaches is that presentational accounts take the content of that observation to have been already given to us in our experience of the tree, and that the statement just makes it explicit, whereas representational accounts hold that only the observation statement has content, and that, strictly speaking, there is no such thing as a 'content' of experience.

The crucial difference between these approaches is that representational accounts emphasise the way in which we are responsible for how we take things to be, in so far as we must actively represent them as being some way,

7. Ibid., 409.

whereas presentational accounts tend to diminish this responsibility, by treating us as more or less passive.

### *1.2.3 Two Forms of Dependency*

Finally, we can see that the dialectic of correlationism is structured around two different questions about dependence upon the structure of thought.

On the one hand, there is the question of whether the in-itself is ontologically dependent upon the structure of thought. This is the primary dimension of the debate between classical realism and classical idealism. Correlationism sides with classical realism on this issue, holding that the in-itself cannot be dependent upon thought because of its facticity.

On the other hand, there is the question of whether our knowledge of the in-itself is epistemically dependent upon the structure of thought. This is the debate over whether we can know anything absolutely, or whether all knowledge is relative. Correlationism sides with relativism on this issue.

The crucial point is that the correlationist makes the following assumption:

> Sufficiency Thesis: the ontological independence of the in-itself from thought is sufficient to establish the possibility that the in-itself could be different from the way it appears in relation to thought, and thus to establish epistemic dependence.

The problem with this thesis is complicated. To understand it, it is necessary to recognise that the circle of correlation does not tell us how exactly the content of thought is relative to its subjective conditions (or structure). In other words, it doesn't explain what this relativity consists in. The problem with the sufficiency thesis is that it only holds if it is supplemented by such an explanation. This is even more problematic than it initially appears, because the essential features of thought that such an account would take to be potentially absent in the in-itself must be accounted for in ontological terms. In essence, the correlationist requires an ontological account of thought, because only such an account can draw consequences from the ontological fact about the independence of the in-itself from thought. The real problem here is that such an account would undermine the simplicity, and thus the force, of the circle of correlation itself.

The real weakness of Meillassoux's approach is that its understanding of the notion of the in-itself, for all that it is supposed to support an epistemological argument, is always implicitly ontological. This is already indicated in the way Meillassoux situates correlationism between classical realism and classical idealism: the former gives Being primacy over thought, the latter gives thought primacy over Being, and correlationism gives primacy to the relation between the two. The classical positions both view the relation between thought and Being, and thus the question of primacy, in explicitly ontological terms. In defining correlationism in the terms he does, Meillassoux guarantees that whatever its epistemological consequences are, it will always be based on some form of implicit ontology.

Viewing the argument in this way also lets us understand the relationship between Meillassoux's speculative materialism and Graham Harman's object-oriented philosophy (OOP). In effect, both positions try to draw out the implicit ontological assumptions underpinning the correlationist argument. Meillassoux recognises the ontological character of the assumption that thought is factical, and then because correlationism still precludes knowledge of particular entities, he extends this facticity to all entities. Harman on the other hand recognises the ontological character of the epistemic dependence of thought about the object upon its subjective conditions, and then, for the same reason as Meillassoux, he extends this structure to all entities (or objects).[8]

The problem for both speculative materialism and OOP is that their arguments only work if there is some independent reason to accept correlationism beyond the very ontological assumptions they draw out of it. This is because, as we have seen, correlationism requires such ontological assumptions to motivate it. This is not to say that both of these ontological positions are false, only that they need to be motivated by different arguments.

In the next two parts of the essay, I will expand upon this problem with Meillassoux's presentation of correlationism:

(1) I will show that there is a non-ontological way of conceiving the dependence of the structure of the world upon the structure of thought. This allows for a further position between classical realism and classical idealism, which I call deflationary realism.

8. See Harman's contribution to 'Speculative Realism', 367–88.

(2) I will provide an alternative account of thought, which provides us with a way of understanding epistemic dependence in a non-ontological manner. This allows for a further position which I call transcendental realism.

## 2. DEFLATIONARY REALISM

I will now examine a series of different debates in analytic metaphysics, within which I will uncover a common dialectical structure, and use this to introduce **deflationary realism**. Unfortunately, I will have to ignore much of the context and specific detail of these debates, and will present them in a somewhat truncated form. Nonetheless, it should still be apparent that there is a common philosophical theme running through them.

### 2.1 Local Deflationism

Whereas the classical debate between realism and idealism is about the real structure of the world as a whole, each of these debates deals with a specific aspect of this structure. We will thus make a distinction between **global** and **local** metaphysical debates. It should be noted that we still have not yet come across a good definition of this notion of 'the real structure of the world', and so it is even less clear what an 'aspect' of it would be. However, examining these debates will bring us closer to understanding both.

#### *2.1.1 Numbers (Quine)*

The first debate is a disagreement over whether a particular domain of entities *exists*, or whether they are *real*. We'll take numbers as our example, given that they provide the most tried and tested example of such debates in the history of philosophy.

The debate initially takes place between local realism about number (traditionally called Platonism), and local anti-realism about number (traditionally called nominalism). Both are forms of classical realism, in so far as both take there to be a real structure of the world independent of thought, and both hold that there are some domains of entities that are real, and are therefore part of this structure. For instance, both tend to think that physical objects are real. The difference is that the Platonist thinks that numbers are just as real as tables and chairs, whereas the nominalist thinks they are not.

Now, the **deflationary realist** steps into this traditional debate and opposes both forms of classical realism. In this instance, the deflationist is none other than Quine. Quine holds that there is nothing more to existence than existential quantification, and that there is no notion of reality distinct from existence.[9] In effect, Quine denies that either form of classical realism can make good sense of what they mean by 'real'.

The major consequence of Quine's view is that all ontological questions about whether or not a given domain of entities exists (or is real) become trivial questions about whether we take there to be true statements which quantify over that domain. For instance, if we take it to be true that 'There are infinitely many prime numbers', we are thereby committed to the existence of both numbers and prime numbers more specifically. In essence, if we take there to be true mathematical *statements*, then we're committed to the existence of mathematical *objects*.

Quine does qualify this idea somewhat: he thinks we should only work out existential commitments from those statements that do genuine explanatory work. This means that we work out what exists only on the basis of the claims made by our best scientific theories. Nonetheless, it is to point out that he does not take scientific claims to possess a different kind of truth.

There are many problems with this qualification, and with Quine's characterisation of ontological questions more generally. Kit Fine has perhaps provided the most comprehensive critique of the Quinean position.[10] What is most interesting is that he uses this to motivate a *thick* notion of reality in opposition to Quine's *thin* notion. However, Fine does not shake the problem of classical realism. His definition of reality (in the sense of realness) appeals to an intuitive but ultimately unexplained notion of Reality (in the sense of the world as it is in-itself). I will adopt something similar to Fine's approach later on, but I will explicate the intuitive notion of Reality to which he appeals (and which I will call the Real). The other problem with Fine's account is that he does not show how his notion of reality can be extended outside of debates about the reality of

9. W.V. Quine, 'The Problem of Interpreting Modal Logic', *Journal of Symbolic Logic* 12:2 (1947): 43–48.

10. K. Fine, 'The Question of Ontology', in D.J. Chalmers. D. Manley, and R. Wasserman, *Metametaphysics: New Essays on the Foundations of Ontology* (Oxford: Oxford University Press, 2009), 155–77.

particular domains of entities. As we shall see from the two subsequent debates, this is a very significant issue.

Leaving all this to one side, we can translate Quine's basic idea as follows:

Quine Thesis: There is no *thick* notion of reality for entities, but only a *thin* one. An entity is real in this sense *iff* we take there to be something true of it.

### *2.1.2 Values (McDowell vs. Blackburn)*

The second debate is a disagreement over whether certain kinds of predicates pick out real properties. The predicates in question are values such as 'good', 'beautiful' and 'funny'. In this debate, Simon Blackburn plays the role of the local antirealist. He opposes his position, which he calls **quasi-realism** about value, to what he calls **naïve realism** about value, which is the corresponding local realism.[11]

The naïve realist supposedly holds that entities in the world are really imbued with values, independently of the way we take them to be. This means that a sunrise could be beautiful even if sentient creatures had never evolved, in just the same sense that it would still last the same amount of time even if no systems of time measurement had ever been invented. In opposition to this, Blackburn claims that the properties studied by the natural sciences are real, but that values are not. Instead, he holds that values are projected onto the world by us. The sunset is beautiful just in the sense that we project some positive reaction it produces in us upon certain genuine properties it possesses.

The deflationary realist in this debate is John McDowell, who classifies his position as anti-anti-realism. The crux of the debate between McDowell and Blackburn is whether or not statements which predicate values of objects are truth-apt. For a statement to be truth-apt is just for it to be able to be true or false. Blackburn effectively tries to deny truth-aptness to value statements by showing how the ways we identify and argue about values fall short of the paradigm case of those properties studied by the natural sciences.[12]

11. S. Blackburn, 'Truth, Realism, and the Regulation of Theory,' in *Essays in Quasi-Realism* (Oxford: Oxford University Press, 1993), 15–34.

12. S. Blackburn, 'Rule-Following and Moral Realism', in S. Holtzman and C. Leich (eds.), *Wittgenstein: To Follow a Rule* (London: Routledge, 1981), 167–70.

In response to this, McDowell has a number of good points, but his central argument is that even if value discourse can never have the form of natural scientific discourse, it nonetheless displays all the features characteristic of assessing the truth and falsity of claims. We can give detailed reasons for and against value-ascriptions, deploying whole networks of interconnected value concepts. For instance, assessment of whether something is funny does not simply depend upon our dispositions to laugh at it, but can involve appeals to complex concepts such as satire and irony.[13]

In essence, McDowell establishes deflationary standards for what kinds of discourse count as truth-apt, and then denies that there is anything more to the reality of properties than there being true claims about them. On this basis, we can locate a parallel of the Quine Thesis:

> McDowell Thesis: There are only *thin* notions of reality and truth. A property is real *iff* we take some ascriptions of it to entities to be true.

### *2.1.3 Modality (Lewis vs. Blackburn and Price vs. Brandom)*

The third debate is harder to classify than the first two. It regards the reality of the **modal** dimension of the world, or the reality of *possibility* and *necessity*. The problem with classifying this is that, although it can potentially be interpreted as a debate about whether or not a certain kind of entity exists, namely, possible worlds, or as whether there are real modal properties, such as dispositions, it is really more general than this. This can be demonstrated by considering two different versions of the debate, between David Lewis and Simon Blackburn on the one hand, and between Huw Price and Robert Brandom on the other.

Taking the former debate first, Blackburn initially attacks Lewis, who is famous for advocating the reality of possible worlds, as if he occupies the local realist position. Blackburn's own view is that modal discourse is projective in a similar way to his view of value discourse.[14] However, Lewis's response to Blackburn reveals that he is in fact a deflationary realist. In effect, he accuses Blackburn of ascribing a thick notion of reality to the actual which he denies

13. J. McDowell, 'Values and Secondary Qualities', *Mind, Value, and Reality* (Cambridge, MA: Harvard University Press, 2001), 147–50.

14. S. Blackburn, 'Morals and Modals', in G. MacDonald (ed.), *Fact, Science and Morality* (Oxford: Oxford University Press, 1986), 119–41.

to the possible.[15] By contrast, he is not claiming that possible worlds are real in the thick sense, but deploying a uniformly thin sense of reality in which the possible and actual are on an equal footing. Lewis argues that we take modal claims (e.g., counterfactuals) to be true, and that we must thereby commit ourselves to the existence or reality of whatever is required to properly interpret their truth. This means that we are committed to the reality of the elements we use to formulate the semantics of modal discourse. For Lewis, this means the reality of possible worlds.

The debate between Price and Brandom runs in parallel to this. Price takes up a similar quasi-realist position to Blackburn, from which he criticises Brandom's own modal realism.[16] The question of whether Price is actually a classical realist is not straightforward, but we needn't answer it. This is because it is Brandom's defence of his position against Price that gives him an affinity with Lewis. He explicitly denies that we can make any sense of the idea of a real structure of the world distinct from the structure of our thought and talk about it.[17] He then maintains precisely the same position as Lewis: we are committed to whichever features of the world we need to make sense of the semantics of modal discourse. The main difference between Brandom and Lewis is that he takes incompatibility relations between propositions (and the facts they represent) as his semantic primitives, and thus is not committed to the reality of possible worlds.

What comes out of these related debates is that there can be aspects of the world not straightforwardly reducible to questions about entities and their properties. We can translate the basic ideas of Lewis and Brandom as follows:

> Lewis-Brandom Thesis: There is only a *thin* notion of reality with respect to aspects of the world. An aspect of the world is real in this sense *iff* we take there to be true claims about it. The nature of this aspect is determined by the semantics of those claims.

---

15. D. Lewis, 'Quasi-Realism is Fictionalism', in M.E. Kalderon (ed.), *Fictionalism in Metaphysics* (Oxford: Oxford University Press, 2005), 314–21.

16. H. Price, 'Will There Be Blood? Brandom, Hume, and the Genealogy of Modals,' *Philosophical Topics* 36:2 (2008), 87–97.

17. R. Brandom, 'Responses', *Philosophical Topics* 36:2 (2008), 135–55.

## 2.2 Global Deflationism

Now that we've had a look at the way deflationary realism functions within local debates, we can try to work out the general character of the position. An important point to make is that it is not possible to be a deflationist in one debate and not in another. This is because the deflationist's tactic involves substituting a thick notion of reality for a thin one, and it is the same notion which is deployed in all these debates. This means that if one is a deflationary realist, one ought to be a global deflationary realist.

I think we can pick out three essential insights of deflationary realism from the debates just considered:

1. There is a crucial link between a *thin* notion of reality and the notion of truth (from the Quine Thesis).

2. To be genuinely deflationary, this notion of truth must be equally *thin* (from the McDowell Thesis).

3. The structure of the world is reflected by the *semantics* of our truth claims. This means that the structure of the world is reflected by the *structure of our thought and talk* about it (from the Lewis-Brandom Thesis).

### *2.2.1 Brandom's Deflationism*

Now, just because all of the deflationary realists discussed above *should* have a coherently articulated global deflationist position doesn't mean that they do. The exception is Robert Brandom, who articulates a systematic position that incorporates all three insights just discussed.[18] Brandom does this by explicitly addressing the question of the dependency of the structure of the world on the structure of thought.[19] However, he articulates a dependency thesis which is non-ontological, and which therefore does not collapse into classical idealism. To do this, Brandom introduces the notions of **sense-dependency** and **reference-dependency**:

18. R. Brandom, 'Holism and Idealism in Hegel's *Phenomenology*,' in *Tales of the Mighty Dead: Historical Essays in the Metaphysics of Intentionality* (Cambridge, MA: Harvard University Press, 2002), 255–309.
19. Ibid., 283.

Sense-Dependency: 'Concept P is sense dependent upon concept Q just in case one cannot count as having grasped P unless one counts as grasping Q.'

Reference-Dependency: 'Concept P is reference dependent upon concept Q just in case P cannot apply to something unless Q applies to it.'[20]

In short, P is sense-dependent upon Q if one cannot understand P without understanding Q, and reference-dependent upon Q if there cannot be P without Q. The former is a kind of *epistemic* dependence, whereas the latter is a kind of *ontological* dependence.

Brandom then points out that there can be sense-dependence without reference-dependence.[21] He also notes that sense-dependence is by default an asymmetrical relation, meaning that there can be one-way sense-dependence. For example, one cannot understand the concept 'nail' without the concept 'hammer', but it is entirely possible that we could destroy all hammers, and yet there would still be nails. Equally, one can understand 'hammer' without understanding 'nail', because hammers may be used to do things other than hitting nails.[22]

We can then articulate Brandom's position as follows:

1. The *world* is all that is the case, or the totality of what is true. This is the same definition of world with which Wittgenstein opens the *Tractatus Logico-Philosophicus*.

2. *Thought* is just the rational process through which we update and revise what we take to be true.

3. The concept of world is reciprocally sense-dependent upon the concept of thought. This means that one cannot understand the structure of the world without understanding the structure of this rational process, or vice versa.

20. Ibid., 278.
21. Ibid., 279–80
22. Ibid.

The consequence of this is that Brandom takes there to be various pairs of fundamental concepts that must be understood together or not at all. For instance, he thinks that we cannot understand what *objects* are apart from understanding what *singular terms* are, that we cannot understand what *properties* are apart from understanding what *predicates* are, that we cannot understand what *facts* (or states of affairs) are apart from understanding what *claims* (or assertions) are, and he thinks that we cannot understand what *laws* are apart from understanding what **counterfactual robustness** is.[23]

This then allows him to make various claims about the structure of the world, on the basis of claims about the structure of thought (which for him is just the semantics and pragmatics of language). For instance:

1. Propositions necessarily have a subject-predicate structure; therefore, the world must be composed of objects and properties.

2. Facts are just true claims, and there are normative truths, therefore there are normative facts.

3. There are modal incompatibility relations between propositions, and between predicates, therefore there are modal incompatibility relations between states of affairs, and between properties.

Now, it should be noted that Brandom actually calls this position '**objective idealism**', and he takes it to be Hegel's position, as well as his own (even if he does take himself to disagree with Hegel on the possibility of providing an exhaustive account of logic, and thus metaphysics).[24] However, I think that Brandom is incorrect in ascribing this deflationary position to Hegel, since Hegel most definitely has more classical metaphysical ambitions when it comes to the applicability of his *Logic*. I therefore take myself to be justified in classifying Hegel as a classical idealist (albeit the most powerful and subtle of them) and Brandom as a deflationary realist.

23. Ibid., 282–3.
24. Ibid., 281.

Moving on, Brandom provides us with the resources to posit the general definition of deflationary realism we are seeking:

> Deflationary Realism: Any position which denies that there is a *thick* sense of reality, and which holds that the structure of the world and the structure of thought are reciprocally sense-dependent, without being reference-dependent.

### *2.2.2 Deflationism vs. Correlationism*

I have thus shown that it is possible to have a position between classical realism and classical idealism that is not correlationism. Moreover, the possibility of this position tells against the **Sufficiency Thesis** upon which the correlationist argument depends. This is because the deflationist can accept that the world is ontologically independent from thought, and thus that there could be a world *without* thought. In short, the deflationist can accept the facticity of thought and still hold that the structure of the world is dependent upon the structure of thought (albeit reciprocally).

It is thus the case that deflationary realism trumps correlationism. This means that the only way to avoid deflationary realism is to answer the deflationist's challenge to classical realism, by providing a genuinely thick notion of reality. However, this thick notion of reality must not appeal to the ontologically defined notion of the in-itself deployed by correlationism, lest it collapse back into correlationism. I think that the only position capable of meeting this task is what I call transcendental realism. The rest of the essay will be devoted to expounding this position.

## 3. TRANSCENDENTAL REALISM

Deflationary realism is an impressive position, especially when it is explicitly articulated in the form Brandom presents. However, I don't think that it is right. There are a variety of reasons for this, some of which are specific to the various local debates we've considered (see Fine's critique of Quine on existence), but the simplest and most compelling is that we seem to have an intuitive grasp of a genuinely *thick* notion of reality. This is obvious when we look at the debate between Platonism and nominalism. We have a good understanding of the difference between the positions, the problem is simply that no one has managed to make explicit the role that the term 'real' is playing in the debate. This is what allows the deflationist to claim that the argument makes no sense.

The task before us is therefore to explicitly define a thick notion of reality. However, in doing so we must also avoid defining reality in *ontological* terms. This is because the notion of reality is actually supposed to make sense of what ontology is, not vice versa. The only way to do this is to define reality in *epistemological* terms. This means providing a non-ontological account of the structure of thought, and then showing that there is a thick notion of reality *implicit* within it. I take this to be the essence of a genuinely *transcendental* approach to realism. I will thus define **transcendental realism** as follows:

> Transcendental Realism: Any position that shows that the structure of thought itself implies that there is a *real* structure of the world in *excess* of the structure of thought.

This position is actually a development of deflationary realism, rather than a simple return to classical realism. This can be seen if we look at the dependence relations this definition implies.

For transcendental realism, the structure of the world is sense-dependent upon the structure of thought, but this dependence is not reciprocal. This looks strange, until one realises that understanding the structure of thought is a *necessary* but not *sufficient* condition for understanding the structure of the world. In short, one must understand the structure of thought in order to understand what it would be to give a proper account of the real structure of the world. This is what Kant would call the 'critique of metaphysics,' which is supposed to come before metaphysics itself.[25]

## 3.1 Rethinking Thought

I'm now going to suggest a way of motivating transcendental realism, and I'm going to do this by sketching an alternative account of thought to the one Meillassoux provides. The account of thought I'm going to present is based on

25. I. Kant, *The Critique of Pure Reason*, tr. P. Guyer and A.W. Wood (Cambridge: Cambridge University Press, 1998).

the historical successor to Fichte's account of consciousness, namely, Hegel's account of **Natural Consciousness** in the *Phenomenology of Spirit*.[26]

### *3.1.1 Hegel Contra Fichte*

Hegel's account is almost as simple as the Fichtean one we considered above. It posits two basic features of consciousness:

> 1. Consciousness relates itself to its object, or takes its object to be a certain way. What this means, is that it makes a claim about its object.
>
> 2. Consciousness distinguishes between its relating (or its claim) and the object as it is in itself. In essence, consciousness allows for the possibility of error.

These then have two implications:

> 1. Because consciousness *itself* makes the distinction between its claim and the object it is about, the object cannot be truly *in-itself*, but must be *for-consciousness*. This means that consciousness must have a concept of its object.
>
> 2. However, consciousness cannot be aware that the object is for-it without ceasing to be consciousness, and thus must *suppress* this fact. This means that consciousness cannot recognise that the concept of the object is dependent upon it, without undermining the possibility of error.

The first thing to recognise is that this account solves the two problems we identified with Meillassoux's account of thought. First, the proposition/concept ambiguity of the Fichtean approach is resolved by having a role both for propositional claims about objects (1 and 2) and for concepts of objects (3 and 4). Secondly, although it is misleadingly named 'consciousness', this is most definitely a **representational** account of thought. Consciousness is *active* in making claims about its object, and is thus *responsible* for those claims. Moreover, it undertakes this responsibility by establishing the object as an independent

26. G.W.F. Hegel, *The Phenomenology of Spirit*, tr. J.B. Baillie (Edinburgh: Pantianos Classics, 2016), 'Introduction'.

standard distinct from its claim. It is precisely by giving the object authority over whether its claim is correct that consciousness opens up the possibility of error.

The next thing to note is that Hegel has effectively split Fichte's notion of 'positing as not posited' into two distinct subjective acts: what I will call withdrawing authority (2), and suppressing the concept (4).

Withdrawing authority is just a different way of talking about the way consciousness opens up the possibility of error. The reason I am using this term is that granting authority to the object over whether one's claims about it are correct can also be viewed as a matter of withdrawing one's own authority over one's claims. In doing so, one thereby undertakes a responsibility to provide reasons why one's claim is correct if challenged. It is precisely by undertaking a responsibility to give reasons for one's claims about an object that one thereby undertakes a responsibility to that object. In effect, what all of this means is that all claims are essentially open to debate.

In contrast to this, the *content* of concepts is not always open to debate. This is because mutual grasp of a concept is a condition of the possibility of disagreement about anything. For example, we can only have a genuine argument about whether 'Bill Clinton is a ladies' man' if we both understand who Bill Clinton is, and what being a 'ladies' man' entails. The point is that in order to open up the possibility of error, we must nonetheless exclude some things from the resulting debate. So, while we accept the possible difference between our claim and the object in itself, we suppress the possible difference between our concept and the object it stands for.

### *3.1.2 Mind Independence vs. Attitude Independence*

This account of the basic structure of thought gives us the resources to properly articulate epistemic dependence in a non-ontological manner. We can do this by distinguishing between two different ways of understanding the notion of the in-itself: in terms of **mind-independence** and in terms of **attitude-independence**.

> Mind-Independence: Something is in-itself if it can *exist* independently of the existence of minds.

> Attitude-Independence: Something is in-itself if *the way it is* is independent of *the way we take it to be*.

The former is an ontological understanding of the in-itself, whereas the latter is non-ontological. Importantly, it is the fact that this is a *representational* account of thought, rather than a *presentational* one, that makes this possible. This is because it enables us to conceive of the relation between subject and object in terms of authority and responsibility. In essence, the withdrawal of authority is a matter of establishing a form of attitude independence.

I would suggest that Meillassoux's indifference to the distinction between presentation and representation, and Harman's dependence upon a phenomenological, and thus presentational, account of thought, is what leads them to adopt the ontological understanding of the in-itself. By contrast, the Hegelian model of thought enables us to adopt the epistemological understanding of the in-itself, and thus to undercut the arguments for their respective ontologies.

On this basis, we may also reformulate the *intuition* underlying correlationism in more exacting terms:

> Correlationist Intuition: The suppression of the concept prevents us from ever establishing the absolute attitude-independence of the object of representation. This means that whether or not our claims about the object are true is never completely up to the object, but is always mediated by something that we, either as individuals or as a community, have authority over.

### *3.1.3 Types of Truth*

Let us call this absolute attitude-independence **objectivity**. For a claim to be objectively assessable is for its truth to be independent of any attitudes that anyone has ever had or will have. This means that no claims about anyone's attitudes can count as good reasons for taking it to be true. The correlationist intuition can then be understood as the claim that we are unable to objectively assess the truth of *any* claim.

Now, some truth claims are obviously not objectively assessable in this way. For instance, the claim 'Bilbo Baggins is a hobbit' is not assessable independently of our attitudes about Bilbo Baggins. Indeed, there are claims such as 'Bilbo

Baggins has a secret half-sister' that we would take JRR Tolkien's attitudes to have special authority over. In these cases, we can nonetheless have arguments about whether the claim is true, because we can still withdraw our own authority, even if we cannot withdraw JRR Tolkien's.

In these cases, we have established a form of *relative* attitude-independence.

What this indicates is that in contrast to the position of deflationary realism, which holds that there is only a single notion of truth, there are at least two kinds of truth: objective and non-objective truth. There thus is a *thin* concept of truth which functions as a genus and a variety of *thick* notions of truth which function as its species. The withdrawal of authority and the attitude-independence it establishes is the common *form* of truth, and the various ways this withdrawal is modified, producing a variety of forms of relative and absolute attitude-independence, constitute the variety of *types* of truth.

It is this insight which gives us the leverage we need not only to overcome deflationism, but to resolve many of the issues involved in the various local debates we considered:

1. The problems with Quine's attempt to distinguish a privileged set of truth claims from which to work out ontological commitments can be overcome if we posit a distinct type of truth. Instead of working out our ontological commitments from the set of *scientific* claims we take to be true, we can work it out on the basis of the set of claims we take to be *objectively* true.

2. The debate between Blackburn and McDowell can be resolved once we recognise that it is not a matter of whether both scientific and value discourse are truth-apt in the same sense, but a matter of determining the differences in the structure of these discourses which differentiate the *types* of truth-aptness they exhibit.

3. This will give us the resources we need to extend the notion of aspects of the structure of the world we uncovered in the debates over modality, and the connection between these and the semantics of discourse, by allowing us to break the reciprocal sense dependence of Brandom's pairs of fundamental concepts.

However, we will only be able to achieve any of these goals if we can fight off the challenge to objectivity that the reformulated correlationist intuition represents.

### *3.1.4 Conceptual Revision*

The key to this is another insight drawn from Brandom, consisting in two interconnected points.[27] First, that our concepts are not fixed, but are *revisable*. Second, that the world itself can sometimes *force* us to revise our concepts. This makes the assessment of those concepts independent of our attitudes in a principled way.

First, the suppression of the concept is not irrevocable. It is possible for us to argue about the content of our concepts, but doing so suspends the initial debates which those concepts were a condition of. In short, we always perform a *suspension* of representation in order to examine the *conditions* of representation. The important point is that we can never perform a global suspension, but only local suspensions. This is just to say that if we disagreed about *everything* then we couldn't disagree about *anything*. If we are to examine some concepts, we must always use others.

Second, we must distinguish between two types of commitments one can undertake by making claims (and thus two types of claims):

> Objectual Commitments: Undertaken by claims about specific objects (e.g., 'this liquid tastes sour', and 'everyone in this room has excellent taste in philosophy'). These constitute the content of *singular* concepts (e.g., 'Bill Clinton is male', 'Bill Clinton was president of the US', etc.).

> Conditional Commitments: Undertaken by claims which make explicit inferential rules. These constitute the content of *general* concepts (e.g., 'if something *tastes sour* then it is an *acid*' and 'if something is an *acid* then it *turns litmus paper red*').

27. R. Brandom, *Between Saying and Doing* (Cambridge, MA: Harvard University Press, 2008), 184–9.

It is to some extent obvious that we can be forced to revise our objectual commitments about objects on the basis of either perception, wherein further objectual commitments are acquired, or inference, in virtue of the rules relating the predicates used in them. It is thus to some extent obvious that we can be forced to revise our singular concepts.

However, we can also be forced to revise the inferential rules that constitute the content of our general concepts on the basis of perception. So, let us take the above example of the concept 'acid', which we will take to be constituted by the two inferential rules:

> If something *tastes sour* then it is an *acid.*

> If something is an *acid* then it *turns litmus paper red.*

Now, say that through perception we then acquire an objectual commitment of the form:

> This liquid tastes sour *and* it turns litmus paper blue.

We are now in a position where our perceptually acquired commitments contradict the content of our concept. This means that if we accept the truth of the observation statements, we are forced to revise our concept of acid, by abandoning or modifying one or more of these rules. This example of objective concept revision is deliberately very simple. The truth is that there is a lot more to the content of concepts, and thus a lot more to the structure of the process of revision. I cannot provide an exhaustive account of this structure here, but I will provide an overview of how this picture needs to be supplemented.

### *3.1.5 Dimensions of Conceptual Content*

First of all, we have to get a bit clearer about what concepts are. It is important to recognise Kant's insight that concepts are **rules** for making judgments. It is also important to recognise Brandom's pragmatic insight that we must understand the propositions that form the contents of judgments in terms of the assertions that express them. Since assertions are principally linguistic, this means we must understand them in terms of the **sentences** deployed in those assertions. We thus have a threefold distinction between the **pragmatic** (assertion), **syntactic** (sentence), and **semantic** (proposition) dimensions of thought and talk. Kant's insight thus becomes Sellars's insight that to understand a concept is to understand the rules governing the use of a word in forming sentences which can be asserted, through which we express propositions.[28] This is not only a representational, but a properly linguistic account of thought.

Given this, we can see that there is more to the content of concepts than the rules made explicit by inferential commitments. This is most evident in the distinction between concepts governing the use of singular terms and predicates. The obvious move would be to understand their content as being exhausted by objectual and conditional commitments, respectively. However, at the very least, familiar Kripkean problems with proper names (which are a type of singular term) imply that the content of singular concepts cannot be understood as what is made explicit by objectual commitments alone.[29] Indeed, as Putnam has shown, the problem is more general than this, in so far as it extends to natural kind terms (which are a type of predicate).[30] What underlies both of these problems is a general worry about how it is possible for us to argue about the rules governing the use of the same word (or the content of the corresponding concept), if what *individuates* that word (or concept) from its homonyms (which have distinct concepts, e.g., the 'bank' of a river from the 'bank' on the high street) is just these rules. In essence, there must be more to the individuation of concepts.

These semantic externalist challenges require us to posit some additional mechanism whereby we can have some minimal grasp of the use of a word which fixes its identity, allowing us to argue about how that very word (as distinct from its homonyms) should be used. The classical way to do this is to posit a special set of claims that one must accept in order to count as understanding the concept. These are *analytic* claims, and there can be no genuine disagreement about them. Only the opposing *synthetic* claims can support such genuine disagreements. I take Quine to have adequately demonstrated that there is

28. W. Sellars, *Empiricism and the Philosophy of Mind*, in H. Feigl and M. Scriven (eds.), *Minnesota Studies in the Philosophy of Science, Volume I: The Foundations of Science and the Concepts of Psychology and Psychoanalysis* (Minneapolis: University of Minnesota Press, 1956), 253–329.

29. S. Kripke, *Naming and Necessity* (Cambridge, MA: Harvard University Press, 1980).

30. H. Putnam, 'Meaning and Reference', *Journal of Philosophy* 70 (1973), 699–711.

no in-principle way of drawing this distinction, and thus take all claims to be synthetic.[31] In the account I am presenting, the intuitive boundary between analytic and synthetic is captured by conceptual suppression, wherein we hold the content of the concept to be fixed in relation to those claims that we open up for debate. The boundary is thus *dynamic* rather than *static*, shifting relative to the focus of the debate. Rejecting the analytic/synthetic distinction in this way is a condition of accepting full-blown conceptual revisability.[32]

The crucial point is to recognise that the additional mechanism required to respond to the semantic externalist challenge must also make possible semantic deference, such as cases in which we use words of which we have a partial grasp, but can nonetheless defer to experts who have a fuller grasp. For example, it is possible for two laypeople to have a fairly interesting discussion about black holes, even though they only have a partial understanding of what black holes are. It is even possible for them to disagree about bits of what they do understand, and nonetheless be still talking about the same thing. This is because they have the ability to defer to physicists about the correct ways to use the word, or about what is true of black holes. There can be similar kinds of debates about particular objects. For example, it's entirely possible for me to talk about Bill Clinton, even if I've never met him, indeed, even if I couldn't pick him out of a crowd, as long as I can defer to the way others use the name 'Bill Clinton'.

The answer to these problems, which Brandom goes a long way toward articulating, is that language use depends upon an ability to keep track of relations of anaphoric dependence between different uses of words.[33] The simplest kinds of such relations are exhibited by uses of anaphoric pronouns within and between sentences, such as in the sentence '*Bill Clinton* is a ladies' man, but *he* is a mediocre saxophonist'. Here there is a simple anaphoric relation between my use of the name 'Bill Clinton' and the pronoun 'he', where the latter inherits its significance from the former. This is true regardless of who I pick out with the name 'Bill Clinton'. I could be speaking about a different Bill Clinton than the former president of the US, but I'd still be claiming *both* that he is a ladies'

31. W.V.O. Quine, 'Two Dogmas of Empiricism', *The Philosophical Review* 60:1 (1951): 20–43.

32. My views on this matter have shifted to some extent, as shown in 'On Computational Asymmetry', in this volume.

33. R. Brandom, *Making It Explicit: Reasoning, Representing, and Discursive Commitment* (Cambridge, MA: Harvard University Press, 1997), chapter 7.

man *and* that he's a mediocre saxophonist. The important point is that these kinds of relations, where one use of a word can inherit its significance from another, can extend between the uses of different speakers. Thus, if a friend of mine has never heard of either Bill Clinton, but I tell him that he is a mediocre saxophonist, when he goes on to tell other people about a saxophonist called Bill Clinton, he'll be referring to whoever I was referring to, in virtue of a dependence relation between our uses of the term. This holds equally of predicates as it does of singular terms. It is by virtue of being able to track these kinds of anaphoric dependence relations that we can take each other to be using the same concept, even if we disagree about particular features of its content. It is also what enables semantic deference of the kind just discussed.

There is a further dimension of conceptual content which needs mentioning, which is the role that our *practical* understanding of things contributes to the content of our concepts of them. This is an idea common to both Heidegger and the later Wittgenstein. As we've already noted, grasping a concept is understanding how to use a word. This is already a kind of practical understanding. Although this understanding might be to some extent *explicit*, for instance, we might have conditional commitments that codify the inferential rules we follow in using the word, it will always depend upon some understanding that is *implicit*. This is the import of Wittgenstein's rule-following regress. What it means is that shared *concepts* will always be dependent upon shared *practices*. Heidegger's insight is that these shared practices for using words are in turn dependent upon our shared practices of dealing with the things that those words refer to.

The real significance of this is that whereas it is possible for us to engage in *explicit* concept revision, by first making explicit the content of our concepts and then calling them into question, it is also possible for there to be *implicit* concept revision, since our practices for dealing with things, and thus the practices for using words that are dependent upon them, can adapt to the things themselves. In the implicit case, the world indirectly forces us to revise our concepts by causing us to change our practices. In the explicit case, the world directly forces us by providing us with good reasons to do so. The distinction is precisely one between *causal* and *normative* force.

On this basis, we can hold that in order to be counted as a rational subject, or as something that can genuinely think and talk about the world, one must be-in-the-world in something like Heidegger's sense, or have a form-of-life in something like Wittgenstein's sense. This is because we are only in touch with the world in so far as it objectively constrains our thought about it, and this is the case only in so far as it can force us to either implicitly or explicitly revise the concepts we apply to it. This means that one needn't be able to explicitly revise one's concepts in order to be a rational subject, but that the potential for acquiring the logical vocabulary (conditionals and negation) required to do so is nonetheless implicit within the abilities of such nonlogical rational beings.

To conclude this section, we can thus draw a distinction between the *primary* and *secondary* dimensions of conceptual content. *Objectual* and *conditional* commitments make explicit the rules constituting the primary dimension of conceptual content. These provide the representational core of the content of *singular* and *predicate* concepts respectively. The secondary dimension of both kinds of conceptual content is articulated by the *anaphoric* relations between particular uses of words and the *practical* relations between the way we use things and the way we talk about them. These provide the nonrepresentational periphery of conceptual content, but they are no less essential to it. The reason for this is that the secondary dimension is what makes possible the revision of the first, and thus what lets it be properly constrained by what it aims to represent. On the one hand, tracking anaphoric relation is what enables us to disagree about the primary content of the same concept, and thus to revise that primary content through argument. On the other, tracking practical relations is what enables the things we deal with to constrain the way we use the words that correspond to them.

Providing a detailed story about the relation between the primary and secondary dimensions of conceptual content is just describing the way the latter structures arguments about the former. Doing this is just a matter of giving a much more detailed account of the suspension of representation.

### 3.2 Objectivity

Moving on from the discussion of the content of concepts, we can now properly articulate a defence against the correlationist challenge. The first thing to recognise is that although we can never *completely* withdraw authority in any given debate, or perform a *global* suspension of representation, there *is* an ideal subset of our truth claims in which:

1. There is no claim for which we cannot perform a *local* suspension, and thus bring the concepts it deploys into question.

2. There is no claim about the primary content of these concepts that cannot itself be suspended, bringing the concepts deployed in it into question. In principle (if not always in practice) there may be recursive suspension.

3. There are no claims about attitudes (e.g., 'Pete *believes that* Bill Clinton is a ladies' man', 'Most people *believe that* unicorns are white', 'The Norse people *believed that* Thor is the son of Odin', etc.).

4. There are no claims the assessment of which bottoms out in claims about attitudes (e.g., 'Blibo Baggins *has* a secret half-sister', 'Unicorns *are* white', 'Thor *is* the son of Odin', etc.).

This subset is just the set of **objective truth claims**, i.e., those things we take to be true independently of the attitudes anyone ever had or will have.

### *3.2.1 Bottoming Out*

To unpack this a bit more, this means that all objective assessment, or arguments about claims within this subset, including all arguments about the primary content of the concepts deployed within these claims (and by *recursion*, all arguments about the primary content of concepts that these depend on), cannot deploy claims about attitudes as reasons. The only exceptions to this are claims in which there are further reasons why those attitudes are authoritative that do not ultimately depend upon claims about attitudes for which we cannot in turn supply such further reasons. This is what it is to say that arguments should not bottom out in claims about attitudes.

An argument bottoms out in this way either when it must appeal to the ultimate authority of some group or individual, or when it is not possible to make a claim without pragmatic contradiction. In those cases, we can say that the claims being made are non-objective. In the former case they are *interpretative* claims and in the latter case they are *transcendental* claims. The former are non-objective because they appeal to *specific* attitudes, and the latter are non-objective because they provide the structure of attitudes *as such* (because they furnish the conditions of possibility for having attitudes). It is interesting to note that, because we have rejected the possibility of analytic truth, these transcendental claims are by definition synthetic *a priori* claims.

This 'bottoming out' should not primarily be understood as a matter of reaching *indubitable* claims about which there can be no debate. Although there are interpretative cases in which there is a sole authority that can settle the debate directly through *stipulation*, these are not necessarily the norm. We can engage in very complex interpretative debates about the beliefs and intentions of those who have such authority if they cannot enter the debate directly (e.g., interpreting the works of dead authors), and we can engage in similar interpretative debates about matters that are determined by *communal*, rather than *individual* authority (e.g., communal norms, and claims such as 'Thor is the son of Odin'). The structure of these debates is just the structure of hermeneutic rationality. Similarly, in the case of arguments about the transcendental structure of thought itself, although there are obvious cases of pragmatic contradiction, there can equally be arguments wherein the proof that the denial of a claim leads to pragmatic contradiction will be very elaborate (and thus debatable). We might call the structure of these debates the structure of reflective rationality.

What 'bottoming out' consists in is thus not a regress to claims about which there can be no debate, but rather, a fundamental shift in the structure of the debate itself. The only way to understand this properly is to examine the structure of those debates that don't bottom out in this way. The major thing we have identified about these debates is that all of the concepts deployed within them are subject to revision, and that they are subject to revision in a way which is not dependent either upon *specific* attitudes (as in the interpretational case) or upon the structure of attitudes *as such* (as in the transcendental case). In the absence of these, the only thing that can force us to revise our concepts is the world itself. However, there are two different forms that this kind of revision can take, and thus two different kinds of objective claims: *empirical* claims and *mathematical* claims.[34]

### *3.2.2 Varieties of Discourse*

What differentiates empirical from mathematical discourse is the respective kind of claims to which they give priority. Empirical discourse gives priority to **perceptually acquired objectual commitments**, since these can force us to revise the contents of our concepts, as we saw in the simplified example of the concept of 'acid' above. Mathematical discourse, on the other hand, gives priority to its axioms, from which all particular mathematical truths must be derivable. These axioms are a set of claims which specify the rules of mathematical deduction (conditional claims), and a few basic premises from which these can proceed (objectual claims). Most importantly, the axioms are revisable, but they are not revisable on the basis of anything like observation claims about independently accessible mathematical objects, since everything about these objects is derived from the axioms. It is not exactly clear how the world forces us to revise our axioms, but I take this not to be a problem, but rather to indicate the possibility of a deeper understanding of the metaphysical status of mathematics.

It is interesting to point out that at least some of mathematics is transcendental or synthetic a priori in so far as the structure of quantification is a necessary part of the structure of rationality. The important point is that the axioms modify the basic structure of quantification, and in doing so extend it beyond simple arithmetic (e.g., by allowing quantification over infinite sets). It is thus possible to revise these modifications, but to understand precisely how these revisions take place is a matter of giving a full account of the structure of mathematical reason. It is the tension between truth and proof demonstrated by Gödel—the fact that given any set of axioms, there will always be some mathematical truths that cannot be derived from them—which makes mathematics objective.[35] We might say that, far from bringing about the ruin of mathematics, Gödel discovered the very essence of the mathematical itself.

---

34. My views on the relation between the mathematical and the empirical have also changed quite significantly, as can be seen in 'On Transcendental Logic', in this volume.

35. K. Gödel, *Collected Works I. Publications 1929–1936*, ed. S. Feferman et al. (Oxford: Oxford University Press, 1986).

Returning to empirical discourse, we can show how it is possible to deploy claims about attitudes in a way which does not bottom out. This is in virtue of the way observation claims (or perceptually acquired objectual commitments) function. We owe this insight to Sellars, whose account of perception refuses to take there to be some special dimension of content (what seems to be the case for-us) over which the perceiver has a special form of authority. If this were the case, and we needed to justify claims about what is by appealing to claims about what seems to be, then empirical discourse would bottom out in claims about the attitudes of whoever has this special authority in each case. Sellars's real insight is that claims about seeming play no important role in empirical discourse. When we endorse the observation claims that others make (e.g., 'It is snowing outside'), we do so on the basis of a kind of authority we ascribe to them, namely, a testimonial authority that we give to anyone who can reliably identify the sort of state of affairs in question (e.g., reliably discriminating between types of weather). However, this kind of authority is provisional, and this means that it is possible to call into question the inference from an observer's reliability under usual conditions to the conclusion that their attitude reflects the way the world is in some particular case.

The crucial point is that arguments about whether an observer's reliability warrants endorsing their observations in a given case are arguments about the observer's causal dispositions, the environmental factors which affect them, and the objects by which these dispositions are triggered. These are not claims about attitudes, and this means that empirical discourse does not bottom out in the way that interpretational or transcendental discourse does. Of course, such arguments will inevitably have to depend upon further observation claims, but all such claims can in principle be called into question, even if they cannot all be called into question at once. This is a special and rather limited case of suspending representation, since it involves a revoking of provisional authority over observation commitments in precisely the way that we revoke the provisional authority we have over the content of our concepts. There can also be more general cases of suspending the use of empirical concepts in order to examine the mechanisms underlying their application. For example, we might suspend all uses of the concept of 'aura' to examine whether there are *any* reliable mechanisms underlying its common usage. In the absence of such mechanisms we would do well to deny that it is a genuine empirical concept at all.

So, the question remains: What exactly about the structure of argument shifts in cases of bottoming out? In the case of interpretative discourse, something is *added*, namely, the ability to use claims about attitudes as reasons on the basis of non-testimonial forms of authority. In the case of transcendental discourse, something is *subtracted*, namely, the ability to use any claims other than those about the structure of thought itself. Reflective reason involves a bracketing of all claims other than those about the very structure of reason itself. On this basis, we can now see that the four forms of discourse we have so far identified form a hierarchy, in which claims from the higher forms of discourse may be deployed as reasons in the lower forms, but not vice versa. They are ordered from highest to lowest as follows: transcendental discourse > mathematical discourse > empirical discourse > interpretative discourse. We can also represent this as a partitioning of the set of truth claims:

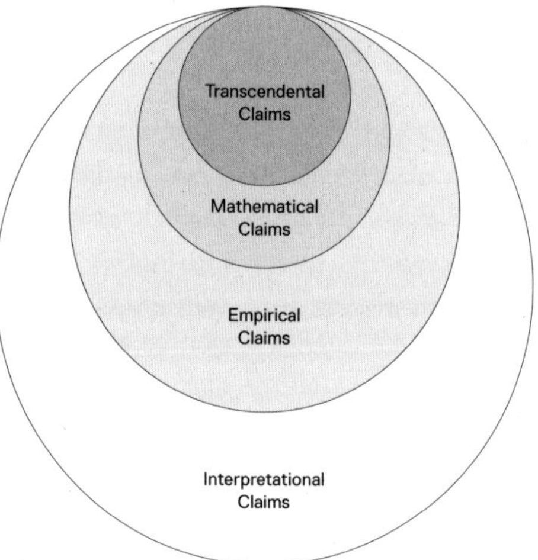


One could take this setup to suggest that we could do away with interpretative discourse entirely, but this is not exactly true. All discourse necessarily involves the possibility of interpretation, by both individuals and groups. On the one hand, discourse depends upon the possibility of navigating the commitments one's interlocutors undertake by their utterances. On the other, discourse depends upon the possibility of navigating the communal norms constituting the secondary dimension of conceptual content discussed above. Strictly, one need only be able to do these things implicitly. However, just as in the case of concept revision discussed earlier, the potential for acquiring the vocabulary necessary to do so explicitly, namely, by engaging in interpretational discourse about individuals and groups, is implicit within these abilities.

### *3.2.3 The Ideal of Objectivity*

Moving on, it is necessary to show why the set of objective truth claims is an ideal subset of what we take to be true. The reason for this is that claims are not *included* within the set, but rather *excluded* from it, and the process of excluding them is potentially indefinite. What this means is that we take claims to be objectively true by default, but we are under an obligation to continuously separate out whatever non-objective claims we find within this default set. This process of separation is potentially indefinite, not only because it involves recursively suspending our claims in order to examine the concepts deployed in them, but because, as noted earlier, such suspensions must always be performed locally, and thus require that one use some concepts to examine others. This means that although there is nothing that cannot *in principle* be suspended in this way, *in practice* we will never be able to suspend and examine all of our concepts. The task of separation is never finished.

What we can take from this is that objectivity is an ideal implicit within the very structure of truth. All discourse aims at truth, and the basic structure underlying this is what I've called the withdrawal of authority. This involves all of those engaged in the discourse giving up authority over their claims in order to grant such authority to the object of their claims. This is always abrogated to some extent by conceptual suppression, wherein we hold fixed the primary content of some of our concepts, in order to make this withdrawal possible. However, we can see that the underlying ideal is that of *maximising* withdrawal. This is why we strive to remove authority from absolutely everyone by default, and thus why claims are taken to be objective by default. It is only when debates bottom out in the ways discussed above that we separate them out, but even here we still strive to limit the relevant authority as much as possible. The very structure of truth compels us to divest ourselves of authority over the claims we make to the greatest extent possible. This means that we are compelled to talk about the world as it is in-itself.

Now, one could still maintain that it's possible to be involved in no objective discourse whatsoever, by holding that one could just engage in transcendental and/or interpretational discourse to the exclusion of all else. However, there is a good argument against this. As we've explained, some form of interpretation is implicitly involved in all discourse (including transcendental discourse), and interpretational discourse just makes this explicit. We've also shown that interpretational discourse can deploy objective claims as reasons, but not vice versa. The additional insight is then that, in order to be properly explicit, interpretational discourse must deploy such objective reasons. In the interpretational debates about both individuals and communities, one can always be forced to provide objective claims about what they have done that license us to ascribe certain commitments to them. For instance, debates about what an individual believes can always regress to arguments about what sentences they have actually uttered, and debates about communal norms (i.e., about what one should do) can always regress to claims about the practices of that community (i.e., about what they actually do). Interpretational discourse thus always has some grounding in objective matters.

What this means is that one cannot be fully explicit about anything unless one can talk about the way the world is in itself. Given that the potential for such explicitness is contained within all discourse, this means that the very structure of thought and talk implies that there must be a way the world is in-itself. This amounts to something like a transcendental deduction of objectivity.

### 3.3 Towards Transcendental Realism

However, although this is an adequate defence against the correlationist intuition, it does not yet amount to a demonstration of transcendental realism as it was defined above. This is because the latter holds not only that there is a way the world is in-itself, but that there is a real structure of the world in-itself. I'm now going to provide a brief argument for this kind of full-blooded transcendental realism.

First of all, we can agree with Brandom that the world is the totality of what is true, and that our picture of the world is just those claims that we take to be true. However, because we have provided a purely formal account of the distinction between objective and non-objective truth, in terms of an ideal subset of what we take to be true, we can now draw a distinction between the world and the Real:

> The World: All that is the case. The totality of all that is true.

> The Real: All that is really the case. The totality of what is objectively true.

We can then distinguish between the *formal* structure of the Real, which is just the structure of thought about objective matters of fact, and the real structure of the Real, which is the structure of the world as it is in-itself. The former is a transcendental (synthetic a priori) and thus *non-objective* matter, whereas the latter is properly objective (synthetic a posteriori). The former is the object of the *critique* of metaphysics, whereas the latter is the object of metaphysics itself. To repeat the distinction:

> Formal Structure of the Real: The structure of discourse about the Real. It is the structure of our picture of the Real as opposed to the structure of our picture of the world, or the formal structure of the ideal objective subset of what we take to be true, in distinction from the set of what we take to be true.

> Real Structure of the Real: This is the structure of the world as it is in-itself. This is the essential structure of the world as distinct from its contents, or what happens to be in the world.

We can then say that, because the ideal of objectivity is part of the structure of truth as such, we are compelled to move from the formal structure of the Real to the real structure of the Real. Rather than treating the question 'What is the Real?' (or 'What is the world in-itself?') as a question about the structure of our attitudes, we must treat it as an objective question, the answer to which is independent of our attitudes. In short, this means that the structure of thought implies that there is a real structure of the world which is not only independent from, but also in excess of, the structure of thought. This is the essence of transcendental realism.

## 4. KANT'S REVENGE

In the main part of this essay I've provided an analysis of the dialectical terrain of contemporary realism, located the potential for a new position within it—**transcendental realism**—and then provided the outline of an argument for it. In this final part of the essay, I'm going to work out some of the consequences of this position in more detail, and further situate it in relation to the historical tradition. Specifically, I will show how it recapitulates and modifies many of the important insights of Kant's philosophy. The moral I would like to draw from this is that far from *rejecting* the critical turn that Kant instigated, the real aim of contemporary metaphysics should be to *radicalise* it. It is precisely only by properly performing the critique of metaphysics that we may properly attend to metaphysics itself, and we may only do this from a genuinely *transcendental* perspective.

### 4.1 From General to Transcendental Logic

The first point to make is that the move from the formal structure of the world to the formal structure of the Real is analogous to Kant's move from what he calls **general logic** to **transcendental logic**.[36]

Kant identifies general logic as that which describes the form of thought in abstraction from all possible content, which is to say, in abstraction from its applicability to objects. In contrast to this, transcendental logic deals with the form of thought in abstraction from the content of *particular* objects, but in accordance with the content of objects *in general*. The various forms of judgement that constitute general logic, understood in terms of their applicability to objects, are then converted into categories, which constitute transcendental logic. The process by which this is achieved is what Kant calls a metaphysical deduction. Taken together, the categories also constitute the concept of an object in general, or the transcendental object.

#### *4.1.1 The Categories*

The formal structure of the world, as I have defined it, is just the formal structure common to all discourse. It is governed by a *generic* notion of truth, which does not yet discriminate between different kinds of truth. Within it we can find various other **generic concepts**, which play the same role as Kant's logical forms

36. See 'On Transcendental Logic', in this volume.

of judgement. These include **existence**, **predication**, **relation**, **identity**, **essence**, **modality** (in its various forms), **ground** and **consequence**, **number**, **part** and **whole**, among others. These are abstract logical forms which can be deployed within any discourse, including non-objective interpretational discourse such as fictional discourse. The move from the formal structure of the world to the formal structure of the Real involves thinking these notions in their applicability to real objects (or entities).

This means that in each case the generic concept gets split in two, into one concept which applies to constituents of the Real and one which does not. For instance, the notion of generic existence is split into the notion of entity and pseudo-entity, and the notion of generic predication is split into the notion of property and pseudo-property. This split allows us to make sense of the first two classical debates discussed earlier, as the questions become: 'Are numbers pseudo-entities?' and 'Are values pseudo-properties?'. In both cases we can modify the deflationary realist position in a systematic way:

> Entity: An object is an entity *iff* we take there to be some claims about it that are objectively true of it (modified from the Quine Thesis; it is interesting to note that this is very close to Kit Fine's solution to the problems of Quine's approach).

> Property: A predicate is a property *iff* we take some ascriptions of it to entities to be objectively true (modified from the McDowell Thesis).

This also lets us make better sense of the notion of an aspect of the structure of the world, or an aspect of the Real. In effect this breaks down into a question about whether or not some aspect of our talk about the world is also an aspect of our talk about the Real. There can be aspects of the Real which are not reducible to entities and properties just because there are categories other than those of **entity** and **property**, such as that of **modality**.

However, there is a very tricky issue here with regard to precisely how we define the notion of real object (or entity) used to define the notion of category above. The difficulty stems from the fact that there are two kinds of objective truth that constitute the Real—empirical and mathematical—and thus ostensibly two corresponding kinds of objects. My solution here is to say that mathematical objects are not real, or that there aren't any mathematical entities. This might seem like an ad hoc move, but there is a genuine reason underlying it. It regards an important difference between empirical and mathematical discourse. In empirical discourse, we grant authority to objects themselves to force us to revise not only our claims about them, but also the content of the concepts we apply to them in those claims. In mathematics, the objects discussed do not have this kind of authority. Not only what these objects are but which of them exist is completely derived from the axioms, and this means that they cannot play a meaningful role in revising those axioms analogous to the role empirical objects play in revising our concepts of them. One way of looking at this is to say that a mathematical object is not an in-itself in the way that an empirical object is. Another way would be to say that mathematical claims are *weakly* objective, whereas empirical claims are *strongly* objective. We must then modify the above categorical definitions to refer to strong objectivity, rather than objectivity *per se*. This has the consequence of answering the question of the reality of mathematical objects *a priori*: mathematical objects are pseudo-entities.

This move makes sense given the fact that, as I mentioned earlier, mathematics is at least partly transcendental, or synthetic a priori. The structure of quantification is part of the basic logical structure of thought, and this means that arithmetic and the mathematical objects it discusses, namely, the natural numbers, can't be seen as radically independent of our attitudes. This means that there is an important way in which my position is in agreement with Kant, but also an important way in which it breaks with Kant. On the one hand, I am in agreement with Kant in treating the objects of empirical discourse as the primary objects of knowledge, and thus taking the categories as solely applying to them. On the other hand, I am in disagreement with Kant in so far as I take mathematics to be more than simply synthetic a priori, and thus take it to genuinely constitute a part of the Real.

Nonetheless, even if we recognise that the mathematical is part of the Real, there is still the question of how it is part of the formal structure of the Real. My provisional suggestion is that the formal notion of an axiom, which functions to modify the synthetic a priori structure of quantification in a potentially revisable way, is the crucial notion here. However, this notion cannot be a category in precisely the same sense that existence is a category, since it does not have the same direct application to real objects (or entities). Nonetheless, there is a good sense in which mathematics is applicable to entities, as repeatedly evidenced in the natural sciences. As such, I will draw a distinction between **empirical categories** and **mathematical categories**. I will not provide more examples of mathematical categories here, but I suspect that there are others. As should be obvious, a much more thorough study of the structure of **mathematical rationality** in its relation to **empirical rationality** is required in order to properly flesh out this position.

### *4.1.2 Mathematising the Aesthetic*

It is nonetheless interesting to note that this split in the formal structure of the Real between the empirical and the mathematical mirrors Kant's division between the **transcendental logic** and the **transcendental aesthetic**. Whereas the former deals with the categories, or **pure concepts**, which provide the very form of the conceptual, the transcendental aesthetic deals with **space** and **time**, or **pure intuitions**, which provide the very form of intuition. The really interesting point is that not only did Kant take the whole of mathematics to be synthetic a priori, he took it to be derived from the pure intuitions of space and time. The position I am proposing allows us to modify Kant's approach here in at least three ways:

The Sellarsian account of perception allows us to deny that there is a distinct kind of representation, such as intuitions, which must be subsumed under concepts, and thus to deny that there are anything like pure forms of intuition.

We can thus hold that mathematics is properly conceptual, but that there is a distinction between mathematical and empirical concepts (and likewise between pure concepts or categories).

We can thus invert the Kantian story, holding that space and time must be understood in mathematical terms. However, because mathematics is nonetheless an objective discourse, this means that the Real can in some sense force us to revise our mathematical axioms in order to properly understand the real structure of space and time. This resolves Kant's inability to deal with both non-Euclidean geometry and the Einsteinian space-time that requires it.

The final consequence of this position is that although we must perform a metaphysical deduction of the categories in a manner similar to Kant, the corresponding transcendental deduction of the validity of the categories must be very different. Kant's transcendental deduction aimed to show the necessary applicability of the categories to the **forms of intuition**, and thus the necessary applicability of **concepts** to **intuitions**. However, the model provided here contains no such split between concepts and intuitions. Instead, the transcendental deduction, which was already sketched earlier, consists in demonstrating the necessity of objectivity. In essence, it involves demonstrating that we cannot think without thinking about the Real.

There is one remaining problem for this deduction, and it rests upon another question about the interface between mathematical and empirical discourse. We have provided a brief argument to the effect that it is not possible to explicitly engage in transcendental or interpretative discourse without also engaging in empirical discourse, but it might still be possible to hold that one could explicitly engage in mathematical discourse without in turn engaging in empirical discourse. Indeed, I earlier posited a hierarchy in which empirical claims could not be deployed as reasons within mathematical debates. This would seem to suggest that there could be autonomous mathematical reason, in a way that would undermine my attempt at a transcendental deduction of the categories.

The response to this problem is to distinguish mathematical *computation* from mathematical *discourse*. The former simply works out the consequences of a given set of axioms in an algorithmic fashion, but cannot allow for the kinds of axiom revision that are necessary for fully fledged mathematical discourse. If we can then show that axiom revision necessarily involves empirical discourse, we will have shored up the transcendental deduction I have proposed. The key to this is to show that there is a secondary dimension to the content of mathematical claims, just as there is in the content of other claims, and both that this is essential to the structure of axiom revision and that it can only be made explicit through interpretational discourse, which can in turn only be made explicit through empirical discourse. Unfortunately, this can only be demonstrated by carrying out the more in-depth study into the structure of mathematical rationality recommended above.

What emerges from this story is that in order to pursue the genuinely neo-Kantian strategy I have been outlining, we need to tell a much more in-depth story about the relation between the primary and secondary dimensions of conceptual content. There lies the key to the transcendental deduction.

## 4.2 The Question of Being

Kant is remembered more for his critique of metaphysics than for the *actual* metaphysics he expounded.[37] Nonetheless, let's not forget that Kant thought philosophy did not end with critique, but that critique is only a means to the proper pursuit of metaphysical knowledge. This is an idea that I have been advocating strongly throughout the whole of this essay. However, although much has so far been said about what the critique of metaphysics consists in, little has been said about what metaphysics itself consists in. In the last section I outlined the move from the **formal structure of the world** to the **formal structure of the Real**, which is the main part of the critique of metaphysics, in this section I will outline the move from the **formal structure of the Real** to the **real structure of the Real**, which comprises the whole of metaphysics.

### *4.2.1 Heidegger's Project*

The other figure that must be brought in at this point is Heidegger, who perhaps has the deepest vision of the nature of metaphysics after Kant. In order to expound this, it is necessary to be clear about the fact that Heidegger *initially* took himself to be doing **metaphysics**, and indeed, to be doing it more thoroughly than the metaphysical tradition that preceded him. His early work was focused upon **ontology**, which aims to provide an account of the **Being of entities** (*das Sein des Seienden*), or that which defines entities *as* entities.[38] Following the Aristotelian tradition, he took this to be a part of metaphysics, but he deviated from the scholastic variants of this tradition in taking it to be the **core** of metaphysics.

37. I. Kant, *Metaphysical Foundations of Natural Science* (Cambridge: Cambridge University Press, 2011).

38. M. Heidegger, *Being and Time*, tr. J. Macquarrie and E. Robinson (Oxford: Blackwell, 2001), 95–102.

Heidegger also followed the Aristotelian tradition in conceiving the **question of Being** as a matter of unifying the different senses in which 'Being' is said.[39] For Aristotle, these were the being of the **categories** (including **substantiality**, **spatio-temporality**, **quantity**, **quality**, etc.), **potentiality** and **actuality** (**modality**), the possession of **accidents** (**predication**), and **being-true** (**truth**). Despite rejecting Aristotle's manifold of senses, Heidegger never established his own definitive list. Nonetheless, there is good evidence that he saw the problem of defining entities *qua* entities in terms of uniting the different senses in which 'Being' could be said of them.

However, Heidegger's real innovation over this tradition was to see the potential for approaching the question, in a way independent of any given list of senses of Being, within the tradition itself. He did this by carefully reconstructing the idea of metaphysics as that which asks after entities as a whole as such. This means that metaphysics in general is concerned with entities as a whole *and* with entities qua entities in its guise as ontology.[40] Heidegger then diagnosed the inherent problem with the tradition as onto-theology, namely, its tendency to understand both of these in terms of entities. Traditionally, metaphysics ends up understanding entities as a whole in terms of some privileged entity (e.g., God) which functions as the ground of their existence, and understanding entities qua entities in terms of some property of entities (e.g., *Physis*, *Logos*, *Hen*, *Idea*, *Energeia*, Substantiality, Subjectivity, Objectivity, the Will, the Will to power, the Will to will, etc), which he calls beingness (*Seiendheit*). Heidegger's own strategy was to try and locate the structure of entities *qua* entities (Being) within the structure of the whole of entities.

Now, Heidegger called this structure of the whole 'world', and understood it in phenomenological terms as a temporal horizon projected by the thinking entity, or Dasein, within which entities are given. This is what underlies the early Heidegger's identification of phenomenology and ontology. This early approach failed precisely because, in attempting to locate Being within the structure of this temporal horizon, it made Being completely dependent upon Dasein. Heidegger's mid- to late period work replaces the notion of world with a more complicated structure, in which Dasein's projection of a world is in strife with a fundamental

39. Ibid., 22–23.
40. Ibid., 31–32.

excess (called earth) which it can never fully assimilate. This structure is articulated in various ways (including as the fourfold of gods, mortals, earth and sky), but we will lump all of these together under the heading of *Ereignis*.[41]

Ultimately, Heidegger abandoned the original Aristotelian question, coming to the position that there cannot be an answer to the question of entities qua entities, in the sense of an answer that would overturn all the various conceptions of beingness the metaphysical tradition has provided. Instead, he took it that *Ereignis* presents the structure underlying the succession of historical epochs within which these conceptions of beingness emerge, and that we must overcome metaphysics by describing this structure. The development of Heidegger's thought can thus be understood in terms of the way he switches the reference of the term 'Being' from the unifying structure of entities qua entities to the structure of the *givenness* of entities as a whole. This is a move from the Being of entities to Being as such, from *Sein* to *Seyn*, or from *Sein* to *Ereignis*.

### *4.2.2 Beyond Heidegger*

Now, we must reject Heidegger's position both early and late, as in both cases it collapses back into some form of correlationism. However, we can accept many of Heidegger's innovations over the Aristotelian tradition. The parallels between these insights and the position I've so far been articulating will become clear shortly, but I will first point out where the most important divergence from Heidegger is to be found. The position I've been articulating advocates a thoroughly representational account of thought, as opposed to the presentational account of thought that Heidegger inherits from Husserl. This means that we cannot view the structure of the whole of entities as a phenomenological horizon within which entities are given. We must nonetheless accept Heidegger's point that whatever this structure is, it cannot be understood in terms of some kind of privileged entity.

The natural way to move beyond Heidegger can be found by attending to the other name he gives to this structure of the whole in both his early and late periods: *truth*. What this indicates is that the natural replacement for the presentational notion of world/*Ereignis* is the account of the world that

41. M. Heidegger, *Contributions to Philosophy (From Enowning)*, tr. P. Emad and K. Maly (Bloomington, IN: Indiana University Press, 1999).

Brandom takes over from Wittgenstein's *Tractatus*. On this account, the world is all that is the case, or the totality of what is true, and the totality of what we take to be true is our representation of the world. We can then understand the Heideggerian strategy for answering the question of Being as seeking to unify the different senses in which 'Being' is said of entities in the *real* structure of the Real. Moreover, we can understand the question itself as seeking the underlying unity of the various aspects of the *formal* structure of the Real, which is to say the unity of the various categories in their applicability to entities (or real objects). This allows us to formulate the question of Being in a way independent of any given list of categories or senses.

In essence, what this shows us is that Heidegger's question of Being, when stripped of its phenomenological trappings, coincides with the task of metaphysics as we have so far defined it—to move from the formal structure of the Real to the real structure of the Real. Furthermore, we can draw a series of additional insights from this fact:

1. The move from the formal to the real structure of the Real can be understood as uncovering the underlying unity of the various categories in their applicability to entities. This indicates that we cannot properly understand the various aspects of the Real that the categories correspond to in isolation from one another.

2. Heidegger's claim that we must have some pre-ontological understanding of Being in order to answer the question of Being is satisfied by this account, in so far as the formal structure of the Real is implicit within the structure of thought as such. Indeed, we can identify this pre-ontological understanding with what Kant calls the concept of an object in general, or the transcendental object.

3. We must avoid understanding the real structure of the Real in terms of a privileged entity (i.e., onto-theology). For example, this means we must reject both Leibniz and Spinoza's account of the world, in which God either plays a privileged role (Leibniz) or is taken to be identical to the world itself (Spinoza).

However, although these insights help us flesh out the account of metaphysics provided above, we still do not have an adequate idea of what it is to move from the formal to the real structure of the Real, or, indeed, how to do it. The rest of this section will try to sketch an answer to these questions.

### *4.2.3 Metaphysical Concepts*

The answer to the first question lies in the fact that, if it is to get at the real structure of the Real, metaphysics must be an objective discipline. This means that there must be some sense in which the world can force us to revise our **metaphysical claims** and the **metaphysical concepts** that constitute their content. The relevant question is: What are these metaphysical concepts? The answer is that they are the concepts that pick out the aspects of the world to which the various categories correspond. The categories provide the form of these concepts, to which metaphysics adds content, and it is this content that the world can force us to revise, even if the categories themselves are fixed. Metaphysics is thus a matter of interpreting the content of the categories, or developing our pre-ontological understanding of Being into an understanding of Being as it is in-itself.

It is helpful at this point to provide an example. I will pick the category of modality, since it highlights the difference between the *transcendental* realist approach and the *deflationary* realist approach discussed earlier. The deflationary realists about modality (Lewis and Brandom) take the world to have a modal structure, but they take this structure to be exhausted by the semantics of modal discourse about the world. As such, Lewis takes there to be possible worlds and Brandom takes there to be incompatibility relations between predicates and between states of affairs. The transcendental realist, on the other hand, is able to interpret the metaphysical significance of the semantics of modal discourse, rather than simply taking it to reflect the structure of the world.

For example, one could be a Spinozist about modality, and hold that there is strictly speaking nothing other than the actual world, and that whatever happens is strictly determined, but that there are nonetheless real modal features of entities, such as capacities (or affects). This position holds that whichever capacities are actualised are in some sense necessarily actualised, but that our talk about possibility nonetheless makes sense, because it plays the role of individuating the capacities of both individuals and general kinds. A Deleuzian might then add that capacities are not the only modal (or virtual) feature of entities, but that there are also tendencies, which are individuated by our talk about probabilities. This would be a further example of interpreting the metaphysical significance of a category implicit within the structure of our thought and talk about the world.

What all of this means is that there are a series of metaphysical questions corresponding to whichever categories we locate through the metaphysical deduction: What are entities *really*? What are properties *really*? What are essences *really*? What relations *really*? What *is* modality *really*? etc. In each case, the 'really' indicates that what is sought is the real structure of the corresponding aspect of the Real, rather than the formal structure of the aspect of thought about the Real.

We can see that this schema is the consequence of breaking the reciprocity of the sense-dependence Brandom posits between the structure of the world and the structure of thought. Just as understanding the structure of thought is *necessary* but *insufficient* for understanding structure of the world, so it is for the various pairs of fundamental concepts Brandom located: we must understand the concept of singular term to understand the concept of entity, but there is more to understanding the latter than understanding the former; we must understanding the concept of predicate to understand the concept of property, but again there is more to properties than the structure of predication, and so on for the various other concepts. There is thus a correspondence, and an essential gap, between *logical* concepts and *metaphysical* concepts.

However, a proper critique of metaphysics should not only give us an idea of what it is to do metaphysics, but also how we should go about doing it. It is in relation to this that the first insight we drew from Heidegger rears its head. We can't properly understand any of these various metaphysical concepts in isolation from one another. We require a *systematic* picture of the real structure of the Real, or a *unified* account of Being. The critique of metaphysics must thus be able to show us how metaphysics can be approached in such a systematic way. I do not claim to be able to fully answer this question here, but I believe that I can point to where metaphysics must begin.

### 4.2.4 Metaphysics and Ontology

The crucial point is that the task of metaphysics, or the question of Being, is to unify the various categories in their applicability to entities. This is a point common to the Aristotelian formulation of the question of Being and the Kantian conception of categories. What it means is that the category of real existence (or the concept of entity) has some form of priority in relation to the other categories. It is by first asking 'What are entities?' that we can get a grip on the other metaphysical questions we must tackle. This does not mean that this question can be answered independently of the others, only that it should be our entry point into thinking about them.

However, this seems to contradict Heidegger's Aristotelian interpretation of the question regarding entities qua entities. Surely, this can only be answered by the question of Being as a whole? The answer to this is yes *and* no. As we have just admitted, the question of what entities really are cannot be answered properly in isolation from the various other questions that make up the question of the underlying unity of the categories. However, there is a way of understanding the question that gives it a kind of relative autonomy from the question of unity. This is to understand it as asking after the beingness of entities, in precisely the way that Heidegger castigated the metaphysical tradition for doing. This means understanding the narrow form of the question 'What are entities?' as a matter of abstracting a general concept of entity from the totality of entities given to us by empirical discourse. For example, one might take all entities given by the natural sciences to be understandable in processual terms, and therefore take it that entities *are* processes. One would then proceed to answer the various other metaphysical questions in relation to this, for example, by working out how the properties and modal features of processes must be understood.

In short, all of this means that we can accept half of Heidegger's critique of onto-theology, namely, that Being (or the real structure of the Real) should not be understood in terms of a privileged entity, but that we must reject his claim that one cannot genuinely inquire into Being by inquiring into beingness. This is because beingness (or real existence) is a genuine aspect of Being.

On this basis, we can formulate a neat division between the various questions of metaphysics and ontology:

The General Question of Metaphysics: What is Being? What is the real structure of the Real? What is the structure of the world in-itself?

The Particular Questions of Metaphysics: What are entities? What are properties? What is essence? Etc.

The Question of Fundamental Ontology: What are entities? What is the real structure of entities *qua* entities?

The Questions of Regional Ontology: Are numbers entities? Does God exist? Do fundamental particles exist? Etc.

This means we have rejected the Heideggerian definition of ontology in favour of its more classical definition as a sub-discipline of traditional metaphysics, although we accept Heidegger's thesis that it is the core of metaphysics. It is also helpful to note that what analytic metaphysics calls meta-ontology (not to be confused with what Heidegger calls metontology) is here labelled **fundamental ontology**, and what it calls ontology is **regional ontology**. Another way of drawing this distinction, advocated by Dale Jacquette, is in terms of **pure ontology** and **applied ontology** respectively.[42]

What emerges from this section is that although on the one hand the radicalised Kantian project I am recommending does not reject metaphysics, but must be seen as a continuation of the metaphysical tradition to some extent, on the other hand it must nonetheless be seen as pursuing a genuinely post-Heideggerian metaphysical project. I have so far painted the critique of metaphysics as a matter of making explicit what was already to some extent implicit within classical metaphysics, in order to pursue such metaphysics properly. However, we could also view this in more Heideggerian terms, as the attempt to formulate the question of Being that the classical tradition has forgotten, but which nonetheless provides its hidden impetus.

42. D. Jacquette, *Ontology* (London and New York: Routledge, 2014).

## 4.3 Science and Metaphysics

The other interesting feature of Kant's philosophy is the privilege he gives to the natural sciences, and thus his forging of an explicit relationship between science and metaphysics. We are now in a position to work out the consequences of the account I've been providing for this relationship.

### *4.3.1 The Structure of Science*

The first thing to note is that the account of thought and talk I have been advocating is committed to some form of **semantic holism**. This is because I follow Quine and Brandom in rejecting the analytic/synthetic distinction, although I take myself to have improved upon their accounts, in so far as the Hegelian account of thought I have introduced allows me to explain the intuitions underlying the notion of analyticity. What this means is that, at least with regard to the set of claims we take to be strongly objective (remembering that the set of what we take to be true is partitioned, and that these partitions have a hierarchical relationship), we can see our commitments as constituting what Quine calls a **web of belief**. This is a nice visual metaphor, where we understand our observational commitments to sit at the edge of the web, facing what Quine calls the **tribunal of experience**, and then both the commitments which these depend on, and those which constitute the contents of the concepts deployed within them, to sit further in, so that the further we get into the web, the more distant we get from experience. Quine held that in principle we could always make changes to commitments further towards the *core* of the web in order to hold fixed commitments at the *periphery*.

Now, Quine initially held that logic could be found at the very core of the web, but he later retracted this idea. The reason for this is that logic provides the very structure of the web itself. Brandom has emphasised this very strongly: the structure of revision cannot itself be revisable (at least not *entirely*). Another way of putting this is to say that the structure of the web is *transcendental*. The important question then is this: If logic does not lie at the core of the web, what does? On my account, it is metaphysical concepts which lie at the core. This nicely mirrors Quine's initial intuition, in so far as these are not *logical* concepts, but the metaphysical interpretations of these concepts.

Now, in order to understand the consequences of this idea, we have to understand that the sciences are the principal discourses through which we acquire objective knowledge. This is because they structure themselves around the ideal of objectivity. In the case of the natural sciences (or empirical sciences) they are structured around the ideal of **strong objectivity**, that is, they make experiment the final arbiter of all claims. In the case of the mathematical sciences, they are structured around the ideal of **weak objectivity**, that is, as they attempt to derive all of their claims from axioms which are nonetheless potentially revisable. Now, there has been plenty written in Philosophy of Science about how the actual practice of science fails to live up to these ideals, or even how these ideals are approached in incommensurable ways through the use of differing methodologies. I don't wish to go into these debates in much detail. I accept that these ideals can be realised in a variety of ways and that for this reason science will always have to address methodological questions. This is what it means for the structure of revision to itself be **partially revisable**. There is an interesting story to tell about how these methodological questions interface with what I earlier called the **secondary dimension** of conceptual content, but I will not attempt to tell it here. The important point is simply that nothing about the difficulties of realising the ideal of objectivity detracts from the ideal *qua* ideal.

### *4.3.2 Reciprocity and Continuity*

Now, in so far as metaphysics is a matter of interpreting the categories in their applicability to entities, and the notion of entity is defined in relation to the notion of strong objectivity, there must be an important relationship between metaphysics and natural science. Indeed, we can see that metaphysics depends upon natural science. This is because metaphysics does not describe the *Real*, but the *real structure of the Real*. Describing the Real is the job of science, and metaphysics is thus dependent upon it for its material. To describe this more concretely, since metaphysics must begin by abstracting a general concept of real existence from the totality of real entities, it requires science to provide it with the set of entities it can abstract from. It is only in virtue of this connection to natural science that metaphysics can claim objectivity, because it is only through this connection that it can potentially be forced to revise its concepts.

However, the relationship is more complex than this. Metaphysics is not something that appears *after* natural science, but something that is always already *implicit* within it. This can be seen by appealing to the metaphor of the web of belief, which provides the ideal structure of natural scientific inquiry. The transcendental structure of the inquiry implies that the core of the web is always there, even if it is more or less developed, or more or less explicit. Metaphysics is implicit within the ideal of objectivity, and science is structured by this ideal, therefore metaphysics is implicit in science. We can even see this in the practice of science itself. Einstein's supplanting of the Newtonian picture of the universe is a truly metaphysical revolution, obliterating the absolute conception of the metaphysics of space and time that were more or less implicit within the latter. The Darwinian revolution in biology continues to challenge the way we think about the very notion of types of entities (and thus that of essence), and complexity theory is forcing us to revise the way we think about part-whole relations. These are all cases in which science is already doing metaphysics—it is simply not doing it in a fully explicit manner. The task of the critique of metaphysics is precisely to make it explicit, so that it can be done properly.

What all of this means is that **metaphysical discourse** is actually a well-defined subset of **empirical discourse**. It also means that the relationship between natural science and metaphysics is not **one-way**, but is a matter of reciprocal influence. Metaphysics plays the role of organising the most fundamental concepts deployed within the natural sciences, and thus can play a very positive and explicit role within them, but in doing so it must also be sensitive to the results of those sciences, because experimental results and the theoretical innovations which follow them can ultimately force its revision. In essence, we can say that metaphysics and science are continuous, but this need not imply that the distinction between them is at all vague.

### *4.3.3 Mathematics and Metaphysics*

The final question to explore is that of the relation between **mathematics** and **metaphysics**. There is not too much that can be said here, given that I have already admitted that a more in-depth study of the structure of mathematical reason is required, so as to describe the structure of the revision of both **mathematical concepts** and **mathematical axioms**, through which we can determine precisely what the **mathematical categories** are. However, there are a few remarks that can be made. First of all, it must be the case that mathematical categories play some role in metaphysics, given that mathematical concepts can be applied to entities and metaphysics is just a matter of unifying the categories in their applicability to entities. Indeed, there is a good sense in which the primary content of many of the empirical concepts deployed within the natural sciences is in part mathematical (e.g., waveform, chemical equilibrium, allele frequency distribution, etc.). This is possible because **mathematical discourse > empirical discourse**.

Now, the applicability of mathematics to entities *in themselves* is an important issue in contemporary Continental metaphysics, and is ostensibly the problem that motivates Meillassoux's speculative materialism. I think there is at least one point of common ground between Meillassoux, Badiou, and the position I am articulating here. Both of them hold that mathematics does not describe a special domain of entities (i.e., mathematical objects), but that it instead describes the Being of all entities. This is in broad agreement with my position, in so far as I take mathematics to describe the Real without describing any entities. The difference between our positions is that they take Being to be exhausted by the mathematical, which I think misses the real point of metaphysics.

## 4.4 Fundamental Deontology

The most powerful of the criticisms originally levelled at Kant, by none other than Fichte, was that the *Critique of Pure Reason* could not account for the possibility of the very form of knowledge it exemplified. This led to a series of attempts by different figures to establish both an account of the *nature* of critical knowledge and a *method* for achieving it, culminating in Hegel's attempt to create a completely **presuppositionless** philosophy, and Husserl's attempt to create a purely **descriptive** phenomenology. Each of these in its own way strove to achieve a kind of critical **immanence** lacking in Kant's work. I will bring the essay to a close by contemplating how the project I have outlined can meet this ideal of immanence.

### *4.4.1 Pragmatic Contradiction Revisited*

I have already provided a partial account of the nature of critical knowledge. This is because I have provided a description of the basic structure of transcendental discourse. On this account, transcendental discourse is at the top of the discursive hierarchy, meaning that transcendental claims can be deployed in all other discourses, and that the **criterion of truth** of transcendental claims is that the negation of the claim implies a pragmatic contradiction. Strictly speaking, this criterion is too broad. The kind of pragmatic contradiction involved must be one which is not dependent upon anything about the person making the claim, meaning that claims such as 'I am talking', the negation of which is such a pragmatic contradiction, should not come out as transcendental claims.

Instead, the kinds of pragmatic contradiction we are concerned with are those which undermine the very structure of rationality itself, or the structure in virtue of which anyone can have an attitude about anything. Another way of saying this is that transcendental claims are those the negation of which would make rationality impossible, and thus those that represent conditions of possibility for rationality.

For example, the claim that one need never provide reasons for one's claims undermines the very structure of justification. It is tantamount to licensing bare assertion, in which the very fact that one takes something to be true is meant to ground its truth. This would amount to saying that authority is never withdrawn from the speaker. The corresponding transcendental claim is then that there must be at least some cases in which bare assertion is not permitted. These are all cases in which the speaker does not have some form of stipulative authority over the matter at hand. From this ban on bare assertion it is very easy to derive a ban on circular reasoning, because it involves justifying a claim by appeal to itself, which ultimately collapses into bare assertion.

So, when we say that the kinds of pragmatic contradiction that we are interested in are those that undermine the structure of rationality, what we are really interested in are those pragmatic contradictions which undermine the possibility of truth. The crucial point is that the possibility of truth is also dependent upon the possibility of falsity, and this possibility is established by the withdrawal of authority. This is why the withdrawal of authority provides the basic structure common to all types of truth. The kinds of pragmatic contradiction we are interested in are principally those that undermine this withdrawal.

### *4.4.2 Radicalising Scepticism*

The account so far provided also suggests the beginnings of a method for elaborating the transcendental structure of rationality, because it suggests that if one brackets all other claims, one is left with transcendental discourse. This follows from the place of transcendental discourse within the discursive hierarchy sketched earlier. This idea presents an interesting connection with the projects of both Hegel and Husserl.

Husserl's phenomenological method is predicated upon the idea of bracketing all evidence *given* in experience in order to provide an immanent description of the structure of *givenness* itself. He calls this the *epoché* and takes it to be a radicalisation of Cartesian scepticism. In contrast to this, my alternative method would bracket all reasons, in order to provide an immanent description of the structure of rationality itself.[43] This could equally be described as a radicalisation of Pyrrhonian scepticism, which is an *inferential* scepticism, rather than an *evidential* scepticism. This form of scepticism is more fundamental, both because the phenomenological position can itself be bracketed from within the Pyrrhonian standpoint (but not vice versa), and because, as Sellars has showed us,[44] we can provide an account of experience from within the structure of reason that has no need of notions such as givenness or evidence (it's also interesting to note that the very notion of the *epoché* originates with the Pyrrhonians). Nonetheless, any attempt to construct a counter-phenomenological method has plenty to learn from Husserl's methodological rigour .

It is now a matter of immense interest that Hegel's attempt to create a truly presuppositionless philosophy is motivated by his encounter with Pyrrhonianism. Although this philosophy only comes to fruition in the *Science of Logic*, in which he forces thought to immanently think its own structure starting from the least it can possibly think (which he names Being), the project of the *Logic* is justified by the *Phenomenology of Spirit*. The goal of the *Phenomenology* is to prove that

43. E. Husserl, *Ideas Pertaining to a Pure Phenomenology and to a Phenomenological Philosophy—First Book: General Introduction to a Pure Phenomenology*, tr. F. Kersten (Boston: Kluwer, 1998).
44. Sellars, *Empiricism and the Philosophy of Mind*.

what Hegel calls Science is the correct mode of knowing, as opposed to the mode of knowing he calls Natural Consciousness. We gave a brief description of the structure of this mode of knowing earlier, and most of the results so far produced are dependent upon it. Situating the current project in relation to Hegel's own project would thus be doubly enlightening.

There are two important features of Hegel's project:

> (1) The concept of Natural Consciousness is for Hegel just the concept of the separation of subject and object (or thought and Being), whereas the concept of Science is just the concept of their unity. One is the negation of the other, meaning that there is no ground in between the two. This means that one must adopt the standpoint of either Natural Consciousness or Science.
>
> (2) Hegel takes it that Science cannot justify itself without circularity, and that it must instead be justified from within the standpoint of Natural Consciousness. The *Logic* begins from standpoint of Science, and thus has a single assumption: the *unity* of subject and object, or the *identity* of thought and Being (i.e., classical idealism). The *Phenomenology* justifies this assumption by attempting to show how the concept of Natural Consciousness systematically undermines itself, thereby negating itself and becoming its opposite—the concept of Science.

However, the point that is not made explicit in all of this is that Hegel is taking up the challenge of Pyrrhonian scepticism. This challenge is best presented by the Agrippan trilemma:

> <u>Agrippan Trilemma</u>: How does one justify any claim, without recourse to (a) bare assertion, (b) circular reasoning, or (c) appealing to another claim which itself must be justified *ad infinitum*, i.e., regress?

The Pyrrhonian initiates this challenge by asserting the negation of any claims their interlocutor makes, thus creating a state of **equipollence**, where we must choose between the claim and its negation. We are then confronted by the trilemma, because to break equipollence, we must provide reasons to accept one or the other of the claims, and for whichever reasons we give for either claim, the sceptic will assert their negation, reintroducing equipollence and leading us into a vicious regress.

Hegel recognises that if he can justify the assumption of the identity of thought and Being, he will be able to carry out an immanent deduction of the structure of thought (and thus also of Being) that requires no further assumptions (this is why the *Logic* is also a metaphysics). The important thing to note is that this presuppositionlessness arises because the very form of Science does not allow for the introduction of equipollence at all. Each point in the dialectical development (Being, Nothing, Becoming, etc.) is necessitated by the last, making it impossible for the sceptic to assert its negation. However, Hegel must still justify the initial assumption which constitutes the structure of Science (or absolute knowing), and he must do this on the sceptic's own turf, so to speak.

Hegel's real innovation is that he realises that the Pyrrhonian is not without his own assumptions. To realise this, one must recognise that if one were confronted with a sceptic who merely asserted the negation of all of one's claims, one would not have a philosophical problem, one would have a heckler. The sceptical problem is only a genuine problem when it is *posed*, as it is in the form of the trilemma. The sceptic must show how the very structure of justification undermines itself, so that what we aim at in making claims is by its own nature impossible. However, in order to do this, the sceptic must actually describe the structure of justification. Hegel attempts to defeat the sceptic by beating him at his own game, namely, by describing the structure of justification, knowing, or claiming, *better* than the sceptic does, and then showing how that structure—which supports the very equipollence that makes scepticism possible—systematically undermines itself, and thus justifies Science.

As we have already seen, Hegel does an excellent job of defining this structure. I would even go so far as to say that he describes the essence of claiming with a clarity and precision unparalleled in the history of philosophy. However, this does not mean that he has gotten it right. The pertinent question is this: how do we know that the structure cannot be described in a manner more adequate than Hegel's account? What this question demands is a genuine method to immanently describe the structure of rationality. This is where Hegel falls down, in so far as he simply posits his concept of natural consciousness without presenting us with anything like criteria for assessing its adequacy.

To refute Hegel is to develop such a method and to show his account of natural consciousness wanting. This would not be to declare it incorrect, but simply to show that it is insufficient, to show that there is more to the ordinary (non-dialectical) structure of justification than he countenances, and that the argument of the *Phenomenology* fails because of this. The proper anti-Hegelian maxim is this: Natural Consciousness contra Science.

What we can take from this encounter with Husserl and Hegel is that we require a method for the immanent description of the structure of rationality itself, and that the way to achieve this method is by radicalising Pyrrhonian scepticism. This method involves bracketing all claims, only to leave those that are immune from bracketing, namely, transcendental claims about the conditions of the possibility of rationality itself. The question that remains is this: What kind of claims are these?

### *4.4.3 Transcendental Normativity*

The answer to this is to be found by returning to Kant's fundamental insight that thought is conceptual, and that concepts are essentially rules. For Kant, thought is an essentially rule-governed activity. The more modern way of putting this is to say that thought is an essentially normative matter. This lets us characterise precisely where Husserl went wrong. The systematic rigour of his phenomenological epistemology is admirable, as is the radicality of the phenomenological *epoché*. The problem is that he picked the wrong object to describe: **evidence** rather than **inference**, **givenness** rather than **bindingness**. The counter-phenomenological method we require concerns itself precisely with this bindingness or **normativity**. Rather, than describing the fundamental structures of consciousness, it aims to describe the fundamental norms of rationality—those norms by which we are bound simply in virtue of making claims at all, or those norms that provide the conditions of the possibility of rationality itself. In contrast to Husserl's phenomenology, I call this descriptive enterprise **fundamental deontology**.

It is only by immanently describing these transcendental norms that we can uncover the subset of these norms which we are bound by in so far as we make claims about the Real. These latter norms are just what we have called the categories. This allows us to extend the narrative I have given so far about the primacy of epistemology in relation to ontology. We can now see that, in turn, deontology has primacy in relation to epistemology. The practice of critique must begin with deontology, even if it does not end with it. The maxim here is: deontology is first philosophy.

This does not mean that, as Levinas claims, ethics is first philosophy. There are different forms of normativity, and not all norms we are bound by are strictly transcendental ones. Fundamental deontology deals only with these transcendental norms, and thus must be distinguished from other normative discourses, including ethics, which would be interpretative rather than transcendental. This does not mean that fundamental deontology is completely isolated from ethics. There is a good sense in which there must be a critique of ethics, just as there must be a critique of metaphysics, and it must also proceed by describing transcendental norms. Kant obviously recognised this himself (though we needn't accept his own deontological conclusions). This critique plays the role of what is usually called meta-ethics.

Now, ideally, I should posit some basic methodological principles governing fundamental deontology and then proceed to derive all of the results provided so far from them. Ultimately, this is the form that the project must take, but I shall not begin it here. I shall however give a working outline of what these methodological principles should be:

> The Primary Bind: This is the principle that there are some transcendental norms. It is demonstrable by pragmatic contradiction, since one cannot deny that one is bound by the same norms of argument as one's interlocutors without destroying the argument itself. There can be disagreements about what we might call subsidiary norms of argument, but the fundamental norms must be held in common, as these are what define the argument qua argument. For example, if an interlocutor points out that one cannot justify one's claims via circular reasoning, one cannot simply hold that this norm doesn't apply to oneself, without thereby undermining the very structure of argument itself (i.e., by collapsing the structure of the withdrawal of authority, and thus undermining the possibility of truth).

> The Principle of Correction: This is the principle that by default, one is entitled to explicitly correct one's interlocutors. Argument would not be possible if one

were not able to correct one's interlocutors in the manner of the above example, because pragmatic contradiction could never be made explicit. However, if one is to do this, one must therefore be able to explicitly state the transcendental norms from which the pragmatic contradictions follow. It is this principle which underlies the fact that transcendental claims can be deployed in all other forms of discourse. Although there are some cases in which transcendental claims might play some kind of positive role (e.g., mathematics, metaphysics, ethics), their ubiquity derives from this corrective role.

The Principle of Autonomy: This is the principle (inherited from Kant), that one can only be bound by commitments to which one somehow binds oneself. This means that one has a unique authority over which commitments one undertakes, both theoretical (objectual and conditional) and practical (individual and collective). Norms are just collective practical commitments.

Now, this last principle is the most complicated. It has a host of consequences. First, although one has a unique authority over which commitments one undertakes, one does not have complete authority. If one could simply specify in every case what one was committed to, one could not genuinely be bound by anything. For example, if one could retroactively specify the content of one's theoretical commitments in every case, one would be in the position of Lewis Carroll's Humpty Dumpty, able to mean anything by anything, and thus not able to mean anything at all (this is also the thrust of Wittgenstein's private language argument), whereas if one could retroactively specify the content one's practical commitments, one could simply redefine one's obligations so as to get out of any contract one is part of. What this means is that, in both cases, there must be a distinction between the force and the content of one's commitments. One is uniquely authoritative over the force of one's commitments (i.e., *whether* one is bound), but one must to some extent withdraw one's authority over the content of those commitments (*what* one has committed oneself to).

This has the result that one must be able to undertake commitments that one does not fully understand the consequences of. One undertakes commitments both through what one says and through what one does. The relevant question is to what extent one must grasp the consequences of what one is saying or doing in order to be counted as undertaking the commitment. There is a very complex debate to be had here, which I will not go into in depth. The important point is that whatever the criteria of commitment are, they can vary from case to case. However, there is one very special case in which one can have no theoretical grasp of what one is committing oneself to, and nonetheless still be committed. This is the case of the transcendental norms themselves. These norms form the limit-case of autonomy: one commits oneself to them in virtue of doing anything that can be counted as rational. This is to say, one is committed to them in so far as one can be committed to anything. This is because they are the norms which specify what it is to be committed to anything.

What all of this means is that arguments about force will always be matters of interpretation, because they always concern authority. Arguments about the content of our commitments will always involve interpretation to some extent (this is partly what is involved in the secondary dimension of conceptual content), but whether or not they count as interpretative will depend upon whether and how they bottom out in claims about attitudes.

Arguments about the content of objective theoretical commitments don't bottom out, arguments about the content of non-objective theoretical commitments do bottom out, and arguments about the content of practical commitments split in two directions, one of which bottoms out and one of which can go either way.

Arguments about what it is to do what the commitment entails can either bottom out or not bottom out, depending upon whether the content is made explicit by objective or non-objective theoretical commitments (e.g., what it is to heat steel to melting point and what it is to score a goal in a football match, respectively). Arguments about which thing we are to do must bottom out, but they can either bottom out in claims about the attitudes of the individual who undertakes the commitment (individual interpretation), about the attitudes of the group that determines the norm (collective interpretation), or about the structure of attitudes *as such* (transcendental reflection).

Ultimately, what emerges from the principle of autonomy is a further principle:

> The Principle of Reflexivity: The structure of normativity can only be described in normative terms. This is what underlies the fact that transcendental discourse

> is at the top of the discursive hierarchy. John McDowell gets at the essence of this principle with the phrase: 'It's norms all the way down.'

So, what we find is that the primary bind codifies the existence (but not the reality) of transcendental norms, the principle of correction codifies their ubiquity in relation to other forms of discourse, and the principle of autonomy (via the principle of reflexivity) codifies their independence in relation to these other forms.

### *4.4.4 Nature and Culture*

If we assume that we can manage to reconstruct the results of the main part of the essay within the framework just presented, then we can posit an additional principle:

> The Principle of Asymmetry: The distinction between the natural realm and the normative realm, between Nature and Culture, is neither a natural distinction, nor a distinction in some higher term (e.g., Being), but is itself a normative distinction. From the side of culture there is a sharp divide between the two, yet from the side of nature there is none.

What this means is that we can conclusively respond to Heidegger's challenge to Kant. At the beginning of *Being and Time* Heidegger claims that Kant has done a good job of giving an account of the kind of Being belonging to Nature, but that he has failed to inquire into the kind of Being belonging to subjectivity, upon which his whole philosophy is predicated. This is why Heidegger's project begins with an analytic of the Being of Dasein, which is his successor to the notion of the subject. Against Heidegger, and in favour of Kant, we can claim that **the subject has no Being**. The transcendental subject is a purely formal 'I', and although it may need to be indexed to some real entity (e.g., a human being), this index is not a genuine property of that entity. Nor is the structure of rational subjectivity a real essence. This is because none of these are properly objective matters.

This also enables us to revive some version of the distinction between facts and values. Facts are just objective truths, whereas values are non-objective truths.

However, this does mean that there is a distinction between transcendental and historical values.

In essence, the **Real** is nothing but **Nature**, albeit a nature that is intrinsically mathematical, because objective discourse is nothing but talk about Nature and the mathematical structures embedded in it. We are compelled to talk about the world as it is **in-itself**, but in doing so we are also compelled to leave all of the **normative machinery** (both transcendental and historical) required to talk about it out of the picture.

### *4.4.5 Varieties of Criticism*

The final issue to address is the status of critique itself. At the beginning of this section, I said that the account of thought presented in the rest of the essay provided a partial account of the nature of critical knowledge. Despite fleshing out the nature of transcendental discourse, this is still the case. The reason for this is that although transcendental critique is its most fundamental form, it is not the only one. The last part of this section will be devoted both to defining the more general concept of critique, and to highlighting the other forms it can take: *historical* critique and *empirical* critique.

To do this I'm going to try and trace a critical tradition that begins with Kant and extends well into the twentieth century. The figures I have in mind are Kant, Nietzsche, Wittgenstein, and Foucault, although there are almost certainly others who could be fitted into this tradition in some way. What unifies these thinkers is the attempt to analyse the structures of thought in order to diagnose systematic errors or illusions that these structures create, so as to free us from these illusions. For Kant, this is a matter of preventing the overextension of reason; for Wittgenstein, it is a matter of preventing us from running our heads up against the limits of language; for Foucault, it is a matter of uncovering the 'historical limits of necessity'; and for Nietzsche, well, it's somewhat more complicated....

Each of these figures is in some sense concerned with the conditions of representation, and how these conditions might distort our view of the very things we are trying to represent. Kant and the early Wittgenstein are concerned with the specifically transcendental conditions of representation—the ahistorical structure of thought and language. Nietzsche, Foucault, and the later Wittgenstein are all concerned with the specific *historical* conditions of representation—the language-games, epistemes, and networks of power relations that constitute the *social* dimension of representation. Nietzsche is then somewhat unique among these thinkers (although he would find many allies in contemporary philosophy) in also concerning himself with the empirical conditions of cognition—the psychological and biological structures which make thought possible.

The account of thought I've so far provided gives us a way of describing each of these different projects in a unified way, in virtue of the notion of the suspension of representation. Representation is suspended when we hold in abeyance the assessment of a claim about an object in order to examine the conditions which make it possible to represent the object. Now, in Part 3 this was mainly described as a matter of bringing into question the commitments which constitute the primary content of the concepts that constitute the claim. However, as has been suggested at times, suspension has a far broader range than this. What is common to the various forms of critique is that they implement suspensions of representation that abstract from primary content, whereas what differentiates them are the different kinds of conditions of representation that they examine.

Transcendental critique is the most fundamental form of critique, in so far as the bracketing it must perform is the closest thing we can get to a global suspension of representation. As has been noted, such global suspensions cannot be used to examine the content of our objective concepts, since one must always use some concepts to examine others. The deontological *epoché* is not quite a global suspension of the kind discussed earlier, given that transcendental claims about the normative structure of discourse are immune to it. Nonetheless, in bracketing all other claims, it abstracts from the content of all ordinary concepts in order to describe the structure of concepts as such, including the structure of concept revision. This is to say that it abstracts from the primary content of all concepts, leaving only the form of the conceptual.

By contrast, historical and empirical critique deal with the structures of specific concepts (or networks of concepts). However, they don't suspend the claims these concepts are deployed in so as to examine the primary content of these concepts, but so as to examine the secondary content that structures the process of conceptual revision in each case (as opposed to the general structure of such revision). Historical critique examines both the networks of deference which constitute the anaphoric dimension of content, the social practices underlying the practical dimension of content, and the sociological structures in relation to which both of these dimensions are situated. Empirical critique examines the way in which other empirical factors shape our practices of dealing with things and using words, and by extension the sociological structures they are tied up in. As such, it is harder to draw a crisp distinction between these two forms of critique than between them and its transcendental form. Both deal with historically contingent structures, and both may deal with specifically social structures. The real distinction lies in whether they describe these structures in normative (interpretational) or causal (empirical) terms, or rather, the extent to which they use either. In truth, both are required to some extent, and this is why it is hard to draw the distinction properly. In essence, the distinction depends upon whether the emphasis is placed upon hermeneutic or natural scientific forms of explanation.

Once more, I must admit that without a more in-depth account of the nature of secondary content and the nature of the suspension of representation, I am unable to provide a more detailed account of the nature of critique. Nonetheless, we are in a position to glimpse the general character of the critical impulse. Critique aims to pick apart the various structures underlying the process of knowledge acquisition, which is both the process of acquiring claims and the process of revising our concepts, in order to differentiate legitimate constraints on this process from illegitimate ones. It is a kind of conceptual technics through which we both uncover the properly transcendental limits of knowledge and remove historical and empirical impediments to it. The project outlined in this essay is thus doubly critical: critical in so far as it is transcendental, and critical in so far as it seeks to give a transcendental account of the process of empirico-historical criticism, so as to facilitate critique in all its forms.

The final point to make is that, just as we saw that scientists are already doing metaphysics to some extent implicitly, so it is that philosophers are already doing critique to some extent. This is the whole purpose of the schema 'philosophy of X' (e.g., philosophy of science, philosophy of art, philosophy of law, etc.). Philosophers are already conceptual technicians, even if this is not all that they are. Following the ideal of explicitness, our goal should be to make explicit precisely what philosophers are already doing in these cases, so that it might be done properly, just as it has been the goal of this essay to make explicit what scientists are already doing.

On this basis, we can draw a distinction between the *critical* and the *constructive* dimensions of philosophy, the former exemplified by transcendental philosophy and the latter exemplified by metaphysics. The former dimension maintains the structure of knowledge, while the latter aims to actually produce knowledge, by creating new concepts which order existing fields of inquiry.

## 5. CONCLUSION

The aim of this essay has been to announce the possibility of something like a transcendental realism, and to do so by engaging both with contemporary debates about realism and with the historical tradition more broadly. In the course of it, I have not only defined what such a transcendental realism would be, but also provided an argument for it, and worked out many of the details and further consequences of it. What has emerged across all of this is the necessity of once more returning to the philosophy of Kant, as it seems we are destined (or doomed) to do every fifty years or so. However, this call for a renewed take on the Kantian project is motivated neither by nostalgia, nor by some deep-seated frustration with the contemporary philosophical terrain. It is neither a call for novelty for its own sake, nor a call for tradition for its own sake. It is motivated by a problem that is deeper than such trite narratives.

On the one hand, against deflationists, anti-realists, correlationists, and all other anti-metaphysicians of the twentieth century, we seem to genuinely understand the significance of metaphysical questions. On the other, against the pre-critical metaphysicians and those who would return us to the era of unconstrained speculation, we are not so sure that we know what this significance really is. The only response to this is a critique of metaphysics, which defines its exercise and its limits, and the progenitor and most powerful exponent of that critique is Kant.

However, as I have also demonstrated, this renewal of Kantianism should also be critical in the more common sense of the word. There is as much in Kant that is ripe for revision as there is that is ripe for appropriation. First of all, following the last wave of Neo-Kantians, we must excise the transcendental aesthetic and the dependence upon nonconceptual forms of representation that it embodies.

Secondly, we must also update both the theories of and the perceived relation between logic, semantics, and pragmatics underlying Kant's conception of thought, to adopt the insights of Hegel, Heidegger, Wittgenstein, Quine, Sellars, Brandom, and others. These two changes amount to a substantive revision of the whole of Kant's account of thought, along the lines already discussed.

On the basis of this, we must revise the Kantian architectonic of reason. This must be done by distinguishing the various forms of rationality in terms of the way they modify the withdrawal of authority, and thus in terms of the types of truth to which they correspond. It is possible to use the insights provide above to furnish such a taxonomy of truth:

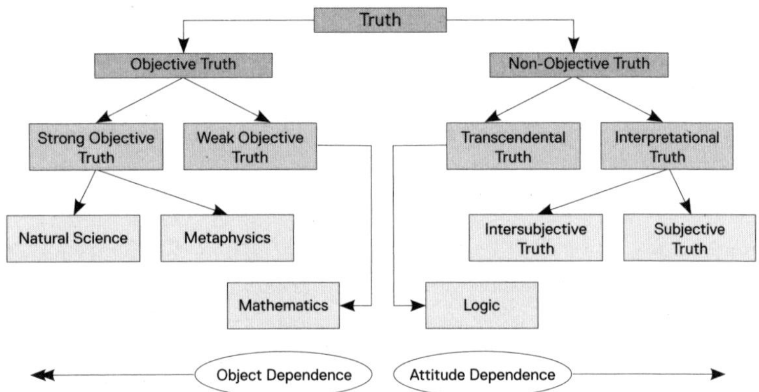


Here we can see that the various types of objective truth can be ranked in terms of the extent to which they grant authority to objects, and thus the extent to which they are **object-dependent**, and the types of non-objective truth can be ranked in terms of the extent to which they grant authority to individuals attitudes, and thus the extent to which they are **attitude-dependent**. For instance, natural scientific truth is more object-dependent than metaphysical truth because the former can depend upon specific kinds of entities, whereas metaphysical truth is dependent upon all entities equally. In a similar vein, subjective truth depends upon the attitudes of a specific individual who has unique authority, whereas intersubjective truth depends upon the attitudes of groups of individuals, none of which need have this kind of authority. Mathematical and logical truths are distinctive in so far as they are not dependent upon **any** specific objects or attitudes.

This schema is not exhaustive; there are many further subtypes of truth that are not presented in it. For instance, we could distinguish **ethical truth** and **aesthetic truth** (the major concerns of Kant's second and third Critiques) as further types of intersubjective truth. We could equally break down mathematics into its logical (quantificational) and non-logical (axiomatic) parts, as well as breaking down logic into its general and transcendental parts. There is thus much work to be done in extending this taxonomy of truth and the corresponding architectonic of reason.

Beyond this, we must do something about the infamous notion of the thing-in-itself, the poor reception of which has haunted Kant's philosophy since its inception, in order to retain the kernel of insight it represents while banishing its more problematic connotations. This means rejecting any ontological understanding of the difference between phenomena and noumena and reconceiving the latter as the concept of the ideal limit of the rational process of revising our theoretical commitments, which can be thought in relation to any given entity. However, far more needs to be said about precisely how to understand this limit-concept, and the relation between it and the notion of the Real.

Finally, we must establish a method (which I have called fundamental deontology) to recapitulate all of these insights in an *immanent* and *systematic* fashion. This is a daunting task, but it is one that is undoubtedly worthwhile. If nothing else, the promise of working out both what *thought* demands of us, and what the *world* demands of us, is too good to pass up.

# Ariadne's Thread: Temporality, Modality, and Individuation in Deleuze's Metaphysics

## 0. INTRODUCTION

By his own admission, Gilles Deleuze was a pure metaphysician.[1] Of course, his thought is broader than this. He made interesting and potentially lasting contributions to social theory, ethics, politics, and aesthetics, to name but a few other philosophical fields. However, it's important to understand not only that his deepest and most significant insights come from his work on metaphysics, but also that most of his insights in other domains flow from these metaphysical innovations. If we wish to understand the real import of Deleuze's work, then we must be willing to plumb the depths of his metaphysical system. Moreover, we must be willing to approach Deleuze's metaphysics as a system. It's all too easy to focus on one thread of his innovative metaphysical tapestry to the exclusion of others, thereby isolating it from the complex interweaving themes that determine its true significance. This means that we have to be willing to take the road less travelled and approach Deleuze's metaphysics holistically—to tackle his system qua system.

This is a tall order for a single paper. I'm simply not able to present the whole of Deleuze's metaphysics in the present context. However, it is possible to pick out certain fundamental structural features that tie the whole together—the skeleton of the system, as it were. This is the goal of this paper, then: to trace the metaphysical bones from which the meat of Deleuze's philosophy hangs.

The principal difficulty we face in taking this holistic approach to Deleuze's metaphysics is that, for all that Deleuze's work is systematic in content, it is not necessarily systematic in form. Deleuze has a metaphysical system, but it is not clear that he has a systematic methodology for either expositing or justifying it.

1. See A. Villani, 'I Feel I am a Pure Metaphysician: The Consequences of Deleuze's Affirmation', in R. Mackay (ed.), *Collapse* vol. 3 (Falmouth: Urbanomic, 2012), 45–63.

Once one is inside Deleuze's system, the landscape is beautiful, but there's no clear point of entrance by which to bring others in to enjoy the view. The solution here can only be to provide our own methodological supplement: to devise some expressive and explanatory principles by means of which to reconstruct the key features of his metaphysics. Put differently, a holistic approach demands a reconstructive approach. We must treat Deleuze in the same way he treated Spinoza, Kant, Nietzsche, and especially Bergson: we must aim to present him in a more accessible and consistent fashion than he himself ever managed.

## 1. THE PROBLEMS OF METAPHYSICS

Bearing this injunction in mind, then, we should begin by addressing the question of precisely what metaphysics is. Once more, this question is too big a topic to be adequately tackled in this essay, but it will be useful to present a provisional answer to it in order to organise our approach to Deleuze's metaphysics. We must be able to say something general about the nature of metaphysical problems, if we are to say anything specific about those problems that Deleuze takes up and the solutions he proposes to them.

So, let's make a few sweeping claims that can be marshalled into the form of an argument:

i. The aim of metaphysics is to describe **the fundamental structure of nature** (or Being).

ii. This task is essentially continuous with that of **natural science**, even if it can be methodologically distinguished from the vast part of the practice of natural science.

iii. Although the fundamental structure of nature is **unitary**, this does not prevent us from distinguishing its different aspects, and thus articulating distinct metaphysical problems.

iv. These are distinguished by examining the **logic** of our pre-theoretical grasp of the structure of nature (or pre-ontological understanding of Being).

v. Therefore, we understand **metaphysical categories** in terms of **logical**

**categories** and thus the **methodology of metaphysics** by way of the **architectonic of reason**.

This is the condensed version of a much larger story about the history of metaphysics that I have told elsewhere, focusing on the relationship between *logic*—as the study of the structure of thought—and *metaphysics*—as the study of the structure of Being.[2] The moral of this story is that although there is certainly more to metaphysics than logic, there is an important sense in which logic constrains metaphysics.

Metaphysics seeks to understand what nature is, whereas logic seeks to understand what 'nature' means. This extends to the discussion of particular categories and the problems that correspond to them: identity, difference, individuality, universality, quantity, quality, relation, essence, space, time, causation, etc. Each of these corresponds to a metaphysical problem, but the scope of this problem is determined by the logical analysis of the relevant category in each case. For instance, if we wish to understand the metaphysics of causation, we had better start with the logic of causal reasoning, because it is only by understanding the latter that we can understand what it would be to understand the former. To put this in different terms: metaphysics must be accompanied by a critique of metaphysics, through which the distribution of problems and the constraints upon potential solutions are understood.

I will not defend this view any further, but will instead attempt to demonstrate its expressive and explanatory power in the course of reconstructing a number of classical metaphysical problematics to which Deleuze makes decisive contributions. I'm going to explain three long-running problems from the metaphysical tradition in the terms just provided: the problem of *universals*, the problem of *possibilia*, and the problem of *time*. The problem in each case is essentially how we are to understand the relevant phenomena as aspects of a unitary nature, or how we are to understand their reality.

## 2. THE EXISTENCE OF UNIVERSALS

The problem of universals has the most noble heritage. It has motivated countless philosophical debates and caused untold confusion since the time of Plato, whose theory of Ideas is the exemplar against which all alternative solutions

2. See 'Essay on Transcendental Realism', in this volume.

to the problem are judged. The problem has traditionally been framed in terms of whether or not universals exist, e.g., does universal doghood exist in an analogous sense to the way particular dogs exist? There are many different answers to this question, but they all turn upon precisely what we mean by 'existence' here.

The affirmative answers are traditionally grouped under the heading of Platonism, and they differ in so far as they offer distinct accounts of the special sense of 'existence' unique to universals. The core issue that each account has to address is the nature of the relation between the existent universal and its existent instances. Famously, Plato locates universals within an independent intelligible realm.[3] They exist as archetypes that individuals may participate in. Aristotle famously tries to invert this picture, by eliminating the intelligible realm in favour of the sensible realm.[4] The universals are thus supposed to be immanent to the individuals that instantiate them. The success of this original inversion of Platonism is debatable, but there is another important contribution Aristotle makes here, in the form of his distinction between substance and accident, e.g., between a dog and the unique red shade of its fur. This combines with the distinction between universal and singular to produce a fourfold schema:

| | SUBSTANCE | ACCIDENT |
|---|---|---|
| UNIVERSAL | Sortals (Secondary Substance) | Qualities |
| SINGULAR | Individuals (Primary Substance) | Tropes |

Table 1

The real contribution here is the distinction between types of universals this produces, i.e., between *sortals* such as doghood and *qualities* such as redness. This distinction is based upon the role such universals play in individuating their instances. What we mean by 'individuation' here is a logical matter of distinguishing an individual from all other individuals, or a matter of settling those

3. Plato, *The Republic*, tr. G.M.A. Grube, rev. C.D.C. Reeve, in *Complete Works*, ed. J.M. Cooper (Indianapolis: Hackett, 1997), 971–1223.
4. Aristotle, *Metaphysics*, tr. C.D.C. Reeve (Indianapolis: Hackett, 2016).

conditions that uniquely identify it. The difference between sortal properties and qualitative properties is that although both can be used to distinguish between distinct individuals (e.g., if this dog is naturally red and that dog is naturally brown, then they cannot be the same dog), only sortal properties can be used to determine quantities of distinct individuals, or to count instances of the property (e.g., there are a determinate number of dogs in Manchester, but not a determinate number of coloured instances).

There is more to the category of quantity than what is provided by sortal individuation. There are all sorts of quantities that aren't reducible to sets of distinct individuals, such as quantities of mass, energy, distance, and even particles in the framework of quantum theory. However, we're going to stick to sortal individuation for the moment, because it touches upon another important historical debate: that between Leibniz and Kant over the principle of the identity of indiscernibles (PII).

This is a disagreement about the nature of sufficient conditions for complete individuation. Leibniz holds that every individual thing (or monad) has a corresponding individual concept that is sufficient to completely individuate it, and that this concept incorporates all the determinations of the thing, as if it were an infinite list of its universal properties.[5] Leibniz's really challenging claim is that the thing's spatiotemporal location is unnecessary for individuating it, and that it can be deduced entirely from the list of its nonspatiotemporal properties. By contrast, Kant holds that some grasp of spatiotemporal location is necessary to completely individuate a thing, but that this is nevertheless insufficient without the addition of a general concept.[6] This ties back to the distinction between sortals and qualities: not just any general concept will do here. Sortal concepts are just those general concepts whose combination with some grasp of location is sufficient to completely individuate something. This is precisely because they are tied to procedures for counting the number of instances of a universal in a given location (i.e., what Kant would call schemata). All you need to completely individuate a thing is enough information about its location to get the relevant counting procedure to give you the answer '1'. This idea is developed by Frege,

5. G.W. Leibniz, *Discourse on Metaphysics and Other Essays*, tr. D. Garber and R. Ariew (Indianaopolis: Hackett, 1991), 1–40.

6. I. Kant, *Critique of Pure Reason*, tr. P. Guyer and A.W. Wood (Cambridge and New York: Cambridge University Press, 1987), 116–69.

Russell, and Quine as the claim that there is nothing more to existence than the instantiation of such a sortal concept.

Returning to the question of whether universals exist, the negative answers are usually grouped under the heading of nominalism; they offer different accounts of the sense in which there is a 'relation' between universals and individuals without the former term existing in any sense. Now we've addressed the relationship between universals and individuation, we can precisely specify the issue that motivates nominalism: the problem of **universal individuation**. This problem is actually at least as old as Platonism, and is posed in Plato's own work (the *Sophist* and the *Parmenides*, specifically).[7] It is the issue of how we can distinguish between universals in such a way as to determine precisely which universals exist, what features they have, and what relations they stand in to one another, in order that we can stop appealing to nonexistent universals (e.g., *sophism*) and mischaracterising those that do exist (e.g., misunderstanding the relationship between truth and beauty).

Plato and Aristotle give us different accounts of where existent universals are located: either in a distinct intelligible space, or somehow in the same sensible space in which ordinary individuals are located. Their accounts are unsatisfactory, however: they fail to provide us with a good account of the meta-sortals we would need to adequately count and thereby differentiate between the various located universals. The common strategy of most nominalisms is to overcome this problem by retreating to the problem of the individuation of concepts, as opposed to worrying about whatever it is that concepts are traditionally supposed to grasp. They treat the problem of universals as one of how we articulate the world into different groups of things, rather than as a problem of how the world is articulated in itself. This strategy produces all sorts of problems of its own, usually epistemological problems regarding how we are supposed to judge whether the way in which we articulate the world is any good. However, I'm not going to go into these in any further detail.

Instead, I'm going to briefly address the nominalist aspect of Manuel DeLanda's interpretation of Deleuze, as it will provide a useful contrast both to traditional nominalism and to the account of Deleuze's solution to the problem of universals

7. Plato. *The Sophist*, tr. N.P. White; *The Parmenides*, tr. M.L. Gill and P. Ryan, in *Complete Works*, 293, 359–97.

I shall present below. DeLanda's nominalism is implied in his doctrine of flat ontology, or the idea that the species to which individuals belong are themselves individuals, rather than universals (e.g., that the species 'lion' is nothing more than the population of individual lions understood as a larger-scale ecological process composed out of smaller-scale biological processes).[8] I'm not going to assess this view so much as call attention to its nominalist pedigree. It eliminates universals as transcendent things by insisting that if they exist, then they must exist in the same sense that other spatiotemporally located individuals do. This naturally collapses into the idea that whatever it is we're talking about in talking about universals must simply be individuals themselves. Such an approach avoids many of the problems of traditional nominalism by refusing to see the individuation of species as a matter of our *concepts* of them, while still refusing to acknowledge special existent universals.

## 3. THE POSSIBLE AND THE PROBABLE

The problem of possibilia has almost as noble a heritage as the problem of universals. It goes back at least as far as Aristotle's discussion of the relation between *potentiality* and *actuality*, but it really came into its own with the debate between Spinoza and Leibniz regarding the interpretation of the **principle of sufficient reason** (**PSR**) and the debate between Hume and Kant regarding the nature of causal necessity. This positively exploded in the twentieth century following Russell's debate with Meinong over the reality of possible individuals, along with Kripke and Lewis's rigorous formalisation of the Leibnizian notion of possible worlds. All of these debates are facets of the problem of how to make sense of what we're talking about when we use modal language (e.g., 'that's *impossible*', 'I *could* have had a sister', 'A *always* follows B', etc.).

The Aristotelian solution is that modality is an intrinsic feature of things, such that specific possibilities (e.g., the possibility that I stop writing this essay) inhere in the form of given individuals as capacities to produce effects (e.g., my capacity to stop writing).[9] This means that general possibilities (e.g., the possibility that humans can write or not write essays) inhere in the form of the

8. M. DeLanda, *Intensive Science and Virtual Philosophy* (London and New York: Bloomsbury, 2013).

9. Aristotle, *Physics*, tr. R.P. Hardie and R.K. Gaye, in *Complete Works of Aristotle, Volume 1: The Revised Oxford Translation*, ed. J. Barnes (Princeton, NJ: Princeton University Press, 1984).

universals that these individuals instantiate (e.g., the universal human). A similar account of **intrinsic modality** is defended by Spinoza.[10] The problem for this position is that it has difficulties in dealing with possibilities involving non-actual individuals (e.g., the possibility that I might have been inspired to write a better essay by a nonexistent associate, had they existed).

Leibniz overcomes this problem by providing an account of **extrinsic modality**, in which we focus on states of affairs rather than the individuals that compose them. He subordinates the distinction between possible and actual individuals to the distinction between possible and actual states.[11] The consequence of this is that the reality of possible states is understood by analogy with the reality of actual states, much in the way that the reality of universals is traditionally understood by analogy with the reality of individuals. The actuality of the actual is equally understood by analogy with the existence of the existent. Possible states and individuals are those which do not exist. Leibniz combines this with his commitment to PSR by making each possible state maximally determinate, such that the only true possible states are possible worlds (i.e., if I were to have stopped writing already, then the whole history of the entire world would have had to have been different). Leibniz thus pictures reality as if it were a die, with as many sides as there are fully formed possible worlds. Only the side which turns up when it is thrown will be actualised, but luckily, the dice is weighted by God's benevolence, so that the best side always faces upward. If God plays dice, he cheats.

This brings us to the dark side of modality, the problem of probabilities. As the example of Leibniz's divine die indicates, the problem of the reality of probabilities emerges out of the problem of the reality of possibilities. The latter is the condition of the former. However, the historical genesis of this problem occurs much later than the corresponding problem of possibility, along with the rigorous mathematical study of probability. We have obviously engaged in probabilistic reasoning for a lot longer than this, but the ever-increasing success of statistical methods for regimenting this sort of reasoning (e.g., the ongoing Bayesian revolution) has brought to the fore the question of just what aspects of

10. B. Spinoza, *The Collected Works of Spinoza*, ed., tr. E. Curley (Princeton, NJ: Princeton University Press, 2 vols., 1985–2016).

11. G. Leibniz, *The Monadology*, tr. R. Latta (Oxford: Oxford University Press, 1898).

reality we're talking about in using this language. This question received sustained attention in the twentieth century from thinkers such as Keynes, Popper, and, even more recently Quentin Meillassoux.[12]

The mathematical understanding of probability has always been linked with the history of games. This is because games offer idealised sets of rules which determine fixed sets of possible states between which the total sum of all probabilities, the number 1 as the correlate of certainty, can be divided. This is most obvious in games of chance, for instance, where a die has six possible and roughly equally probable outcomes, dividing certainty six ways. However, there are also games that are not immediately based on chance, such as chess, wherein there are a fixed number of possible first moves for either side, and as such a fixed number of possible second moves, etc., thus creating a space of all possible games within which only certain possible states can follow from certain others. Here, the probability of a given state is not determined purely on the basis of the distribution of possible states, but also on the players' skill in choosing between moves. Nevertheless, the rules prevent the players from deviating from the fixed distribution of possibilities, say by moving a rook diagonally or shooting the other player through the chest.

In all such games, chance only enters at predetermined points, and at these points finite sets of possible states branch out, between which probabilities, or shares of chance, are apportioned. So a game of dice may involve three distinct throws, with the probability of the overall result being a function of the probabilities of each taken separately, but this always excludes 'outside chances' which interfere with the ideal distribution at the points in between throws. The understanding of any system on the basis of probability involves this kind of idealisation, through which it is broken down into strict causal regularities, providing the necessity exhibited by transitions between the fixed points of chance, and the eruptions of contingency which these chances represent.[13] Once these points are isolated, the total set of all possible outcomes is delimited as the product of the sets of outcomes of each fixed pint of decision.

The real measure of probability is introduced by the constraints placed upon these fixed points, understood as extrinsic to the possibilities themselves.

12. Q. Meillassoux, *After Finitude*, tr. R. Brassier (London and New York: Continuum, 2008).
13. G. Deleuze, *The Logic of Sense*, tr. M. Lester and C. Stivale (London: Athlone, 1990), chapter 10.

In reality, the die as a whole is constituted by billions of molecules, each with its own motion and its own possibilities, all feeding back into the whole. At each moment, all of the interactions of the die with the molecules of air, and each bump on the rough surface of the table upon which it is rolled, introduce contingencies into the throw. Of course, it is correct to say that no system at all can be modelled on the basis of the totality of such constraints. If chance were to be introduced at every point there could be no calculation of probability, because there could not even be the delimitation of the set of possible outcomes. As such, probabilistic models of phenomena always involve restrictions of relevant factors and estimations of their effects and interactions. We must give our dice a determinate number of sides, and even though we may weight them to some extent by reapportioning chance between outcomes as we see fit, this will always be based on a sort of retrojection of actual statistics.

The metaphysical debate regarding the nature of probability tends to focus upon whether or not the latter is reducible to our ignorance of the totality of causal constraints, or whether there is something like real chance over and above this ignorance. The core issue here is the question of whether every determinate state has a sufficient reason, i.e., PSR. If one accepts PSR, then it is far easier to maintain that chance is purely epistemic, even if it is based upon an ignorance that only an infinite intellect could overcome (e.g., Spinoza's Substance or Leibniz's God)—but this threatens to collapse into and undermine the metaphysics of possibility on which it is founded. Once one acknowledges that there is always a reason why the actual world is in one state rather than another, it becomes hard to defend the thesis that possible states are any more real than probable ones. This is the fine line across which Spinoza and Hume stare at one another. If on the other hand one denies PSR, then it is far easier to maintain that chance is properly metaphysical, even if it is something extrinsic to possible states that selects which ones to actualise—but this threatens to collapse the various local points of chance into a single global chaos which determines everything. One risks trading an epistemology of ignorance for a theology of contingency. This is the slippery slope at the top of which sits Leibniz's cheating benevolent God (Yahweh), and at the bottom of which sits Meillassoux's mad indifferent Hyperchaos (Azathoth).

## 4. THE TEMPORAL TRINITY

The problem of time is at once impressively ancient and strikingly contemporary. On the one hand, it goes back to some of the earliest recognisably metaphysical speculations of Presocratic philosophers such as Heraclitus, Parmenides, and Zeno, and passes through many of the great thinkers of the tradition, such as Aristotle, Augustine, Aquinas, Leibniz, Kant, Hegel, Schelling, and Heidegger, before reaching the present day. On the other, it is one of the most pressing theoretical concerns of physics in the present age, pervading everything from thermodynamics and complexity theory to the tortuous interface between general relativity and quantum mechanics. One cannot take a view on either traditional metaphysics or cutting-edge physics (not to mention their intersection) without coming face to face with questions regarding the reality of time.

There is so much to these various debates that I have no choice but to be merciless in boiling them down to a few simple features. I'm going to focus on the holy trinity of temporal phenomena: dimensionality, directionality, and flow. The important metaphysical options regarding the nature of time will then be differentiated first of all by which of these they treat as temporal epiphenomena, and secondly by how they aim to explain those they take to be genuine phenomena. I will not examine all possible positions that one can occupy here, but merely sketch the rough outline of the historical dialectic of temporality.

**Temporal dimensionality** is the idea that individuals are located in time as well as in space. This is incredibly intuitive to us, if only in so far as we use tense operators to locate both individuals and the states of affairs they compose in the past, present and future (e.g., 'I *am* here *now*', 'You *were* there *before*', 'She *will be* coming round the mountain *when she comes*'). Nevertheless, some have tried to claim that dimensionality is epiphenomenal. Parmenides defended this thesis by holding that individuality is itself an epiphenomenon, and his disciple Zeno tried to back this up with his ingenious paradoxes. This is not the only way to go about it, though—as we have already mentioned, the most radical champion of individuality in the history of metaphysics, Leibniz, took both space and time to be epiphenomenal. The real difficulty for these thinkers is that it is hard to reconcile their positions with the sheer explosive progress in physics since Galileo popularised the mathematisation of the temporal dimension. There are many contemporary physicists who are willing to give up direction and flow as temporal epiphenomena,[14] but I am unaware of any who are willing to give up dimensionality.

**Temporal directionality** is famously referred to as 'the arrow of time'. It is also incredibly intuitive to us in so far as there is a notable asymmetry in the way we talk about the things we locate on either side of the now: the past is closed, but the future is open. There are various ways to account for this asymmetry, but once one acknowledges the dimensionality of time, they inevitably collapse into distinguishing the temporal dimension (or dimensions) from spatial dimensions by placing restrictions on the way things may be located along it. This is where physics takes charge of the debate. For example, thermodynamics is usually interpreted as placing a constraint upon the way in which ordered states may be situated in relation to one another, namely, entropy. The more ordered states must be put before the less ordered ones, and this seems to require that we ascribe metaphysical reality to directional notions such as before and after. However, this example is complicated by the fact that, even if the basic equations of general relativity and quantum mechanics don't agree with one another, they at least seem to agree that time is reversible. The equations can be run in either direction just fine, and this seems to indicate that any thermodynamic directionality that emerges out of the interactions they describe must be epiphenomenal.

**Temporal flow** is the *holy spirit* of the trinity: even those who believe in it usually have difficulty explaining just what it is. The difficulty here is that whereas dimensionality and directionality are global phenomena, flow is usually described in local terms. This means that whereas dimensionality and directionality are understood as universal conditions of individuation, flow is usually understood as a particular condition of individuation, namely, as a condition which applies to the individuation of those things located in the present. Far worse, this particularity is usually not even discussed in terms of individuation at all, but in terms of the phenomenology of those specific individuals who can describe their experience of the present and its passing (i.e., philosophers). This is obviously the perspective from which Husserl and Heidegger address the question of flow, and it is often the way that Kant and Bergson are interpreted as addressing the issue. This interpretation is not without support, but it misses important nonphenomenological aspects of their positions. The insurmountable

14. M. Tegmark, 'Life is a Braid in Space-Time', *Nautilus* 9 (2014).

problem for those who approach the metaphysics of flow in phenomenological terms is that their concerns can be easily dismissed as epiphenomenology by physicists. The reality of flow can only be addressed as something other than the experience of flow.

We can draw three questions from these debates, corresponding to each member of the temporal trinity in turn:

i. **Dimensionality:** Is time a *necessary* condition of individuation?

ii. **Directionality:** Is time a *unique* condition of individuation?

iii. **Flow:** Is the *interface* between the past and future *also* a unique condition of individuation?

We can separate the important insights of Kant and Bergson from their phenomenological trappings if we consider how they would respond to these questions. It seems to me that they would answer each question in the affirmative, but that the reasons they would offer for these answers would be significantly different.

The support for a phenomenological reading of Kant's theory of time comes from the fact that he is concerned with individuation from the perspective of finite subjects who are themselves located within time. However, this is not a phenomenology of time so much as a logic of time. It is simply that this logic is one of intratemporal individuation, rather than extra-temporal individuation. This becomes clear when we consider that Kant's account of individuation in terms of sortal concepts is essentially an account of procedures for counting individuals. These procedures take place within time, and as such they must comprehensively distinguish a thing from all other things using spatial and qualitative data whose temporal extent is necessarily limited. Put differently, sortal concepts are tied to procedures to completely individuate things on the basis of limited information about their past, and absolutely no information about their future. This is what it means to say that the heart of Kant's theory of time is the *schematism*. What makes time unique as a condition of individuation is that it is the dimension along which the steps of a procedure are mapped, making it finite in the sense that it must be able to operate under the condition of an open future. If we take

Kant's transcendental psychology seriously, then we must conclude that the proper study of what 'time' means is carried out by the mathematical study of time-bound procedures. To cash this out in a neat formula: Kant's pure and empty form of time is the time of computation.

The support for a phenomenological reading of Bergson is very similar, and is bolstered by Bergson's explicit reliance on introspective methods (which he names 'intuition').[15] However, Bergson's real metaphysical insight can be freed from this by building upon Kant's procedural logic of individuation. The point is essentially that digital computation based upon procedures that can be broken down into discrete steps is always grounded in analog computation based upon dynamic information-processing systems. The informational inputs we receive from our environment needn't be conceived as discrete data—divided into quantitative differences in degree and qualitative differences in kind—but can at least also include signals that continuously vary in their qualitative character. This modifies the Kantian picture significantly. To cash it out by modifying our Kantian formula: the pure and empty form of time is not the discrete time of procedural processing, but the continuous time of information dynamics.

## 5. THE ORIGINS AND ENDS OF DELEUZE'S SYSTEM

We are now on the cusp of examining Deleuze's contribution to these three metaphysical problematics. By examining the nature and history of metaphysics, we have developed the explanatory side of our reconstructive methodology. However, we must still develop the expressive side of this methodology, by providing ourselves with some further reconstructive principles. To this end, I'm going to suggest two ways of framing Deleuze's work that will guide the way we present it: a narrow, albeit rough interpretation of its historical origins, and a broad, yet more precise interpretation of the theoretical ends that motivate it.

Deleuze's relation to the history of philosophy is notoriously complicated. There is almost no thinker he has touched upon from whom he did not draw something important to integrate into his own system (e.g., Plato, Spinoza, Leibniz, Kant, Nietzsche, Bergson, etc.). The minor tradition of philosophy from which he draws his central concepts is built with exceptional exegetical skill, and it is so broad that to choose any one thinker as a lens through which to view

15. H. Bergson, *The Creative Mind*, tr. M.L. Andison (New York: The Philosophical Library. 1946).

his work risks eliding important details. However, in presenting the history of metaphysics through the explanatory filters already developed, we've inoculated ourselves against this risk to some extent. What we require is a narrative that will allow us unite the various concerns already presented in the right way. My suggestion is that we do this by viewing Deleuze's system as an attempt to rewrite Spinoza's metaphysics after Heidegger's critique of onto-theology. There are a number of good exegetical reasons for doing this, ranging from Deleuze's persistent obsession with and fidelity to Spinoza, to the various cryptic remarks he makes about overcoming Spinoza in the direction of a more univocal account of Being than Spinoza himself provided.

I will address the latter point shortly, but it's first important to grasp the upshot of this way of framing his work: it allows us to ask to what extent any given metaphysical innovation builds upon or revises existing elements of Spinoza's project. This gives us direct purchase upon the motivations guiding the construction of Deleuze's system, in so far as they are an evolutionary adaptation of Spinoza's own motivations. I'm going to propose three principal motivations that build upon one another: PSR, the principle of the univocity of Being (PUB), and the principle of immanence (PIM).

Sufficient reason is at the core of both Spinoza's and Leibniz's rationalism, and it is no exaggeration to say that Deleuze takes his philosophical task to be to make this principle compatible with atheism. Although we have already indicated that Spinoza's interpretation of the principle is preferable to Leibniz's, in so far as the pure actuality of Spinoza's Substance is preferable to the rigged possibility of Leibniz's God, this does not get Spinoza off the hook. He still interprets Substance as analogous to individuals (or modes), using a single category of causation to describe both: Substance is still a ground, even if it is a self-grounding ground. The reason for this is that Spinoza makes the same mistake as Leibniz in interpreting the regress of reasons implied by PSR as an actual infinity.

This mistake forces both of them to posit some ultimate ground at the beginning of the chain, and some infinite intellect capable of thinking the whole of it, in order to make the principle consistent. They each thus posit an absolutely unique thinking entity as the dual ground of the existence and intelligibility of everything. This is the metaphysical essence of theism and thus espouses what

Heidegger will later call onto-theology. By contrast, Deleuze aims to make PSR compatible with atheism by interpreting the regress of reasons as a potential infinity. This means that, on the one hand, although there is a reason for every specific determination, there is no single reason for all determinations, and also that, although we can never run out of reasons, this is not guaranteed by the ability of some superior thinker to grasp the whole chain of reasons at once.

The principle of univocity is at minimum the idea that every entity is said 'to be' in the same sense. This idea originated with Duns Scotus, was taken up by Spinoza, and is pushed even further by Deleuze. The crucial point to understand here is that there are at least two ways of interpreting the principle: as the univocity of predication (e.g., that the property of intelligence is ascribed to God in the same way it is ascribed to humans) and as the univocity of existence (e.g., that God is said to exist in the same sense as humans are said to exist). Each of these is opposed to an analogical conception of Being, in which we take some things 'to be' in a sense that is merely analogous to the sense in which a privileged category (e.g., the *divine*) is said to be. As we should be able to see, Spinoza follows Duns Scotus in restricting univocity to predication. He takes Substance to share the same attributes as its modes in a non-analogical way. However, this is founded upon viewing Substance and modes as distinct types of existent to which other logical categories apply analogically: as supernumerary and enumerable (quantity), self-grounded and other-grounded (causation), atemporal and temporal (time), etc. Deleuze's atheism demands that this deeper equivocity be eliminated, along with the residual privileging of Substance it represents. In order to champion the univocity of existence Deleuze must ensure that his own equivalent of Substance cannot under any circumstances be said to exist.

Finally, we can see that Deleuze's insistence upon immanence follows naturally from his insistence on sufficient reason and univocity. The principle of immanence is the idea that there is a unitary space of individuation in which all things are located. There is one and only one whole. This means that all individuals, relations, and the states of affairs these things compose, are to be understood in terms of their situation on this unitary plane of immanence. The principle is violated when we aim to explain things within the immanent sphere by appeal to things that cannot be located within it, with the sole exception of the conditions of location itself. The fact that space is not located within itself in so far as it is coextensive with itself is no obstacle here. We thus call such violations appeals to transcendent principles the character of which is entirely independent of either contents or the structure of the plane. This plane of immanence is Deleuze's post-Heideggerian transformation of Spinoza's Substance. It is his attempt to make Substance turn around the modes, by conceiving it not as analogous to individual modes, but as the condition under which modes can be individuated.[16] We will now see the extent to which this transformation of analogical relations into relations of conditioning is at the heart of Deleuze's metaphysical innovations.

## 6. THE SPACE OF UNIVERSALS

Let us begin then by looking at how Deleuze applies this transformation to the problem of universals. Put simply, his aim is to successfully invert Platonism where Aristotle failed, by reframing the terms of the dispute between Platonism and nominalism. His key insight is that we should not be asking whether universals exist in some sense analogous to the sense in which individuals exist, because this regresses to the problem of how these universals are themselves individuated, but rather that we should be asking whether universals are conditions of individuation in a way similar to space.[17] His answer is that they are indeed such conditions, and that their relation to space and time as the fundamental conditions of individuation can be specified in a precise and non-analogical way. This is without doubt the single greatest contribution to the metaphysics of universality since Plato. However, it is not an insight that is entirely without precedent. To understand this, we must quickly return to Leibniz's picture of individuation, and describe what is so unique about it.

The crucial point here is that there are fundamentally two different types of spatial individuation: occupying a location in a space and being a location in a space. The best way to demonstrate the latter is to look at the primordial example of individuation: the natural numbers. These are an infinite series of perfectly distinct objects, standing in precise relations of succession to one another, that tails off into infinity. But the numbers do not *occupy* points along the line of succession, as if their mathematical properties could somehow be pulled apart

16. See G. Deleuze, *Difference and Repetition*, tr. P. Patton (London and New York: Bloomsbury, 2014), 395.

17. Ibid.

from their location. They simply *are* the points along the line of succession, and nothing more. The link between their location and their properties is purely necessary. It is not that there is a specific procedure for counting them, so much as that they are the immanent condition of every such counting procedure. By contrast, we normally think of physical objects as standing in contingent relations of occupation to their locations, and assume that they have at least some properties that are not dependent upon their location. It is precisely this contingency that demands intratemporal procedures for individuating them in the face of the open future: we only see things as occupying space in so far as we take them to be unfixed in time.

Leibniz's ambition is encapsulated in the idea that he thinks the subjects of our propositions (monads) may be individuated in precisely the same way that numbers are, and that this may be done without appeal to either space or time as they are traditionally understood.[18] The best way to demonstrate this is by showing how it is possible to graph the propositions expressing the properties individuals possess, and showing how Leibniz transforms this into a qualitative space capable of individuating monads.

| | F | G | H |
|---|---|---|---|
| a | Fa | Ga | Ha |
| b | Fb | Gb | Hb |
| c | Fc | Gc | Hc |

Table 2

This table lists pre-individuated subjects down one side, and the predicates which express the properties these individuals possess across the top. These two discrete dimensions produce a propositional space containing all possible combinations of subject and predicate. These spaces are what traditionally condition our individuation of actual states of affairs, by delimiting all possible states of affairs. We treat each proposition in this space as a location (or *possibility*) which can be occupied (or *actualised*), i.e. true or false. This information can be incorporated into the space itself by treating it as a surface embedded in

18. G. Leibniz, *The Monadology and Other Philosophical Writings*, tr. R. Latta (Oxford: Clarendon, 1898).

a higher dimensional space, curving through an additional binary dimension of truth and falsity (0, 1 : underlined). This is a rigorous procedure for converting any form of propositionally articulated information into a mathematical manifold.

Leibniz transforms this propositional space into a qualitative space by removing the dimension along which the preindividuated subjects are arrayed, and turning each predicate into its own binary dimension (0, 1). We can display this in an incredibly simplified form by assuming there are only two such predicates.

| | F | ~F |
|---|---|---|
| G | a | b |
| ~G | c | d |

Table 3

This table represents the four-place qualitative manifold one gets from combining only two predicates. Leibniz's **spatiotemporal epiphenomenalism** boils down to the idea that each location in such a space (corresponding to a series of predicates, e.g., F & ~G, ~F and G, etc.) corresponds to a completely individuated possible monad (e.g., c and b, respectively). Leibniz simply thinks that the number of predicates is infinite, making for an infinite number of monads. Possible worlds are nothing but infinite sets of such monads that are compossible with one another. The actual world can thus be seen as a surface derived from this space by curving it through a binary dimension of existence (0, 1 : underlined). This curvature selects one set of compossible points as the set that is actualised. This is the basis of Leibniz's idea that the best possible world is the most continuous world: the principle of selection is a principle of ideal curvature. God cheats using differential calculus.

What Deleuze realises is that this way of understanding the actual world as a surface or manifold can be pulled apart from understanding it in propositional terms. The procedure for graphing propositional information makes it very clear that it is convertible into digital information, and, following Bergson, Deleuze is very aware of the fact that there are forms of analog information that are not convertible in this way. Our linguistic ability to represent the actual world using propositions has been exceeded by our mathematical ability to model it using graphs and more complex symbolic tools. This is what motivates Deleuze to develop a metaphysics of the subrepresentational.[19]

The principal consequence of this shift in perspective is that Deleuze allows for more than just binary qualitative dimensions. He allows us to incorporate all of the myriad qualities and quantities that would be used in the most outlandish graphs we could possibly dream up. This gives the qualitative space a far more interesting structure, and, since it allows for the incorporation of continuous variation in quality and quantity, it escapes the possibility of lossless conversion into digital information. The other consequence of this is that Deleuze breaks with Leibniz in rejecting his epiphenomenalism. Deleuze takes seriously the progress that the sciences have made in modelling the world using these mathematical techniques, and the fact that these models deploy space and time in complex ways which make it impossible to separate them from the quantities and qualities that they interact with. The interaction of space, time, and quality is something that can only be understood by providing a metaphysics for contemporary mathematical science, as opposed to Leibniz's fantasy mathematical science. We at last find a *mathesis universalis* in the language of dynamic systems, chaos, and complexity theory, but it is quite unlike what Leibniz imagined it would be.

Nevertheless, this gives us the outline of Deleuze's strategy in dealing with the problem of universals: universals are constituted by the dimensions through which the actual world, qua informational surface, curves. When Deleuze says that the Idea of *Fire* is present wherever there is fire, he is deadly serious. At this location the world expresses the complex mix of qualitative and quantitative determinations constitutive of fire, as the surface of the actual world curves through the appropriate dimensions.

## 7. REGIONAL POSSIBILITIES

We can now turn to the way in which Deleuze transforms the problem of possibilia. His aim here is to make Spinoza's account of intrinsic modality consistent, allowing us to affirm the reality of both the possible and the probable without having to appeal to any transcendent principles. He does this by combining these two aspects of modality in his theory of the virtual. This is meant to account for the inherent capacities (Spinoza) and tendencies (Bergson) of

19. Deleuze, *Difference and Repetition*.

individuals that we attempt to grasp in our talk of, respectively, possibilities and probabilities. The innovation is that it is supposed to do this without understanding virtual states by analogy with our retrojective ways of representing them by recombining propositions about actual states. Ultimately, the virtual should be immanent to the actual in so far as it requires no transcendent supplement to actualise itself. The modal features of the world should be woven together like a complex mathematical tapestry upon the plane of immanence.

Deleuze draws his theory of the virtual from the structure of dynamic systems theory (DST), which is the principal tool used by the sciences to extract information about the tendencies of individual systems from plots of their actual states. This is what enables him to convert Leibniz's theory of monads into his own theory of nomads. DST does this by taking a graph of the actual history of a system and collapsing the time dimension. It uses a series of complex mathematical techniques to retain relevant information about how the various variables representing the different dimensions tend to interact with one another, while jettisoning the irrelevant information about how they actually interacted in particular cases. Overleaf is an example of this being done with a pendulum. What this produces is a surface with one less dimension than the graph, whose curvature nevertheless describes the tendencies of this system in the form of the differential relations between the various variables that draw it. The topologically significant features of this surface are called **attractors**, and they are often drawn as points or lines on a flattened version of the surface, in order to capture the most important tendencies of the system in a simplified format (see fig. 1).

The crucial point to appreciate here is that the virtual surface is not the actual surface. The actual could only be said to traverse the virtual surface in real time. If we think of a universal Idea as the set of qualitative and quantitative dimensions that are relevant to capture the modal features of a given type of individual, and if we think of these dimensions as real features of nature rather than merely as convenient ways of modelling nature, then the Idea is a virtual surface swarming with points, corresponding to all the individual instances of its type. Deleuze calls these nomads, because they traverse the space in real time, guided by the tendencies encoded in the curvature of the virtual surface. If one were to reintroduce the temporal dimension here, one would simply see these points drawing the actual trajectories of the graphs from which we extract our

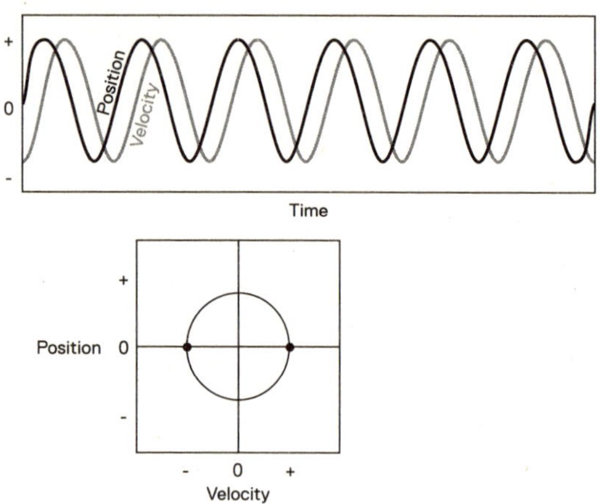


Figure 1

dynamic models of the virtual. This is the basis of the immanent actualisation of the virtual.

However, to view Ideas in this way is still to view them as abstract universals, which is to say that they are still insufficient to individuate their individual instances. This becomes clear when we realise that any number of nomads could occupy the same position on the virtual surface at once. This means that, although their position on the surface provides important information about their present state, this information must be supplemented if it is to completely individuate them. This is where Deleuze sides with Kant over Leibniz. The information required to turn an abstract universal into a concrete universal capable of completely individuating its instances is *spatial* information. We must add extensive spatial dimensions to the Idea, and in doing so encode information about the spatial relations between the various instances in the ways the nomads move. What this does is effectively to turn the disparate set of points traversing the virtual surface into an actual surface in its own right. The way this actual surface curves as it traverses the higher-dimensional virtual surface thereby encodes the relevant information about the spatial relations between the points that compose it. This has the added effect of meaning that each and every individual has its own unique Idea encoding its own modal features, in so far as this is simply a region of the concrete universal.

Nevertheless, Leibniz has his revenge, for there is no single system of spatial dimensions common to all concrete universals. Deleuze sides with Leibniz in thinking that extensive spatial dimensions are inseparable from the qualities and quantities that are expressed within them. They are not exactly epiphenomenal, but they emerge simultaneously with systems of quantitative and qualitative dimensions. The importance of this becomes clear when one realises that individuated quantities can themselves be collapsed and transformed into further dimensions, as we find in the classic DST graph of an ecosystem containing a population of foxes and rabbits, whose numbers tend to vary in relation to one another in a regular way (see fig. 2).

The complex interplay between different qualities, quantities, and extensities is the reason Deleuze is fond of suggesting that Leibniz's plurality of possible worlds all exist at once, unhinged from God's unsporting obsession with continuity. In truth, there is a multiplicity of divergent worlds of possibility, or a plurality of perspectives from which to divide the continuous informational surface of the world into discrete individuals.

## 8. THE UNITY OF TIME

Finally, we come to the title of this paper, **Ariadne's thread**—the tortuous line that leads us through the labyrinth. Deleuze's Spinozism gives us good reason to think that this picture of disparate disconnected Ideas is not the whole picture.

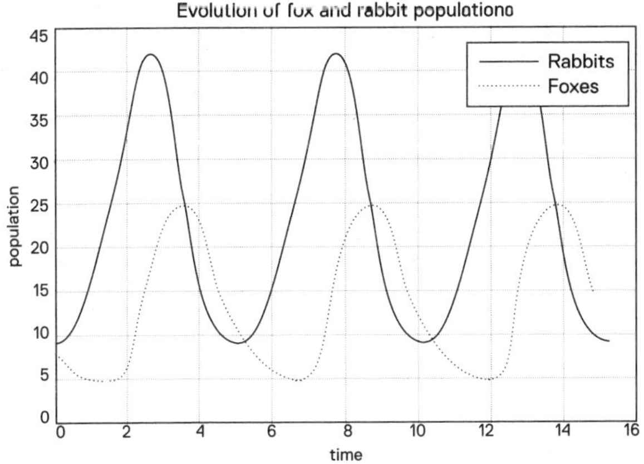


Figure 2

The principle of immanence demands that these all be brought together and flattened to constitute a single plane of immanence, or perplicated to create a single **intensive spatium**. The divergent worlds must somehow be contained within a single universe. This is indeed the case, and it is where Kant gets the last laugh. What breaks the analogy between time and space is that whereas there are many spaces, there is a unitary time common to them all. No Idea contains a time dimension, because this would collapse the virtual back into the actual. DST shows us that we can only think the real modal features of things by collapsing the time dimension. Time becomes coiled up on the virtual surface, in the erratic yet continuous movement of the actual surface. What makes all these spaces attributes of the same world, or perspectives upon the same immanent informational surface, is thus that they share the same coil of time. This is what Deleuze calls the pure and empty form of time, **Aion**, or **the eternal return**. It is the *univocal* metaphysics of time underlying the *plurivocal* metaphysics of space. This is Ariadne's thread: a single temporal line leading us through the labyrinth of overlapping qualitative, quantitative, and extensive spaces.

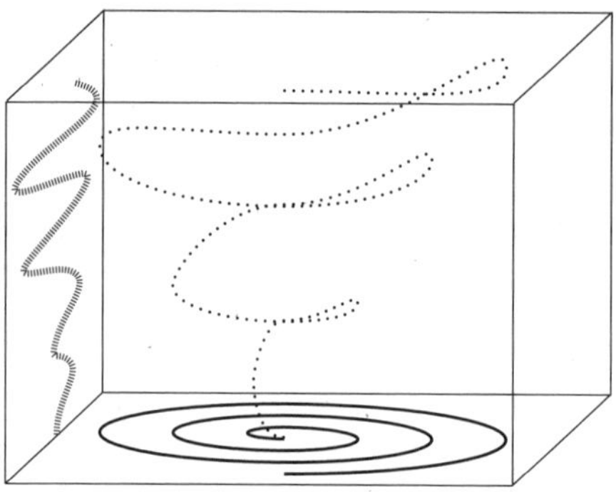

Figure 3

LOGOS

# Is There a TV in My Head?: Content, Functional Mapping, and the Myth of the Given

Just what are we talking about when we talk about the *content* of perception? There are a number of different questions which are often asked about the precise nature of this content, such as to what extent it is *representational*, and to what extent this representation is *conceptual* in character.[1] However, these questions usually gloss over what it is to talk about perceptual content *qua* content, in their haste to talk about it *qua* representation or conception. On this basis, it is all too tempting to account for not only the specific character of the content, but also how it is individuated, in *phenomenological* terms.[2] This is to say that perceptual content is understood as whatever is contained within an *introspective domain* to which we have some sort of special access. Wilfrid Sellars's attack on the myth of the given has provided us with good reason to doubt the epistemic authority such special access to our inner states purportedly provides, and thus to doubt the efficacy of any account of perceptual content that gives introspection such a fundamental role.[3] This is his critique

---

1. I am here lumping together a number of different though overlapping debates the terminology of which diverges in various ways. I do not wish to give a complete taxonomy and genealogy of the phrases 'mental content', 'phenomenal content', and 'sensory content' within the literature and the various degrees to which they have (or haven't adequately) been distinguished. However, it is worth noting that there is a distinct thread of debate that reserves the word 'content' for cases of representation (see S. Siegel, 'The Contents of Perception', *The Stanford Encyclopedia of Philosophy*, 2010, <http://plato.stanford.edu/entries/perception-contents/>). The question is then whether the 'phenomenal character' of perception constitutes a form of representational content, and the extent to which this is conceptual or otherwise.

2. The reference to 'phenomenology' here is meant to include both those loose discussions of what perceptual experience 'is like' that have proliferated in the analytic philosophy of perception and the more methodologically defined introspective study of consciousness that derives from Husserl's work.

3. This is most famously presented in 'Empiricism and the Philosophy of Mind' (hereafter *EPM*), in *Science, Perception, and Reality* (Atascadero, CA: Ridgeview, 1963), 127–96.

of what Jim O'Shea has called the *epistemic given*.[4] However, there is a further side to the myth that Sellars critiques, which O'Shea calls the *categorial given*. The aim of the present paper is to articulate and explain the latter by building upon Sellars's critique of the former and the account of perception that ensues from it. This involves demonstrating some constraints governing accounts of perceptual content on the basis of the explanatory demands placed upon them as accounts of perception on the one hand, and the explanatory resources available to them as accounts of content on the other. The result will be an account of the myth of the categorial given that explains both why it is tempting and why we must resist its temptation.

## 1. PERCEPTION AND EXPLANATION

To begin with the explanatory demands, it seems to me that there are two distinct explanatory enterprises to which any account of perceptual content must contribute. On the one hand, there is the *epistemological* enterprise of explaining the general role that perception can play in empirical justification independently of variations in the causal structure of perceiving agents. This means telling a story about how the sensory inputs fed into a causal system can gain the normative significance of warranting moves within the space of reasons, in a way that could apply not only to different human beings, but to stranger creatures such as aliens or artificial intelligences whose sensory capacities and overall causal economy diverge radically from our own. On the other hand, there is the *psychological* enterprise of explaining the specific role that perception plays in the causal economy of particular perceiving agents. This means telling a story about how the sensory inputs fed into a causal system contribute to the production of *behavioural outputs*, in such a way as to give us predictive purchase upon the behaviour of creatures with particular types of causal structure.

Although these enterprises are distinct, they are also importantly intertwined. Any epistemology that cannot account for the way differences in the causal structure of our sensory capacities can affect their role in empirical justification will have failed to get a grip on the causal dimension of perception, or its

4. J.R. O'Shea, *Wilfrid Sellars: Naturalism with a Normative Turn* (Cambridge: Polity, 2007), chapter 5.

connection to *sensation*, and any psychology that cannot account for the way perception can supply us with reasons that cause us to act one way rather than another will have failed to get a grip on the normative dimension of perception, or its connection to *rational agency*. We only have an account of perception, be it epistemological or psychological, when its causal and normative dimensions are properly connected. Any account of perceptual content as something that plays a role in both epistemological and psychological explanations must couch it in terms amenable to both of these dimensions. The first insight that we can take from Sellars here is that the proper interface between these two dimensions is the use of *functional explanation* in empirical psychology. To use a phrase he is fond of, we must understand perceptual content in terms of the way it fits into the 'wiring diagram' of the perceiver.[5]

Causal explanation in general works by applying *explanatory schemas* to systems that facilitate the development of *predictions* about the way that they would behave under various possible conditions. These schemas provide us with more or less general ways of organising *counterfactual reasoning* about these possibilities, thereby enabling us to draw specific conclusions about how they would behave in any given set of circumstances.[6] A *functional schema* enables us to develop predictions by treating a system on analogy with *practical reasoning*. For instance, by allowing us to treat its *parts* as *means* in relation to the *whole* as an *end*. This lets us describe the causal role of the systems' components in terms of *success* and *failure*, and thereby to organise our counterfactual reasoning about the causal relations between them in terms of the way failure cascades throughout the system.[7] The explanatory power of a functional schema thus lies precisely in its introduction of the possibility of *malfunction*. It is the fact

5. W. Sellars, 'Being and Being Known' (hereafter *BBK*), in *Science, Perception, and Reality*, 41–59 [§37].

6. One way of cashing this out the idea of 'organisation' is to say that explanatory schemas provide us with methods of grouping beliefs about a system's circumstances that would, if true, act as defeasors for those material inferences that encode particular aspects of the system's behaviour. This is to say that they provide us with cognitively tractable ways of carving out ranges of *counterfactual robustness* for these inferences. The need for such tractable ways of sorting relevant from irrelevant information about causal systems (be they implicit practical abilities or more explicitly formalised methods) is discussed by Robert Brandom in chapter 4 of *Between Saying and Doing* (Oxford: Oxford University Press, 2008) (hereafter *BSD*).

7. These cascade patterns neatly group defeasors in the manner noted in the previous footnote, thereby revealing the modal structure of the system's possibility space.

that this is an essentially normative notion which enables functional explanation to connect the epistemological and psychological dimensions of perception.

It remains to say something about the role of introspection in relation to these explanatory demands. One crucial consequence of Sellars's critique of the epistemic given is that introspection must be understood as a genuine species of perception, rather than *sui generis*.[8] This means that whatever epistemic authority we possess in relation to the objects of introspection is *de facto* rather than *de jure*, insofar as they are potentially otherwise observable even if they are not in fact otherwise observed. It is because of this that there is no need for a distinct phenomenological enterprise of describing what perception 'is like', nor any good reason to think that our epistemological and psychological theories of perception should be beholden to it. This is not to say that introspection can play no role in the development of these theories, only that it plays no privileged role in the process of assessing them. Instead, the capacity for introspection and the associated language games involving 'looks', 'seems', and 'what it is like' are themselves to be accounted for by our epistemological and psychological theories insofar as they constitute a novel class of sensory inputs and behavioural outputs, which play a derivative role in the practice of empirical justification insofar as they enable us to *modulate* our observational claims (e.g., by introducing information about our propensities to assert claims about observables into empirical discourse while withdrawing commitment to those claims) and *calibrate* the perceptual capacities from which they ensue (e.g., by comparing, identifying, and adjusting our responses to features of my sensory system).

## 2. CONTENT AND EXPLANATION

Moving on to the explanatory resources, it strikes me that the purpose of the notion of content is to talk about how two seemingly *different* states of distinct systems (the *vehicles*) can nevertheless be the *same* in another sense (through sharing *content*). There's obviously a trivial sense in which this can be the case without warranting the ascription of content at all, such as the sense in which

8. The consequences of this idea are initially presented by Sellars in his 'Myth of Jones' (*EPM*, section XII), in which he dramatises the origin and conceptual development of perceptual capacities to introspect internal states.

two houses may be in a state of disrepair, even while the precise nature and extent of their disrepair may differ. But to say that they both share a content here would be to say nothing more than that they share a *property*, and thus entirely redundant. This is not to say that states whose similarity consists in common properties cannot share content on that very basis. Two VHS tapes that share precisely the same magnetic properties will share precisely the same informational content. The question is how we can say that an information storage medium that works on different causal principles, such as a Betamax tape or a DVD could share the same content as the VHS tapes. I'm going to use this comparison with information storage media as the guiding analogy through which to think about the explanatory role of perceptual content. I think we should aim to think about what it would be for states of distinct perceiving subjects *qua* causal systems to have the same content, in much the way that states of distinct information storage devices can have the same content, before we address what it would be for this content to be perceptual, and in what sense this makes it representational and/or conceptual.

In order to extend the individuation of the content belonging to states of causal systems beyond mere similarity of properties, we must consider relations of *isomorphism* between them. This means breaking down states into the features of which they are composed and the relations between them, and then developing a way of *mapping* these to the features and relations that compose the corresponding states. This *mapping schema* (or *morphism*) allows us to count some feature of one state as equivalent to a feature of another despite differences in their properties, insofar as it occupies the same role within the system of relations that constitute it. We can then determine if two states share the same content on the basis of some sufficient degree of correspondence between their components. This would let us see a VHS and a Betamax tape as possessing the same content in so far as there is some way of mapping the magnetic properties of one to the other, despite the differences between these properties. However, the problem with such *pure isomorphism* is that it can be arbitrarily extended in ways that undermine any possible explanatory role it could have. We can potentially construct arbitrary mappings that pair the magnetic traces on the VHS tape with price patterns in the stock market, or pair the digital encoding of the DVD with a sequence taken from the binary expansion of pi.

In so far as it completely severs the individuation of content from any concern with the causal capacities of systems and their states, pure isomorphism precludes identity of content from playing any role in causal explanation.

We can avoid these problems of pure isomorphism by using the *functional roles* of the states and their components to constrain the mapping schema. In order for this to work the relevant states must be *variable* features of the wiring diagram of the system; and their variations must be functionally correlated with *variable outputs* of some sort. For example, the VHS tape contains a length of material whose electromagnetic properties vary in delimited ways, which will produce suitable variations in the patterns of light emitted by a TV set to which it is appropriately connected.[9] On this basis, it is possible to produce a *functional mapping* from the components of the one set of variable states to another in terms of *common outputs* to which they are functionally correlated. For example, we can produce a functional mapping from VHS to Betamax that maps their distinct variations in electromagnetic properties onto one another in terms of similarities in the patterns of light they engender when suitably connected to a TV set. In essence, we treat the states possessing content as isomorphic with one another in so far as their components can be mapped onto the same set of functional roles, which are themselves isomorphic with the output they are supposed to produce. It is this dependence upon a common output mechanism that allows functionally individuated content to play a useful role in causal explanation.

However, there are still questions regarding the fineness of grain of such isomorphisms. As an illustrative example, consider the way that the contents of a VHS tape can be copied from one tape to another. This process never reproduces the electromagnetic properties of the first tape exactly, with serial copying eventually introducing so much distortion as to completely eradicate the original pattern. There is thus a legitimate question as to where precisely in a series of copies the tapes cease to bare the same content as the original, or precisely how much variance the mapping relation will tolerate. Similar problems emerge if we consider intrinsic differences between storage mediums and

9. I am not the first to use an analogy with a TV set to try and elucidate elements of Sellars's account of perception. Edmond Wright deploys the same analogy in trying to explain Sellars' account of sensory contents, or what he calls 'sensa' or 'raw feels' (E. Wright, 'A Defence of Sellars', *Philosophy and Phenomenological Research* 46:1 [1985], 73–90).

formats, such as the difference between analog and digital encoding, or the difference between higher and lower resolution digital encoding. This suggests that there are many possible mapping relations corresponding to different sorts of fineness of grain, insofar as they permit different sorts of variance between the outputs to which the relevant component states are correlated. The lesson to learn from this is that individuating content can be more complicated than it initially seems, and that discussions of content often make appeals to implicit criteria for selecting mapping relations. There is nothing troubling about this per se, any more than there is about implicit restrictions on quantification in natural language. However, it should make us cautious about assuming that there is a natural way of individuating the contents of perception that we can easily appeal to in order to secure a common object of debate.

There are two final points to make about functional mapping. The first point is that we need not yet characterise content individuated this way as representational. It is all too tempting to say that the content represents the output that it is functionally correlated with. For instance, it can be tempting to suggest that two VHS tapes represent the same movie, or that two records represent the same piece of music.[10] Here it is important to remember that 'movies' or 'pieces of music' are just as abstract as shared contents, and that their correct showing or performance is subject to their own additional norms. One might nevertheless think that content represents raw output, such as the patterns of light or sound with which the information storage media are correlated. However, we should resist the temptation to identify representation with mere functional correlation, as it arises principally because the analogical character of functional explanation invites us to treat the relevant states *as if* they were instructions for performing certain actions. The second point is that it gives us a way of talking about *form* as well as *content*. The ways in which the components of the relevant states can vary may be classified in terms of more general functional roles they play, and these classifications provide more or less abstract forms that correspond to the content of their specific variations. Put another way, form consists in the *functional invariants* that delimit the variations in which content consists. It is the structure of those elements of the wiring diagram in which the range of variation of the content bearing states are encoded.

10. Sellars himself is guilty of claiming this at one point in *BBK* (§40).

## 3. PERCEPTION, REPRESENTATION AND CONCEPTION

We can now turn to considering which states of a causal system deserve to have something called perceptual content ascribed to them, and to what extent they are representational and/or conceptual. Here I am going to follow Sellars, who takes perception to be the transition from a causally efficacious sensory input to a normatively significant propositional output, or from *sensation* to *conception*. I'm also going to endorse his account of the nature of this conceptually articulated output, which is modelled upon the assertion of a declarative sentence.[11] For Sellars, conceptual content is primarily to be understood as the functional role that a sentence and its component expressions play in the language game of giving and asking for reasons. This is a linguistic practice composed by three distinct types of sentence-involving behaviour: *language-entry* transitions (perception), *intra-language* transitions (inference), and *language-departure* transitions (action).[12] Language-entry transitions are the result of behavioural dispositions to endorse sentences on the basis of non-linguistic sensory input (e.g., to assert 'it's raining' in response to the presence of rain) and language-departure transitions are similarly the result of behavioural dispositions to produce non-linguistic behavioural output on the basis of endorsed sentences (e.g., to use an umbrella given endorsement of 'it's raining', 'the rain will ruin my shirt', and 'I have an umbrella to hand'). Intra-language transitions (e.g., inferring 'the ground will be wet' from 'it's raining') may be counted as genuine *moves* in the game insofar as they can be performed in accordance with rules of inference (*ought-to-dos*) rather than merely assessed in accordance with functional norms governing the relevant dispositions (*ought-to-bes*). However, that each type of transition is subject to

11. The nature of the connection between language and thought presupposed by this methodological stance remains contentious. In his early work, Sellars restricts himself to discussing private thought episodes as derivative upon linguistic 'thinkings-out-loud' insofar as the former can be understood in terms of their functional role in producing the latter (cf. *BBK*, 'Some Reflections on Language Games', in *Science, Perception, and Reality*, 321–58. Hereafter *SRLG*.), but in his later work he attempts to account for the existence of private thought episodes (such as those belonging to non-linguistic animals) that have no such functional connection to linguistic expression ('Mental Events', *Philosophical Studies* 39:4 [1981]: 325–45). However, others who have adopted the methodological stance of the early work have rejected this later move (R. Brandom, *Making It Explicit* [Cambridge, MA: Harvard University Press, 1994], chapter 3, §5). I will not endeavour to resolve this issue here.

12. A more detailed presentation of these ideas can be found in *SRLG*.

normative assessment of whatever kind is sufficient to provide sentences with a unified functional role within the overall economy of perception, inference, and action. Two sentences have the same content just insofar as they are properly involved in the same transitions, and two component expressions have the same content just insofar as their contribution to the roles of the sentences they compose is the same. In so far as system states can derivatively possess conceptual content insofar as they are appropriately functionally connected to the possibility of producing linguistic behaviour, the sense in which the transition from a causal input to a conceptually contentful state counts as perceptual is to be understood in terms of the sense in which a language-entry move is perceptual. Finally, I'm going to take for granted that conceptual content is representational insofar as I agree with Sellars that it *signifies* things in the world, but I'm not going to go any further into the tortured question of how representation can be reconstructed out of inference here.[13]

On this basis, I think that anything worth the name perceptual content will be have to be possessed by states of the mechanisms involved in the whole process of moving from sensation to conception. Borrowing another term from Brandom, we could say that perceptual content must be possessed by some state of the *perceptual mechanism* underlying a rational agent's *reliable differential responsive dispositions* (RDRDs).[14] However, there are potentially many candidates for this, insofar as there can be numerous subsystem states with variable functional outputs involved in the processing of sensory information into conceptual content. Restricting ourselves to our own visual systems for the moment, this can range from the pattern of activation on the back of the retina (Quine's infamous *stimulus meaning*)[15], through neurological states of the various information processing systems in the visual cortex, to neurological states of a global system that integrates information from various sources and makes it available to other cognitive processes (such as Thomas Metzinger's

13. In *BBK* (section II), Sellars draws a distinction between two types of representation: *signification* and *picturing*. The former is unique to conceptually articulated representations of language users, whereas the latter is common to the sorts of environmental mapping and signalling that we share with non-linguistic animals. We will say more about the latter notion below, but it is worthwhile noting that Brandom's attempt to explain representation in terms of inference in *MIE* can be seen as an attempt to articulate the former notion.

14. *MIE*, chapter 4.

15. W.V.O. Quine, *Word and Object* (Cambridge, MA: MIT Press, 1960), chapter 2.

*phenomenal world model*)[16]. Moreover, because content baring states can compose into further states, it is equally possible to talk about combinations of any or all of these. There are multiple layers of information processing between sensation and conception any and all of which can be the subject of functional mappings insofar as they output to other layers or to the ultimate conceptually articulated product. This panoply of options should give us further reason for caution in assuming that there is a natural way of individuating perceptual content.

The question is now what it would be to say that any of these states possessed representational yet non-conceptual content. This is what Sellars calls *picturing* as opposed to signifying.[17] The obvious thing to do here is to reach for the notion of isomorphism once more, and to say that content which is already individuated by functional mapping is representational just insofar as there is also an isomorphism between it and some state in the world, which it is thereby taken to represent. For example, the content of the VHS and Betamax tapes may be the same in so far as they record the data from the same security camera, and they may then be taken to represent the same events insofar as there is an isomorphism between this content and the relevant events. However, this suffers from the same problems with arbitrary mappings we discussed earlier, insofar as we can conjure up isomorphisms with other potentially stranger events or states. We might then suggest that this isomorphism is constrained by the causal origin of the relevant states. However, this would leave us saying that if the tapes were warped in precisely the same way by the same magnetic field, that they thereby represent that magnetic field. Sellars's solution to this problem is that the isomorphism must be more deeply tied into the functional role of the content bearing state.

In 'Being and Being Known', he illustrates this using the example of a robot that stores information on a similar magnetic tape, which he takes to picture its environment in virtue of an isomorphism between the state of the tape and the state of the environment. However, he also claims that:

> This picturing cannot be abstracted from the mechanical and electronic processes in which the tape is caught up. The patterns on the tape do not picture

16. T. Metzinger, *The Ego Tunnel* (New York: Basic Books, 2009), chapter 2.

17. See footnote 13 above.

> the robot's environment merely by virtue of being patterns on the tape. In Wittgenstein's phrase, the 'method of projection' of the map involves the manner in which the patterns on the tape are added to, modified, and responded to by the other components of the robot. It is a map only by virtue of the physical *habitus* of the robot, i.e., by virtue of mechanical and electronic propensities which are rooted, ultimately, in its wiring diagram.[18]

To summarise, the constraints upon an isomorphism that allows us to produce a *representational mapping* between the states of two systems does not merely concern similarity of functional output, but a more complex relation of *projection* in which the state mediates between functionally specified inputs and outputs. For example, we can understand a variable state of the wiring diagram of a bee as representing the path to a source of nectar insofar as it varies appropriately when the bee discovers the source of nectar and produces the behaviour of returning to it with other bees. Moreover, the dance that the bee performs in order to direct other bees to that source represents the path insofar as its variations are appropriately correlated with the behaviour of travelling to it.[19]

So, for a state of our perceptual mechanisms to be non-conceptual and yet representational in this sense would be for it to play a functional role in a process of systematically guiding *behaviour* in relation to sensory input that is to some extent independent of any role played by conceptual content in guiding *action*, insofar as the latter is derivative upon the role of sentences in language-departure transitions in much the way that perception is derivative upon the role of sentences in language-entry transitions. The question is thus to what extent such states can play an active role in the move from sensation to conception (perception) without their role in the move from sensation to behaviour being mediated by conception. This is not a question I aim to completely resolve here.[20] However, I do take it to be plausible to assume that there are some such states,

18. *BBK*, §40.

19. This example originates in Sellars (SRLG, §§14–15), but it, and the associated account of picturing, are developed in more detail by Ruth Millikan (*Language: A Biological Model* [Oxford: Clarendon Press, 2005], 96–8).

20. This is one area in which Sellarsian work in philosophy of mind could be fruitfully crossbred with Heideggerian ideas, in so far as the latter's emphasis upon abilities to practically *cope* with one's environment that need not involve inference, but can nevertheless be interrupted and adjusted in accordance with it, provides a way of thinking about how such states might be involved in the mechanisms underlying our behavioural dispositions.

in so far as our perceptual capacities are not created out of whole cloth, but are built upon aspects of our psychology that we share with non-linguistic animals and pre-linguistic infants.

## 4. UNIVERSAL AND PAROCHIAL CONTENT

Having distinguished between the non-representational, non-conceptual, and conceptual contents that states of our perceptual mechanisms can bare in terms of the functional roles of their components within these mechanisms, I now want to make a further distinction between types of content on this basis, and see how this distinction can shed some light on the myth of the categorial given. The distinction I want to draw is between what I'll call *parochial* and *universal* forms of content. The former covers all forms of content whose individuation is *dependent* upon functional mappings that are specified in terms of particular causal mechanisms, whereas the latter covers all forms of content whose individuation is entirely *independent* of any particular causal mechanism. We've already made this sort of distinction in considering the difference between contents individuated in terms of functional mappings and contents individuated in terms of pure isomorphisms. The characterisation of the latter is entirely mechanism independent, but ultimately cannot play a useful role in any causal explanation, psychological or otherwise, whereas the characterisation of the former, along with the representational mappings we have discussed depends upon the causal structure of the mechanisms in terms of which the output is specified.

However, it is important to see that although the conceptual content that results from perception is functionally individuated, it is nevertheless universal in the sense just defined. This is because the language games from which these functional roles are derived are intrinsically *extensible*. Though any given speaker's ability to perform language-entry transitions is tied to the structure of their own perceptual mechanisms, the concepts that they apply are not thereby indexed to those mechanisms. Although the process through which we challenge and justify observational reports concerns the proper functioning of the mechanisms that produce them, the assessment of this functioning is open to arguments about the causal relationship between the states observed and the system observing them. For example, arguments about colour observations are open to information about colour illusions that depend upon our theoretical grasp of how cone receptors interact with different wavelengths of light and the way the information they produce is integrated by the visual cortex. This same theoretical understanding of the causal relationship between colour and light has enabled us to incorporate new and more accurate measurement devices into our practices. The same applies with regard to concepts such as temperature, pressure, weight, and the like, for which empirical science has enabled us to create superior means of observation and measurement, thereby bootstrapping our ability to apply empirical concepts on the back of our parochial perceptual mechanisms. In short, a concept that could only be applied in one way would not be an empirical concept, insofar as that concept is supposed to inferentially encode the causal regularities upon which the relevant perceptual mechanisms depend.[21] It is thus entirely possible for speakers with entirely distinct causal economies to *non-inferentially* apply the same concept as long as their behaviour can be appropriately triangulated from within the game of giving and asking for reasons itself, insofar as the causal structure of any given perceptual mechanism is something amenable to analysis through *inference*.

Nevertheless, this extensibility and the universality it implies does not detract from the fact that our concepts are achievements of a distinct sort. The theoretical understanding of causal structure encoded in the inferential role of our empirical concepts is hard won. This inferential role is thus something that changes and grows as the scientific enterprise revises and refines our understanding.[22] This point is crucial for making sense of Sellars's account of *categorial form*, and thereby the myth of the categorial given. In so far as they are individuated in terms of functional role, concepts display relatively fixed forms of functional invariance in much the way that forms of functionally individuated content do. Just as form in general consists in more general functional roles that

21. This connection between empirical concepts and causal modality is worked out in detail in Sellars's 'Concepts as Involving Laws and Inconceivable Without Them' (*Philosophy of Science* 15 [1948]: 287–313) and explored further by Brandom in *BSD*, chapters 4–6.

22. This raises questions about the degree of similarity of functional role required for sameness of conceptual content that must remain beyond the scope of the present paper, lest we be dragged into the debates about sameness of meaning that have raged in the philosophy of language at least since Quine's 'Two Dogmas of Empiricism' (*The Philosophical Review* 60 [1951]: 20–43.) and the related debates about sameness of reference for theoretical terms between different theories that have followed them in the philosophy of science.

group other functional roles by means of these sorts of invariances, so categorial form consists in those more general functional roles common to specifically conceptual roles. For Sellars, *categories* are just concepts that classify other concepts in this way. The importance of recognising concepts as achievements is that it forces us to recognise a difference between categorial form that belong to our concepts *qua* concepts, and categorial form that belong to our concepts *qua* particular attempts to inferentially encode structure of the world. This produces a distinction between *logical categories* that remain invariant across the various revisions of our conceptual models of the world (e.g., singular term, predicate, quantifier, etc.) and *empirical categories* that uncover invariant features of these models that may nevertheless be revised along with them (e.g., physical object, occurrent property, process, etc.).

This puts us in a position to explain the myth of the categorial given and to account for its seductive character. I'll begin by quoting Sellars' succinct description of this form of the myth:

> To reject the Myth of the Given is to reject the idea that the categorial structure of the world—if it has a categorial structure—imposes itself on the mind as a seal imposes an image on melted wax.[23]

The first thing to unpack here is the notion of the *categorial structure* of the world. This is the subject matter of traditional metaphysics, but for all of the competing sets of categories to be found in the tradition there is scant explanation of their function beyond 'carving nature at its joints'.[24] For our purposes it is easiest to hold that it is whatever empirical categories *signify* by means of classifying empirical concepts. Importantly, this raises the question of whether categorial structure can be *pictured* by the non-conceptual forms of representation that we share with animals and pre-linguistic infants. To admit this would be to draw a parallel between the categorial form of our conceptual systems and what we might call the *phenomenological form* of the relevant representational mechanisms.

23. W. Sellars, 'Foundations for a Metaphysics of Pure Process: The Carus Lectures of Wilfrid Sellars' (hereafter *FMPP*), *The Monist* 64:1 (1981), 3–90, Lecture I, §45..

24. This is a metaphor with a long history, originating in Plato's *Phaedrus* (tr. R. Waterfield [Oxford: Oxford University Press, 2002], §§265d–266a).

Leaving this to one side for the moment, I think we can reformulate the myth as follows: it consists in the idea that there is some form of *universal perceptual content* that is distinct from *empirical conceptual content* as Sellars describes it. This is just the claim that there is some specific sense in which absolutely any two sentient creatures could be said to have the same *experience* without having the same *conceptual grasp* of this experience. To put this in terms of our guiding metaphor, this amounts to treating ourselves as if we have TVs in our heads that have no particular causal-functional structure. It means supposing that there is a kind of content that is self-individuating insofar as it cannot in principle be individuated by means of a functional mapping between its vehicles. This is where the temptation to treat perceptual content as that which is available to introspection leads, insofar as it slides all to easily into treating introspection as in principle the only mode of access to content. It is treating introspection as *sui generis* in this manner leads to treating perceptual content as *sui generis* in its self-individuation. The illusion of self-individuation is maintained by illicitly individuating perceptual content on the basis of *what* we take it to represent (e.g., the pink ice cube we're both looking at), rather than *how* it represents it (e.g., the functional role the relevant states play in a wider behavioural economy that incorporates the pink ice cube). This makes the posited content universal in the manner described above, but only insofar as it becomes parasitic upon the conceptual content of sentences we use to describe what it represents. It is on this basis that our ability to discriminate features of the phenomenological form of our perceptual mechanisms through introspective apprehension appears to us as unveiling a categorial structure that the world itself has impressed upon us.

What is distinctive about the categorial form of the myth of the given is that those who endorse it can insist that even if introspective reflection on the manner in which the world appears to us cannot provide us with epistemological foundations for specific claims about the world (the epistemic given), it can nevertheless play a more general epistemological role in organising the process of making claims about the world by delineating the categories we should use to organise our empirical concepts.[25] The problem with this is not so much that this

25. Husserl's phenomenological project and the role that the notion of categorial intuition plays within it is paradigmatic of this approach (cf. *Ideas Pertaining to a Pure Phenomenology and to a Pure Phenomenological Philosophy: First Book* [Dordrecht: Kluwer Academic Publishers, 1982]).

sort of epistemological project is misguided. If nothing else, it is clear from Sellars later work on process metaphysics that he took such work to be both possible and necessary.[26] The problem is the idea that studying the phenomenological form of our parochial perceptual mechanisms through any means has anything interesting to contribute to this task.

26. See *FMPP*.

# On Computational Asymmetry

## 0. INTRODUCTION

Chomsky and others have rightly made a big deal of the fact that a good number of the sentences produced by the speakers of any given language are unique, as in, they've never been spoken before in the history of that language. I'd wager that when you take into account writing, this proportion becomes even larger, just because we tend to write longer sentences. It's all about how big the possibility space is. Let's take an extreme example: What are the chances that, if you took a number of Spanish words at random, the same length as *Don Quixote*, you would somehow recreate the novel? As Pierre Menard understood, the chances are infinitesimally small unless one can discover some principle through which to generate it, something better than mere randomness, something like Cervantes's original inspiration.[1]

Some problems are like *finding* a rule, and some problems are like *following* a rule. Some are unavoidably confronted with a space of *possibility* and some can collapse this space into *necessity*. It's immeasurably harder to discover a novel mathematical proof than it is to check one. It's far harder to write a great novel than it is to read one, and far harder to compose a brilliant song than to enjoy one. In case it looks like this is always an asymmetry between production and consumption, here's something that seems to go in the opposite direction: it's far harder to decrypt something than to encrypt it. But wait, this only works if you haven't got the encryption key, which means you have to find the rule! The lesson is that in asymmetric interactions the sender and receiver can play different roles. Consider the fact that it's often (though not always) harder to learn something than it is to teach it. Scott Aaronson thinks cryptography and

1. J.L. Borges, 'Pierre Menard, Author of the Quixote', in *Labyrinths* (London: Penguin Classics, 2000).

learning are dual problems.[2] From this perspective, trying to learn something is like trying to decrypt the world.

## 1. SEMANTIC SYMMETRIES

One way to look at our cognitive comfort zones is as regions of the information processing possibility space in which these asymmetries collapse, either because we're using more or less deterministic recipes that are as easy to follow as they are to check, as easy to learn as they are to teach, or because we've all got enough computational resources not to worry about them, when it's so easy to create/discover a workable rule that it makes no functional difference. Another way of understanding this is to say these are regions in which communication becomes possible— where sender and receiver achieve something resembling computational symmetry. What I mean by communication here is more than mere information transmission. When one looks at language from an information-theoretic perspective, just how complex a signal it is once more depends on the size of the possibility space in terms which you calculate the relevant probabilities.

Let's take English. Are we looking at strings of *letters* (and punctuation), some thirty-odd possible symbols bunched into pseudo-sentential chunks? Are we looking at series of *phonemes*, forty-four in all, combined in various limited ways? Or are we looking at sequences of *sentences*, each some combination of a near two hundred thousand words, according to some more or less implicit set of grammatical rules? Even at this level, we're still not talking about semantics, only syntax, and the amount of Shannon information will vary with what we pick. Chomsky's famous example—'Colourless green ideas sleep furiously'—is still grammatically well-formed and still completely meaningless.[3] We have to see that in one sense, language transmits an incredibly small amount of information, and in another, it transmits a potentially vast amount. For example, a sign that reads 'Beware the Dog' is only fourteen characters long, but it means an awful lot in certain situations. The presence of a dangerous dog in your immediate environment is a very significant and informationally rich signal to be looped

---

2. S. Aaronson, 'Why Philosophers Should Care About Computational Complexity', in *Computability: Gödel, Turing, Church, and Beyond*, ed. B.J. Copeland, C.J. Posy, and O. Shagrir (Cambridge, MA: MIT Press, 2013).

3. N. Chomsky, *Syntactic Structures* (The Hague: Mouton, 1957), 15.

through your various predictive layers. The semantic content begins to look like it's hidden in the symmetric capacities of the sender and receiver to compress and decompress the syntactic signal with so little effort they don't even notice.

It's about now that I get to sneak in a little computational Kantianism.[4] Kant would characterise these cognitive comfort zones in terms of what he calls analytic judgments, or those judgments that express the content of the concepts through which we understand the world (*Verstehen*). For instance, 'cats are mammals' and 'mammals are animals' are both analytic judgments. Taken together they allow you to infer the seemingly banal fact that any given cat is an animal. Kant thinks that there are other, synthetic judgments such as 'water boils at 100 degrees centigrade at one atmosphere of pressure', which enable us to draw far more interesting inferences (e.g., about how we should go about making a cup of tea), and whose truth is not dependent on the content of the concepts that compose them (i.e., water, temperature, and pressure). Indeed, once we know that 'mercury expands when heated' and by precisely how much, we can make a nice little thermometer to check our water temperature, and thereby just how much its boiling point changes as we vary atmospheric pressure. I've cheated a bit here, because it's likely that the unit of measure (degrees centigrade) was defined through using facts about the expansion of mercury, but I think you get the drift.

It would seem that synthetic judgments are in some important sense asymmetric. If nothing else, when you send one to someone else, you can communicate information they don't already have. Whereas an analytic judgment is less like useful information and more like a test of whether someone understands the concepts needed to receive informative judgments. Seeing if someone else's understanding of where your cat sits in the hierarchy of genus and species matches yours is one way of checking whether you're talking about the same thing (e.g., 'You know sphynxes are a type of cat, right?'), and thus whether you can tell them that cats have a toxic reaction to theobromine, and so they shouldn't give Chairman Meow chocolate (e.g. 'You know, the sweet stuff made from cocoa?'). There's another asymmetry here though: it seems as if synthetic judgments are like rules that must be discovered, whereas analytic judgments are like rules that can only be followed. How does this work?

4. See also 'On Transcendental Logic', in this volume.

## 2 SYNTHETIC ASYMMETRIES

One of the great philosophical ironies is that 'Analytic' philosophy has for the most part completely misunderstood the distinction between analytic and synthetic judgments. The relevant debates are dominated by philosophers who think that tame definitions of purely conventional terms such as 'Bachelors are unmarried men' are sufficient examples of analyticity,[5] while slightly more subtle thinkers such as Quine and Brandom use the inadequacy of these tame examples to reject analyticity altogether, advocating some sort of unrestricted semantic holism. I think Mark Wilson has provided the correct response to Quine, which is that, since unrestricted semantic holism is computationally intractable in practice, there can be nothing whose meaning is globally dependent on everything else, but only more local, if revisable, regions of significance.[6] However, the best thinkers in this regard are two of the great modernist logicians: Per Martin-Löf and Jean-Yves Girard (I'd claim that the third is William Lawvere, but he's not relevant here).

Martin-Löf has shown in an simple and elegant way what Kant's claim that mathematics is synthetic *a priori* really means.[7] Those who, since Frege, have attempted to treat maths as purely analytic have simply failed to appreciate Gödel's incompleteness results, and, in their blind fidelity to classical logic, have refused to stop viewing mathematics through the lens of completeness, despite their claims to the contrary. They are so blinded by the sheer obviousness of arithmetic judgements such as '5 + 7 = 12' that they cannot but see them as analytic, and on this basis, they pretend that famous open problems in number theory such as Goldbach's conjecture must be analytic in the same sense, even though we know of no rule that could decide the question.

Here's where we return to my claim that novel mathematical proofs are immeasurably harder to discover than they are to check. This all depends on what we mean by 'novel'. We can work out precisely how much harder it is to solve a certain mathematical problem than another if we have algorithmic

5. Cf. P. Grice and P.F. Strawson, 'In Defense of a Dogma', *Philosophical Review* 65:2 (1957), 141–58; J. Fodor and E. Lepore, 'Why Meaning (Probably) Isn't Conceptual Role', *Philosophical Issues* 3 (1993), 15–35.

6. M. Wilson, *Wandering Significance* (Oxford: Oxford University Press, 2008), 279–86.

7. P. Martin-Löf, 'Analytic and Synthetic Judgements in Type Theory', in P. Parrini (ed.), *Kant and Contemporary Epistemology* (Berlin: Springer, 1994), 87–99.

procedures for solving them. However, there are further ways of breaking down problems into more complicated computational complexity classes that enable us to reason about possible solutions.[8] The most significant of these are P and NP: deterministic polynomial time and nondeterministic polynomial time. These articulate a precise difference between problems for which there are algorithmic solutions better than randomly exploring some possibility space, and problems for which there are not. As such, if one is confronting a genuinely open mathematical problem for which there is no way of enclosing the space of possible solutions in advance, then the computational difference is essentially unmeasurable.

What Martin-Löf makes clear is that the content of the concepts we use to pose these problems, the inductive definitions of the types that specify ranges of values for variables (e.g., natural numbers, rational numbers, real numbers), and the functions that specify operations on variables of the relevant types (e.g., addition/subtraction and multiplication/division), are precisely what we need to recursively check solutions to judgements formulated using them (e.g., '5 + 7 = 12'). Contra Kant, one might admit that if the definition of the operation of addition is all you need to compute the results of these judgments (e.g., written in lambda calculus notation: $(\lambda sz.s(s(s(s(s(z))))))$ $(\lambda abc.b(abc))$ $(\lambda xy.x(x(x(x(x(x(x(y))))))))$ reduces to $\lambda xy.x(x(x(x(x(x(x(x(x(x(x(x(y))))))))))))$, then this makes them analytic. The difference between solving the problem and checking the solution has collapsed. However, something like Fermat's last theorem is still a synthetic judgment, because of the fact that the concepts sufficient to pose the problem are insufficient to solve it and need to be supplemented by whole new clusters of types, culminating in extravagant abstractions such as elliptic curves and modular forms.[9] This provides a delightful way of understanding the paracompleteness of the (intuitionistic) logic of mathematical justification. As we keep adding new types in order to solve problems we were able to pose with the previous ones, we open up whole new ranges of problems we can pose but not yet solve. The answers to our questions keep inviting us to ask new ones.

8. See footnote 2 above.

9. A. Wiles, 'Modular Elliptic Curves and Fermat's Last Theorem', *Annals of Mathematics* 141:3 (1995), 443–551.

By contrast, Jean-Yves Girard has been trying to explore the analytic/synthetic distinction in more general terms.[10] In order to relate Girard's work to Martin-Löf's it's important to briefly mention the Curry-Howard correspondence, which is a correspondence between type theory and intuitionistic logic.[11] This means that one can view propositions as types whose instances are proofs, and conditionals (if P then Q) as functions that take a proof from one type (P) and return a proof of another type (Q). Martin-Löf built his version of type theory (MLTT) using this correspondence, extending it to include quantifiers as dependent types.[12] This has gained new significance in recent years, as it is the basis for Homotopy Type Theory (HoTT), a new approach to the foundations of mathematics that provides an alternative to set theory.[13] It's important to understand that, though all propositions are types, not all types need be propositions. Hence Martin-Löf's inductive definitions of types whose instances are things like natural numbers, rather than proofs.

Girard's work can be seen as an attempt to derive types from more fundamental interactive dynamics, rather than simply defining them.[14] However, this was first and foremost an attempt to see how propositions emerge out of the abstract structure of dialogical interaction, along with the logical operators of linear logic. Girard is interested in more than just propositional types, and it's possible to reconstruct MLTT within his ludics framework.[15] What's interesting about his more recent, explicitly Kantian work on transcendental syntax, in which he aims to study 'the conditions of the possibility of language' is that he has developed a new conception of the computational dynamics out of which types emerge, one that can in some ways more easily be extended beyond the

10. J.-Y. Girard, 'Transcendental Syntax I: Deterministic Case', *Mathematical Structures in Computer Science* 27:5 (June 2017): 827–49.

11. See P. Wadler, 'Propositions as Types', *Communications of the ACM* 58:12 (December 2015): 75–84.

12. P. Martin-Löf, *Intuitionistic Type Theory* (Naples: Bibliopolis, 1980).

13. See *Homotopy Type Theory: Univalent Foundations of Mathematics*, <https://homotopytypetheory.org/book>, and J. Ladyman and S. Presnell, 'Does Homotopy Type Theory Provide a Foundation for Mathematics?', *British Journal for the Philosophy of Science* 69:2 (2016): 1–44. See also the coda to 'On Transcendental Logic', in this volume.

14. This goal is common to both his transcendental syntax project and his earlier work on ludics. See his 'Locus Solum: From the Rules of Logic to the Logic of Rules', *Mathematical Structures in Computer Science* 11 (2001): 301–506.

15. E. Sironi, 'Type Theory in Ludics', <https://arxiv.org/abs/1402.2511>.

mathematical cases Martin-Löf is describing, to the empirical and practical cases necessary to think about communication and cognition.[16] Ludics was about finding the dynamics hidden in the syntax of proof trees, and transcendental syntax is about finding the dynamics hidden in the syntax of proof nets.

How does this help us? Because Girard begins to conceive of types as bundles of tests, which are no longer restricted to processes like checking proofs. These tests can now involve interaction with the world and with one another, in addition to interaction with other language users. Types are no longer restricted to mathematical structures but can incorporate those computational behaviours involved in interacting with the world, and can do so in ways that need neither be linear nor entirely fixed. Precisely the sort of information-processing behaviours involved in the predictive processing model, with its interacting loops of upstream and downstream signals; loops that extend into the environment as sensation feeds into simulation and simulation feeds into action.[17] The way in which these processes communicate thus begins to look like a microcosmic model of linguistic communication, and the tests required to establish and calibrate communication begin look like analytic queries.

This is not something I wish to explore in too much more detail, but I do want to tie up the point: we can see the symmetric compression and decompression involved in communication as something like functionally bisimilar behaviours.[18] The bundles of such behaviours that constitute sortal concepts[19] (qua types) enable us to individuate empirical objects (qua instances) in ways that are sufficiently similar to talk about them, and condense aspects of behaviour (that we can interactively test for) in such a way that we can ascribe properties (qua predicates) to them. The high-bandwidth semantics riding the low-bandwidth syntax comes from our ability to sync our simulations of the world sufficiently. This almost seems like a trite point: I say 'My cat is a sphynx' and you develop certain expectations that shape your simulation of the world and my cat's role

16. For an overview, see B. Eng, 'A Gentle Introduction to Girard's Transcendental Syntax for the Linear Logician', <https://arxiv.org/abs/2012.04752>.

17. See A. Clark, 'Whatever Next? Predictive Brains, Situated Agents, and the Future of Cognitive Science' *Behavioural and Brain Sciences* 36:3 (2013): 181–204.

18. See D. Sangoria, 'On the Origins of Bisimulation and Coinduction' in *ACM Transactions on Programming Languages and Systems* 31:4 (2009): 1–41.

19. See R.E. Grandy, 'Sortals', *Stanford Encyclopedia of Philosophy*, 2010, <https://plato.stanford.edu/entries/sortals>.

within it. But this is way more interesting because it neither involves idealised representational contents that are merely exchanged (I'm looking at you, model theorists), nor a requirement that the neurological correlates of our simulations be innate and isomorphic (I'm looking at you, Fodor), nor a structureless play of signifiers where meanings not only bleed into one another, but semiotically haemorrhage in such a way that we can no longer say anything about meaning at all (I'm looking at you, Derrida). There are definite data structures here: adapted information schemas that are getting synced up through training and calibration.[20]

We've got a marriage of structure and behaviour organised through symmetries (not unlike that proposed by Tia Trafford).[21] Moreover, we can see how something like analyticity emerges out of the underlying behavioural bisimilarities. For instance, the basic interactions through which we bundle other tests, the ones that correspond to the conditions of individuation through which objects (qua behavioural invariants) get picked out and reidentified, are inherited in a manner that is expressed by analytic judgments such as 'cats are animals', 'oil is a liquid', and 'I am a person'. This provides a logical basis for the perennial distinction between properties that inhere in substances and those that are merely accidental; a distinction discovered by Aristotle, reworked by Kant, forgotten by Fregeans, and given back to us by Martin-Löf in the form of type definitions (essence), typing judgements (individuation), and the subtle complexities of subtyping (genus/species). There's a deeper story I could tell here about logical and computational dualities, but I've got to stop somewhere. I'll leave you with a last thought. If this hierarchy of relations through which information schemas (data structures) and interactive behaviours (methods) are inherited looks a bit like object-oriented programming to you, there's a reason for that. (The irony involved in me describing experience in object-oriented terms is not lost on me.)[22]

---

20. Cf. P. Grietzer, 'A Theory of Vibe', *Glass Bead*, Site 1 (2017), <https://www.glass-bead.org/article/a-theory-of-vibe/>.

21. T. Trafford, *Meaning in Dialogue: An Interactive Approach to Reasoning* (Berlin: Springer, 2017).

22. See P. Wolfendale, *Object-Oriented Philosophy: The Noumenon's New Clothes* (Falmouth: Urbanomic, 2014).

# On Transcendental Logic

## 1. BACK TO KANT (AGAIN)

### 1.0 Kant Contra Aristotle

I am a Kantian. I believe that there is a difference between **general logic** and **transcendental logic**. I'm not unique in this, but it is not a common position to hold. I also think that some who hold it don't really understand its significance. For instance, Sebastian Rödl is a brilliant thinker, but he thinks that transcendental logic starts where inferential behaviour ends.[1] This means he's not really doing logic, he's doing what Husserl would call formal ontology.

Kant describes the distinction between general logic and transcendental logic in terms of a difference between *form* and *content*. He thinks that the inferential behaviours encoded by general logic, which for him was a customised variant of Aristotelian term logic, could be used to reason about anything at all. General logic prescribes certain ways of manipulating and transforming symbols, but these symbols need not refer to anything, even if they capture some of the patterns of reasoning we apply to symbols that do refer. This is manifest in the difficulties of reasoning about individuals in Aristotelian logic. There's no formal difference between primary and secondary substances (e.g., Socrates and Man) even though we might make judgements that relate one to the other (e.g., 'Socrates is a Man'). These are essentially the same as judgements relating secondary substances as species and genus (e.g., 'Man is an Animal'). There is no relation between the singular and the general in Aristotelian logic. Transcendental

1. S. Rödl, *Categories of the Temporal: An Inquiry into the Forms of the Finite Intellect* (Cambridge, MA: Harvard University Press, 2012).

logic is supposed to bridge this divide, by relating it to the difference between the **senses** and the **intellect**.[2]

I could say a lot about Kant here. Too much, in fact. His transcendental psychology has too often been dismissed as fanciful introspection, when it was to a large extent motivated by logical constraints.[3] In my view, this amounted to working on the problem of artificial general intelligence about two hundred years before anyone else, but this isn't the place to justify that claim. A complete account of computational Kantianism is going to have to wait for another time, but I will have to give you a thorough overview. To begin, we must explain Kant's guiding question: How is it possible for us to be responsible for our judgements about objects? How is it possible for them to be subject to assessments of truth and falsity? Given that ought implies can, what capacities must we have in order to be counted as so responsible? This is what Kant would call **the problem of objective validity**. His provisional answer is that there must be some way of securing the relation between judgements and the objects their truth is beholden to. This becomes a new question: How is it that singular objects are given to us in intuition, such that they can be subsumed under general concepts?

There are three more things to be said about Kant's relation to his Aristotelian inheritance.

First, he inherits the scholastic distinction between the doctrine of concepts, the doctrine of judgements, and the doctrine of syllogisms; between general concepts (e.g., Liquid, Water, Temperature, Pressure, etc.), the judgements that they compose (e.g., the analytic judgement 'Water is a liquid' and the synthetic judgement 'Water boils at 100 degrees Celsius at one atmosphere of pressure'), and the inferences between these judgements (e.g., if 'the boiling point of Liquids decreases alongside Pressure', and 'Water boils at 100 degrees Celsius at one

2. The best and most illuminating account of the formal structure of Kant's transcendental logic has been provided by Michiel van Lambalgen and Theodora Achourioti in 'A Formalization of Kant's Transcendental Logic', in which they reveal it to essentially be the *geometric logic* studied most extensively in category theory. For a simple introduction to geometric logic and its potential uses, see S. Vickers, 'Geometric Logic in Computer Science', in G. Burn, S. Gay, and M. Ryan, *Theory and Formal Methods 1993* (Berlin: Springer, 1993), 37–54. For a more detailed discussion, see S. Mac Lane and I. Moerdijk, *Sheaves in Geometry and Logic: A First Introduction to Topos Theory* (Berlin: Springer, 1992). For a more in depth use case, see S. Abramsky, 'Domain Theory in Logical Form', *Annals of Pure and Applied Logic* 51:1–2 (14 March 1991), 1–77.

3. See P.F. Strawson, *The Bounds of Sense* (London: Routledge, 2018).

atmosphere of Pressure', then 'at less than one atmosphere water will boil at less than 100 degrees Celsius'). These are the types of representation managed by the faculties of understanding, judgement, and reason, respectively. Furthermore, judgements have primacy over concepts: concepts are to be understood in terms of their role in judgements, which is essentially to be understood through (but not reduced to) their contribution to the latter's role in inference.

Second, he inherits and reworks the connection between primary and secondary substances: every object is experienced as a type of object (e.g., this Cat on my lap, this oncoming Storm, this sample of Liquid). The singular is constrained by the general. This also means that there is a distinction between concepts that individuate objects and concepts that merely classify them, between what are usually called sortal and non-sortal concepts.[4] The former enable not just demonstrative judgements (e.g., 'This Cat on my lap is sleepy', 'That Storm is a big one' etc.), but also quantitative ones (e.g., 'There are two Cats in this Room', 'There is no Liquid in this Flask', etc.); while the latter enable qualitative and relational ones (e.g., 'Cats are furry' and 'Hurricanes are worse than Storms'). We'll forget about modal judgements for now.

Third, he rejects Aristotle's idea that substances are simply given as individuated, it is a nontrivial problem to go from unstructured sensory data to classified objects (as anyone working in machine vision will tell you). Aristotle treats substances as primitive individuals. They form the substratum of the referential framework through which we can individuate everything else (i.e., qualities, quantities, relations, places, times, positions, states, causes, and effects). For Aristotelians (as well as Lockeans, and Leibnizians), the world is already divided into neat chunks which we then stumble across. This is precisely what Kant denies. There is some work to be done in cutting it up, even if there might be some joints to carve at. This point is going to be important, because it's crucial for understanding vagueness.

## 1.1 Schema of Individuation

I can now explain what separates transcendental logic from general logic: transcendental logic is logic as if individuation mattered. The relation to an

4. See R.E. Grandy, 'Sortals', *Stanford Encyclopedia of Philosophy* (2010), <https://plato.stanford.edu/entries/sortals>.

object that makes a judgement objectively valid (and thus contentful) is to be understood in terms of how objects are synthesised. How do we go from more or less unstructured sensory data to typed particulars? Kant's answer is what he calls a **schema**. There are some who think this is an arbitrary notion designed simply to bridge the gap between concept and intuition. They are wrong. There are two things you need to know about schema.

First, they can mediate between concepts qua inferential rules, and intuitions qua data, because they are rules for processing data. You see a dynamic pattern first, a substance in motion second, an animal in transit third, a bounding dog fourth, and finally end up judging that there's a German shepherd running past you, and then inferring that it's gotten away from its owner. This is why time is privileged over space in Kant's transcendental psychology, because this processing takes place in time, even when it's not processing of spatiotemporally organised data.

Second, this mediation is what enables the singular to constrain the general, and thereby what makes objective validity possible. Every object must be individuated as an instance of a type, in so far as it is synthesised using intuitive data following suitable (series of) schematic rules. However, it is only by manipulating such instances that we can extract new information relating to the type. Schemas are rules through which instances become representative.

Here is a section from the introduction to the *Critique of Pure Reason* whose full significance is generally not appreciated:

> Mathematics and physics are the two theoretical cognitions of reason that are supposed to determine their object *a priori*, the former entirely purely, the latter at least in part purely but also following the standards of sources of cognition other than reason.[5]

I won't quote the following sections at length, but they go on to contrast the *constructive method* of mathematics, exemplified by Euclid's axiomatisation of geometric constructions (as distinguished from Hilbert's formalisation thereof),[6]

5. I. Kant, *Critique of Pure Reason*, tr. ed. P. Guyer and A. Wood, 'Preface to the second edition <B>', 107.

6. For a detailed examination of this difference, see A. Rodin, *Axiomatic Method and Category Theory* (Berlin: Springer, 2014).

with the *experimental method* of the empirical sciences (including but not limited to physics). This is not a haphazard contrast on Kant's part. He is not merely describing the mathematical and empirical as two unrelated species that happen to fall within a wider genus. Kant thinks that there is a duality between the mathematical and the empirical, and that this duality structures the way in which empirical cognition involves mathematical cognition, from the familiar objects of everyday experience to the unfamiliar objects of experimental science.

Schema are the key to this duality. To explain this, it's first necessary to dispel the temptation to describe the synthesis of objects as the construction of instances. All objects are synthesised, but only mathematical objects are constructed. This is because they are intuitively generated in accordance with certain rules, be it internally in imagination (e.g., visualising a plane figure whose edges are equidistant from its centre at all points) or externally by means of an imaginative prosthesis (e.g., drawing a circle on paper with a compass). It is the fact that an instance is constructed in accordance with certain rules that enables us to prove things involving the types they belong to (e.g., the irrationality of pi).

There are some scholars who claim that Kant's mathematical constructivism is motivated by logical inadequacy: that an inability to formulate the axioms and theorems of geometry in his revised term logic forced him to shift the burden from concepts to intuitions. They are wrong.[7] Kant's constructivism was motivated by a principled interpretation of the proof procedures followed both by Euclid and the mathematicians of his own era. Furthermore, Kant's ideas were a significant influence on Brouwer's intuitionism, and through this, Heyting's development of intuitionistic logic as a means of articulating mathematical reasoning. I'll explore this in more detail below, but for now, I should like to emphasise both the ongoing influence and the contemporary viability of Kant's philosophy of mathematics, as there are still many who are so comfortable assuming its antiquation and nonviability as an unjustified premise in other arguments.[8]

We need to get a grip on empirical schema, as these are far less well understood than their mathematical counterparts, to some extent because

7. See R. Pinosio, 'Kant's Transcendental Synthesis of the Imagination and Constructive Euclidean Geometry', MSc Thesis, University of Amsterdam, 2013, <https://eprints.illc.uva.nl/id/eprint/879/1/MoL-2012-13.text.pdf>.

8. Cf. J. Macfarlane, 'Kant, Frege, and the Logic in Logicism', *Philosophical Review* 3:1 (January 2002): 25–65.

Kant does not say as much about them. One of the more concrete examples he gives us is of the empirical schema of a plate, which he says is dependent upon the mathematical schema of a circle. This is an example of the relationship between what Kant would call the **productive** and **reproductive imagination**, where our ability to process a geometric data structure enables us to organise our simulation of our environment and the concomitant sensorimotor behaviour. For instance, we anticipate that as we move around the plate its profile will deform, circle becoming ellipsis as we modulate our own sensory input. We can equally anticipate what might happen when the plate is struck in a certain way, breaking into fragments whose shapes can be raggedly aligned.

This is a fairly simple example, but it might strike some readers as unusual. This is because I am describing Kant's account of perception as somehow bound up with action. The contemporary popularity of action-oriented accounts of perception and related accounts of embodied cognition tend to pass quite harsh judgements on their philosophical forebears, among which Kant is such a titanic figure that he invites much unjustified ire.[9] Of course, the fact that Kant is one of the original exponents of indirect realism does not help his case as far as many are concerned. Some people are just very attached to the idea that they're really touching the world, I suppose. This has perhaps lessened as the predictive processing paradigm has gained popularity in cognitive science and philosophy of mind alike.[10] I'm not the only one to have noted that Kant's insistence that perception essentially involves not only imagination but also anticipation suggests an affinity between his ideas and the idea that perception is predictive simulation.[11]

Still, the suggestion that Kant was not simply concerned with detached observations about 'moderate-sized specimens of dry goods' strikes some as unorthodox. Despite the fact that the 'Analogies of Experience' presuppose active perceptual modulation and that the 'Refutation of Idealism' is at pains to situate us within the world as a substance whose variations are causally tied to

9. See 'Artificial Bodies and the Promise of Abstraction', in this volume.

10. See A. Clark, 'Whatever Next? Predictive Brains, Situated Agents, and the Future of Cognitive Science' *Behavioural and Brain Sciences* 36:3 (2013): 181–204.

11. See L.R. Swanson, 'The Predictive Processing Paradigm Has Roots in Kant', *Frontier Systems in Neuroscience* 10 (2016), <https://www.frontiersin.org/journals/systems-neuroscience/articles/10.3389/fnsys.2016.00079/full>.

the dynamics of their environment, there persists an image of Kant as simply a fancier version of Descartes for whom minds are but lightly tethered to the world around them. If that doesn't convince you, then here is the killer point: Kant explicitly insists that the ideal of empirical knowledge is experimental science, and that this is no passive matter, but a complex and ongoing process of observation and manipulation. Moreover, he draws no line between the logic of mere perceptual judgement and the logic of thoroughgoing experimental science. They are governed by the same rules, or rather, the same sort of rules.

Empirical schema are rules for observing and manipulating our environment in such a way that features of it become representative, such that we can extract and apply general rules for understanding and acting upon them. They can as easily be simultaneous (e.g., running our hands over a surface as we feel its contours) as sequential (e.g., diagnosing symptoms then testing medication). They apply as much to the contents of my house as to experimental samples of gasses, as much to the creak in my neck as to as cultured swabs of microorganisms, and as much to my love life as to explosive encounters in particle accelerators. The caveats are that no one set of rules covers every context (transcendental schema are another issue), and that the main difference between familiar and scientific contexts is that it is usually so easy to spontaneously invent rules in the former that we never need to formalise them in the fashion of the latter, or thereby make explicit any relevant mathematical data structures or proof procedures.

This is why we do not say that empirical objects are constructed: the dual of construction is interaction. Observation and manipulation of our environment are invariably connected, even when we prioritise one (theory) or the other (practice). We interact with the world in ways that uncover stable patterns. Some of these patterns have mathematical structure that we can capitalise on, but it is dynamically realised: the dual of structure is behaviour.[12] Our behaviour interacts with environmental behaviour, and out of this we extract objects qua behavioural invariants. Of course, just as we simulate the objects that are really there around us, updating them in accordance with sensorimotor input/

12. This is most cleanly expressed by the mathematical duality between *algebras* (which model structure and its active construction) and *coalgebras* (which model behaviour and its interactive observation). See B. Jacobs, *Introduction to Coalgebra: Towards Mathematics of States and Observations* (Cambridge: Cambridge University Press, 2016).

output, we can equally simulate objects that aren't. This isn't quite the same as construction, though. We're generating behavioural interaction. Can we extract useful information from such simulations? Sometimes, sure. Just because we're generating the interaction ourselves doesn't mean it can't do anything interesting, but don't expect this to always work. Still, there are a lot of people trying to build climate simulations in elaborately outsourced computational imaginations, so there's got to be something to it.

### 1.2 From Logic to Psychology

Here's a further point about Kant's account of the faculties. If you're thinking that sense, imagination, understanding, judgement, and reason, are distinct psychological modules that Kant claims are somehow bundled together in every human skull, then you've got the wrong end of the stick. Kant is trying to understand what it is to be a system exchanging information with one's environment in such a way that one becomes capable of thinking and saying things about it that could possibly be true or false, reasoning with and revising them, bundling them into theories; acting and reacting, desiring and demanding, and more or less living through them. In short, what it is to have a mind and be a person. He doesn't do a perfect job, but his picture is a distinctly logical one, in which we can distinguish various functions that must be performed for such a system to work. It's not necessary for these functions to be parcelled out into isolated components, anymore than respiration, digestion, and excretion need to be (a subtle point in the philosophy of biology that Kant didn't quite get right).[13]

I've talked a decent amount about understanding, imagination, and even gestured vaguely at inner and outer sense (and thus space and time qua forms of intuition). What I haven't really done is to explain the functions of judgement and reason. I've described their characteristic forms of information (judgements and inferences), but I haven't really said anything about what they do with them. Here's a very important point. For all that Kant is obsessed with rules, he doesn't think that these rules are always exceptionless, deterministic, or unrevisable. If nothing else, he thinks that we creatively synthesise objects on

13. See H. Ginsborg, 'Kant's Biological Teleology and its Philosophical Significance', in G. Bird (ed.), *A Companion to Kant* (Oxford: Blackwell, 2006), and W. Wimsatt, 'Functional Organisation, Analogy, and Inference', in A. Ariew, R. Cummins, and M. Perlman (eds.), *Functions: New Essays in the Philosophy of Psychology and Biology* (Oxford: Oxford University Press, 2009).

the fly, testing out existing rules and inventing new ones as we go. You see that dynamic pattern and try out a bunch of rules until you've got a reasonable range of expectations, regardless of whether you've ever seen a German shepherd or even a dog for that matter. Syncing this up with the existing rules managed by the understanding (e.g. 'Is it an Animal?', 'Is it a Mammal?', etc.) is the process of creating a new concept that can then enable inference.

This creative process of finding rules is what Kant calls the technical exercise of judgement. It is technical in the sense that it's all about technique, rather than blind obedience to an algorithm. It is judgement in the sense that judgements are about combination (i.e., binding terms together with a copula) and this is, in the last instance, a matter of choice, or good judgement (i.e., 'Is it a Mammal? Yes, why not. This Animal is a Mammal'). For Kant, the question is whether judgement is finding a rule or following one, whether it is technical or schematic.[14] Every act of judgement involves a bit of both, but if the former dominates it produces a technical judgement (e.g., 'The purpose of a Heart is to beat', 'That Sunset is sublime', etc.) and if the latter dominates it produces a determinate judgement (e.g., 'That Heart has stopped beating', 'That Sunset is caused by airborne Particles that are scattering shorter wavelengths of Light'), etc. What happens in the aesthetic judgement of beauty is something like a limit case of this whole process, where the technical exploration of the space of possible rules runs away with itself, trying different ways of synthesising sensory data without settling on any, such that all we can say is 'That's beautiful!'.

What about reason? Reason is not just about performing inferences in accordance with the inferential rules encoded in the concepts of the understanding, but also about finding, articulating, and revising these rules. Reason extends beyond deductive syllogism into the wider realm of abductive exploration. On this basis, it is also responsible for the wider economy of knowledge and desire. It is responsible not just for pushing us to expand our stock of judgements about the world (e.g., by asking 'Why do airborne Particles only scatter the shorter wavelengths of Light?' or inferring 'That Heart stopped beating because of a Myocardial Rupture'), aiming towards a complete picture, but also for forcing us to revise our judgements and the concepts that compose them (e.g., 'Electrons behave like Particles', 'Electrons behave like Waves', and then 'Electrons aren't

14. See 'On Computational Asymmetry', in this volume.

Point Masses, they're Probability Distributions', etc.), aiming towards a consistent picture. I don't quite buy into Kant's account of the transcendental ideas (i.e., the World, the Soul, and God), but I think the notion that there are something like inferential patterns that can be articulated independently of the specific concepts deployed in them is a good one. If nothing else, how would we get from the logical structure implicit in our judgements to the logical vocabulary we use to make it explicit?[15]

Furthermore, the claim that this is a matter of economy is entirely literal. The principles governing our cognitive activities must not only aim for completeness and consistency, they must also be computationally tractable. We constantly need to find better ways to arrange and compress the whole armamentarium of concepts, judgements, and inferences that we're somehow keeping track of. This is one way of looking at Fichte's claim that practical reason has priority over theoretical reason in the last instance. It's not just that reasoning is something we do. It's that, even if we have to make choices about nothing else, we still need to make choices about how to deploy our cognitive resources. There is no getting around this fundamental computational fact, unless you restrict yourself to following rules laid out in advance. If there's one other thing we might articulate better than Kant did, it's that the disparate theories and associated inferential procedures that we try and piece together into an account of the world as a whole don't always fit together neatly.[16] We're always trying to integrate them, but this is not always as simple as having a consistent set of premises from which to reason. It doesn't necessarily matter that our manifest image of the world (those moderate sized dry goods) doesn't perfectly line up with our scientific one (those pesky particles), but it does matter that general relativity and quantum mechanics don't fit together.

Finally, it's necessary to say something about the elephant in the room: the distinction between phenomena and noumena. This is the aspect of Kant's philosophy that I disagree the most with. I even wrote a whole book trying to dissect its problematic legacy.[17] Nevertheless, it's possible to present a

---

15. See R. Brandom, *Making It Explicit* (Cambridge, MA: Harvard University Press, 2008).

16. See M. Wilson, *Wandering Significance* (Oxford: Oxford University Press, 2008), and *Physics Avoidance* (Oxford: Oxford University Press, 2017).

17. P. Wolfendale, *Object-Oriented Philosophy: The Noumenon's New Clothes* (Falmouth: Urbanomic, 2014).

charitable reading of the distinction that recovers its methodological purpose without endorsing its metaphysical conclusions. This is where we return to the question of individuation. The methodological purpose of the phenomena/noumena distinction is to force us to explain how it is possible for us to make objectively valid judgements (which are truth-apt, rather than true), without presupposing that the world is cut up in advance. If you explain the relation of our judgements to objects by constitutively assuming that they are already individuated, rather than regulatively assuming that they can be so individuated, you have presupposed that which you need to explain. Take that, direct realists.

I'll finish my overview of Kant with a suitably gnomic remark. I'm increasingly of the opinion that there is one way in which Kant got things exactly wrong. I think we need to be **empirical idealists** and **transcendental realists**.[18] I think my Platonism is showing.

## 2. TRANSCENDENTAL LOGIC, SIMPLIFIED

### 2.1 Aristotle, Locke, Leibniz, and Kant

I know what you're thinking. If I'm going to simplify transcendental logic, then why did I make you read several thousand words on Kant? Well, beyond the fact that I like to give credit where credit is due, I think that Kant's original concerns are still the best introduction to the overall shape of the ideas about logic and computation I'm going to outline. If nothing else, it puts the question of individuation front and centre, and suggests that there might be something that the partisans of precision actually have to argue for, rather than merely arguing against various forms of vagueness (ontic, epistemic, and semantic). We can see that they adopt something like a default position, in which they assume that the world is already individuated in some way.

Attempts to think through this assumption inevitably move from logic to metaphysics, or to set-theoretic model theory, although there's really not much difference.[19] The classical and early modern alternatives to Kant lay out the metaphysical options best: Aristotle, Locke, and Leibniz. There is something to be said for understanding Descartes's and Spinoza's respective reworkings of

18. See 'Essay on Transcendental Realism', in this volume.
19. The work of David Lewis exemplifies this indistinction.

the scholastic notions of substance, attribute, and mode, but that's for another essay altogether. When it comes to conditions of individuation, both Aristotle and Locke permit only sufficient conditions of discernibility. Aristotle's primary substances are typed by secondary substances, which determine those variations outside of which they can no longer be themselves (e.g., the youthful Socrates is identical to the old Socrates, but not his hemlock-laden corpse). By contrast, Locke distinguishes a few fundamental types of entity (e.g., physical object, material stuff, biological system, etc.) and then establishes generic conditions under which one instance is discontinuous with another (e.g., spatiotemporal discontinuity, differing corpuscular composition, differing functional composition, etc.). His account of personal identity is slightly more complicated, but I won't discuss that further here. Essentially, Aristotle and Locke need to appeal to some primitive identity that cannot entirely be explained. Things simply are what they are.

Leibniz is the first person to really tackle the problem of individuation head on, by insisting on the need for necessary conditions of identity. This is why it's called Leibniz's Law: he doesn't just formulate the principle that underwrites Aristotle's *maximalist* and Locke's *minimalist* type systems (**the indiscernibility of identicals**), he supplements it with its converse (**the identity of indiscernibles**). Leibniz stares into the abyss of individuation and then makes exactly the wrong decision. Leibniz's logic has essentially only one type, which means it is implicitly quantifying over everything and every possible predicate those things can have. The question of whether he restricts these predicates to nonrelational ones (i.e., monadic predicates), and precisely how he understands relations, especially with regard to the ideality/reducibility of spatiotemporal relations, is a matter of some controversy.[20] Regardless, the resulting move from logic to metaphysics results in a world constituted by infinitesimal pointlike substances (monads) arranged in hierarchies through which they express the properties of those parts of the hierarchy over which they preside. This is a psychedelic vision of the world, and it's not without its own innovative insights.[21] However, it very much makes the best of a bad logical choice. Monads are self-identical because they cannot

20. See R.T.W. Arthur, 'Leibniz's Treatment of Relations', in *Monads, Composition, and Force: Ariadnean Threads through Leibniz's Labyrinth* (Oxford: Oxford University Press, 2018), appendix 2.

21. See M. Wilson, 'From the Bending of Beams to the Problem of Free Will', in *Physics Avoidance*.

change—all that can change is the way they are arranged, and even this is in some sense implicit in each and every monad to some degree of clarity and distinctness. Leibniz has solved the problem of individuation by drilling down to the most primitive form of identity possible, a form which is equivalent to containing the rest of the world in microcosm. The individual concept of each entity incorporates everything about the particular possible world it is located in.

Kant's response to Leibniz is thus more subtle than is usually realised. He is not simply arguing against the identity of indiscernibles on the basis of spatio-temporal duplicates, but trying to show how a typed logic can provide conditions of individuation that combine Aristotle's concern with invariance and Locke's concern with continuity, while supplementing them with spatiotemporal conditions sufficient for uniqueness. He is dealing with the problem of individuation in a way that refuses to move from logic to metaphysics.

Kant has a far more nuanced account of invariance than Aristotle, and a far more interesting account of continuity than Locke. On the former account, Kant's interpretation of the category of substance is much more fluid than Aristotle's, as is clear from his example of the invariance of substance across the combustive transition from wood to smoke and ash. There are different layers of invariance, rather than a fundamental level of discrete entities on which all questions about variation are founded. On the latter account, Kant's conception of continuity across variation is based on a more thoroughly mathematical appreciation of continuous variation (Leibniz had invented calculus by this point, and Kant was obsessed with Newton). This means that the types of quality (qua reality, negation, and limitation) can be far more interesting, and we can articulate relations between their variations in the form of empirical laws. Furthermore, all of this is articulated not as a pre-given type system, but as a basic set of principles for building one through observational and experimental interaction with the world. These are what Kant calls **transcendental schema**. They are the computational principles through which we learn to extract behavioural invariants (objects) and to identify and relate their behavioural variations (predicates). They are the base types of a generative system of empirical types.

## 2.2 Kant on Logical Explanation

Given all this, it is no surprise to me that once the prohibition on metaphysics in the Analytic tradition was punctured by Quine, weakened by Kripke, and blown apart by Lewis, most variants of analytic metaphysics have tended to be Aristotelean, Lockean, or Leibnizian in shape; with numerous additional bells and whistles, and varying degrees of self-consciousness.[22] What do you expect from a tradition which has entirely rejected the logical resources that Kant deployed to resolve these issues? Bad logic must be supplemented with bad metaphysics. Good metaphysics demands good logic.

Don't worry, I'll try to justify these sweeping judgements shortly. For now, I want to address an issue that may be obvious given what I've already discussed but is certainly not obvious in Kant's own work. Given what I said above about the duality between mathematical construction and empirical interaction, it would seem that mathematical objects and empirical objects should be individuated in different ways. If this is so, why is there only one transcendental logic?

This is an absolutely crucial question. One of the defects of Kant's account of mathematical construction is that he limits it to construction in intuition. One of the often-noted effects of this is a difficulty in dealing with non-Euclidean geometries. The more significant flaw is that it enables him to interpret mathematics as the purely formal study of any possible object of experience, which makes perfect sense given his view of the dependence of empirical upon mathematical schema. There is even a certain logical dimension to this, in so far as mathematical discoveries can always have empirical consequences, whereas the effect of empirical discoveries on mathematics (e.g., the relation between developments in physics and analysis) is more complex and contentious. Nevertheless, there must be some sense in which we're using constructed instances to represent specific mathematical objects, or conditions for determining whether two such instances represent the same object. This means that we need to be able to talk about identity and individuation in mathematics, and how these are articulated by mathematical types.

---

22. See S. Kripke, *Naming and Necessity* (Cambridge, MA: Harvard University Press, 1972); D. Wiggins, *Sameness and Substance Renewed* (Cambridge: Cambridge University Press, 2001); M. Ayers, 'Ordinary Objects, Ordinary Language and Identity', *The Monist* 88:4 (October 2005), and D. Lewis, *On the Plurality of Worlds* (Oxford: Blackwell, 1986).

I'll examine this duality between mathematical and empirical types below, and hopefully recover Kant's own transcendental logic as expressing something like the point where the two meet. For now, I want to focus on the fundamental concepts that these different logics of individuation share, and show how these concepts are elided or collapsed by the logical paradigms that have come to dominate Analytic philosophy of logic, language, mind, and metaphysics since the advent of Frege's *Begriffsschrift*. This is not to say that Frege was oblivious to concerns about individuation. He was certainly interested in criteria of identity, especially in the case of mathematical objects; and his account of informative identities in terms of sense and reference is not only influential but remains a hyper-intensional thorn in an extensional paw.[23] However, these concerns took a back seat to his formulation of first-order classical logic and his associated interpretation of concepts as functions from objects to truth values.

These days, we customarily think that there are three logical layers: **propositions**, **concepts**, and **objects**. Propositions are things that can be true or false. Objects are things of which propositions can be true or false. The tendency is to think of propositions and objects as logical primitives and then to explain concepts in terms of them. On the one hand, modifying Frege's extensionalism, we tend to think of them either directly as functions from objects to truth values or indirectly as functions from objects to propositions (e.g., sets of possible worlds). On the other, cutting against Frege's intensionalism, we tend to think them either directly as sets of objects, or indirectly as sets of sets of objects (e.g., sets of possible objects) or sets of other concepts (e.g., intersecting sets of conceptual primitives). There have been some attempts to give independent substance to the concept of concept, either through the metaphysics of properties or the epistemology of conceptual capacities. Both tend to collapse back into extensionalism of one sort or the other.

In the days of term logic, we took concepts as logical primitives, and tried to understand propositions and objects in terms of them. This reversal of explanatory direction is apparent in both Aristotle and Leibniz. Aristotle divides the conceptual layer between substance and accident but loses purchase on the third layer in the process. Leibniz's conception of the distinction between substance and accident is undermined by his single typed approach to substances.

23. See P. Tichý, *The Foundations of Frege's Logic* (New York: De Gruyter, 1988).

On the one hand, this produces a conception of propositions as simply expressing inherence relations between subject and predicate, producing a distinction between types of truth (i.e., truths of essence and truths of existence) based on whether this inherence can be deduced finitely or infinitely (i.e., by us or by God). On the other, this produces the conception of objects explained above: monads as infinitesimal point structures whose complete individuation demands that they simultaneously individuate every other monad they are compossible with.

The aim of Kant's transcendental logic is to retain Aristotle's division of the second layer without losing the third, and this means endorsing Leibniz's commitment to complete individuation without abandoning the type system that mediates identity. The result is something that looks more like modern type theory than it does like contemporary philosophical logic:

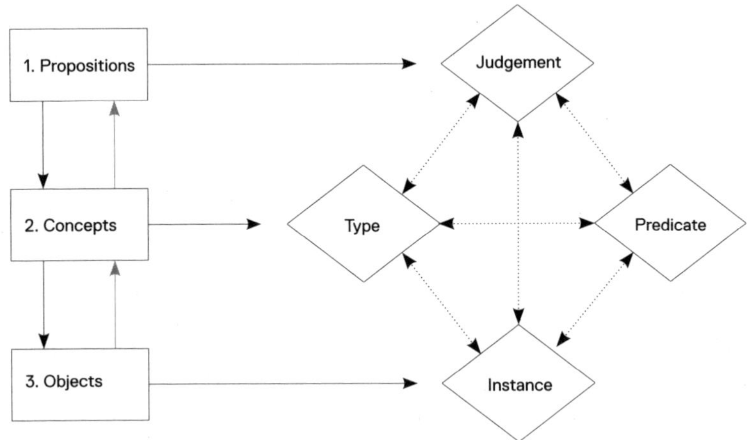


Kant separates and transforms the fundamental logical notions: propositions (into judgements), concepts (into types and predicates), and objects (into instances). This then enables us to ask the full range explanatory questions: How does an object instantiate a type? How does an object fall under a predicate? How does an object validate a proposition? These questions can all be flipped around: How does a type determine a range of instances? How does a predicate subsume its objects? How is a proposition beholden to its objects?

We can even add to this a couple of cross-hatched questions: How does a type constrain its predicates? and How can predicates define new types?

Some of these questions were already asked by Aristotelian logic: How do attributes inhere in substances? How do substances support their accidents? However, Aristotle literally birthed the discipline of metaphysics in his attempt to answer these questions in nonlogical terms. Contemporary Analytic philosophy tends to follow Aristotle when it is confronted with these issues, bolting ontology onto logic in haphazard attempt to halt the paradoxical collision that ensues when classical logic crashes headlong into the empirical world.[24] By contrast, Kant recognised that these were genuinely logical questions, and that answering them required moving from Aristotle's general logic to his own transcendental logic. What I now need to show is how Analytic philosophy is trapped in its own, more contemporary form of general logic, and how we enact our own transition to an equally contemporary transcendental logic.

However, before I get into the details, it's worth recapitulating Kant's strategy for approaching the above logical questions. As I have already noted, Kant treats judgements as primary. However, he does not treat their capacity to be true or false (truth-aptness) as an explanatory primitive. This is why his whole project turns around the question of objective validity, or the relation between judgements and objects. Nevertheless, explaining how it is possible for our judgements to be about objects without simply assuming objects as a corresponding logical primitive requires beginning with judgements, rather than adopting Aristotle's and Leibniz's strategy of beginning with concepts. Kant needs to somehow get explanatory purchase on types, predicates, and objects through their role in judgements, without begging the question by understanding judgements through them. Although he thinks judgements combine concepts, there must be more to them than such combinations. Although he thinks judgements are validated by objects, there must be more to them than such validations. Kant escapes these explanatory circles by understanding judgements in terms of their role in inference, gaining purchase on the remaining notions through their distinctive

24. I particularly have in mind the problems faced in squaring the indiscernibility of identicals with the possibility of change, vagueness, and similar cases that potentially undermine the absoluteness of the identity relation. For an overview see H. Deutsche, 'Relative Identity' (2022), *Stanford Encyclopedia of Philosophy*, <https://plato.stanford.edu/entries/identity-relative/>.

contributions to this role.[25] This is why we are dealing with transcendental logic, rather than formal ontology.

## 2.3 Metaphysics, Epistemology, and Semantics

I want to wrap up this section by showing how two other Kantian problems fit into this framework, and, on this basis, why they have generally been misunderstood: the distinction between *analytic* and *synthetic* judgements, and the distinction between the *pure* and the *empirical*.

It's often noted that 'Kant's cleavage between analytic and synthetic truths was foreshadowed in Hume's distinction between relations of ideas and matters of fact, and in Leibniz's distinction between truths of reason and truths of fact'.[26] But this statement says more about how the distinction can be misunderstood than about how it should properly be understood. Hume's and Leibniz's distinctions have different flavours: Hume is more concerned with explaining the epistemic difference between the a priori and the a posteriori, whereas Leibniz is more concerned with explaining the modal difference between the necessary and the contingent. Note here that I do mean 'explain' in both cases. The relevant distinctions are not simply restatements of a priori/a posteriori and necessary/contingent distinctions but attempts to explain their source. Hume's is a psychological explanation in terms of associations, whereas Leibniz's is a metaphysical explanation in terms of compossibility.

Kant's transcendental psychology and its foundation in transcendental logic supersede these prior explanatory frameworks, by interposing a semantic difference between epistemic and modal ones. This is where Kripkeans have a tendency to start talking about how all three levels (semantic, epistemic, modal) can be interspliced, using semantic externalism and possible worlds to dream up examples of analytic a posteriori statements (e.g., 'Water is $H_2O$'). This is not entirely off the mark, as we'll see, but it's wrapped up in a mishmash of Aristotelian and Leibnizian metaphysics so thick it can no longer tell the difference between logic and model theory, although this is merely one more example of the negligible difference between model theory and metaphysics. However, I'm

25. See R. Brandom, *Reason in Philosophy* (Cambridge, MA: Harvard University Press, 2013), chapter 1.
26. W.V.O. Quine, 'Two Dogmas of Empiricism', *The Philosophical Review* 60 (1951): 20–43.

going to have to return to these issues later, after we've gone over a bit more type theory.[27] For now, it suffices to say that Quine's arguments against the analytic/synthetic distinction rest upon an impoverished view of logical structure that gets him into no end of trouble.

The real issues here are Quine's unwavering fidelity to first-order classical logic supplemented by set theory, and thereby extensionality (the foreclosure of modality); and his tendency, following Russell rather than Carnap, to collapse the analytic/synthetic distinction back into Hume's epistemological concerns (the foreclosure of semantics). The contrasting approaches to the semantics of identity taken by neo-Aristotelians/neo-Leibnizians (e.g., Wiggins, Lewis, or both: Kripke) and neo-Fregeans (e.g., Evans, McDowell, Brandom, or Tichý) demonstrate the two ways in which the Analytic tradition has tried to grapple with these problems post-Quine. On the one hand, one rejects Quine's foreclosure of modality, either by reconstructing intensions out of modal extensions (semantic internalism) or by insisting on the metaphysical primacy of the identity relation in a manner that bends everything else to its will (semantic externalism and/or applied ontology). On the other, one rejects Quine's foreclosure of semantics, by refusing to collapse the distinction between sense and reference into that between intension and extension, and copes with the hyper-intensional consequences as best one can (mediating internalism/externalism). Alternatively, one can remain faithful to Quine by following Davidson, who resolves the issue by dissolving it entirely. You let the world take care of the details for you.[28] Semantic externalism becomes indistinguishable from semantic nihilism. Davidson's pragmatism is often admirable, and he has subtle post-Quinean thoughts on rationality, interpretation, and action; but Davidson's 'semantics' is a philosophical abomination.

---

27. In my view, the correct reading of Kant's analytic/synthetic distinction, at least as it pertains to mathematical judgements, is provided by Per Martin-Löf in his seminal paper 'Analytic and Synthetic Judgements in Type Theory' (in P. Parrini [ed.], *Kant and Contemporary Epistemology* [Dordrecht: Kluwer, 1994], 87–99). Martin-Löf defends Kant's claim that mathematics is synthetic a priori by showing that there is an asymmetry between what one needs to know in order to *prove* a conjecture and what one needs to know in order to *verify* this proof. Only the latter understanding is encoded in analytic type definitions. This is another example of the difference between *finding* and *following* rules discussed earlier. See also 'On Computational Asymmetry', in this volume.

28. D. Davidson, 'On the Very Idea of a Conceptual Scheme' in *Proceedings and Addresses of the American Philosophical Association* 47 (1973–1974): 5–20

Leaving these issues to one side then, we can turn to the distinction between the *pure* and the *empirical*. This loosely aligns with the distinction between the a priori and the a posteriori, but it has a few curious features that can make it hard to interpret. Firstly, although it includes judgements, it is not limited to them. There are also pure/empirical intuitions (sense), pure/empirical schema (imagination), pure/empirical concepts (understanding), and pure/empirical ideas or principles (reason). Secondly, although the pure is always understood in terms of form, the empirical is understood in opposition to this sometimes as *matter* (intuitions) and sometimes as *content* (concepts). This difference can be discerned in Kant's famous dictum that 'thoughts without content are empty (form without content), intuitions without concepts are blind (matter without form)';[29] the formal bridge between the two being the connection between the pure forms of conception (categories) and the pure forms of intuition (space and time) established in the 'Transcendental Deduction of the Pure Concepts of the Understanding' (transcendental schema). This is made more complicated by the fact that pure forms of conception qua functions of judgement can have content in virtue of providing the form of content as such, in so far as they make possible relation to an object; and that the pure forms of intuition are themselves intuitions, and as such can be constructively operated on by the productive imagination in accordance with pure schema.

However, the most important thing to understand is that the pure includes both the transcendental and the mathematical. This causes no end of confusions, and these should be nipped in the bud if we are going to explore the mathematical/empirical duality from the perspective of transcendental logic. The main confusion arises from the fact that the a priori is often interpreted in two different ways: as that which can potentially be discovered independently of experiential knowledge, and as that which is already known independently of experiential knowledge. Kant adopts the former interpretation. The latter interpretation then divides into the innatist theories of Plato and Descartes, and their nativist descendants such as Chomsky and Fodor. Kant's account of the transcendental conditions of experience is often confused with both of these positions.

29. Kant, *Critique of Pure Reason*, 193–4 [A51/B76].

Kant's position differs from innatism in so far as he has no need to treat transcendental structures as something given to a mind that could in principle be separated from them (e.g., by God or a sojourn among the Forms), and he has no need to treat mathematical structures as something remembered by a mind in which they are already implicit (e.g., memories teased out by geometric constructions). It differs from nativism in that he has no need to tell any just-so-stories about the evolution of minds, or to lean upon such stories in order to justify his peculiar conception of their structure. Transcendental structures are uncovered by arguments to the effect that mindedness is impossible without them, and mathematical structures can be embedded in minds by biological evolution, cultural learning, or personal innovation. The weakness in Kant's account that encourages these misinterpretations is the methodological laxity of his notion of **transcendental reflection**, which has allowed subsequent readers to confuse the undoubtedly introspective inspiration for his transcendental psychology with an illicitly introspective justification. I do believe that there are such slippages in Kant's arguments, and that they themselves inspire the subsequent phenomenological tradition. However, it is possible to correct these slippages by developing a more precise account of transcendental method.[30]

There are two final questions, each raised by Kant's original problem: How are synthetic a priori judgements possible?

In what sense do we know the synthetic a priori judgements that articulate the transcendental conditions of the possibility of empirical knowledge (e.g., 'In all change of appearances substance persists and its quantum is neither increased nor diminished in nature')?[31] I don't think Kant has a good answer to this question, but it is not too hard to find such an answer. These principles can be implicit in things we must know how to do to be minded, without us being able to explicitly say what we're doing.[32]

How does the discovery and justification of the synthetic a priori judgements of mathematics differ from the discovery and justification of the synthetic a posteriori judgements of empirical science? This is to return to the question of

30. See 'The Greatest Mistake: A Case for the Failure of Hegel's Idealism', in this volume.

31. The ultimate elaboration of this idea is to be found in Noether's theorem.

32. This idea is developed in detail by Robert Brandom in *Between Saying and Doing* (Cambridge, MA: Harvard University Press, 2008).

how transcendental logic is refracted through the duality between the mathematical and the empirical, between structure and behaviour.

*

It is hard to do justice to an unfinished and perhaps unfinishable project without attempting to finish it, at least in part. I must resist the temptation to do so here. More detailed discussion of type theory and category theory, and related philosophical debates, would be necessary. However, I do think it worth trying to convey some of the key ideas and intuitions driving the project outlined above.

To begin with, my understanding of Kant's thought was entirely upturned by Achourioti and van Lambalgen's revelation that his transcendental logic could be interpreted as geometric logic, a system studied in detail in category theory and computer science, but largely unknown in philosophical circles.[33] This logic is loosely intuitionistic in flavour, but it has a deeper connection to topology, in so far as it is the internal logic of Grothendieck topoi, which is to say that it is implicit in a certain conception of generalised space.[34] Given Kant's essentially spatial intuitions about concepts (he talks of 'spheres' and 'limits') it seemed possible that he had intuitively stumbled upon an inherently spatial logic.[35] This combined with two other mathematical ideas: (i) Michael Robinson's contention that 'sheaves are the canonical structure for data integration'[36], and (ii) Steve Vickers conjecture that geometric logic has a natural observational interpretation.[37] As categories of sheaves on a site, we might then interpret Grothendieck topoi as

33. See footnote 2, above.

34. For a conceptual overview, see S. Vickers, 'Generalised Point-free Spaces, Pointwise', <https://arxiv.org/abs/2206.01113>.

35. This is clearest in Kant's account of infinite judgements (e.g. 'The car is non-blue') which differ from negative judgements (e.g. 'It is not the case that the car is blue') in so far as they *positively delimit* the range of features an object possesses on the basis of the type it belongs to. For example, 'It is not the case that gravity is blue' is as true as 'It is not the case that the car is blue', but to say that 'The car is non-blue' is to affirm that cars are a coloured type of object (unlike gravity), and on that basis carve out a region of the *colour space* that the car might be found in.

36. M. Robinson, 'Sheaves are the Canonical Structure for Data Integration', <https://arxiv.org/pdf/1603.01446.pdf>.

37. S. Vickers, 'Geometric Theories and Databases', in M.P. Fourman, P.T. Johnstone, and A.M. Pitts (eds.), *Applications of Categories in Computer Science* (Cambridge: Cambridge University Press, 1992), 288–314; and 'Geometric Logic as a Specification Language', in Burn, Gay, and Ryan (eds.), *Theory and Formal Methods*, 321–40.

something like spaces of possible experience in which heterogeneous types of sensory data are synthesised into coherent observations with an implicitly propositional structure, complete with objects, predicates, and types. The underlying site (or base space) corresponds to Kant's pure forms of space and time. The observations that populate it are open-ended but essentially cumulative. This means that, although there are things we have not yet experienced, once they are experienced there is no disputing them. The information about the world that we take in through sensation grows steadily, without correction or loss.[38]

However, such informatic infallibility is a significant problem. Not only does it exclude the large-scale conceptual changes that experimental science forces upon us through the cycle of hypothesis and test, but it overlooks the extent to which even the small-scale adjustments that run through our everyday experience are constituted by the interplay of prediction and error.[39] Yet geometric logic works fine as long as we assume that there are at least some basic observational judgements that are effectively reliable and unproblematic, and whose inferential consequences are entirely clear-cut. Another way to think about this is that it works fine as long as we assume that there is no difference between the rules we use to predict their behaviour and the laws they are supposed to capture, either at the level of imaginative schema or mathematised theory. Yet another way is that this amounts to collapsing the difference between behaviour and structure, or rendering interaction as close to construction as possible. It is this collapse that leaves Kant with a single transcendental logic spanning both the empirical and the mathematical, despite the fact that their objects are individuated in entirely different ways.

How then do we pull this apart into two distinctive logics? The good news is that the project of mathematical transcendental logic is already well under way in the form of Homotopy Type Theory (HoTT) and its offshoots.[40] The putative aim of this project is to provide a new foundation for mathematics by creating a

38. This monotonic increase of information is also what allows geometric logic to fit the domain-theoretic semantics of the full range of computations possible in untyped λ-calculus (see Abramsky, 'Domain Theory in Logical Form'), as even though some of these computations will never terminate, they will continue to accrue information indefinitely (e.g., a program that calculates the digits of pi).

39. See footnote 10 above.

40. See 'Homotopy Type Theory: Univalent Foundations of Mathematics', <https://homotopytypetheory.org/book>, and J. Ladyman and S. Presnell, 'Does Homotopy Type Theory Provide a Foundation for Mathematics?', *British Journal for the Philosophy of Science* 69:2 (2016): 1–44.

framework in which all proofs are computationally verifiable, exploiting the Curry-Howard correspondence between proofs and programs and its extension into categories by Lambek.[41] It is built upon the **intuitionistic type theory** developed by Per Martin-Löf, which suspends the identity of indiscernibles (LL1) by locally restricting identity to objects of the same type. For example, the definition of the type of integers provides the conditions under which any two expressions whose values are integers might be judged identical (e.g., 5 + 7 = 12), but it does not even make sense to ask whether expressions corresponding to objects of different types are the same (e.g., integers and manifolds). HoTT then globally reimplements LL1 in a new form: the **univalence axiom**. By treating types as spaces (infinity-groupoids), identities can be seen as paths, which themselves can be identified by means of further paths, and so on ad infinitum. On this basis it becomes possible to talk about identity between types in terms of equivalence, and thereby treat unrestricted identity as equivalent to equivalence. What this promises is not just that proofs will be directly checkable qua programs, but that we can prove that different computational frameworks represent the same mathematical objects. This amounts to something like a natural theory of mathematical intentionality.[42]

Another way of looking at HoTT is as uniting two different roles that logic has traditionally played in computer science: knowledge representation and computational structure. Formal ontologies built using custom description logics (e.g., OWL) are the paradigm example of knowledge representations, allowing information about specific domains to be regimented in a way that facilitates automated reasoning.[43] Curry-Howard correspondences are the paradigmatic use of logic to express computational structure, beginning with intuitionistic logic and typed lambda calculus and extending into other logics and calculi (e.g., in ways that slowly capture additional features of computation, such as state, concurrency, and control).[44] HoTT is in the unique position of doing both:

---

41. This three-way correspondence leads to a perspective that Robert Harper has dubbed 'computational trinitarianism': R. Harper, 'The Holy Trinity', *Existential Type*, 27 March 2011, <https://existentialtype.wordpress.com/2011/03/27/the-holy-trinity/>.

42. This is the ultimate realisation of the promise of abstraction discussed in 'Artificial Bodies and the Promise of Abstraction', in this volume.

43. See R.J. Brachman and H.J. Levesque, *Knowledge Representation and Reasoning* (Burlington, MA: Morgan Kaufman, 2004).

44. See P. Wadler, 'Propositions as Types', *Communications of the ACM* 58:12 (December 2015): 75–84. It is important to make a distinction between logics that *intrinsically* correspond to

providing an integrated type system that organises the range of mathematical objects about which we might form conjectures and construct proofs, while circumscribing the computational behaviour of those processes which operate upon them. To describe this in more Husserlian terms, it manages to articulate both the *noematic* and *noetic* dimensions of mathematical thought.

How would we go about dualising this to the empirical case?

There are roughly three points of leverage we might exercise here. The first is the duality between Leibniz's Laws: the identity of indiscernibles (LL1) and the indiscernibility of identicals (LL2). It might make sense to suspend and reimplement LL2 in a manner similar to what type theory and the univalence axiom do with LL1. This is compelling for at least three reasons: (i) unlike mathematical objects, empirical objects change in ways that seemingly violate LL2, (ii) unlike mathematical objects, empirical objects involve vagueness in ways that seemingly violate LL2, and (iii) the dialogical structure of both synchronic communication and diachronic revision requires that we can stipulate we are referring to the same objects even as our conceptual schemes differ or change, permitting identity relations that fall outside of fixed 'types' (e.g., electrons as corpuscles and as probability distributions), but also forcing us to be selective about which predicates these identities let us transport from one presentations of the object to the other.[45] However, this is to leap directly to the level of predicate calculus, and there are pressing questions to be answered at the propositional level.

This leads us to our second point of leverage: the duality between proof and refutation. If intuitionistic logic is the logic of proofs, as evidenced in the BHK interpretation and the Curry-Howard correspondence, then one might conjecture that the dual co-intuitionistic logic is the logic of refutation, and so might provide a suitable propositional foundation.[46] The main merit of this

computational structures in this manner and those that have been *extrinsically* constructed in order to reason about computations (e.g., Hoare logic, dynamic logic, etc.). The latter are in a certain sense knowledge representation systems for representing computations.

45. This is the core of Brandom's account of double-book scorekeeping and the de re/de dicto vocabulary that makes it explicit (*Making It Explicit*, chapter 8). See also 'Prometheanism and Rationalism', in this volume.

46. If the algebraic semantics of intuitionistic logic is given by Heyting algebra, then that of co-intuitionistic logic is given by co-Heyting or Brouwerian algebra. Cf. T. Trafford, 'Co-constructive Logic for Proofs and Refutations', *Studia Humana* 3:4 (2014): 22–40; D. Miller, 'Making Falsificationism Bite', in *Out of Error: Further Essays on Critical Rationalism* (London: Routledge, 2017); A.B.M. Brunner and W.A. Carnielli, 'Anti-intuitionistic Logic and Paraconsistency', *Journal of Applied Logic* 3:1 (March 2005): 161–84.

proposal is that co-intuitionistic logic is naturally paraconsistent: it invalidates the law of noncontradiction in a manner precisely dual to the law of excluded middle in intuitionistic logic. This means that it supports nontrivial contradictions with specific meanings or consequences. In more informal terms, we might characterise this as the difference between questions for which you cannot guarantee there is an answer, and questions for which you can receive answers that tell you to ask better questions. The main problem with this proposal is that co-intuitionistic logic does not contain an implication operator ($P \to Q$) and its dual co-implication operator ($P \succ\!\!- Q$) does not have an obvious discursive interpretation (though it is sometimes read as 'P excludes Q'). Thus far, every attempt to simply dualise the syntax of intuitionistic logic has failed to produce anything that might truly be useful from the perspective of knowledge representation, either providing a sterile interpretation of refutations as constructed objects too much like proofs, or offering a superficial inversion of topos-theoretic semantics in which symbols are read backwards but structures are not dualised.[47] However, things are more promising in the case of computational structure, in so far as the co-implications present in co-intuitionistic (and bi-intuitionistic) logic and implicit in classical logic have been used to provide interpretations of control operators and even the π-calculus used to describe concurrent computation.[48] This affinity for concurrency and control suggests that we should try to interpret this logic dynamically, rather than statically.

This leads us to our third and final point of leverage: the duality between structure and behaviour. In mathematics, this is neatly captured by the duality between algebra and coalgebra, where the latter are naturally used to represent dynamic systems of various sorts.[49] In computer science, coalgebra have been used to make sense of notions of state, concurrency, and control,[50] while the duality has been used to articulate the distinction between *data* (e.g., lists) and

47. See T. Trafford, *Meaning in Dialogue: An Interactive Approach to Reasoning* (Berlin: Springer, 2017) for the most interesting and sustained attempt to pursue both strategies.

48. T. Crolard, 'A Formulae-as-Types Interpretation of Subtractive Logic', *Journal of Logic and Computation* 14:4 (August 2004), 529–70; G. Bellin and A. Menti, 'On the π-calculus and Co-intuitionistic Logic. Notes on Logic for Concurrency and λP Systems', *Fundamenta Informaticae* 130:1 (2014), 21–65.

49. See footnote 12.

50. J. Rutten, 'Coalgebra, Concurrency, and Control' in *Discrete Event Systems: Analysis and Control* (Boston: Springer, 2000): 31–38.

*codata* (e.g., streams),[51] which is relevant here to the extent that sensory input and observation more generally are more naturally conceived as codata, in so far as they are potentially open-ended. These all utilise the notion of bisimulation,[52] a form of behavioural equivalence that is weaker than classical identity and as such may provide some purchase upon the suspension/reimplementation of LL2 suggested above. However, the key point is that it is not simply the fact that empirical objects are themselves subject to change that motivates appeal to this duality, but the fact that experience/experiment and the reasoning associated with it is essentially dynamic, subject to revision through interaction with the world. Whatever are analogous to types in the empirical domain not only have to bundle streams of interaction into simulated objects (qua instances),[53] but also change themselves in response to these interactions. In this regard they are less like the fixed type systems deployed by functional programming than the mutable class hierarchies deployed by object-oriented programming, which blur the boundary between code and data and articulate modular knowledge representation systems more suitable for piecemeal revision.[54] However, this is invariably extrinsic revision, in which the programmer changes the classes and the code they contain, whereas what we wish to discover is the logic of intrinsic revision, wherein these changes are engendered by the interactive process of execution itself. This sort of productive circularity is incredibly hard to reason about correctly.[55]

One way to pull together some of these threads is through the concept of **exception handling**. This is a type of control structure in which a computation identifies an error (exception) and performs an appropriate response (handling).

---

51. J. Rutten and B. Jacobs, 'A Tutorial on (Co)Algebras and (Co)Induction', *Bulletin of The European Association for Theoretical Computer Science*, 1997.

52. See D. Sangoria, 'On the Origins of Bisimulation and Coinduction', *ACM Transactions on Programming Languages and Systems* 31:4 (2009): 1–41.

53. See 'Artificial Bodies and the Promise of Abstraction' and 'On Computational Asymmetry', in this volume.

54. See R. Kowalski, 'Computational Logic in an Object-Oriented World', in O. Stock and M. Schaerf (eds.), *Reasoning, Action and Interaction in AI Theories and Systems*. (Berlin: Springer, 2006), and B. Jacobs, 'Coalgebraic Reasoning about Classes in Object-Oriented Languages', *Electronic Notes in Theoretical Computer Science* 11 (1998): 231–42.

55. See D. Hofstadter, *I Am a Strange Loop* (New York: Basic Books, 2008), and J. Barwise and L. Moss, *Vicious Circles: On the Mathematics of Non-Wellfounded Phenomena* (Chicago: Centre for the Study of Language and Information, 2004).

This can be as simple as halting the computation entirely when anything goes wrong, but it can encompass a wide range of potential errors and nested strategies for continuing the computation while managing them. This is some sense isomorphic to the logic of contradiction. Having a single trivial contradiction from which everything follows is effectively having only one exception, which halts by default, while a logic which permits nontrivial contradictions supports distinct exceptions with distinct responses. However, much as with extrinsic revision, these responses are invariably hard-coded by programmers, sometimes to ensure that the program continues to behave within acceptable parameters in unusual situations, and other times to provide feedback that helps them revise the code to avoid terminal errors. Ideally, we want exceptions to be intrinsically meaningful, and so determine or at least delimit the range of appropriate responses. Transposing this back into a logical key, this would be to supply a semantics for both non-monotonic inference[56] (reasoning in unusual situations) and conceptual revision (revising the rules for reasoning in usual situations), allowing the knowledge representation itself to determine how it is applied and/or modified when faced with uncertainties.

There are roughly two lines of inquiry I have been pursuing in this regard.. Working from the predicate level down, I am exploring the possibility of a genuine dual of the Heyting topoi used to give semantics for intuitionistic type theories, co-Cartesian co-closed categories equipped with a quotient classier dual to the subobject classifier.[57] The nascent idea here is that we can treat the quotient classifier as supplying an internal co-algebra in a manner exactly dual to the way that the subobject classifier supplies an internal algebra.[58] Instead of a lattice of subobjects determined by predicates, we would then have a lattice of quotient objects determined by behavioural invariants, which is to say a lattice of bisimulation partitions of some underlying set of behaviours. Perhaps counterintuitively, both such lattices are Heyting algebras. However, my intuition is that, rather than simply reading the co-algebra morphisms in reverse to give us

56. See R. Brandom, *Between Saying and Doing* (Oxford: Oxford University Press, 2008), chapter 4.

57. The most detailed work done on both the motivations for and difficulties involved in pursuing this strategy is William James's *Closed Set Logic in Categories*, a thesis submitted to the philosophy department at the University of Adelaide in 1996.

58. This point is almost noticed by James (ibid., 100), who notes that the operator arrows are the wrong way around ($Q \rightarrow Q + Q$ rather than $\Omega \times \Omega \rightarrow \Omega$) and so chooses to read them backwards.

a intuitionistic internal logic, we might somehow invert the quotient lattice into a co-Heyting algebra to provide us with a co-intuitionistic predicate calculus, using it to model something like the inheritance tree of object-oriented class hierarchies.[59] The connection between multiple inheritance and non-monotonic inference is by now well documented, and my hope is that there might be useful non-trivial contradictions produced by overlapping inheritance.

Working from the propositional level up, I am exploring the idea that anything like a co-intuitionistic dual of the Curry-Howard correspondence would be concerned with computation not from the perspective of *languages* (e.g., lambda calculus) but from the perspective of *machines* (e.g., Turing machines). The nascent idea here is that we can begin by building the equivalent of the BHK interpretation upon which Curry-Howard was built, wherein implications are interpreted as functions from proofs of one proposition to proofs of another. But where this interprets implication statically, we should interpret co-implication dynamically, as something like a channel connecting propositions conceived as signals. This means that a collection of sequents forms a **state transition system**. Channels are conceived as either open (0) or interfering (1), either adding or subtracting the value (0/1) of one proposition from another. Moreover, the fact that co-intuitionistic negation is not a primitive means that it can be interpreted as a channel from the constant signal ( $\top$ ) to a proposition (P), while the infinite hierarchy of negations (¬P, ¬¬P, ¬¬¬P...) modulates this channel in a manner that equips each proposition with a stream (e.g., 0100101) that advances with each time step. This simple model should be able to build basic binary stream processors, though there are certain technical difficulties involved,[60] and I have not determined precisely how expressive it is. My hope is that this model could be extended to include other kinds of signal, perhaps including more complexly typed streams or continuous signals, and that it might even be extended to deal with asynchronous communication.

59. P. Rychlik, 'Multiple Inheritance Systems with Exceptions', *Artificial Intelligence Review* 3 (1989), 159–76.

60. The main technical difficulty concerns the logical closure of the theories (and co-theories) used to build the transition systems. If one accepts weakening, then channels appear everywhere and eradicate all useful structure instantly. Though there are logics which disallow weakening (e.g., relevance logics), I would prefer a more principled reason for its removal here.

Both lines of inquiry are still underdeveloped, as they stray into mathematical waters somewhat outside of my depth. They are also quite far from reconnecting, beyond the basic observation that they are both concerned with coalgebra, at least insofar as state transition systems can be interpreted as coalgebra. They are even further from validating the initial intuition regarding the relation between the duality of the mathematical and the empirical and the duality of the Leibniz Laws, beyond the loose suggestion that coalgebra involves bisimulation and this may provide a basis for the weakened identities a modified LL2 requires. Nevertheless, I remain convinced that the challenge posed by Kant's notion of transcendental logic requires that we philosophers wade into this deep mathematical sea. Our goal should be nothing less than a computational account of intentionality as such, or the structure of those cognitive processes that secure the objective validity of our judgements, which is to say the possibility that they might be true. It should not surprise us that structural differences in our modes of cognition go hand in hand with logical differences in the relevant type of truth,[61] but it may still surprise us just how much the latter might tell us about the former. This is to say that transcendental logic may yet give us new purchase on **transcendental psychology**, and thereby on the problem of building better minds.

61. See 'Essay on Transcendental Realism', in this volume, for a discussion of types of truth.

ETHOS

# The Artist's Brain at Work

## 0. INTRODUCTION

What's going on in the artist's brain during the creation of a work of art? Before we can even begin to answer this question, we must recognise that it contains a hidden normative dimension. It's obvious that we aren't interested in every neural episode that occurs during the creative process, but only those that are somehow relevant to this process. The threshold of relevance may extend deep below the threshold of consciousness, encompassing nuanced emotional responses and faint traces of memory of which the artist is unaware, but it can't include everything. For instance, even if one acknowledges the importance of synaesthetic effects in the composition of visual works, this import only makes sense if it's limited to specific connections between the visual and other sensory modalities, e.g., alignments of colours and temperatures, shapes and sounds, etc., no matter how minimal the intensity of these connections. More generally, this notion of relevance makes no sense unless we understand the creative process as resulting in a genuine work of art, or, at the very least, as aiming at such a work. If nothing else, we are entirely uninterested in the brains of anyone trying to pass something off as art, however fascinating they might be in other respects. Herein lies the question's normative supposition.

Of course, this opens onto a far more difficult and controversial question: What is a genuine work of art? Or perhaps even: What is the purpose of art? Giving anything resembling an adequate answer to this question would involve more than just an account of the institutional reality of contemporary art. It would require addressing the historical process of self-definition through which art got where it is now, tracing the various moments of its self-imposed split from *craft*: as propaganda, decoration, or entertainment, and examining the gradual reinforcement then sudden collapse of the barriers between *mediums*:

the dialectic of concrete figure and abstract form in painting and sculpture, the subsequent rise of performance and installation, and the eventual emergence of the exhibition as its own medium under the banner of 'relational aesthetics'.[1] It would also mean exploring its tumultuous relationship with literature, music, drama, cinema, and other institutionalised practices that covet the title of *arts*. I will have something to say about parts of this history, and what it tells us about the nature of art, but a truly comprehensive answer to the difficult question is going to have to wait for another time.

Nevertheless, in looking for some purpose of the artwork from which to work backwards into the artist's brain, sheer symmetry invites us to consider the work's effect, not simply on the eye, but on the brain of the beholder. If anything, this concern with the mind of the beholder is a more classical topic in aesthetics and philosophy of art, which has been readily absorbed by the discourses of the brain and transformed into what is now called neuroaesthetics.[2] As much as this new discipline has to tell us about the peculiarities of different modes of sensory processing and their implications for the corresponding modes of composition—such as the connection between supernormal stimulus in visual pattern recognition and caricature in painting—we must avoid being drawn any deeper into its details than we are into those of art history. What we must focus on is the ideal relationship between the production and consumption of the artwork, which is to say, on the circuit that the genuine work forms between the artist and the beholder, from brain to brain.

## 1. AESTHETICS AND SEMANTICS

Leaving the language of brains to one side for the moment, there are two opposing ways of understanding the relation between artist and beholder that have dominated thinking about art since the middle of the last century. I'll call these the **aesthetic model** and the **semantic model**. The central difference between these two models lies on the side of consumption, in the effect that the work is supposed to have upon the beholder: in the aesthetic model, the work is supposed to stimulate a sensory or emotional response, whereas in the

1. See N. Bourriaud, *Relational Aesthetics* (Dijon: Les Presses du Réel, 1998).
2. See A. Chatterjee, 'Neuroaesthetics: A Coming of Age Story', *Journal of Cognitive Neuroscience* 23:1 (January 2011): 53–62, and *The Aesthetic Brain: How We Evolved to Desire Beauty and Enjoy Art* (Oxford: Oxford University Press, 2015).

semantic model, the work is supposed to communicate a message of some kind. The consequence of this is a difference on the side of production, in the nature of the artist's creative activity: in the aesthetic model, the artist's mind is focused on the *design of an effective form*, whereas in the semantic model, the artist's mind is focused on the *articulation of a significant content*.

These general positions harbour a great deal of potential variation, with many otherwise opposed theories falling on the same side of the divide. The aesthetic model includes the perennial view of aesthetic taste as an immediate source of sensory pleasure, but also the formalist concern with the technicalities of aesthetic composition, and the myriad champions of intensities of feeling beyond mere pleasure, from sublime awe to visceral disgust. The semantic model includes the traditional view of artistic value as an immediate source of religious, moral, or even political understanding, but also the anti-formalist concern with the artist's subjective expression, and the originators, defenders, and inheritors of the tradition of conceptual art.

Equally, most variants of these positions do not deny that art can both stimulate and communicate, but rather that they subordinate one (as means) to the other (as end). For example, the Catholic Church commissioned aesthetically skilled painters to communicate religious messages precisely because the rhetorical effectiveness of these messages depended upon the power of their compositions to stimulate sensory and emotional responses. The converse might be said for certain cases of shock art and kitsch, in which the work is made to communicate a message for emotive effect, such as a frisson produced by breaking a taboo, or a nostalgia induced by invoking cliché. We can see these modes of subordination as ways of configuring the relation between form and content, and although they may not account for every possible configuration to be found in the realm of genuine art, they do allow advocates of each model to explain many of their opponent's preferred examples in their own terms.

Finally, a focus on form or content doesn't prevent either model from incorporating a corresponding concern with matter. It's all too easy to explain the design of form as isolated from the matter it's imposed on (excessive hylomorphism), or the articulation of content as independent of the medium in which it's expressed (excessive idealism). In each case, the temptation is to see the essence of the artwork, be it form or content, as an idea contained in the artist's mind, and its matter or medium as something inessential which contributes nothing to the idea but its realisation. However, it's entirely possible for either model to treat the matter upon which the artist works as presenting positive, productive constraints upon the process of creation, and in doing so to replace the image of a determinate idea, fixed in the mind, with that of a plastic pattern, embroiled in the interactions between the brain and its environment.

## 2. CRITIQUE

Despite these qualifications, I think that both models face intractable difficulties. Here, I shall address a single, crucial problem with each of them. It is by addressing these problems that we will find a superior model of the relationship between artist, work, and beholder, and uncover a path leading back into the artist's brain.

The crucial problem with the aesthetic model is that it ultimately fails to distinguish art from craft, differentiating it from decoration, entertainment, and propaganda only by means of the types of sensation and emotion it aims to induce, but for which it has no principled criterion. As articulated by figures such as Joseph Kosuth and Arthur Danto, it fails precisely in so far as its unable to incorporate those cases of nakedly conceptual art that effectively enacted art's secession from craft, such as Duchamp's *Fountain* and Warhol's *Brillo Boxes*.[3] Whatever minimal aesthetic character these possessed was entirely insufficient to distinguish them as works of art, and their acceptance as art thus demands that we recognise a dimension of art orthogonal to sensation and feeling. Of course, for Kosuth and Danto this dimension is meaning, and they take it to define art, thereby subordinating aesthetics to semantics.

The corresponding problem with the semantic model is that it ultimately fails to distinguish art from other forms of communication—not just from poetry and literature, but equally from journalism and philosophy. Art refuses any constraints on expression, either on the topics it can address or the types of messages it can convey, and this makes it impossible to distinguish art from other forms of communication on the basis of its content. Moreover, the very same gestures that free it from craft eventually dissolve the barriers between mediums that might have distinguished it on the basis of its form. As explained

3. See J. Kosuth, 'Art After Philosophy', *Studio International*, October 1969, and A. Danto, *The Abuse of Beauty* (Chicago: Open Court, 2003).

by figures such as Susan Sontag and Gilles Deleuze, what comes to define art in the absence of aesthetic forms is not so much the contents communicated by the work but the practices of interpretation through which they are retrieved, practices which, for all their theoretical armaments, are essentially distinguished by the particular historical community to which they belong.[4] Nevertheless, the proposed alternatives of these thinkers—erotics against hermeneutics, and composition against communication—return us directly to the aesthetic model already considered.

## 3. CONSOLIDATION

We now have some sense of the dialectical impasse in which the aesthetic and semantic models are caught. The only way to dissolve this impasse, and to work our way towards a properly synthetic position, is to explore the common assumptions about the mind of the beholder upon which both models are built. The most important of these is the received distinction between sensibility and intellect, which has continued to organise the dialectic of aesthetics and semantics long after it had been complicated by both philosophy and psychology.[5]

There are three main oppositions that constitute this distinction: sensibility is understood as *passive*, as supplying the intuitive matter of thought, and as responsible for noncognitive effects such as feelings, whereas the intellect is understood as *active*, as supplying the conceptual form of thought, and as responsible for cognitive products such as beliefs. The underlying idea organising these oppositions is that cognition is essentially discursive, meaning that conceptual understanding is essentially modelled on linguistic competence. This is not an entirely terrible idea. The significance of language is that it provides us with a general capacity to represent the features of our environment that outstrips the specific capacities to simulate certain features of our environment made available by our senses. Language is extensible, it allows us to think and

4. See S. Sontag, 'Against Interpretation', in *Against Interpretation and Other Essays* (New York: Farrar, Strauss, and Giroux, 1961); G. Deleuze and F. Guattari, 'Percept, Affect, Concept' in *What is Philosophy?* (London and New York: Verso Books, 1994).

5. The crucial source from which this distinction springs is Immanuel Kant's transcendental psychology, developed in his *Critique of Pure Reason*, tr. ed. P. Guyer and A. Wood (Cambridge: Cambridge University Press, 2002).

talk about electrons, capitalism, and justice, while our sensory capacities are limited to the range of environmental stimuli for which they evolved.[6]

The problem with the discursive account of cognition is that it gives language a monopoly, covering over the crucial cognitive activities occurring beneath the linguistic level. The philosophical tradition mitigated this to some extent by appealing to the imagination—understood as a more active faculty of simulation that mediates between sensibility and intellect—but this remains little more than a placeholder for the specific cognitive capacities upon which our more general, discursive understanding depends.[7] It's here that the study of the brain comes to the fore, revealing as it does the various neural mechanisms involved in processing and integrating our sensations into a map of our environment, and the specific competencies that they enable, from motion tracking to facial recognition.

However, the crucial innovation in all this is the description of the brain as an *information processing system*, to which these various mechanisms belong as subsystems, processing certain sorts of sensory input and contributing towards certain sorts of behavioural output. This is significant because the language of information bridges the gap between sensibility and intellect, and thereby provides a common framework in which to address aesthetic and semantic issues. In essence, we can reframe the opposition between the form and content of art as a distinction between two types of content: the information processed by various specialised cognitive subsystems, and the information processed at the more general discursive level. This enables us to treat meaning as information, even though not all information is meaningful.[8]

## 4. THE COGNITIVE ROLE OF ART

Already, this suggests a rough picture of the circuit between artist and beholder as a flow of information, but as yet it tells us nothing about what distinguishes this from any other flow, be it the *emotional information* transmitted by a facial expression or the *semantic information* communicated by a text message. If we are going to provide a genuine alternative to the aesthetic and semantic models, we can't distinguish the information flow the artwork instigates by

6. See 'The Reformatting of Homo Sapiens', in this volume.
7. Again, Kant's work is the source of this idea.
8. See 'The Reformatting of Homo Sapiens'.

limiting it to one type of information, which means that we must locate an effect that genuine art has upon the beholder that isn't restricted to a given type of information processing.

It's at this point that I can't avoid making some positive claims about the purpose of art. I've already said a few things about the historical process of art's self-definition in examining the dialectic between aesthetics and semantics, but it's obvious that I don't think either side of the debate captures the important lessons of the passage from modern to contemporary art. The truth in the aesthetic model lies in its fidelity to stimulation, and the truth in the semantic model lies in its fidelity to cognition. The error of the aesthetic model is its focus on the noncognitive dimension of stimulation, and the error of the semantic model is its focus on the communicative dimension of cognition. The simple truth about the purpose of art that has been revealed by the history of art's struggle to define itself is the minimal condition of contemporary art: that it makes us think.

Put simply, my positive claim is that the purpose of art is cognitive stimulation.[9] To explain this properly requires a further distinction between *cognitive process* and *cognitive product*, or between the information-processing subsystem that a given work activates and its results. In those examples favoured by the aesthetic model, the artwork aims to stimulate our nondiscursive information processing capacities, elevating their exercise by testing their limits, disrupting them, or simply pushing them beyond their everyday use. Colour discrimination, visual pattern recognition, emotional intelligence, etc., are all subject to stimulation in their own ways, the point being not to produce any particular understanding of their object, but to exercise them for their own sake. In those examples favoured by the semantic model, the artwork aims to stimulate our discursive information processing capacities, inviting us to explore conceptual connections, resolve theoretical tensions, or indeed juxtapose interpretations, without demanding that we arrive at any particular conclusion. It's entirely possible for art to stimulate our communicative capacities for purposes other than communication, so that its success doesn't depend on whether we interpret it in the right way, but on whether the call to interpretation inspires us.

9. This idea is, in outline, a development of Kant's aesthetics that identifies the common denominator of his accounts of the beautiful and the sublime (in the *Critique of the Power of Judgment*).

## 5. INSPIRATION, INVITATION, AND EXPLORATION

This idea of cognitive stimulation, or inspiration, is the informational thread we must follow from the brain of the beholder to the brain of the artist. What is going on in the artist's brain if not the design of an effective stimulus, or the articulation of an interesting thought? Well, there's a sense in which these are perfectly adequate descriptions of what is going on in an artist's brain when they compose a cognitively stimulating work. On the one hand, although art is more than craft, it almost always involves crafting, working its materials to specific effect. If we acknowledge that art has a purpose, then we must also acknowledge that it's possible to design works to meet this purpose. On the other hand, although art does not aim at a particular cognitive product, its materials invariably include established cognitive forms, using determinate abstractions, invoking particular concepts, and representing specific states of affairs. If we aim to understand art in terms of information processing, then we must be willing to explain how artists articulate this information as form and content. Nevertheless, there remains something more to the creative process that these descriptions fail to capture, a connection between the artist's own inspiration in creating and the inspiration the work induces in its audience. If there is anything that characterises the information flow proper to art, it's this transmission of inspiration.

Perhaps the best way to approach this is via an anecdotal observation: for all the emphasis placed on research in contemporary art practice, artists generally prefer initiating lines of thought to completing them. This is often reflected in artists' descriptions of their work, where we are told that they set out to explore a certain theme—e.g., the space of exhibition, the agency of things, or the history of a community—but are never quite given a finished map of the terrain explored. And there's nothing wrong with this. If an artist's investigations were to produce important theoretical results—e.g., mathematical theorems, philosophical concepts, or political principles—then they would be better off communicating them in a book than encoding them in a work of art. The artwork is less a determinate thesis than an invitation to think along certain lines. The question is, what does this involve?

Crucially, any such invitation presupposes a common set of cognitive capacities, shared between artist and audience.[10] The precise extent and nature of this commonality varies, depending on the sorts of information processing that are involved. For instance, as I've already hinted, portraiture is predicated on the existence of specialised cognitive subsystems for facial recognition and discrimination of associated emotional states that are more or less hardwired into our common neural architecture, even if their exact parameters and effectiveness vary from individual to individual.[11] By contrast, although conceptual art is predicated upon the discursive capacities I've suggested are characteristic of conceptual thought in general, different works will appeal to different conceptual competencies—e.g., a grasp of concepts from geometry, social theory, or even art criticism itself—whose acquisition depends upon various forms of adaptation, socialisation, and education.[12] There are many ways in which our abilities to process perceptual and semantic information can diverge, but we constitute an audience to which art can be addressed only when our capacities converge in some way.

This network of overlapping similarities in information processing suggests an alternative metaphor through which to frame these issues: a shared cognitive landscape, or an overarching space of possible cognition whose different regions, from the familiar terrain of facial feature mapping to the wild fringes of higher-dimensional geometry, are subtended by convergences in our capacities to think the thoughts they comprise. Only those with the right cognitive capabilities can enter a given region of the landscape, and even then, only some of them ever will. This gives a new sense to the artistic language mentioned above: we can see the artist as exploring our shared cognitive landscape—uncovering regions within and navigating paths through the immense space of possible information-processing states characteristic of our collective cognitive architecture.[13] This in turn suggests a way of understanding the idea of invitation:

---

10. This is an important aspect of what Kant called the *sensus communis*.

11. See B.J. Balas and P. Sinha, 'Portraits and Perception: Configural Information in Creating and Recognizing Face Images', *Spatial Vision* 21:1–2 (2007): 119–35, for an empirical investigation of relationship between capacities for facial recognition and techniques in portraiture.

12. See M. Wilson, *Wandering Significance* (Oxford: Oxford University Press, 2006) for a detailed study of the complex social underpinnings of conceptual competence.

13. This spatial conception of aesthetic cognition is similar to the conception of vibes as manifolds developed by Peli Grietzer (P. Grietzer, 'A Theory of Vibe', *Glass Bead*, Site 1 [2017], <https://www.glass-bead.org/article/a-theory-of-vibe/>).

we can see the artwork as less a map than a point of entry into the cognitive landscape, a site from which others can set out to think on their own, not so that they can reach the same conclusions as the artist or one another, if any present themselves, but so they have the opportunity to explore the exercise of their own cognitive powers in certain loosely delimited ways.

## 6. INSIDE THE ARTIST'S BRAIN

This spatial metaphor will no doubt break down if pushed too far, but it gives us better purchase on the normative dimension of our original question: Which neural processes are relevant to the creation of a genuine work of art?

As I suggested earlier, this question presupposes a minimal degree of sincerity on the part of the artist—we are not interested in the cognitive processes involved in passing something off as an artwork. However, although we have recognised that, in so far as art has a purpose, it's possible for artists to consciously aim at this purpose, we should reject the idea that sincerity requires such consciousness. It must be possible for an artist to create a genuine artwork without any explicit theoretical understanding of what it means to do so, and this implies that sincerity can be implicit in their practical understanding of the act of creation. The cognitive similarities between artist and audience presupposed by the landscape metaphor provide a way of accounting for this: an artist requires no theoretical grasp of their audience's cognitive capacities; they only require the ability to exploit the similarities between them—sincerity is implicit in the fact that they use what inspires them to inspire others.

Given this, it would seem obvious that the aspects of the artist's brain we are interested in—those relevant to the creative process—are principally those information-processing subsystems that their work aims to stimulate in their audience: facial recognition in portrait painting, object reidentification and event tracking in cinematography, discursive reasoning in conceptual art, or some complex of such faculties in post-medium compositions. However, this will equally seem trivial if it's not qualified.

On the one hand, we should recognise that divergences between the artist's and audience's cognitive systems can play a productive role in the composition of stimulating works. There are many cases of synaesthetic, partially sighted, and even blind painters whose peculiar abilities to process visual, tactile, and related data provide them with unique perspectives on the forms of visual information that stimulate 'normal' perceptual subsystems, since they share some basic functional architecture.[14] The phenomenon of neuroplasticity reinforces this point, ensuring as it does that even such 'normal' cognitive functions can be realised by different neurological structures.[15] This potential for multiple realisation only becomes more pronounced as we move along the spectrum from innate to acquired capacities. It's reasonable to expect that the extensibility of linguistic function underlying the representational generality of discursive cognition permits significant neuroanatomical divergences, and that these can play a similarly productive role in conceptual art.

On the other, we shouldn't expect the artist's more or less active use of these cognitive capacities—extending beyond simple introspection to incorporate myriad forms of practical experimentation—to simply mirror the more or less passive excitation of the same capacities in their audience. If we push the convergence between artist and audience too far, we risk collapsing back into the semantic model, the transmission of inspiration reverting to the communication of a determinate content indexed by a common cognitive result. The artist's inspiration doesn't merely prefigure that of their audience. The audience is free to let the cognitive processes begun by a stimulus take their course, but the artist must arrest, control, or even reverse these processes, recovering, modulating, and capturing the images, themes, and other information that send and maintain them in motion. It's one thing to seek one's own inspiration, and another to capture that inspiration in a way that can be shared with others. In attending to their own cognitive processes in this way, the artist effectively, if unconsciously, uses their own brain as a window into the brains of their audience.

14. See C. van Campen, *The Hidden Sense: Synaesthesia in Art and Science* (Cambridge, MA: MIT Press, 2010) and J.M. Kennedy, *Drawing and the Blind: Pictures to Touch* (Newhaven, CT: Yale University Press, 1993).

15. See D.M. Maino, 'Neuroplasticity: Teaching an Old Brain New Tricks', *Review of Optometry* 146:1 (January 2009).

# What's in a Game?

## 0. DEFINING 'GAME'

Games are more culturally important than they have ever been. As an example, the videogame industry now generates more revenue than the music and film industries combined. The prevalence of videogames raises some interesting philosophical questions. One of the most common is: Can games be art? However, all too often, because of the outsize prevalence of videogames, this question is limited to whether they can be art, at the expense of the various other forms of games played throughout history and in the present. This inevitably turns into a comparison between videogames and cinema, which invites us to analyse their artistic merits purely in terms of visual beauty or narrative complexity, and on that basis find videogames wanting.

However, the increasing cultural significance of games is not limited to that of videogames. There are also board games and tabletop roleplaying games (e.g., *Kolejka*, *Twilight Imperium*, and *Dungeons and Dragons*), whose popularity and wider cultural influence has grown steadily over the last few decades. If we want to ask the question of whether games qua games are art, or to put it another way, whether the features specific to games can be seen as being artistic, then we first need to ask what actually makes something a game, or what the characteristic features of games are. This turns out to be a far more difficult question than it initially appears.

Let us begin by considering Wittgenstein's challenge:

> Consider, for example, the activities that we call 'games'. I mean board-games, card-games, ball-games, athletic games, and so on. What is common to them all? [...] Are they all '*entertaining*'? Compare chess with noughts and crosses. Or is there always winning and losing, or competition between players? Think of

> patience. In ball-games, there is winning and losing; but when a child throws his ball at the wall and catches it again, this feature has disappeared. Look at the parts played by skill and luck, and at the difference between skill in chess and skill in tennis. Think now of singing and dancing games; here we have the element of entertainment, but how many other characteristic features have disappeared! And we can go through the many, many other groups of games in the same way, can see how similarities crop up and disappear.
>
> And the result of this examination is: we see a complicated network of similarities overlapping and criss-crossing [...].[1]

Wittgenstein's fundamental claim here is that it is impossible to define 'game' by means of some common set of features that all games share. Rather, he thinks we can only identify ranges of overlapping similarities: there is only a family resemblance between specific games, not an overarching essence.

However, there are a variety of responses to this challenge from different disciplines. There have been attempts to define what games are in sociology, mathematics, and philosophy itself. There is even now an entire field of game studies. In light of these responses, we should begin by asking what counts as a good definition of a game? I propose three criteria:

i. **It should aim to cover most, but not necessarily all games.** If it turns out that gladiatorial combat should not be called a game, we are not really missing out.

ii. **It must take account of the reasons why we play games, even if these reasons are not unique.** Games can be *interesting*, *challenging*, and *fun*, but for some people, so can climbing Mount Everest, and we do necessarily want to define the latter as a game.

iii. **It should identify edge cases.** There will be practices where it is not clear if they are or are not a game. We do not need to decide the matter in each case. But we do need to be able to explain why they are edge cases. The

1. L. Wittgenstein, *Philosophische Untersuchungen/Philosophical Investigations*, tr. G.E.M. Anscombe, P.M.S. Hacker, and J. Schulte (Oxford: Wiley-Blackwell, revised 4th edition 2001), 36e [§66].

edges that we might want to keep our eyes open for are the distinction and overlap with *play*, *sport*, and *hobbies*. The distinction between games and play is particularly important here because, although we say we *play* games, play is actually a broader concept and has a longer philosophical history.

## 1. SOCIOLOGY AND 'THE MAGIC CIRCLE'

Johan Huizinga, the author of *Homo Ludens*, and French sociologist Roger Caillois, who built upon the former's work, between them developed what is generally called 'The Magic Circle Theory' of games.[2] Huizinga's key idea is that play involves a 'magic circle' which constitutes a temporary world concealed within but separated from the rest of the ordinary world. This circle is defined by four essential conditions:

i. **Freedom** of action.
ii. **Independence** from the rest of life.
iii. **Governance** by some fixed rules.
iv. **Delimitation** in space and time.

The problem with this theory is that, on the one hand, it includes practices that we don't necessarily think are games, such as ritual and legal debate, while on the other hand it excludes practices that we do, such as cooperative games and gambling. The reason for these problems is essentially that what Huizinga provides is not really a theory of games, but a theory of play. *Homo Ludens* is so titled because he thought the play drive is what distinguishes humans from other animals and forms the root of all cultural practices. As such, he cannot really distinguish between games and these other practices.

Caillois later attempted to improve Huizinga's definition by making certain alterations:

i. Rather than freedom of action, games require **uncertainty of outcome**. This precludes rituals from counting as games.

2. J. Huizinga, *Homo Ludens: A Study of the Play-Element in Culture* [1938] (London: Granada, 1970); R. Caillois, *Man, Play, and Games* [1958], tr. M. Barash (Champaign, IL: University of Illinois Press, 2001).

ii. Independence from the rest of life is redefined as **unproductivity**. For example, gambling has consequences but produces nothing that might contribute to the wider world.

iii. Games are defined by **roles**, which can either be specified by rules or acquired by imitation. For example, when kids play at sword fighting, their sticks become swords. There are not rules governing how to use them, but their use is restricted by a certain representational role.

According to Caillois, there are four different styles of play that constitute different types of game:

i. **Agon**, or competitive games.
ii. **Alea**, or games of chance.
iii. **Mimicry**, or games of imitation.
iv. **Ilinx**, or games of vertigo and/or dizziness.

There are problems with Caillois's formulation as well. On the one hand, this definition includes both dances and lotteries. The former because it is free, purposeless movement and the latter because they depend upon pure chance, even though the only choice is whether or not to enter. On the other hand, it excludes things like composition games, such as the Dadaists' *Exquisite Corpses* or any type of collective story-writing constrained by specific rules, as well as alternate reality games (ARGs) such as Pokémon Go which can be played anywhere and anytime, overlaid on the regular world.

The critical problem with Caillois's approach is twofold and stems from the philosophical history of the concept of play. The drive to play is seen as something we share with animals (e.g., the play of kittens), even if we express it with a unique degree of intensity. Caillois's definition would place the activity of the Chessmaster (*ludus*) and the kitten (*paidia*) on different ends of a continuous spectrum of play which is all essentially irrational and purposeless, even if one side is more rule-bound than the other. Freedom here is fundamentally interpreted in negative terms as the absence of constraint.

## 2. MATHEMATICS AND GAME THEORY

In mathematics, Game Theory is the study of strategic interaction between rational agents. From this perspective, a game is a rule-governed interaction between several players. Its rules must describe:

i. **The Space of Possible Actions** to choose between (e.g., a decision tree).

ii. **The Available Information** used to make choices (e.g., choices, resources, etc.).

iii. **The Payoff** associated with each outcome (e.g., points, victory, loss, etc.).

The aim of Game Theory is to study strategies, which are ways of choosing paths through the possibility space or decision tree in response to other player's choices. In particular, game theorists aim to find winning strategies, which are those that always produce the optimal outcome.

What are the problems with the definition of games offered by game theory? Once again, it tends to include certain things that we do not think of as games and exclude certain things that we do. It includes things like purchasing negotiations, the prisoner's dilemma, and, my personal favourite, nuclear war. It excludes things like solo games because they are noninteractive, roleplaying games because they do not necessarily have easily defined payoffs, and nonstrategic sports (e.g. weightlifting and other pure competitions of strength or skill).

The most significant problem is that the very practice of game theory breaks games. Tic-tac-toe is the perfect example here, because if both players know the optimal strategy in Tic-tac-toe, then every game ends in a draw, which vitiates any interest we might have in playing it. This is because strategic analysis reduces uncertainty to the point where it is no longer interesting, challenging, or fun.

## 3. PHILOSOPHY

The philosopher Bernard Suits, author of *The Grasshopper: Games, Life and Utopia*, also aimed to respond to Wittgenstein's challenge. Unfortunately, his work is something of a cautionary tale because it shows just how wrongheaded a definition can be while still more or less covering the class of things it is supposed to define. His definition is as follows:

> To play a game is to engage in an activity directed towards bringing about a specific state of affairs, using only means permitted by rules, where the rules prohibit more efficient in favor of less efficient means, and where such rules are accepted just because they make possible such activity.[3]

To break Suits' definition into its component parts, a game is an activity with:

i. **Constitutive Rules** (e.g., the rules of golf).
ii. **A Prelusory Goal**, meaning a goal that could be achieved *outside of the game* (e.g., dropping a ball in a hole).
iii. **Lusory Means** (e.g., hitting the ball with a club).
iv. **Lusory Attitude** (i.e., doing it for its own sake).

What are the problems with Suits's formulation? Not only does it include non-strategic sports like weightlifting, but it extends to puzzles and most hobbies in general. Anything that one can do in a deliberately inefficient way for its own sake, such as cooking a pizza rather than buying one, becomes a game. The definition further excludes things like simulation games and roleplaying games because they do not have a single defining goal. More significantly, their goals cannot be described as prelusory—this applies even to some popular games including chess: checkmate does not make sense independently of the rules of chess and cannot be seen in terms of deliberate inefficiency.

The greatest problem with this definition is that it simply fails to capture why we play games. We can recognise that deliberate inefficiency is a part of certain games, but there is no conception of why one would want to do these specific things in deliberately inefficient ways.

## 4. LEARNING FROM FAILURE

What have we learned from the failures of each of these theories? Let us address each in turn.

3. B. Suits, *The Grasshopper: Games, Life and Utopia* (Toronto: Broadview Books, 2005), 34

## 4.1 Magic Circle Theory

What alternate reality games like *Pokemon Go* teach us is that the separation between games and life is more fundamental than a spatiotemporal boundary. The separation involved in the Magic Circle is not literally about drawing a circle in the sand. What lotteries teach us, on the other hand, is that although the choice to play a game must be free, there must be more to one's freedom within the game than that choice alone. There must be more than the simple negative freedom of not being influenced. If all that happens in a game is that the player chooses to use a particular piece, then it is barely even a game.

## 4.2 Game Theory

When discussing Game Theory, we learned from Tic-tac-toe that uncertainty is essential. Solved games are simply not true games anymore, in the lived sense of the term. From roleplaying games we learned that there is more to rationality than just strategy. While Game Theory is genuinely studying some facet of practical rationality, it is not for that matter studying all of it. In roleplaying games, one does not simply reason instrumentally about already decided ends, one can also decide to change one's goals and develop new ones. There is reasoning about ends, not just about means.

## 4.3 Suits's Theory

When discussing Suits's Theory, we saw that for simulation games (e.g., SimCity, Minecraft, etc.), rules can be constructive as well as restrictive. This is a matter of positive freedom. The rules don't simply limit actions we can already perform, but actually constitute new actions that would be impossible outside of the game. Furthermore, we learn that the satisfaction of playing a game does not come from everyday difficulty. This is why focusing on deliberate inefficiency misses the point. Rather, satisfaction arises from a vicarious sense of personal agency in which we are able to see and own the consequences of our actions.

# 5. CONCLUSION: GAMEPLAY AS ENCAPSULATED AGENCY

Synthesising these insights, we might offer the following definition: a game is an activity in which we are free to own the consequences of our own actions and which we may play principally for this reason. This is appealing because life is not fair. In life we can own the consequences of our actions, but there can also be perfectly justifiable mitigating factors which limit our responsibility for outcomes, both good and bad. As Heidegger and Sartre have observed, we do not choose the range of choices we have in life, but when we enter into a game, we do choose the range of choices available to us, and in doing so we are able to freely own the consequences of our actions.

There are four conditions that make this possible:

i. **Possibility**: a structured range of meaningful choices.
ii. **Uncertainty**: a gap between intention and outcome.
iii. **Liberty**: no *external* motivations to make in-game choices.
iv. **Desire**: distinctive *internal* motivations to make in-game choices.

Crucially, the motivations identified above need not be to achieve a single overarching goal, but can be more complex and multifarious.

Furthermore, this definition exhibits the tendency towards greater separation between games and life in so far as the first two conditions gradually evolve into **game worlds**. We cease simply to have closed-off spaces and instead create new realms within which we can live and interact. Similarly, it transforms the second two conditions into **game selves**, such as roles and characters. This makes roleplaying games exemplary, since they exemplify this tendency toward the separation inherent within the process of constituting new spaces of freedom.

Finally, we can return to the question of whether games can be art. If games can be said to be an art form, then freedom is their medium. Games allow us to freely experiment with freedom itself. This is what is distinctive about games, and they should be considered an art form on that basis.

# Art and Value

## 0. WHAT IS THE VALUE OF CONTEMPORARY ART?

What is the point of asking this question?

i. To justify the existence of art institutions.

ii. To critique the character of the institutions we have.

Any account of the *value* of contemporary art that's indexed to the interests of these institutions can't play this critical role, and so can't be expected to play a justificatory role either.

Any account of what contemporary art is that indexes it to institutional validation precludes a satisfactory account of its value. This means that, in order to ask about the value of contemporary art, we have no choice but to ask about its *essence*.

The problem here is not simply that contemporary art is difficult to define, but that this difficulty concerns its fraught relationship with its essence. Contemporary art is haunted by the question of what it is, sometimes obsessed by it and sometimes outright hostile to it, but never truly free from it.

'Contemporary art' is less a name for a genre of works than for the corresponding practices of creating and appreciating such works. It is the terminus of a historical process of self-definition, through which these practices liberated themselves from the confines of *craft*—as propaganda, decoration, or entertainment—and differentiated themselves from the broader range of *arts*—such as literature, music, and theatre. It is what is left after the era of modern art, after the collapse of the barriers between mediums, and after the exhaustion of purely conceptual art.

However, these determinations—*post-modern*, *post-medium*, and *post-conceptual*—are almost entirely negative. They distinguish, but they don't define. They nevertheless point to the impasse reached by the process of self-definition: in the process of freeing artists from the constraints imposed by existing mediums, conceptual art transmuted the modernist tendency to explore these constraints within the mediums themselves, into the contemporary tendency to explore the nature of art through art itself.

The problem with this is its own essential premise: art is not a medium. It's not possible to experimentally explore the constitutive constraints of those practices named 'contemporary art' in the same way one can within a given medium, because there aren't any constraints that can't be transgressed in the name of 'art'. The constant threat of performative transgression thus reduces the historical process of self-definition to the perpetual affirmation of autonomy. This is the impasse of contemporary art.

It's not entirely surprising that some mistake this impasse for a positive definition. For such people, contemporary art is defined by its freedom to experiment and to insist on anything else is to curtail this freedom. To quote Joseph Kosuth: 'Art's only claim is for art. Art is the definition of art.'

However, if contemporary art is nothing but the enactment of its own autonomy, then it can't but be indexed to its institutions and their history, in such a way that these can't be criticised or justified. The problem is that there seems to be no competing definition that does not simply provide a further opportunity for transgression. The qualifier 'contemporary' does not give us purchase on any concrete temporality that could define artworks or art practices, it simply announces the perpetual present of the impasse.

If we are to have any hope of answering our original question, we must abandon the qualifier, and ask about art as such: *What is it* and *What is its value?* My aim is to show how intimately entwined these questions of essence and value are.

## 1. WHAT IS ART?

What does an account of art have to do?

If nothing else, it must articulate the continuity and discontinuity between art and:

**Nature**: sublime vistas, awesome skies, and the many wonders of plants, animals, and human life.

**Craft**: elegant decoration, forceful rhetoric, and the many pleasures of fashion, gastronomy, and similar practices.

## 1.1 History

The earliest accounts of art in the Western tradition identify it as the peculiar craft of *mimesis*, or the imitation of nature. This makes what distinguishes artworks from other artefacts precisely what they share with the natural things they represent. This account faced two problems:

i. It does not actually explain what is shared by art and nature, or why it is valuable.

ii. It becomes increasingly irrelevant as the non-representational elements of art come to be appreciated on their own terms.

Its most obvious successor is the idea of art as the craft of *expression*. On this account, art reflects the internal life of the artist rather than the external state of the world, understood in terms of feelings, character, and sometimes simply will. This creates a strict discontinuity between art and nature, but in doing so it gives art its own distinctive value: the cultivation of self-understanding. This essentially humanist account of art and its value is largely responsible for the continuity between 'fine art' (e.g., painting and sculpture) and the broader range of 'arts' (including literature, music, theatre and cinema). However, it faces its own problems:

i. It ignores previous examples of obviously mimetic art.

ii. It becomes increasingly irrelevant as non-expressive forms of art are deliberately cultivated.

As discussed above ('The Artist's Brain at Work'), it's the critical deadlock between two models—the aesthetic and the semantic—that produces the institutional approaches with which we began. It dissolves the problems of the previous models by asserting a radical discontinuity between art and everything else. The idea that art is autonomous becomes the idea that art is *sui generis*.

## 1.2 Nominalism

Let's consider one of the most influential institutional theories of art: Thierry de Duve's nominalism. De Duve introduces this theory by taking the perspective of an alien anthropologist trying to interpret the meaning of the word 'art'.

He upholds Duchamp's *Fountain* as representative of the impossibility of any such interpretation, in so far as it constitutively refuses any classificatory grouping with other examples from the history of art. On this basis he proposes a *nominalist* theory, in which the word 'art' has no meaning over and above the gesture through which we choose to name things as art.

What this means is that the meaning of the word is determined by the role it plays in an ongoing cultural conversation in which we dispute its applicability, articulating the possibilities of artistic practice by producing, analysing, and integrating novel examples. It is this conversation that is conserved and curated by the art world and its institutions.

I propose to invert de Duve's perspective and use it against itself. I'm going to take a specific example: consider the signs of a possible alien megastructure surrounding KIC 8462852, also known as Tabby's star.[1] We might propose several reasons why an alien civilisation would build such a thing, including for energy, for habitation, to signal their existence to other such civilisations, or all of the above.

But what if it is a work of art, either in addition to these other reasons, or entirely on its own terms?

It seems that we can make sense of such a suggestion without knowing anything about this civilisation, its sensory and intellectual capacities, its history, or its institutions. The important question is: Why does this make sense? I think that this has something to do with the nature of value itself.

---

1. See e.g. S. Shostak, 'Have We Detected an Alien Megastructure in Space? Keep an Open Mind', *The Guardian*, 12 August 2016, <https://www.theguardian.com/commentisfree/2016/aug/12/alien-megastructure-tabbys-star-kepler-telescope>.

In suggesting that this epic structure is a work of art, we imply that it was in some sense a work performed for its own sake. There is something about the actual performance of the act that exceeds the content of its idea. In this we see a fundamental connection between art and value that cannot be effaced.

On the one hand, there are always more possibilities than we can realize, and the choice to realize some rather than others, even conceived as an experimental process of chance and refinement, implicitly commits itself to the value of those that are chosen.

On the other, the form of value this performance commits itself to can't be reduced to use value, exchange value, nor any notion of economic value. This excess is precisely what is indicated by the phrase 'for its own sake'.

Du Duve's mistake is opposing nomination to classification, when the use of the word 'art' is at heart a matter of evaluation. What is required is a description of the specific kind of value that it is concerned with.

## 2. WHAT IS VALUE?

In trying to identify the form of value specific to art we need to distinguish it from other forms of value in the vicinity:

i. From economic values such as *utility* and *price*.

ii. From epistemic values such as *truth* and ethical values such as *goodness*.

iii. From subjective values such as *personal preference*.

Nevertheless, we need to understand what all of these have in common. We need to describe the genus of value as such if we are to describe the species of value that distinguishes art. And here, the key idea is that *value is what provides reasons for action*.

If you are stuck in a burning gallery and can only save one work, all else being equal, you should save the most valuable.

The question is whether we can make sense of reasons why a work could be most valuable that would have such consequences for action, independently of other concerns. These reasons must be:

i. **Formally**: non-instrumental and intersubjective.

ii. **Substantively**: motivations for both the creation and appreciation of art works.

The traditional name for this sort of value, in contrast to truth and goodness, is *beauty*.

## 3. WHAT IS BEAUTY?

### 3.1 History

There are two sides to the traditional concept of beauty: beauty as *value* and beauty as *quality*. The former can still be seen in expressions like 'What a beautiful goal' or 'That is a beautiful instrument', and the latter in the use of 'attractive', 'pretty', and 'pleasant' as synonyms for 'beautiful'.

These two senses have been intertwined at least since the origin of aesthetics as a discipline, when the concept of taste combined traditional Greek concerns regarding the nature of excellence with early modern concerns regarding the character of experience.

However, when, in the early twentieth century, artists began to reject the aesthetics of the beautiful, rediscovering the aesthetics of the sublime and exploring a wider range of experiential qualities such as the uncanny, the shocking, and even the disgusting, the language of beauty as a distinct form of value was rejected along with it.

This is in part responsible for the additional weight that the term 'art' has acquired, as distinct from the 'arts' and the 'crafts' they had already split from: the term is increasingly needed not just to name a range of specific practices and objects but to evaluate their worth, independently of whether they exemplify classical traits such as symmetry, harmony, or pleasantness.

This is in turn responsible for reframing the idea that art is 'for its own sake', replacing the disinterestedness of beauty qua value with the autonomy of art qua practice. This obsession with practical autonomy then fuels the idea that art is *sui generis*.

## 3.2 Essence

It's worth addressing another prominent objection to the notion of beauty, namely, the anti-essentialist complaint that it is inherently parochial, for instance, upholding the attractiveness of naked European women above all else. It's useful to pursue the parallel between goodness and beauty in responding to this objection.

Obviously, different cultures have different ideas about which actions are good, but this presupposes that there is something about which they disagree, namely, goodness. Similarly, we might have different ideas about which things are beautiful, but there are still things that can be said about what we're disagreeing about, namely, beauty.

## 3.3 Definition

I think that it is possible to provide a definition of beauty as a genus of value within which we can distinguish several distinct, but compatible species. This will enable us to distinguish art from craft and nature while acknowledging its continuity with both, by describing the particular species of beauty that art exemplifies in contrast with them.

This definition has a *formal* and a *substantive* component.

i. **Formally**: beauty can be understood as **unconditional value**. This means that it provides reasons for action that are in some sense independent of other motivations such as personal desires or common purposes. This defines beauty as what is valued for its own sake.

ii. **Substantively**: beauty can be understood as the **enhancement of freedom**. This means that these reasons derive from the expansion of our possibilities for action and satisfaction, enabling new desires and purposes, rather than satisfying existing ones.

To see how this works, its useful to break beauty down into its principal species.

There is a philosophical disagreement about whether beauty is essentially interested or disinterested running back at least as far as Plato, but more famously represented by Hume and Kant's opposing theories of aesthetic judgement.

I think that the two sides in this debate are in fact talking about distinct kinds of beauty: the beauty of craft and the beauty of art, or relatively and absolutely unconditional value.

## 3.4 Craft

Relatively unconditional value encapsulates the range of concerns that I earlier called excellence. It is value that exceeds some given range of desires or purposes, but is nevertheless relative to them. It occurs when something is better than it needs to be according to some existing practices. This can be understood as the enhancement of concrete forms of freedom. What I mean by this is that the beauty of craft consists in its ability to generate new practical possibilities that transcend its initial aims.

This includes everything from the simple provision of unexpected sensuous satisfaction (e.g., a meal that is creatively seasoned), through the extension of existing practices (e.g., a musical instrument with a greater range or precision of play), to the constitution of entirely original modes of living (e.g., the design of a new medium for social interaction). This is demonstrated nowhere better than in the contemporary craft of computer programming. Talk to any programmer for long enough about their code and they'll inevitably bring up questions of beauty, freely contrasting 'elegant solutions' and 'ugly hacks', and deploying a homegrown aesthetic language of surprising subtlety. However, what is most apposite about this aesthetics is the central role played by extensibility, or the ability of code to be expanded upon or transposed into new contexts for novel purposes. In essence, its beauty lies in the as-yet-unexplored opportunities it enables.

## 3.5 Art

What is unique about the beauty of art is precisely that it is not relative to an existing set of practices and their associated desires and purposes. The question is how to understand this absolute unconditionality in terms of the enhancement of freedom. To make sense of this, we need to return to the deadlock between aesthetics and semantics.

The truth in the aesthetic model lies in its fidelity to stimulation, and the truth in the semantic model lies in its fidelity to cognition. The error of the aesthetic model lies its focus on the noncognitive dimension of stimulation, and the error of the semantic model lies in its focus on the communicative dimension of cognition. The simple truth about the purpose of art that has been revealed by the history of art's struggle to define itself is the minimal condition of contemporary art: that it should make us think.

If craft concerns itself with excellence, then art concerns itself with inspiration. It does not aim to satisfy existing desires and communicate existing ideas, but to stimulate the production of new desires and ideas. It aims to expand our horizons of possibility in a way that cannot be anticipated in advance, and thus cannot be restricted to a given domain of theory or practice. Art is less about the freedom to experiment than it is about **experimentation with freedom**.

If craft aims at the local enhancement of freedom, then art aims at the global enhancement of freedom. However, because the structure of our collective horizon of possibility is essentially social, the task of expanding it in a global manner demands its own social infrastructure. This is why art has emerged as a distinctive practice tied to absolutely unconditional value. The purpose of the institutional framework of contemporary art is to constitute and maintain the social imagination. It is on this basis that these institutions must be critically assessed.

## 3.6 Infrastructure

Finally, this notion of infrastructure can account for the value of cultivating self-understanding emphasised by expressionism and the value of articulating the possibilities of artistic practice emphasised by the institutional approach.

On the one hand, if we are to engage with the global horizon of freedom we must understand ourselves and each other as free. Expression maintains the mutual recognition that the social imagination requires.

On the other hand, if we are to preserve and build upon our understanding of what it possible, then we must record, analyse, and appreciate those exemplary works that trace the contours of the possibility space. Articulation maintains the cultural and historical consciousness that the social imagination requires.

To close then, the critical question our institutions face is whether this infrastructural dimension of contemporary art has begun to overshadow the true source of its value, the undefined work of freedom.

# Not So Humble Pie

I'm making a pie. I take pies very seriously, and so should you. A good pie is a work of art. Of course, pastry is a tricky thing to get right, but filling is where the real difficulties lie. Here we confront all sorts of problems to do with taste and texture, and, if some are to be believed, an ethical problem to boot. I'm making a steak and kidney pie (it's very English), and, being frank, that means at least one animal had to live in captivity, only to be killed so I can cook it. How can I be justified in sacrificing a living thing for a humble pie?

Humble pie is precisely what those who think consuming meat is unethical expect us to eat. They think that, when it comes to deciding what we can and can't do to living creatures, meat eaters make an illegitimate distinction between humans and other animals. As far as they're concerned, we can't think it's wrong to eat each other and think it's okay to eat animals.

Utilitarianism provides the strongest argument for this claim, and it goes something like this: (a) *value* is what justifies action, (b) the *source* of all value is pleasure and pain, (c) our *capacity* for pleasure and pain is something we share with all other animals, therefore (d) *distinctions* between types of animal can never justify differences in kind in the way we act toward them, only differences in degree. So, even if we acknowledge that our capacity to enjoy a bit of Shakespeare is worlds apart from a rabbit's orgasm, there must be some standard by which their value can be compared. You can garnish this idea in various ways, but here's the meat of it: there must be a certain number of rabbit orgasms that is worth more than the Complete Works of Shakespeare—and, if we were compelled to choose, we would have to pick the former over the latter.

I think that there is no amount of rabbit gratification that's worth even a single line of Shakespeare, and that explaining why will let me save my pie, if not its humility.

The dodgy utilitarian premise is (b). Although pleasure and pain cause other animals to act, they don't give them reasons to act. While pleasure and pain have value for us, they don't have value for animals. Nothing has value for animals, because there's no sense in which their behaviour could be justified or unjustified. This is the essence of the difference between us and them: animals merely behave, whereas we act. What we have in common with animals is that we both have *biological lives*: we continually metabolise, consuming and digesting sustenance, regulated by nervous systems. What distinguishes us is that we also have *personal lives*: we reason and act, making choices that reflect upon who we are, constructing ourselves as persons.

The true source of value is the capacity for action itself, or freedom. The value which transcends usefulness is beauty, and the beauty that we make for ourselves is art. We are free in so far as we don't just make beauty *for* ourselves, but also *out of* ourselves. We warrant ethical special treatment not because we're a special kind of animal (humans), but because we're our own works of art (persons).

I am a work of art, and so is my pie. Animals can be beautiful, but they are not thereby works of art, either for others or for themselves. Life is cheap. Pies are art. I'll take art over humility any day.

# INDEX OF NAMES

## W



## Y

# INDEX OF SUBJECTS

## D

## Q



## R

## U



## V



## W



## X